Why Do You Need This New Edition?

If you're wondering why you should buy this new edition of *Study and Critical Thinking Skills in College*, here are seven good reasons!

1 **Critical thinking skills are vital to effective reading and problem solving, both key to success in college, at work, and in your daily life.** The seventh edition of *Study and Critical Thinking Skills* has been significantly revised to provide expanded coverage of critical thinking skills and practice in applying them, as well as to provide you with practical advice and strategies for coping with the most common problems college students face today.

2 **"Reading Between the Lines," a new introduction to critical thinking,** spells out the importance of study and critical thinking skills and demonstrates how you can use five key critical thinking skills to understand and evaluate arguments in textbooks, at work, and in your personal life.

3 **A new section, "The College Student's Troubleshooting Guide,"** identifies common academic and personal problems you may find yourself facing as a new college student and offers helpful solutions to them in an easy to read format. Topics covered include how to set goals and priorities, read textbooks and take effective notes, improve your grades and do well on tests, improve your writing skills, use technology, solve interpersonal conflicts, ensure your safety and security, solve living and commuting arrangements, and stay healthy.

4 **New Skills in Action activities in every chapter** provide immediate practice with new skills, show you how these skills can be applied in a wide range of reading situations, and deepen your critical thinking abilities. They appear in a wide range of engaging formats including case studies, checklists, charts, problem-solving scenarios, time analyses, and more.

5 **A new chapter summary, Five Key Points to Remember**—a short five point list of important skills to use and remember—appears at the end of each chapter, for quick and easy review of the main topics you have learned.

6 **A new emphasis on the role of computers in learning** is integrated throughout the book, providing you with advice and practical suggestions on how to use computers as learning/study tools. Topics include taking online courses, using a laptop for notetaking, outlining using a computer, taking an exam on a computer, and using electronic calendars.

7 **Expanded Coverage of Critical Thinking in Chapter 15,** which includes new information on informed and uninformed opinion, types of relevant and valid evidence, sources of information, author's tone, and on how to identify common errors in reasoning, will help you strengthen and expand your critical thinking skills.

PEARSON
Longman

Study and Critical Thinking Skills in College

Study and Critical Thinking Skills in College

SEVENTH EDITION

Kathleen T. McWhorter

Niagara County Community College

Longman

Boston   Columbus   Indianapolis   New York   San Francisco   Upper Saddle River
Amsterdam   Cape Town   Dubai   London   Madrid   Milan   Munich   Paris   Montreal   Toronto
Delhi   Mexico City   Sao Paulo   Sydney   Hong Kong   Seoul   Singapore   Taipei   Tokyo

Acquisitions Editor: Kate Edwards
Development Editor: Gillian Cook
Marketing Manager: Tom DeMarco
Production Manager: Stacey Kulig
Project Coordination, Text Design, and Electronic Page Makeup: Pre-Press PMG
Cover Designer/Manager: John Callahan
Cover Image: iStock; PhotoAlto/Alamy
Photo Researcher: Connie Gardner
Senior Manufacturing Buyer: Alfred C. Dorsey
Printer and Binder: Edwards Brothers
Cover Printer: Lehigh/Phoenix

McWhorter, Kathleen T.
  Study and critical thinking skills in college / Kathleen T. McWhorter. --
7th ed.
      p. cm.
  Includes bibliographical references and index.
  ISBN-13: 978-0-205-73480-1
  ISBN-10: 0-205-73480-4
  1. Study skills. 2. Thought and thinking. 3. Critical thinking. I.
Title.
  LB2395.M445 2011
  378.1'70281--dc22

                                          2009050835

1 2 3 4 5 6 7 8 9 10—EB—13 12 11 10

Longman
is an imprint of

www.pearsonhighered.com

ISBN-13: 978-0-205-73480-1
ISBN-10:   0-205-73480-4

Brief Contents

Detailed Contents

Preface

The seventh edition of *Study and Critical Thinking Skills in College* offers a striking new emphasis on critical thinking skills and provides students with advice and strategies to cope with the most common problems college students face.

■ New to This Edition

This edition of the text has been extensively revised to provide new and expanded coverage of critical reading skills, solutions to common academic and personal problems students experience, practical tips on how to use computers to learn, and enhanced coverage of evaluating textbook content and arguments. New and expanded features include the following:

- ◆ **NEW! "Reading Between the Lines," an introduction to critical thinking**. This introduction provides a rationale for the book's dual emphasis on both study skills and critical thinking and demonstrates the importance of critical thinking in college. It foreshadows the continuing emphasis on critical thinking throughout the book by discussing the immediate practical benefits of critical thinking in both everyday and academic life. Five key critical thinking skills are presented:

  - ◆ Examining opinions and beliefs
  - ◆ Recognizing emotional appeals
  - ◆ Looking for omitted information
  - ◆ Understanding the power of words
  - ◆ Learning how numbers can mislead

  A "Skills in Action" activity is included for each topic to provide immediate relevance.

- ◆ **NEW! "The College Student's Troubleshooting Guide."** This insert identifies common academic and personal problems that beginning college students face and offers helpful solutions. The guide begins with a brief list of contents, identifying the following categories: setting goals and priorities, textbook reading, note taking, grades and taking tests, writing skills, technology, interpersonal conflicts, safety and security, living and commuting arrangements, and wellness issues. Arranged in tabular form, the guide concisely states common problems in each category and offers a range of possible solutions.

- ◆ **NEW! Skills in Action activities.** The new critical thinking introduction and each chapter in the book now contain activities that focus on skill application. The activities offer a wide range of engaging formats: case studies, checklists, charts, problem-solving scenarios, time analyses, and so forth. These activities are intended to demonstrate to students the immediate utility of the skills they have just learned, further expand their critical thinking skills, and model future applications.

◆ **NEW! Review: Five Key Points to Remember.** Each chapter now concludes with a five-point list of important skills to use and remember. The list is purposefully short so as to be accessible to students and easy to remember.

◆ **NEW! Emphasis on the role of computers in learning.** Throughout the book, advice and practical suggestions on using computers as learning/study tools have been added. Topics include taking online courses, using a laptop for note taking, outlining using a computer, taking an exam on a computer, and using electronic calendars.

◆ **Expanded coverage of critical thinking in Chapter 15.** Chapter 15, "Critical Reading and Thinking About Course Content," has been revised and expanded to include new information on informed and uninformed opinion, an explanation of types of relevant and valid evidence, a description of a variety of sources of information, a new section on author's tone, and new material on identifying common errors in reasoning.

■ Goals

Study and Critical Thinking Skills in College was written to enable students to become academically competitive and to prepare them for success in the workplace. It aims to achieve the following goals:

◆ **Active Learning.** A primary purpose of the text is to teach students to approach study as an active thinking process. For many students, learning is a passive assimilation process, and their goal is to acquire as many facts and as much information as possible.

◆ **Critical Thinking.** A basic assumption of this book is that students can learn how to learn and can be taught to think critically. The second major purpose of this book, then, is to teach specific learning and thinking strategies. Learning is approached as a highly versatile and adaptive process. Students are encouraged to analyze learning tasks and to choose appropriate strategies that suit the nature of the task and their prior knowledge and experience.

◆ **Attitudes Toward Learning.** Although a major emphasis is on cognitive skills, skills in the affective and behavioral domains that shape and control learning are also introduced.

◆ **Workplace Applications.** Another purpose of the text is to promote students' success in the workplace as well as in the classroom.

◆ **Metacognitive Skills.** The book applies current research findings in the areas of metacognition, schema theory, and writing as learning. Metacognitive strategies are built into specific learning and study techniques.

■ Content Overview

Study and Critical Thinking Skills in College presents a unique integration of study and critical thinking skills.

◆ **Part One introduces students to college learning and thinking and establishes a focus on student success.** These chapters encourage students to develop specific success strategies: learning the college system, taking responsibility for their own learning, establishing goals and managing their time, reducing stress, communicating effectively in the classroom, and thinking critically to solve problems.

◆ **Part Two teaches students fundamental approaches to the learning process as well as essential critical thinking strategies.** In Chapter 7 students analyze their own learning style, consider how to use their learning style to choose study methods, and discover how to adapt to various teaching styles. Chapter 8 discusses principles of learning and memory and their application to academic tasks.

◆ **Part Three shows students how to apply skills to various academic disciplines.** Techniques for approaching the social sciences, life and physical sciences, mathematics, literature and the arts, and career fields are discussed. The importance of learning specialized and technical vocabulary is stressed, and specific learning strategies are suggested.

◆ **Part Four offers students skills and strategies for mastering course content.** The section begins with a chapter on academic patterns of thought, emphasizing their predominance and use across various academic disciplines. The remaining chapters discuss techniques and strategies for lecture note taking; learning from textbooks, graphics, and online sources; and organization and synthesis of course content; as well as academic thought patterns as organizing features. The SQ3R reading study system is also introduced.

◆ **Part Five equips students with the skills and strategies needed in preparing for and taking exams.** Students learn to organize their review, use thematic study, and develop study strategies for specific academic disciplines. They learn specific strategies for answering objective test questions, writing essay exams, and controlling test anxiety.

■ Special Features

The following features significantly enhance the text's effectiveness as a motivational teaching tool:

◆ **Focus Questions.** Each chapter begins with a brief list of questions that identifies key chapter topics and provides students with purposes for reading. The questions can also serve as a means of checking recall after reading the chapter.

◆ **Thinking Critically . . . About.** These inserts relate critical thinking skills to chapter content and offer practical suggestions and tips for developing critical thinking skills.

◆ **Skills in Action.** These activities provide immediate and practical application of skills taught in the chapter.

◆ **Real Students Speak.** Each chapter contains a student profile that identifies the student, states his or her academic goals, and shares the student's advice for academic success involving the skills taught in the chapter.

◆ **In-Chapter Exercises.** Numerous exercises within each chapter provide students with opportunities to immediately apply and evaluate techniques. While the exercises take a variety of forms, their focus is the practical application of skills in realistic college course situations, and they often require the use of the students' own textbooks or course materials.

◆ **Working Together Exercises and Activities.** Each chapter includes exercises and activities designed for group interaction. Their purpose is to promote collaborative learning, allowing students to listen to and learn from the thinking processes of other students.

◆ **Review: Five Key Points to Remember.** Functioning as a brief summary, this list of key points helps students pull together chapter content and focus on what is important.

◆ **The Work Connection.** This activity, appearing near the end of each chapter, encourages students to explore workplace applications of chapter content. By extending chapter skills to the workplace, students realize the long-term benefits of the skills they are learning.

◆ **The Web Connection.** Each chapter concludes with an interactive activity involving Web sites that present additional information on topics covered in the chapter. A brief description of each Web site is included, along with its URL. The sites may provide helpful tips, offer alternative viewpoints, or contain useful study aids such as worksheets, questionnaires, or checklists. Students interact with the Web site by writing about, discussing, or evaluating its content.

■ Book-Specific Ancillary Materials

Instructor's Manual and Test Bank

The *Instructor's Manual and Test Bank* provide many suggestions for using the text, including how to structure and organize the course and how to approach each section of the book. The manual also contains a ten-item multiple-choice quiz for each chapter of the text.

Expanding Your Vocabulary

Instructors may choose to shrink-wrap *Study and Critical Thinking in College* with a copy of *Expanding Your Vocabulary*. This book, written by Kathleen T. McWhorter, works well as a supplemental text by providing instruction and practice in vocabulary. Students can work through the book independently, or units may be incorporated into weekly lesson plans. Topics covered include methods of vocabulary learning, contextual aids, word parts, connotative meanings, idioms, euphemisms, and many more fun and interesting topics. The book concludes with vocabulary lists and exercises representative of 11 academic disciplines. To preview the book, contact your Longman sales consultant for an examination copy.

■ Acknowledgments

I wish to acknowledge the contributions of my colleagues and reviewers, who have provided valuable advice and suggestions over the course of many editions:

Andy Alexson, Tennessee Temple University

Colleen Angel, Luzerne County Community College

Ann Austin, St. Ambrose University

Sue Burdette, Wichita State University

Doris Burgert, Wichita State University

Chris Butterill, University of Manitoba

Nancy Cannon, Cecil Community College

Deborah Ceppaglia, Medaille College

Julie Colish, University of Michigan, Flint

Ray DeLeon, California State University–Long Beach

Barbara Doyle, Arkansas State University

Peter Geller, Inter-Universities North

Janet Griffin, Howard University

Starr S. Hoover, Tennessee Temple University

Orlando E. Katter, Jr., Winthrop University

Trish LaFlamme, Community College of Southern Nevada

Seana Logsdon, Medaille College

Rose Manzer, Sir Sanford Fleming
   College
Cheryl McLean, Edmonds
   Community College
Patricia I. Mochnacz, University of
   Manitoba
Jayne Nightengale, Rhode Island
   College
Mary Parish, Minneapolis
   Community and Technical College
Sue Pendergast, SUNY, Orange
William Reed, Albany State University
Cheryl Rinker, Rock Valley College
Jim Roth, Spokane Community
   College
Cecilia Russo, St. John's University

Rebecca Sanberg, Housatonic
   Community College
Gladys Shaw, University of Texas–El
   Paso
Barbara Smuckler, College of Mount
   St. Vernon
Helene Stapleton, Cayuga
   Community College
Sharon Stevens, Oklahoma City
   Community College
Gail Watson, County College of
   Morris
Carolyn J. Wilkie, Indiana University
   of Pennsylvania
Donna Wood, Southwest Tennessee
   Community College, Macon

I would also like to thank the students who shared their knowledge and experience to help me create the Real Students Speak feature of this edition:

Ebtisam Abusamak, Central
   Piedmont College
Michael Archer, Greenfield
   Community College
Tony Chatila, Miami-Dade
   Community College
Sophie Crafts, Clark University
Lauren Croce, University of
   Massachusetts
Norah Edge, St. John's College
Lishai Goldstein, McGill University
Rachel Goodman, West Chester
   University
Ben Howard, Brown University
Nakasha Kirkland, Armstrong
   Atlantic State University

Noah Klugman, Kalamazoo College
Christina Olivo, Western New
   England College
Markella Tsoukalas, Fairleigh
   Dickinson University
Marlo Ricotta, Niagara County
   Community College
Corinne Roberts, Modesto Junior
   College
Willy Rutherford, Miami-Dade
   Community College
Adesola Sonaike, Armstrong Atlantic
   State University
Jamie Sturm, Kalamazoo College
Andrew Wilton, State University of
   New York at Buffalo

I am particularly indebted to Gillian Cook, my development editor, for her creative talent, sound advice, and expert guidance and to Kate Edwards, acquisitions editor, for her careful attention, enthusiasm, and strong support of this project.

KATHLEEN T. MCWHORTER

Reading Between the Lines

INTRODUCTION

The title of this textbook, *Study and Critical Thinking Skills in College*, shows that the book has two major components:

◆ Study skills
◆ Critical thinking skills

STUDY SKILLS

There is a major difference between high school and college. In high school, instructors tend to provide a lot of support and individual attention. You probably had no more than 30 students in each of your high school classes. In college, however, you may find yourself in lecture halls with hundreds of other students, so individualized attention from the instructor can be rare.

Study and Critical Thinking Skills in College will introduce you to a wide variety of study tools to help you in all of your college courses. To do well in a class, you should plan to study two hours outside of class for each hour your class meets. For example, if you take a 3-credit course that meets for three hours each week, you should plan to spend $3 \times 2 = 6$ hours per week reading and studying for that class.

Skills in Action

This semester you are taking five classes: biology (3 credits), a biology lab (1 credit), history (3 credits), pre-algebra (3 credits), and freshman orientation/study skills (2 credits). How many hours *each week* should you plan to read and study outside of class?

THINKING CRITICALLY

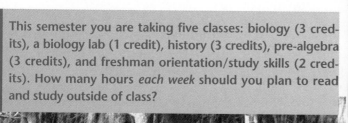

CRITICAL THINKING SKILLS

While there will be some overlap between the study skills you developed in high school and those you'll use in college, the biggest difference between high school and college is the difference in your instructors' expectations of how you *think*.

Elementary and high school education focuses mostly on memorization. In college, however, you are expected not only to learn and memorize new information, but also to analyze what you are learning, formulate your own opinions, and even conduct your own research. In other words, your college instructors expect you to *think critically*—to interpret and evaluate what you hear and read, rather than accept everything you read as "the truth." The term *critical* does not mean "negative." Rather, it means "analytical" and "probing"— that is, thinking more deeply about the subjects you study.

To succeed in college, you will need to combine your study skills with critical thinking skills. This introduction provides you with an overview of critical thinking. It shows you five key ways you can begin to adjust your thinking to match what your instructors expect of you.

Skills in Action

Form groups of three or four students. To start developing new ways to think about what you will be learning in college, discuss each of the following questions and what they mean to the study of the discipline to which they relate. Summarize your responses in a paragraph or an oral presentation to the class.

◆ **HISTORY** There's an old saying that "history is written by the winners." What do you think this means? Can you think of any examples to support your answer? (For example, think of the history of the United States of America.)

◆ **PSYCHOLOGY** One of the big questions in psychology revolves around the topic of "nature vs. nurture." In a nutshell, the *nature vs. nurture* debate asks whether people are who they are because of their genetic makeup ("nature") or because of the way they were raised or what happened to them as children ("nurture"). Do you think this debate can ever be resolved? Just from listening to or watching the news, what do you know about this topic? What do you know about it from your own experiences?

THE BENEFITS OF CRITICAL THINKING

You may be surprised to discover that the benefits of developing your critical thinking skills extend beyond your college courses and into your everyday life. In college, critical thinking skills allow you to

- do well on essay exams.
- write effective essays and research papers.
- evaluate whether print and online sources are reliable.
- distinguish good information from bad, incomplete, inaccurate, or misleading information.

In your everyday life, critical thinking skills will help you

- become a savvy consumer and make good financial choices.
- understand when companies are trying to manipulate you with their advertising or public-relations efforts.
- resolve conflicts or come to acceptable compromises.
- solve problems using a logical, step-by-step process.

Skills in Action

As anyone who follows any sport knows, a huge amount of critical thinking goes into planning game strategy, minute by minute and play by play. Even individual athletes, such as tennis players and swimmers, have to analyze their competitors' weaknesses and think about how to achieve victory. Think about a sport in which you have competed, or one in which you are interested. Write a list of the strategies and critical-thinking activities the coaches and players engage in.

CRITICAL THINKING IN COLLEGE

If you can master the following five essential components of critical thinking, you will be well on your way to becoming a master reader, thinker, and learner.

1 EXAMINE YOUR OPINIONS AND BELIEFS

If you are like many beginning college students, you view the world through the lens of your family, upbringing, friends, culture, and education. Your views are shaped by your experiences, and you take for granted many opinions and beliefs. In college you will meet other students from very different backgrounds, and they may hold very different opinions and beliefs. Your professors will expose you to new ways of thought and present you with different perspectives through lectures, discussions, and assigned readings.

College is about opening your mind to new ways of thinking. These new ways of thinking may challenge some of your opinions or beliefs. Be sure to recognize and analyze these different opinions and beliefs. Avoid the temptation to reject them only because they are different from yours.

> **Skills in Action**
>
> Two students from very different backgrounds are roommates. Sally grew up with politically liberal parents, both professionals, in a small town near Boston. She has several friends with two moms, volunteers at the local recycling center, and was active in Barack Obama's presidential campaign. Veronica is from Detroit, where she grew up in blue-collar household—both her parents work in the auto industry. She has strong conservative religious beliefs, volunteers at the local homeless shelter, and, like her parents, voted for John McCain in the presidential election.

What do you think these two students might say about the following topics?

◆ legalizing gay marriage
◆ bailing out the auto companies
◆ passing stricter environmental legislation

To answer this question you made some assumptions about each of the students, based on the information provided. Do you think you might have answered differently if you knew more about each student? How much do you think your own background and experience influenced your responses to the above question?

2 RECOGNIZE EMOTIONAL APPEALS

Business owners understand consumer psychology, and they use all sorts of techniques (especially words and pictures) to get people to buy their products. Ads for cosmetics show women transformed from Plain Janes into ravishing beauties—and the message to the consumer is "Buy our cosmetics, and you too will look like a model." An advertisement for a sports car shows a handsome young man driving along the highway with a beautiful woman in the passenger seat, implying that men who drive that specific car are highly attractive to the opposite sex. Even nonprofit organizations that have admirable goals (such as animal-rescue operations and save-the-children foundations) use emotional appeals to get you to donate money to their causes.

Thinking critically enables you to recognize the emotional appeal in an argument and step away from it, so that you can evaluate it logically and clearly. This can be difficult to accomplish because emotions can be so powerful.

In college, you need to be on the alert for emotional appeals in both print and online sources. Instructors may assign readings intended to expose you to different viewpoints on an issue. You may encounter emotional appeals on Web sites, in newspaper editorials, and in periodicals.

Skills in Action

Suppose you are working for an animal rights organization on a fund-raising activity. Your organization, PPOF (People for the Protection of Foxes), believes that too many foxes are being trapped in the wild, then killed for their fur. You are writing a letter asking for donations to help end this practice.

Look at the two photos below. You have to decide which one to use on the envelope in which you are mailing your fund-raising letter. Which one would you choose to use? Why? Write a few sentences explaining your reasons.

3 LOOK FOR WHAT IS NOT SAID

Writers and speakers sometimes mislead by omitting information. They deliberately leave out essential details, ignore contradictory evidence, or include only those details that support their position. Consider this example.

A woman who homeschools her children writes an article about the benefits of homeschooling. As an advocate for this method of education, she emphasizes her children's educational progress, as well as the sense of personal fulfillment she experiences through teaching them. However, she omits another aspect of the argument, which is that homeschooled children sometimes feel lonely or isolated from their peers. She also describes a research study that concludes that homeschooled children excel academically, but does not report that other studies have demonstrated that homeschooled children do not differ in academic achievement from traditionally educated students.

In this example, the writer has chosen to ignore contradictory evidence, using only information that supports her argument in favor of homeschooling.

Whenever you encounter material from a source that might be unreliable, ask yourself the following questions to be sure you are getting full and complete information:

◆ Based on my own experiences, how do I evaluate this material? Is there another side to this case that I should consider?
◆ What important information might have been omitted? What am I not being told?
◆ What contradictory evidence is not reported?
◆ Has the author or speaker selectively reported details to further his or her cause?
◆ Where can I go to find out what information might be missing (textbook, journal, newspaper, database, the Internet, and so on)?

To answer these questions, you usually will need to do some additional reading or research. In all of your college courses, be sure to ask questions and make sure you have all the facts. Before you decide a source is credible, learn as much about it as you can. Then, as you use the information you have researched, be sure to present it fairly and honestly.

Skills in Action

Read the following everyday-life scenarios. In each situation, identify what information is being withheld from you. (In other words, what other information would you need to critically evaluate the situation?) Then compare your answers with those of other students.

1. You see a TV ad for a fast-food restaurant, showing a huge, delicious-looking hamburger topped with pickles, onions, and tomatoes. The announcer says, "For a limited time, get your favorite burger for only 99 cents!"

2. You open your mailbox and find a letter from a credit card company. The letter invites you to open a credit card with no annual fee and offers you instant credit just for returning the attached card in a postage-paid envelope.

3. You get an offer from a DVD club that appears to be quite a deal. As part of your introductory package, you get five DVDs for only 99 cents plus shipping and handling.

4 PAY ATTENTION TO THE POWER OF WORDS

Words are powerful. On the positive side, words can inspire, comfort, educate, and calm. On the negative side, they can be used to inflame, annoy, or deceive. Professional writers and speakers know how to use words to influence their readers and listeners. Here are a few key terms related to word choice that will help you think critically:

Denotation

This is the literal meaning of a word. For example, the denotation of the word *obese* is "very fat."

Connotation

This is the set of additional meanings or associations that a word can take on. Saying that someone is obese carries quite a negative connotation. A writer who wishes to be kind to an overweight politician might describe him as "slightly plump" (which carries an almost pleasant connotation) or "quite heavyset" (which is a fairly neutral description). To present a negative image of the politician, however, a writer might describe him as "grossly fat" or "obese."

Look at the photo above. Would you say this man is *lazy*? Or is he *relaxed*? What connotations do these words have?

Euphemism

A **euphemism** is a word or phrase that is used in place of a word that is unpleasant, embarrassing, or otherwise objectionable. For example, a company may say that it is "downsizing" its work force when it is actually firing people. A company that is "internationally outsourcing" is actually eliminating jobs in the United States and sending them overseas. Euphemisms almost always seek to sugarcoat an unpleasant reality, and you should always be suspicious of them.

A current hot political topic is that of immigrants coming to the United States without permission from the U.S. government. Two terms are frequently used to describe this phenomenon: *illegal immigration* and *undocumented immigration*. Both terms describe the same phenomenon. Working with three other students discuss the following questions:

- Which term has a more negative connotation? Why?
- Which seems more neutral? Why?
- Is either of the terms a euphemism? If so, which one?

5 LEARN HOW NUMBERS CAN MISLEAD

The British Prime Minister Benjamin Disraeli once said, "There are three kinds of lies: lies, damned lies, and statistics." Disraeli was referring to the persuasive power of numbers. Numbers and statistics are of prime importance in all aspects of our daily lives, including our personal finances and how our tax dollars are spent. The collection and analysis of numerical data is an important part of nearly every academic discipline, from the physical sciences (such as chemistry and physics) through the liberal arts (such as English).

But numbers can also be used to mislead; and in these cases, they do amount to the types of "lies" that Disraeli referred to. Consider the case of a company that issues an annual report to its investors. When all the accounting is done, the company is shown to have lost $8 million. Rather than saying "Acme Corporation lost $8 million last year," the annual report may say, "We showed a negative profit of $8 million," which means exactly the same thing but looks and sounds a lot better to people who do not have training in accounting terminology.

Statistics are often presented as facts, but the truth is that they are based on small sets of data. While statistics are often reliable, they may also be very misleading. Suppose you read in your local newspaper that "94 percent of the people surveyed are in favor of a new tax to raise revenue to build a new Little League baseball stadium in town." You might ask yourself: What types of people responded to this survey? If the survey was conducted at the site of the existing field and was answered only by fans, then the results could be highly biased in favor of building a new Little League stadium. If, on the other hand, the survey took place at a retirement home where people are living on fixed incomes (and who would therefore not want to pay higher taxes), the survey results might be very different.

The important lesson here is to view statistics and numbers with a skeptical eye. As with all other reading materials, consider their source and determine if the numbers are being quoted to advance a particular agenda or to sway your opinion.

As you will see in Chapter 13 of this book, graphics are often used to summarize numbers and statistics. Sometimes these graphics can be used to mislead by presenting actual numbers in a graphically inaccurate or disproportionate way.

1. Consider Figure 1, which was mailed to all the houses in a particular school district by the local board of education. This graphic was part of a flyer intended to convince people that the school budget must be increased (that is, people must pay higher property taxes to finance the school budget). How is Figure 1 deceptive? What needs to be done to make the figure better represent the underlying numbers? List your solutions and compare them with those of your classmates. What was the most common solution? Why?

2. Consider Figure 2 (page 10), which an antitax group sent to the same group of homeowners to demonstrate how property taxes have increased over a period of ten years. How is Figure 2 deceptive? What needs to be done to make the figure better represent the underlying numbers?

FIGURE 1
Increase in School Enrollments, 2000–2010

2010

2000

6,250 children

8,600 children

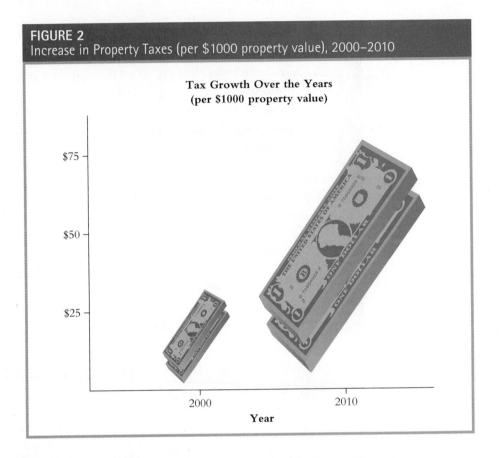

FIGURE 2
Increase in Property Taxes (per $1000 property value), 2000–2010

Tax Growth Over the Years
(per $1000 property value)

STUDY AND CRITICAL THINKING SKILLS IN COLLEGE

As you proceed through this book, you will find many additional opportunities to develop your critical thinking skills. Every chapter offers a "Thinking Critically About . . ." feature to stimulate your thinking. For example, in Chapter 1 you are asked to think critically about your grades, while in Chapter 3 you are asked to think critically about procrastination. Each chapter also contains one or more "Skills in Action" activities that encourage you to apply your skills to a variety of situations.

In addition, two complete chapters of this book offer further instruction on important critical thinking skills. Chapter 6, "Thinking Critically and Solving Problems," offers a step-by-step approach to problem solving. Chapter 15, "Critical Reading and Thinking About Course Content," teaches you how to synthesize information from multiple sources and critically evaluate your course materials.

1 The College System: An Orientation

Do You Know?

How can you find the information you need about your college?

What college services are available on your campus?

How can you learn from the people you will meet in college?

How are different courses organized?

How does the grading system work?

How can you succeed in the classroom?

College is very different from any other place you have studied or worked. It has its own way of operating, its own set of rules and regulations, and its own procedures. To function effectively within any new environment, you have to learn how it works and how to make it work to your advantage. Before continuing with the chapter, assess your knowledge of how your college works by completing the questionnaire shown in Figure 1.1 on page 12.

■ Information Sources

Important official sources of information include the college catalog, the college's Web site, one's academic advisor, and the student newspaper. An important part of learning the college system is knowing where to find needed information.

Using the College Catalog

The college catalog is a primary source of information for staying in and graduating from college. Be sure to obtain a current edition. It is your responsibility to know and work within the college's regulations, policies, and requirements to obtain a degree. Although faculty advisors are available to provide guidance, you must be certain that you are registering for the right courses in the right sequence to fulfill requirements to obtain your degree. Furthermore, be sure to obtain a complete catalog, not a preadmissions publicity brochure. Keep the

FIGURE 1.1
Rate Your Knowledge of Your College

Answer each of the following questions about your college.

1. What are the hours of the college library?

2. What is the last date by which you can withdraw from a class without a penalty?

3. Where do you go or whom do you see to change from one major (or curriculum) to another?

4. How is your grade point average (GPA) computed?

5. Where is the student health office located?

6. Who is your advisor and where is he or she located on campus?

7. Does your college use pluses and/or minuses as part of the letter grading system?

8. Where are computer labs located on campus?

9. How would you contact each of your instructors if it should be necessary?

10. What assistance is available in locating part-time jobs on campus?

catalog that is in effect during your freshman year. It is considered the catalog of record and will be used to audit your graduation requirements. A complete catalog usually provides several types of information:

Academic rules and regulations	Course registration policies, grading system, class attendance policies, academic dismissal policies
Degree programs and requirements	Degrees offered and outlines of degree requirements for each major
Course descriptions	A brief description of each course, the number of credits, and course prerequisites (Note: Not all courses listed are offered each semester.)
Student activities and special services	Student organizations, clubs and sports, student governance system, and special services

Your College's Web Site

Many colleges have a Web site on the Internet that contains useful general information about the college, as well as information about degrees, programs, and services. It may contain such valuable information as course descriptions, schedule planning, course and program information, and financial aid.

Many college Web sites have links to sites that offer grammar hotlines, study skills workshops, library research assistance, and term paper writing tips.

EXERCISE 1.1   ## Learning About Your College

Directions   *Use your college catalog or Web site to answer the following questions.*

1. Does the college allow you to take courses on a Pass/Fail or Satisfactory/Unsatisfactory basis? If so, what restrictions or limitations apply?
2. What is the last date on which you can withdraw from a course without academic penalty?
3. On what basis are students academically dismissed from the college? What criteria apply to readmission?
4. What is the institution's policy on transfer credit?
5. What rules and regulations apply to motor vehicles on campus?
6. List five extracurricular programs or activities the college sponsors.
7. Describe the health services the college provides.
8. What foreign languages are offered?
9. Is a course in computer literacy offered?
10. What courses are required in your major or curriculum? Are any general education courses required?

Course Management Systems

More and more instructors use a computer-based course management system to provide information about their courses and to handle their day-to-day operation. The system may contain the course syllabus (see p. 20), lists of assignments, announcements of quizzes and exams, and so forth. The system may also allow you to communicate directly with classmates and with your professor. With some systems you can submit assignments electronically and receive graded papers back from your professor.

Your Academic Advisor

In most colleges, each student is assigned an academic advisor. Your advisor's primary function is to help you select appropriate courses and make certain that you meet all requirements for your degree. Meet with your advisor early in the semester and get to know him or her. Many advisors on campus have e-mail addresses. Often you can use e-mail to schedule an appointment with him or her or to ask a quick question. Be sure to consult with your advisor before adding or dropping courses or making other important academic decisions. Sometimes he or she can help you resolve a problem by "cutting through the red tape" or knowing whom to call. Your advisor is an important source for a letter of recommendation, which you may need for college transfer, graduate school, or job applications, so it is important to develop and maintain a positive relationship with him or her.

Student Newspaper

The student newspaper is another useful source of information. It provides a student perspective on issues, problems, and concerns on campus. It may also contain important announcements and list upcoming events.

■ College Services

A large portion of your tuition is spent to provide a wide range of academic, social, recreational, and health services. Since you are paying for these services, you should take advantage of them. Table 1.1 lists the most common services offered on college campuses. Check to see exactly what services are offered on your campus.

TABLE 1.1 College Services

Office	Services Offered
Student Health Office	Handles illnesses and injuries; may dispense over-the-counter drugs
Student Activities Office or Student Center	Offers a range of recreational activities; sponsors social events; houses offices for student organizations
Counseling and Test Center	Provides personal and career counseling and testing
Financial Aid Office	Offers assistance with loans, grants, and scholarships
Placement Office	Lists job openings (full time and part time); establishes a placement file that records student references and transcripts
Library	Lends books, CD's and DVD's, provides computer access; provides listening and study rooms; has photocopy machines; offers assistance in locating reference materials; obtains books and research materials from other libraries through interlibrary loans; offers access to electronic databases
Learning Lab/Academic Skills Center	Offers brush-up courses; individualized instruction or tutoring in study skills, reading, writing, math, and/or common freshman courses

EXERCISE 1.2   **Identifying College Services**

Directions   *Answer the following questions about college services on your campus.*

1. What services does the student health office offer?
2. List five student organizations sponsored by the college.
3. Where would you go to find out if tutoring is available for mathematics courses?
4. In what intercollegiate sports does the college participate?
5. Where are computer labs located?

■ Campus Diversity

For many students, college is an opportunity to meet people unlike themselves: students and instructors from different social, cultural, and national backgrounds. This means you are likely to encounter people whose beliefs, values, and experiences differ significantly from your own. If you consider this diversity as an opportunity to broaden your horizons and think from different points of view, you will benefit more than if you socialize only with other students who come from backgrounds similar to your own.

1. **Look for opportunities to meet students from diverse backgrounds who share your interests.** Get involved with sports activities and clubs, for example. Most colleges present many opportunities for students with common interests to meet and think about matters of concern at the local, national, and even international levels. Don't restrict your activities to those that include only others of your own background.

2. **Share your experiences and background when relevant in class discussions.** Most students are interested in the customs, traditions, and viewpoints of others. You possess a unique body of information based on your life experiences. Sharing it adds depth and texture to relevant class discussions.

3. **Consider study and research projects that will give you a chance to learn about unfamiliar cultures.** Take advantage of any course-related opportunities to study unfamiliar cultures, whether in the library, on the Internet, or by conducting person-to-person research on campus. Use academic assignments as a way to move beyond familiar territory and into contact with new people and new ideas.

Thirty years ago, first-year college students typically were 18-year-olds who lived on campus in dorm rooms. Today, 40 percent of college students are age 25 or older, and well over 50 percent are commuters who travel to and from campus daily. As a result of these and other changes in the college population, many colleges and universities now offer services for students with different needs. Be sure to check what services are available on your campus, as well as using the following suggestions.

Commuter Students

Check to see if your campus offers special services for commuter students. Your college may coordinate "ride boards" for sharing rides; it may offer commuter lounges; it may lend laptops to commuters who do not have ready access to the college's computer labs. Table 1.2 on page 16 identifies common problems commuting students experience and offers suggestions for coping with each.

Adults Returning to College

Many adults are returning to education. This means that if you are an adult beginning or returning to college, you are not alone. Many other students on your campus face the same concerns and problems as you do. Get in touch

TABLE 1.2   Tips for Commuting Students

Problem	Suggestions
1. You are trying to balance responsibilities of family, job, and college.	• Time management skills are essential. Pay particular attention to Chapter 3. • Establish your priorities. Once you list what is most and least important to you, you won't feel guilty about choices you must make.
2. Family and friends don't understand your new commitment to college.	• Explain the new demands college has placed on you. • Make clear when you have reserved times for study. • Learn to say "no" to friends and family who expect you to be able to live as you did before you began college.
3. Commuting takes time.	• Use your commute time for learning. • If riding, work on assignments.
4. It's difficult to meet other students; you don't feel as if you belong.	• Talk to others; don't wait for them to talk to you. • Get to know one person in each of your classes. • Exchange phone numbers. • Join clubs and attend student activities on campus. • Spend extra time on campus; don't leave immediately after your last class.

with these students; they can offer moral support, serve as sounding boards, and provide valuable advice for succeeding in college. Your college's activities office may sponsor a club or offer workshops.

Use the following suggestions to make your transition back to education a smooth one.

Make sure your family understands and supports your decision. You may need to ask them to pick up part of the household workload that you had previously carried.

Do not study all the time.   Many adults feel they are behind or out of touch and, consequently, study nonstop. Instead, develop a realistic study plan and stick with it. (See Chapter 3 for specific suggestions.)

Start slowly.   Ease yourself into college. Take courses that you are likely to do well in and that will strengthen your self-confidence.

Recognize that your first semester will be the hardest.   During your first semester you are not only working on each of your courses, you are also working on developing a new lifestyle.

Cultural Diversity

College offers you an incredible opportunity to meet students from many different cultural, ethnic, and religious backgrounds. If you actively seek them out, you'll learn as much about different ways of seeing and being in the world from other students as you will in your college classes. The rich variety of cultural and spiritual practices represented by diverse students and instructors can help you see your own culture from a very different point of view.

Many colleges organize student groups that enable students of color to get in touch with one another and discuss problems, and sponsor activities that encourage students to share their cultural and ethnic heritage with others. If your college does not sponsor such student clubs or activities, consider starting your own group or club or see what is available in the larger community. Also, check for Web sites sponsored by cultural organizations in order to find out about services and resources and activities at the national level. For example, Movimiento Estudiantil Chicano de Aztlan has Web sites at many college campuses around the country, and Hillel is a national Jewish student organization that promotes unity among the members of the Jewish community.

No matter what your background, the following tips can help you get off to a successful start in college.

Consult with a campus mentor frequently.   Try to find a person—either a student or a faculty or staff member—who is familiar with the college and who is willing to guide you through your first semester and offer advice.

Find a role model from your community.   Talk to a relative, friend, or acquaintance who has attended college to find out what strategies helped them succeed. Use their experiences and expertise as a guide to develop your own.

Once you become familiar with college expectations, become a mentor to a younger person from your community.   Define your academic and personal goals (see Chapter 3) and then share them with a junior-high or high-school student who wants to attend college. Share both the problems you encounter and the successes you experience. Doing so will help reinforce a continuing tradition of success in your community.

Students with Disabilities

College is fully accessible to students with physical or learning disabilities. Federal laws mandate that colleges provide specific services to disabled students. Most colleges have an office or counselor designated to assist students with disabilities, as well as a full range of services and equipment, including interpreters for hearing-impaired students, writers, note takers, and so forth.

Student organizations for disabled students may provide social networks or peer counseling, for example. If you are a student with a disability, here are a few suggestions to help you succeed.

Communicate with your instructors.   Explain any kind of assistance or special accommodation you may require or certain preferential treatment you want them to avoid. Most instructors are anxious to assist; it is your job to let them know *how* to help.

Take advantage of available facilities and accommodations.   Some students who have special needs try not to use the services available to them unless absolutely necessary. They do not want to be given an unfair advantage or seem privileged to other students. Your goal is to succeed in college; take advantage of whatever services will help you.

Get to know other students in each of your classes.   Many students are genuinely interested in you, but they are unsure of how to initiate a conversation. Help them along; introduce yourself to them.

Multilingual Students and ESL (English as a Second Language) Students

If you are an international student or from a family or community in which English is usually not spoken, you face the challenge of reading, listening to lectures, writing papers, and participating in class discussions in a language that is not your first, native language. Here are a few suggestions.

Take ESL courses, even if they are not required.   These are taught by specialists in second-language learning; you will learn more quickly and easily than if you try to teach yourself.

Acquire a comprehensive two-language dictionary (English-Spanish, English-Japanese, etc.) and use it regularly.   Carry it with you to classes; refer to it as needed during lectures.

Consider recording lectures.   You can play back the lectures and catch ideas you missed during the lecture.

Discuss problems or limitations with your professors.   Once they are aware of your special needs, most will be eager to assist.

EXERCISE 1.3 | **Identifying Problems and Finding Help**

Directions   *Working with a classmate, brainstorm a list of potential problems—academic, social, or personal—that a student may encounter while attending college. For each problem, identify a source of help.*

■ Course Organization

No two college courses are conducted in exactly the same manner. Each course is tailored by the instructor to best express his or her approach to the subject matter, teaching style, and educational objectives. Two sections of the same course offered the same semester may be structured entirely differently from one another. One instructor may require a text; the other may assign readings. One instructor may lecture; the other may conduct class discussions. One instructor may give exams; the other may assign papers. The key to success in college courses, then, is to understand and work within the instructor's course organization. On the first day of class many instructors distribute a *syllabus* that explains their organization and approach. These, too, vary according to instructor, but they usually list the following:

- ◆ the required text
- ◆ the attendance policy
- ◆ the grading system
- ◆ the course objectives
- ◆ weekly assignments or readings
- ◆ dates of exams or due dates for papers

An excerpt from a syllabus for a human anatomy and physiology course is shown in Figure 1.2 on page 20. One of the most important parts of the syllabus is the course objectives. Objectives state, in general terms, what the instructors intend to accomplish and what they expect you to learn through the course. Objectives state what you are to learn; exams, then, are built to measure how well you have learned it.

Online Courses

Many colleges offer online courses; they require a great deal of independence, self-direction, and the ability to work alone. *Avoid taking online courses during your first semester or first year.* It is better to learn what is expected in college classes by attending traditional classes. Once you are familiar with college expectations, you will be better prepared to take an online course, using the following tips:

Read, read, read.   Reading is your primary source of information. You read textbooks and communications from professors and other students. If you aren't a strong reader or feel as if you need personal contact and in-person support from other students, get in touch with a classmate or find a friend who will register for the same online course.

Keep up with the work.   Most students who fail online courses fail because they fall hopelessly behind with the required reading and written assignments and cannot catch up. Devote specific hours each week to the online course. Make a work/study schedule and follow it as you would for any other class.

FIGURE 1.2
A Sample Course Syllabus Excerpt

Course Syllabus

Course Number: BIO 201

Course Name: Human Anatomy and Physiology I

Instructor: Dr. Jack Eberhardt

Prerequisite: BIO 102 with a grade of C or higher

Office Location: 322 Olympic Towers

Office Hours: MWF 1–3

Course Objectives:

1. To identify the major parts of a cell and know their functions.
2. To understand the structure and function of the human organ systems.
3. To learn the types of human body tissues and understand their functions.
4. To perform laboratory activities for collection and analysis of experimental data.

Your instructor tests you on these objectives. Use this list to test yourself.

....

Course Grade: Grades will be based on 3 multiple-choice exams and weekly laboratory reports. Exam questions are based on lecture notes, textbook assignments, as well as the lab manual. The exams will test factual knowledge as well as critical thinking skills.

Exams test your recall as well as your reasoning skills. Lab is important.

....

Attendance: Regular attendance is required for both lecture and laboratory. If you miss a class, you should get the missed material from a classmate. The instructor will not distribute or post lecture or lab notes. Make-up labs will not be allowed. If you miss an exam, you must provide written documentation to explain your absence. If you fail to do so, a grade of zero will be entered.

Don't miss classes or labs.

....

Tentative Lecture Schedule:

DATE	TOPIC	CHAPTER
Sept. 16	Course Introduction, The Scientific Method	1
Sept. 21	Atoms, molecules, water, chemical bonding	1, 2

Develop a weekly reading schedule based on this list.

....

>>>

Keep your focus.   Turn off music, instant messaging, and e-mail while working on your computer for your online course.

EXERCISE 1.4 **Studying a Syllabus**

Directions   *Study the syllabus for one of your courses and answer as many of the following questions as possible.*

1. What types of thinking are emphasized? (Refer to Chapter 2, p. 43.)
2. How is the subject matter of the course divided?
3. Summarize the grading system.
4. Predict three topics that might be asked on a final exam consisting entirely of essay questions.

■ Grades and the Grading System

Most colleges use a letter grade system in awarding final grades. Each college has its own variations, special policies, and unique designations, so be sure to read the section in your college catalog on grading policies. Specifically, find out about the following:

Pass/Fail Options

Some colleges allow you to take certain courses on a Pass/Fail basis. You earn the credit but receive only a Pass or Fail grade on your record. The Pass/Fail option, if available, allows you to take courses without competing for a letter grade. You might consider electing a Pass/Fail option for a difficult course. If, for example, you are required to take one math course and math has always been difficult for you, then consider taking that course on a Pass/Fail basis. Be sure to check your college catalog and with your advisor to be certain that required courses can be taken on a Pass/Fail basis and how to initiate the process. The instructor's permission may be required. Also, there may be a restriction on the number or types of courses that may be elected using this option.

The Pass/Fail option also provides an opportunity to take interesting elective courses without worrying about grades. Suppose you are interested in taking a history of modern music course but know that it is a difficult course taken mostly by students majoring in the arts. A Pass/Fail option would allow you to enjoy the course without competing for a letter grade.

Course Withdrawal

Most colleges have a provision by which you can withdraw from a course up to a given deadline in the semester without academic penalty. Be sure to check the college catalog for the deadline for course withdrawal. If you know you are doing poorly in a course, discuss the possibility of course withdrawal with your instructor. Some students who think they are in danger of failing learn otherwise by speaking with their instructor. Also, consult your advisor and the financial aid office to learn what impact, if any, course withdrawal will have on your academic and financial aid status.

Incomplete Grades

Many grading systems have a provision for students who are unable to complete a course for which they are registered. This grade, often called an Incomplete, is awarded at the discretion of the instructor when he or she feels the student has a legitimate reason for being unable to complete the course. Instructors may award an Incomplete if you are injured during the last week of classes, for example. Be sure to contact your instructor as soon as possible; offer to provide the instructor with verification of your reason. Many colleges have a deadline by which an Incomplete must be converted to a grade. This means you must arrange with your instructor to complete whatever course requirements he or she specifies by a given date. Be sure it is clear what assignments must be done, how to do them, and when they must be completed.

Grade Point Average (GPA)

Each semester an average is computed using the individual grades you received that semester. This average is computed by assigning numerical values to letter grades. An A may be assigned four points, a B three points, a C two points, a D one point, and an F zero points, for example. Consult your college catalog to discover what numerical values are used at your school and how they are calculated. Find out if pluses and minuses are considered.

A cumulative GPA is computed over successive semesters by averaging all the grades you have received since you began attending college. Many colleges require a specific cumulative GPA for admission to an academic department and for graduation. Grade point average may also influence financial aid eligibility and your academic status. You may be required to maintain a minimum GPA to receive financial aid or to remain in good academic standing.

| EXERCISE 1.5 | **Understanding the Grading System** |

Directions   *Answer each of the following questions about the grading system at your college.*

1. What is the deadline for course withdrawal?
2. Is the Pass/Fail grading option available? If so, is there a limit to the number of courses you may elect using this option?
3. Is there a time limit by which the work for Incomplete grades must be completed?
4. Are pluses and minuses considered part of your grading system?
5. What is the point value of D grades in your college's grading system?

THINKING CRITICALLY

. . . About Grades

Grading is an important part of most college courses. Successful students learn to use the grading system to their advantage. Here are a few questions to consider:

1. **How can you use the grading system to help you organize your study?** Suppose, for example, biweekly quizzes on textbook chapters in your business marketing class constitute 50 percent of your grade. How should you schedule your study?

2. **How can the grading system help you decide what is important to learn?** Suppose that 40 percent of your grade in sociology is based on weekly summaries and critiques of films shown in class. What can you do while watching the film and immediately after each film to improve this portion of your grade?

3. **How can the grading system help you make choices?** Suppose, for example, you have the choice of taking a final exam or writing a paper for your history class. What factors would you consider in making your decision?

SKILLS ⓘ ACTION

Using the Pass/Fail System to Your Advantage

The Pass/Fail system is intended not only to reduce students' stress and anxiety levels but also to encourage them to expand their horizons. The following is a list of courses offered at a typical college. From this list, choose no more than three courses that you would choose to take on a Pass/Fail basis. Explain the reasoning behind each of your choices.

- ◆ Art history survey
- ◆ Introductory statistics
- ◆ Survey of poetry
- ◆ Interpersonal communication
- ◆ American history
- ◆ Principles of chemistry
- ◆ Principles of economics

- ◆ Personal finance
- ◆ American Sign Language
- ◆ History of Russia and the Soviet Union
- ◆ Anatomy and physiology
- ◆ Introduction to health
- ◆ Psychology of children and adolescents

■ Classroom Success Tips

The following suggestions will help you be successful in each of your courses.

Attend All Classes

Even if class attendance is optional or not strictly monitored by your instructor, make it a rule to attend *all* classes. For most students, class time totals 12 to 15 hours per week, except for laboratory and studio courses. This amounts to less than 10 percent of your time each week! If you say you don't have enough time to attend all classes, you are not being honest with yourself. Remember, class instruction is a major part of what your tuition is paying for. You are cheating yourself if you don't take advantage of it. Seldom is a class taught in which you do not learn something new or gain a new perspective on already familiar ideas.

Get Acquainted with Faculty

Get to know your professors; you will find your classes more meaningful and interesting, and you will learn more. Challenging and stimulating conversations

---

REAL STUDENTS SPEAK

Sophie Crafts

Clark University
Worcester,
Massachusetts

Background: Sophie is a senior at Clark University majoring in psychology.

Goal: To obtain a bachelor's degree in psychology.

Advice on Getting Academic Help: If I don't like a class, writing papers is a big chore. I'm a big procrastinator and at the last minute have to do a lot of studying for tests and final exams. It stresses me out. I've found that meeting with a professor and explaining that I'm having a hard time keeping up really helps. They often offer really good advice on how to get through the class successfully. I've also found that teaching assistants help a lot. They can be easier to talk to than professors and more available."

often result, and you can gain new insights into the subject matter that you might never obtain by merely attending class. Talking with your instructors is an opportunity to apply and connect the course with your academic interests and goals. Talking with your instructor will also help you establish yourself as a conscientious and interested student.

Keep Up with Assignments

It is tempting to delay work on projects and assignments until you feel like doing them or until you have an exam or quiz on them. This approach is a mistake and can lead to a failing semester. Students who procrastinate end up with an impossible amount of reading to do within a short time. As a result, they don't do the reading at all or read the assignments hurriedly and without careful thought.

Form a Study Group

Choose several classmates and form a study group. Schedule a regular meeting time and place. Use the sessions to review, quiz each other, and study for exams.

Project a Positive Image

Be sure to approach each class positively and demonstrate that you are a serious student. Unfortunately, some students do behave thoughtlessly or rudely in class. The unspoken message they send is that the class is unimportant and uninteresting, and instructors are quick to perceive this. Work on establishing a positive image by

- ◆ arriving at class promptly
- ◆ asking or answering questions
- ◆ participating in class discussions
- ◆ sitting in the front of the room
- ◆ making eye contact with the instructor
- ◆ completing assignments on time
- ◆ reading assigned material before class
- ◆ saying "hello" when you meet your instructor on campus
- ◆ shutting off your cell phone during class

Take Action If You Are in the Wrong Course

You may find yourself in a course that is either too easy or too difficult. Courses in which this most often occurs are mathematics, foreign languages, and the sciences. If you suspect you are in the wrong course, talk with your instructor immediately. If he or she confirms that you are misplaced, ask for advice. Also consult with your advisor. Generally, it is inadvisable to continue in a course that is too difficult; dropping the course, if possible, is a reasonable alternative. Be certain, however, that dropping the course does not reduce your course load to below the minimum if you are a full-time student. If you make your decision to drop a course early enough in the semester, you may be able to add another course in its place.

Purchase Recommended Materials

While most instructors require a textbook, some make the purchase of other materials optional. These materials include review books, workbooks, dictionaries, or other reference books, manuals, or style sheets. Your instructor would not recommend the materials unless he or she felt they would be helpful. Therefore, make sure you purchase these optional materials. Often you will find that these materials make review easier and/or are helpful in completing required assignments or papers.

Take Action When You Miss an Important Exam or Deadline

Hopefully you will never have to miss an important exam or deadline for a paper. However, if you should wake up with the flu on the morning of a midterm exam, for example, you may have to miss the exam. Be sure to contact your instructor *before* the exam. Leave a phone message in the department office if you are unable to contact him or her directly. Explaining the situation ahead of time is preferable to making excuses later. If a paper is due and you are ill, ask a friend or fellow student to deliver it for you.

Get Involved with College Life

Academic course work is, of course, the primary reason for attending college. However, if all you are doing on campus is taking courses and studying, you are missing an important part of college life. College is more than textbooks, exams, and lectures. The academic environment is a world of ideas, a place where thought, concepts, and values are of primary importance. It is a place where you can discuss and exchange ideas, explore new approaches to life, and reevaluate old ones. College also provides an opportunity for you to decide who you are (or who you want to be) and how you would like to spend the rest of your life.

Considerable research indicates that students who participate in college activities tend to be more successful in college than those who do not. Activities provide an opportunity for you to get involved and to feel part of a group with similar interests. On large campuses, where it is easy to feel lost, involvement is

Working Together

Form groups of two or three students, and compile a list of success tips not included in this chapter that could be included in a tip sheet to be distributed to first-year students. Also include pitfalls to avoid. Include advice on things you've learned so far this semester (hints: registration, parking, dorms, food service, bookstore, add-drop procedures).

especially important. If you are preparing for a career, getting involved with college life is important. Most employers are interested in hiring well-spoken, interesting people who are aware of the world around them and can interact with others effectively. College can help you become well rounded, if you take advantage of it.

To get involved with college life, find out about activities and issues on campus. Many interesting lectures, debates, films, and concerts are sponsored weekly. Make it a point to meet someone in each of your classes; you will feel better about going to class, and a worthwhile friendship may develop. Find out if there is a student group that shares your interests, and join it. You may meet interesting people in the ski club, chorus, nursing students' association, or black students' union, for example.

If You Plan to Transfer

If you are attending a two-year college and plan to transfer to a four-year school after completing your associate's degree, plan accordingly. Do not assume that any course you take at one institution will be accepted for a degree at another. Each college and each academic department has its own policies and guidelines for the acceptance of transfer credit.

To ensure that most or all your credits will transfer, be sure to do the following:

◆ Obtain the college catalog of the institution to which you intend to transfer and read about degree requirements and transfer credit policies and procedures.

◆ Contact an admissions counselor to answer any questions.

◆ Make your current academic advisor aware of your plans. He or she can assist you in determining and selecting appropriate courses for transfer.

SKILLS IN ACTION

Analyzing Your Strengths and Weaknesses

An important component of college success is knowing where your strengths and weaknesses lie. Playing to your strengths is as important as compensating for your weaknesses. Following are some situations that students commonly report as weaknesses. For each, develop and write out a plan for meeting it head on and not allowing it to undermine your studies.

1. I hate studying math, but I need to take the course to get my degree.

2. I am not a morning person. If I could have my way, I'd sleep until noon each day. But I have to take classes in the morning; there's no way around it.

3. I have to take this class because it's required for my major. But I really can't stand the professor—he's snotty and arrogant. Even worse, I find the class boring.

REVIEW Five Key Points to Remember

1 **Learn about campus resources.** Colleges offer a wide variety of valuable services; find out what is available and take advantage of them.

2 **Benefit from campus diversity.** Widen your horizons by taking the time to get to know students, faculty, and staff who represent various social, cultural, and national backgrounds.

3 **Study course syllabi.** These are valuable tools that help you know what to expect and what to study in each course.

4 **Learn about grades.** Be sure to learn your college's policies on grading including Pass/Fail, course withdrawal, Incomplete grades, and grade point average (GPA).

5 **Build classroom success.** Project yourself as serious student by attending all classes and keeping up with assignments and deadlines.

The Work Connection

The workplace of the 21st century, researchers agree, is quite different from the workplace of the past. Corporate mergers, acquisitions, downsizing, new technologies, and global competition are only a few of the factors that are causing a shift in the qualities, skills, and capabilities that employers will expect of successful employees. Research also suggests that the average person will make three to five major career changes in the course of his or her work life. Now is the time to start considering how the decisions you make in college are likely to affect your future employment. Begin by answering the following questions:

1. What are three careers that you might enjoy pursuing during your lifetime?

2. What skills will you learn in this course that relate to your career and life goals? List four or five skills.

3. What college courses might you consider taking that will make you versatile and employable in a variety of career settings?

The Web Connection

Each chapter in this book ends with a list of Web sites that include information and activities helpful to college students. Visit them when you need more assistance with particular topics, strategies, or skills.

1. How to Flunk Out with Style and Grace

   http://em.csuchico.edu/aap/Undergrad/probation/FlunkWStyle.asp

   This site uses humor and irony to tell students how to succeed by telling them how not to succeed. Print out this list and record whether you have been exhibiting any of these behaviors. Jot down strategies to change your behaviors if necessary.

2. Three Credits and a Baby

   https://secure3.electronet.net/RWUniversity/stories.cfm?id=21&action=Show&cid=42

   From the Real World University site, this brief article describes one young woman's struggle as a single mother going to college. Choose one of her tips and explain how it could apply to your own situation.

3. Commuters and College Life

   http://www.wealtheffect.com/icampusa/ic–commuters.htm

   Some tips for commuters are presented here as part of a larger guide to starting college. Interview a commuter about the information presented on the Web site. Are there issues that could be added?

2 Taking Charge of Your College Career

Do You Know?

What is expected of you in college?

How can you take charge of your college career?

What are the early warning signs of academic difficulty?

How can you take an active approach to learning?

What levels of thinking are key to college success?

What is plagiarism and how can you avoid it?

You are now a college student. Reaching this point may have required years of hard work, preparation, and planning. Now that you are here, you are ready to begin the challenging, exciting tasks that college involves. At this point it is only natural for you to be wondering, "How successful will I be?" or "How well will I be able to meet these new demands and challenges?" This chapter describes the new demands of college, offers numerous success strategies, teaches you *how* to learn, and shows you *how* to become an active, involved learner. It also introduces you to critical thinking skills and shows their importance in college success. In addition, the chapter shows you how to avoid plagiarism.

■ Coping with New Expectations

Whether you have just completed high school or are returning to college with a variety of work experiences or family responsibilities, you will face new demands and expectations in college. The following section discusses how to cope with these demands.

Set Your Own Operating Rules

College is very different from lower levels of education and from jobs you may have held because it imposes few clear limits, rules, or controls. There are no

REAL STUDENTS SPEAK

**Markella
Tsoukalas**

**Fairleigh Dickinson
University
Teaneck, New Jersey**

Background: Markella is a junior at Fairleigh University majoring in business administration. She also works halftime as an office manager.

Goals: To go to graduate school and obtain a masters degree in business administration.

Advice on Taking Responsibility: High school and college are completely different. High school is basically spoon fed to you. You get an assignment two weeks before it's due. If you don't do the work, the teacher calls your parents. In college there are no threats; if you don't do the work, OK, you get an F. In high school people feel tied down and smothered. Then they get to college and they feel so free, they forget why they are there, they lose their focus, their reason for going to college. To do well in college you have to a have a love for going to school and want to achieve success. You have to take responsibility for your learning.

defined work hours except for classes; your time is your own. Often, you face no threats or penalties for missing classes or failing to complete assignments. You do *what* you want, *when* you want, *if* you want to at all. For many students, the lack of structure requires some adjustment; at first, it is often confusing. Some students feel they should spend all their free time studying; others put off study or never find quite the right time for it.

One of the best ways to handle this flexibility is to establish your own set of operating rules. For example, you might decide to limit yourself to two absences in each course. Here are examples of rules successful students have set for themselves:

◆ Study at least three hours each day or evening.
◆ Start studying for a major examination at least a week ahead.
◆ Complete all homework assignments regardless of whether you get credit for them.
◆ Make review a part of each study session.
◆ Read all assigned chapters *before* the class in which they will be discussed.

You may feel more committed to the rules you set if you write them down and post them above your desk as a constant reminder.

Take Responsibility for Your Own Learning

In college, professors function as guides. They define and explain what is to be learned, but *you* do the learning. Class time is far shorter than in high school; there is not enough time to provide numerous drills, practices, and reviews of factual course content. College class time is used primarily to introduce what is to be learned, to provoke thought, and to discuss ideas. Instructors expect you to learn the material and to be prepared to discuss it in class.

Develop New Approaches to Learning

College requires new attitudes and approaches toward learning.

Focus on Important Concepts

Each course you take will seem to have endless facts, statistics, dates, definitions, formulas, rules, and principles to learn. It is easy, then, to become a robot learner—absorbing information from texts and lectures, then spewing it out automatically on exams and quizzes. Actually, factual information is only a starting point, a base from which to approach the real content of a course. Most college instructors expect you to go beyond facts to analysis: to consider what the collection of facts and details *means*. Many students "can't see the forest for the trees." They fail to see the larger, overriding concepts of their courses because they get caught up in specifics. Too concerned with memorizing information, they fail to ask, "Why do I need to know this?" "Why is this important?" or "What principle or trend does this illustrate?" Here are a few examples of details from a course in American government and the more important trend, concept, or principle they represent:

Topic	Detail	Importance
Voting Rights Act of 1965	Federal registrars were sent to southern states to protect blacks' right to vote.	This was the beginning of equality in voter registration.
Supreme Court case: *Roe v. Wade*	Court ruling forbade state control over abortion in first trimester of pregnancy; permitted states to limit abortions to protect the mother's health in the second trimester; permitted states to protect fetus in the third trimester.	Established policy on abortions; opened questions of "right to privacy" and "right to life."

EXERCISE 2.1

Identifying Key Concepts

Directions   *Choose one of your textbooks and turn to a section of a chapter you have already read. List six consecutive headings that appear in that text. After each heading, explain why each topic is important. In other words, indicate its significance and the concept or principle it illustrates.*

Focus on Ideas, Not Right Answers

Through previous schooling, many students have come to expect their answers to be either right or wrong. They assume that learning is limited to a collection of facts and that their mastery of the course is measured by the number of right answers they have learned. When faced with an essay question such as the following, they become distraught:

Defend or criticize the arguments that are offered in favor of construction of border fences to control immigration. Refer to any reading you have done.

You can see that there is not *one* right answer; you can either defend the argument or criticize it. The instructor who asks this question expects you to think and to provide a reasoned, logical, consistent response using information acquired through readings. Here are a few more examples of questions for which there are no single correct answers:

◆ Do animals think?
◆ Would you be willing to reduce your standard of living by 15 percent if the United States could thereby eliminate poverty? Defend your response.
◆ Imagine a society in which everyone has exactly the same income. You are the manager of an industrial plant. What plans, policies, or programs would you implement that would motivate your employees to work?
◆ Is the primary purpose of an artist to represent his or her own feelings?

Working Together

Form groups of three or four students and complete the following steps:

1. List the courses taken by each group member. Each group should identify courses that

   a. require new approaches to learning.
   b. focus on ideas and concepts.
   c. focus on logical thinking.
   d. require reaction and discussion.
   e. require evaluation of new ideas.
   f. involve creative thinking.
   g. require problem solving.

2. Each group should present its list to the class; then the class should compare the lists in each category.

EXERCISE 2.2   **Examining Issues**

Directions   *Examine two or three newspapers or magazines to identify controversies—issues people disagree about—currently in the news. Based on what you read, compose a list of five questions for which there are no single correct answers—questions for which different viewpoints or opinions exist.*

THINKING CRITICALLY
. . . About Course Content

To become an active learner, get in the habit of asking critical questions. Critical questions are questions that help you analyze and evaluate what and how you are learning. As you work through this book, you will learn to ask many critical questions. Here are a few to help you get started:

◆ Why was this material assigned?

◆ What am I supposed to learn from this assignment?

◆ How does this assignment relate to today's class lecture?

◆ What is the best way to learn this information?

◆ How will I know I have learned the material?

◆ What levels of thinking does this assignment or exam require?

■ Taking Charge

People who make plans and decisions are more successful than those who do not. People without definite plans and goals drift through life passively, letting things happen and allowing others to control their lives. Active decision makers, on the other hand, know what they want and plan strategies to obtain it. Here's how to take charge.

Accept Responsibility for Grades

Certainly you have heard comments such as, "Dr. Smith only gave me a B on my last paper" or "I got a C on my first lab report." Students often think of grades as rewards that teachers give to students. Thinking this way is avoiding responsibility, blaming the instructor instead of owning up to the fact that a paper or exam failed to meet the standards set by the instructor.

Be honest; you will not always earn the grades you want and you will not always score as well as you expect to on every exam. Analyze what you could have done to improve a disappointing grade, and put this to work in preparing for the next exam.

Don't Make Excuses

Studying is not easy; it requires time and conscious effort. Try not to make it more difficult than it really is by avoiding it. Some students avoid studying by following a variety of escape routes. Here are a few common ones:

- ◆ I can't study tonight because I promised to drive my sister to the mall.
- ◆ I can't study for my physics test because the dorm is too noisy.
- ◆ I can't finish reading my psychology assignment because the chapter is boring.
- ◆ I didn't finish writing my essay because I fell asleep.

If you find yourself making excuses to avoid studying, step back and analyze the problem. Consider possible causes and solutions (see Chapter 6). For example, if the dorm really is too noisy to study, could you study at a different time or find a new place to study? More likely, the problem is that you were just not in the mood to study. Be honest! Before you quit and go on to something else, make a definite commitment to finish the assignment later; be specific about when and where. Postponing study may be better than avoiding it completely, but bear in mind that it probably will not be much easier after it has been postponed.

EXERCISE 2.3

Analyzing Study Situations

Directions   *Analyze your past study performance by answering the following two questions honestly.*

1. What excuses have you used to avoid study?
2. Whom have you blamed when you did not study or did not earn the grade you expected?

Develop Essential, Marketable Skills

Many students enter college with a rigid, narrowly defined, and often limiting academic self-image. They make choices and decisions based on an image they express with comments like these:

"I'm not good with math."

"I've never done well in writing."

"If I have to speak in front of a group, forget it."

If you think you are weak in math, then majoring in accounting may not be a good idea. However, avoiding all courses that involve mathematics or calculations is not realistic. In almost any job, you will sooner or later need to

SKILLS IN ACTION

Taking Charge of Your Learning After Exams

Analyze the following case study; then answer the questions that follow.

A political science professor has just returned graded midterm exams to her class. One student looks at the grade on the first page, then flips through the remaining pages while commenting to a friend that the exam was "too picky." She files the exam away in her notebook. A second student reviews his exam for grading errors and finds one error. Immediately, he raises his hand and asks for an adjustment to his grade. The instructor seems annoyed and says she will not use class time to dispute individual grades. A third student reviews her exam blue book to identify a pattern of error; on the cover of the blue book she notes topics and areas in which she is weak.

1. Compare the three students' responses to the situation.

2. What does each student's response reveal about his or her approach to learning?

3. What alternatives might have been more appropriate for the second student?

work with numbers. Potential employers will look for and expect at least minimum competency.

Work on expanding and modifying your skills by taking courses to strengthen your weaknesses (elect a Pass/Fail grade, if you are worried about grades) and to acquire basic competencies in a variety of areas. For example, an elective course in public speaking will boost your confidence in your ability to present yourself effectively. Build a marketable package of skills that will place you in a competitive position to land that all-important job after graduation.

EXERCISE 2.4

Examining Your Strengths and Weaknesses

Directions   *Define your current strengths and weaknesses as a student. If you find that your strengths and weaknesses vary in different courses, make your list specific for each course you are taking. Chart a course of action to address each weakness.*

■ Early Warning Signals of Academic Difficulty

A major part of getting ahead academically and staying there is monitoring your progress in each course and then adjusting your study strategies accordingly. In courses with weekly quizzes or frequent assignments, it is easy to assess how well you are doing. In other courses, knowing how well you are doing is more difficult. Some instructors give only two or three exams per semester; others may require only a term paper and a final exam. Such courses offer no grades during the term for you to determine if you are doing well; instead, you will have to be alert for the early warning signals of academic difficulty.

Questions That Predict Academic Difficulty

Here are some questions that will indicate whether you are on the right track in a course.

Are you falling behind on assignments?   Do you put off studying by saying, "I'll wait until this weekend to work on calculus; then I'll have enough time to really concentrate on straightening this out"? Meanwhile, you fall further behind as the week goes by. If you are behind on assignments, you may be avoiding them because they are difficult and unrewarding. This is a signal that something may be going wrong with the course.

Have you missed several classes recently?   Most instructors agree that student attendance is a good predictor of success in a course; students who attend class regularly tend to earn good grades. If you have missed several classes in a course without a legitimate reason for doing so, this may be another form of avoidance.

Do you feel lost or confused in any course?   If you are having trouble making sense of what the instructor is doing day to day or cannot see how various topics and assignments fit together, you may be in academic difficulty. The course may be at the wrong level for your current academic background, or you may lack an overview or perspective on the course.

Are you relying heavily on a friend for help in completing assignments?   Depending regularly on a classmate for help suggests that you are not able to handle the course alone. Remember, your friend won't be much help when it comes to the final exam.

Do you feel restless and listless, as if something is wrong but you're not sure what it is?   If you feel anxious and depressed, most likely something is wrong. Look for patterns and discover where and when you feel this way.

Do you feel constantly tired or spend a lot of time sleeping? Overtiredness may be a reaction to a general feeling of stress. It, too, may be a signal that something is wrong. Find out what it is.

How to Handle Academic Problems

If you are like many college students, discovering and admitting that you are having trouble with a course can be difficult and traumatic. The possibility that you may fail a course is a shock and a threat to your self-image. "Could this really be happening to me?" is a very common feeling. Here is some advice to follow if you should have this feeling.

Maintain your self-confidence.   Don't lose your confidence just because you are having trouble with one course. Remind yourself of the successes you have experienced in other courses. Don't start thinking differently about yourself; realize that you are merely gaining additional experience that will help you learn more.

Remember that you are not alone.   The first semester of college is the most difficult one for most students. A review of students' grade point averages throughout their college experience confirms this. The first semester or quarter grades are the lowest; grades gradually rise as students develop skills and acquire experiences in handling college courses. Keep on striving and you will improve.

Take immediate action.   As soon as you suspect you are having trouble in a course, take immediate action. Things seldom improve on their own. In most cases the longer you wait, the further behind you will fall and the more difficult it will be to catch up.

Talk with your instructor.   Before things get too bad, talk with your instructor. Most instructors have office hours each week, times when they are available to talk with students. They are also available by phone. When you talk with your instructor, try to define topics, areas, or skills that are troublesome. Have specific questions in mind. State the steps you have already taken and ask for advice. Your instructor may recommend additional reading to fill in gaps in your background knowledge or suggest a new approach to follow as you read and study.

Many instructors encourage you to use e-mail to ask questions about specific assignments or to discuss your progress in the course.

Explore sources of help.   Many colleges and universities have sources of academic assistance. Find out if there is an Academic Development Center or Learning Center on your campus. Such centers offer brush-up courses and sponsor peer tutoring programs for popular freshman courses. Check to see if the library or media center has DVDs, computer programs, or self-instructional workbooks that deal with the subject matter of your course. For a troublesome course, if free tutoring is not available, consider hiring an upperclass student as a tutor. Ask your instructor to recommend someone. Although this may be expensive, consider what you will lose if you fail and have to retake the course.

Consider withdrawing from the course.   If you and your instructor feel you cannot handle the course or if you have fallen so far behind that it is nearly impossible to catch up, consider withdrawing from the course. (Your college

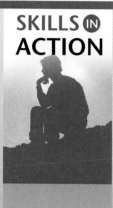

SKILLS IN ACTION

Considering an Instructor's Effects on Your Learning

As a responsible student, you take charge of and accept responsibility for your learning. While you should not "blame" a professor for giving you poor grades, it *is* true that certain instructors may be more in sync with your learning style (or even your personality) than others.

Below, list a course you will have to take in the next two terms and the names of two or three instructors who teach it. Talk to other students, or use the Web site http://www.ratemyprofessors.com to get a sense of each instructor's approach and style. Based on your research, which professor do you think would be the best match for you?

Course Name: _____

Instructor's Name	Strengths and Weaknesses

catalog explains policies and deadlines for course withdrawal.) While it is painful to admit that you were not able to handle the course, withdrawal will free your mind from anxiety and enable you to concentrate and do well in your remaining courses.

If you decide to withdraw from a required course and you must reregister for the course in a subsequent semester, consider taking the course from another instructor whose approach and teaching style may work better for you. Since course withdrawal is an expensive option, use it only as a last resort.

■ Active Versus Passive Learning

A freshman who had always thought of herself as a good student found herself getting low Cs or Ds on her first quizzes and exams. She was studying harder and spending more time but was not earning the grades she expected. After discussing the problems with her professors, she realized that her approach was a passive one. She did what her instructors requested. She read what was

assigned, completed assignments as required, and followed instructions carefully. To be more successful, this student needed to develop a more active approach. She should have interacted with the material she read: asked questions, sorted out what was important to learn, and decided how to learn it. Table 2.1 lists characteristics of the two types of learners. As you read through the list, determine which type you are.

TABLE 2.1 Characteristics of Passive and Active Learners

	Passive Learners	Active Learners
Class lectures	Write down what the instructor says.	Decide what is important to write down.
Textbook assignments	Read.	Read, think, ask questions, try to connect ideas.
Studying	Reread.	Make outlines and study sheets, predict exam questions, look for trends and patterns.
Writing class assignments	Carefully follow the professor's instructions.	Try to discover the significance of the assignment; look for the principles and concepts it illustrates.
Writing term papers	Do what is expected to get a good grade.	Try to expand their knowledge and experience with a topic and connect it to the course objective or content.

Why Become an Active Learner?

Think about the many types of learning you have experienced. How did you learn to ride a bike, make pizza, or play tennis? In each case, you learned by doing, by active participation. While much of what you will learn in college is not as physical as riding a bike or playing tennis, it still can be learned best through active participation. Studying and thinking are forms of participation, as are making notes, speaking up in class discussion, or reviewing chapters with a friend. Active involvement, then, is a key to effective learning. Throughout this text, you will learn strategies to promote active learning. Assess your active learning strategies by completing the questionnaire shown in Figure 2.1.

FIGURE 2.1
Rate Your Active Learning Strategies

Respond to each of the following statements by checking "Always," "Sometimes," or "Never."

	Always	Sometimes	Never
1. I try to figure out *why* an assignment was given.	❏	❏	❏
2. While reading I am sorting important information.	❏	❏	❏
3. I think of questions as I read.	❏	❏	❏
4. I try to make connections between reading assignments and class lectures.	❏	❏	❏
5. I attempt to see how a newly assigned chapter in my text relates to the previously assigned one.	❏	❏	❏
6. I try to see how my instructor's class lectures fit together (relate to one another).	❏	❏	❏
7. I think about how the information I am reading can be used or applied.	❏	❏	❏
8. After writing a paper or completing an assignment, I think about what I learned from doing it.	❏	❏	❏
9. I review a returned exam to discover what types of questions I missed.	❏	❏	❏
10. I react to and evaluate what I am reading.	❏	❏	❏

Each item that you marked as "Sometimes" or "Never" identifies skills you need to work on to become a more active learner. Review the checklist, then gradually introduce the skills into your daily reading and study methods.

Become a More Active Learner

When you study, you should be thinking about and reacting to the material in front of you:

Ask questions about what you are reading.   You will find that this helps to focus your attention and improve your concentration.

Discover the purpose behind assignments.   Why might a sociology assignment require you to spend an hour at the monkey house of the local zoo, for example?

Try to see how each assignment fits with the rest of the course.   For instance, why does a section titled "Consumer Behavior" belong in a retailing textbook chapter titled "External Retail Restraints"?

Relate what you are learning to what you already know.   Use your background knowledge and personal experience. Connect a law in physics with how your car brakes work, for example.

EXERCISE 2.5

Working Together

Analyzing Learning Tasks

Directions   *Working in pairs, consider each of the following learning situations. List ways to make each an active learning task.*

1. Revising a paper for an English composition class
2. Reading an assignment in a current newsmagazine
3. Studying a diagram in a data processing textbook chapter
4. Preparing a review schedule for an upcoming major exam
5. Looking up synonyms in a thesaurus for a word for your sociology term paper
6. Reading the procedures in your chemistry lab manual for the next laboratory session

---

■ Using Levels of Thinking

To give you a better understanding of the variety of thinking skills involved in academic learning, a model is shown in Table 2.2. This model, developed by Bloom (1956), and revised by Anderson (2000), describes a hierarchy, or progression, of thinking skills. These levels of thinking will help you master textbook material, prepare for exams, and predict exam questions. Notice that the levels move from basic literal understanding to more complex critical thinking skills. The first two levels describe information gathering skills—the ability to remember and understand information. The remaining four are critical thinking skills.

TABLE 2.2 Levels of Thinking

Level	Description	Examples
Remembering	Recalling information; repeating information with no changes	Recalling dates; memorizing definitions
Understanding	Understanding ideas; using rules and following directions	Explaining a law; recognizing what is important
Applying	Applying knowledge to a new situation	Using knowledge of formulas to solve a new physics problem
Analyzing	Seeing relationships; breaking information into parts; analyzing how things work	Comparing two poems by the same author
Evaluating	Making judgments; assessing the value or worth of information	Evaluating the effectiveness of an argument opposing the death penalty
Creating	Putting ideas and information together in a unique way; creating something new	Designing a new computer program

When college instructors write exams, most assume that you can operate at each of these levels. Table 2.3 shows a few items from an exam for a sociology course. Notice how the items require different levels of thinking.

TABLE 2.3 Test Items and Levels of Thinking

Test item	Level of thinking required
Define "stereotype."	Remembering
Explain how a stereotype can negatively affect a person.	Understanding
Give an example of a stereotype that is commonly held for a particular age group.	Applying
Study the two attached interviews. Which of the interviewers reveals a stereotypic attitude?	Analyzing
Evaluate a television commercial shown in class, discussing how a stereotypic attitude was revealed and approached.	Evaluating
Construct a set of guidelines that might be used to identify a stereotypic attitude.	Creating

The various categories of thinking are not distinct or mutually exclusive; they overlap. For example, note taking during a lecture class involves understanding, but it also involves analyzing, evaluating, and creating. Taking an essay exam may involve, at one point or another, all six levels. Throughout this book you will learn strategies for improving each level of thinking.

EXERCISE 2.6

Working Together

Using Levels of Thinking

Directions   *Read the following excerpt from an interpersonal communication textbook and then complete the items that follow. Then, working with a partner, use each level of thinking to discuss, understand, and evaluate the excerpt.*

Forms of Nonverbal Communication

Nonverbal elements, as already noted, sometimes work separately from verbal communication; that is, we may receive a nonverbal message without any words whatsoever. But usually the nonverbal domain provides a framework for the words we use. If we think of nonverbal communication as including all forms of message transmission *not* represented by word symbols, we can divide it into five broad categories: emblems, illustrators, affect displays, regulators, and adaptors.

   In their early work in this area, Jurgen Ruesch and Weldon Kees outlined just three categories: sign, action, and object language. Sign language *includes gestures used in the place of words, numbers, or punctuation.* When an athlete raises his index finger to show his team is "Number One," he is using sign language. Action language *includes all those nonverbal movements not intended as signs.* Your way of walking, sitting, or eating may serve your personal needs, but they also make statements to those who see them. Object language *includes both the intentional and unintentional display of material things.* Your hairstyle, glasses, and jewelry reveal things about you, as do the books you carry, the car you drive, or the clothes you wear.

Weaver, *Understanding Interpersonal Communication*, pp. 283–284.

1. *Remembering*	What is the definition of "object language"?
2. *Understanding*	What does object language include?
3. *Applying*	Give an example of object language.
4. *Analyzing*	Analyze and describe the object language used by a friend.
5. *Creating*	Identify objects that are important means of communication among your group of friends. Rank them in order of importance.
6. *Evaluating*	Do you agree or disagree with Ruesch and Kees's categorization of nonverbal communication? Explain your answer.

| EXERCISE 2.7 | **Identifying Levels of Thinking** |

Directions *For each activity or situation described below, indicate the levels of thinking that are primarily involved.*

1. Answering the following short-answer test question: Give an example of defensive behavior.
2. Solving a math problem
3. Taking notes on a college lecture
4. Translating into English a poem written in Spanish
5. Studying a famous painting for an art history course
6. Selecting a topic for a term paper in a criminal justice class
7. Revising a composition to make its thesis clearer and to improve its organization
8. Completing a biology lab in which you dissect an insect
9. Writing a computer program for a class assignment in a data processing course
10. Answering the following essay exam question: Most people would probably be outraged if someone sprayed them with poisonous air or fed them dangerous chemicals. In effect, this is what industrial polluters and many of their products are doing. Why, then, are people not outraged?

Neubeck, *Social Problems*, p.267

■ Building Academic Integrity

It is important to present yourself as a serious and honest student. This involves avoiding cheating and avoiding both intentional and unintentional plagiarism.

Avoid Cheating

There are many forms of cheating and you are likely to see some students engaging in it. Students who cheat on homework or exams are, in the long run, cheating themselves out of the education they are in college to obtain. Obvious forms of cheating involve sharing homework assignments or exchanging information with other students on exams. Other, less obvious, but still very serious, forms of cheating include

◆ using unauthorized notes during an exam
◆ changing exam answers after grading and requesting regrading
◆ falsifying or making up results for a lab report
◆ submitting the same paper twice for more than one course without instructor authorization
◆ not following rules on take-home exams
◆ using someone else's work or ideas as if they are your own (plagiarism)

Avoid Plagiarism

Plagiarism means borrowing someone else's ideas or exact wording without giving that person credit. If you take information on Frank Lloyd Wright's architecture from a reference source, but do not indicate where you found it, you have plagiarized. If you take the six-word phrase "Martinez, the vengeful, despicable drug czar" from an online news article on the war on drugs, you have plagiarized. Plagiarism is intellectually dishonest because you are taking someone else's ideas or wording and passing them off as your own. There are academic penalties for plagiarism. You may receive a failing grade on your paper or you may fail the entire course. At some institutions you can even be academically dismissed.

As you write papers for college classes, you will probably use sources to locate the information you need. As you read and take notes, and, later, as you write the paper, you need to know the rules for indicating that you have taken information or ideas from the work of other people. Consult a writer's handbook for more information. Identifying your sources helps others who want to look further into the ideas of that author to find that source. It also gives credit to the person who originally wrote the material or thought of the idea.

What Constitutes Plagiarism

Plagiarism can be intentional (planned) or unintentional (done by accident or oversight). Either way it carries the same academic penalty. If you buy a paper from an Internet site or deliberately copy and paste a section of an article from a Web site into your paper, your plagiarism is intentional. If you take notes from a source and copy exact wording, forget to enclose the wording in quotation marks, and later use that exact wording in your paper, your plagiarism is unintentional, but it is still serious and dishonest. Here are some guidelines that will help you understand exactly what is considered plagiarism.

WHAT IS PLAGIARISM?

- **Plagiarism** is the use of another person's words without giving credit to that person.
- **Plagiarism** uses another person's theory, opinion, or idea without indicating where the information was taken from.
- **Plagiarism** results when the exact words of another person are not placed inside quotation marks. Both the quotation marks and a citation (reference) to the original source are needed.
- Paraphrasing (rewording) another person's words without giving credit to him or her is still **plagiarism**.
- Using facts, data, graphs, charts, and so on without stating where they were taken from is **plagiarism**.
- Using commonly known facts or information is **not** plagiarism and you need not give a source for your information. For example, the fact that Neil Armstrong set foot on the moon in 1969 is widely known and does not require documentation.

To avoid plagiarism, use the following suggestions:

- When you take notes from a source, place anything you copy directly in quotation marks.
- As you read and take notes, separate your ideas from ideas taken from sources so you do not mistakenly present ideas from sources as your own. One way to do this is to use different colors of ink for each; another is to use different sections of a notebook page for information from sources and for your own ideas.
- Keep track of all sources you use, marking where each idea came from.
- When paraphrasing someone else's words, change as many words as possible and try not to follow the exact same organization. Give credit for where the information came from.
- Write paraphrases without looking at the original text so you rephrase it in your own words.
- When writing your paper, use quotation marks to designate exact quotations.
- Use citations to indicate the source of quotations and all ideas and information that are not your own. A citation is a parenthetical notation referring to a complete listing of sources used at the end of the paper.
- Never copy and paste directly from a Web site into your paper without enclosing the words in quotation marks and listing the source.

Avoid Cyberplagiarism

Cyberplagiarism is a special type of plagiarism; it involves borrowing information from the Internet without giving credit to the source posting the information. It is also called **cut and paste plagiarism**, referring to the ease with which a person can copy something from an Internet document and paste it into his or her own paper. Numerous Web sites offer student papers for sale. The term *cyberplagiarism* also refers to using these papers and submitting them as one's own.

Instructors have access to Web sites that easily and quickly identify papers that have been shared or purchased, so most instructors can easily spot an intentionally plagiarized paper.

EXERCISE 2.8	**Recognizing Plagiarism**

Directions   *Read the following passage from* Sociology for the Twenty-First Century *by Tim Curry, Robert Jiobu, and Kent Schwirian. Place a check mark next to each statement that is an example of plagiarism from this passage.*

Mexican Americans.   Currently, *Mexican Americans* are the second-largest racial or ethnic minority in the United States, but by early in the next century they will be the largest group. Their numbers will swell as a result of continual immigration from

Mexico and the relatively high Mexican birth rate. Mexican Americans are one of the oldest racial-ethnic groups in the United States. Under the terms of the treaty ending the Mexican-American War in 1848, Mexicans living in territories acquired by the United States could remain there and were to be treated as American citizens. Those that did stay became known as "Californios," "Tejanos," or "Hispanos."

_____ a. Mexican Americans are the second-largest minority in the United States. The number grows as more people immigrate from Mexico.

_____ b. After the Mexican American War, those Mexicans living in territories owned by the U.S. became American citizens and were called "Californios," "Tejanos," and "Hispanos" (Curry, Jiobu, and Schwirian, p. 207).

_____ c. "Mexican Americans are one of the oldest racial-ethnic groups in the United States."

_____ d. The Mexican-American war ended in 1848.

SKILLS IN ACTION

Checking Your Academic Integrity

The following list identifies some common behaviors in which students engage in order to improve their grades. Check off those behaviors that would violate academic integrity. In groups of three or four students, compare your results with classmates'; discuss any items on which you disagree.

- ❏ Asking an upperclassman for help with a difficult course
- ❏ Geting a copy of a professor's exams from a fraternity house
- ❏ Buying a copy of the teacher's edition of a text and using it to find answers to homework assignments
- ❏ Visiting an instructor during office hours to get clarification on topics they do not understand
- ❏ Using the Internet to conduct research
- ❏ Purchasing prewritten term papers from a fellow student or the Internet
- ❏ Using their word processor's spell-check and grammar-check functions before handing in a paper
- ❏ Asking an instructor for a better grade because they need that grade to stay on the basketball team
- ❏ Talking to students who have had their instructor in the past about strategies for doing well on assignments and group projects

REVIEW — Five Key Points to Remember

1 **Accept responsibilities.** You are responsible for your own learning; set operating rules, develop new approaches to learning, and focus on and evaluate ideas.

2 **Watch for warning signals.** Pay attention to warning signs of academic difficulty and take immediate action if you spot any.

3 **Be an active learner.** Become an active learner by integrating ideas, questioning, and responding to course content.

4 **Develop levels of thinking.** Use all six levels of thinking as you listen and respond in class, read assignments, and write exams and papers.

5 **Build academic integrity.** Be honest and fair by avoiding cheating and plagiarism.

The Work Connection

What workplace skills will you develop in college? Carolyn Corbin, founder and director of the Center for the 21st Century, has coined a new word for the successful worker of the future: "indipreneur." An indipreneur is a person who is independent and entrepreneurial, even when working for a corporation. Indipreneurs are self-reliant, are flexible, and experience change as a challenge rather than as a threat.[1] Corbin identifies the top three skills most important to a person's workplace success: "Know how to think, how to get along in the workplace with other people, and how to stay current in skills and technology."[2]

1. How will developing active learning skills in college aid you in the workplace of the twenty-first century? List eight to ten ideas.

2. What steps can you take now to ensure that you will have the top three skills Corbin considers most important for career success List at least five steps.

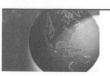

The Web Connection

1. How Realistic Are Your College Expectations?

   http://www.advising.wayne.edu/hndbk/expect.html

   Try taking this true/false quiz from Wayne State University. Evaluate your answers. What areas might you need a "reality check" in?

2. Great Expectations

   http://www.highereducation.org/reports/expectations/expectations.shtml

   Browse the findings of a recent study on the public's opinion of higher education. Write a paragraph describing how these findings compare with your own ideas about the role of college in your life.

3. Setting and Achieving Goals

   The University of Texas at Austin has several worksheets available to help you plan, set and evaluate your weekly goals. Find these tools on this page under "Time Management":

   http//www.utexas.edu/student/utlc/learning_resources/

   Try using these pages for two weeks and then evaluate their usefulness for you.

3 Establishing Goals and Managing Your Time

Do You Know?

How can you decide what you want out of life?

How can you organize your life for success in college?

How can you analyze your existing time commitments?

How can you build a study plan?

How can you make better use of your time?

How can you concentrate to make the most of your study time?

In college assignments, papers, and exams seem to keep coming, and just when you feel as if you've gotten things under control, another assignment or examination is announced. You can learn to cope with the tremendous work-load of college by setting goals, organizing your life, and managing your time.

Time management is a highly marketable skill in career and professional fields as well as in college. Handling the pressures of the workload of a responsible, fulfilling job also requires time management skills. If you develop and apply these skills to college life, you will be able to make an easy transition to career or professional life.

■ Establishing Life Goals

In order to manage your time effectively, you must first decide which things in your life are more important and which are less so.

Let's begin, then, by defining some life goals. Life goals are what you want out of life. They should be statements of where you are headed. They represent focal points of your life and can help you stay on track when life gets confusing, frustrating, or overwhelming.

How to Discover What Is Important

1. Make a list of the ten most joyous moments in your life. A phrase or single sentence of description is all that is needed.

51

2. Ask yourself, "What do most or all these moments have in common?"

3. Try to write answers to the above question by describing why the moments were important to you—what you got out of them. (Sample answers: helping others, competing or winning, creating something worthwhile, proving your self-worth, connecting with nature, and so forth.)

4. Your answers should provide a starting point for defining life goals.

Defining Life Goals

In defining your life goals, be specific and detailed. Use the following suggestions.

◆ **Your goals should be positive (what you want) rather than negative (what you want to avoid).** Don't say, "I won't ever have to worry about credit card balances and bill collectors." Instead, say, "I will have enough money to live comfortably."

◆ **Your goals should be realistic.** Unless you have strong evidence to believe you can do so, don't say you want to win an Olympic gold medal in swimming. Instead, say you want to become a strong, competitive swimmer.

◆ **Your goals should be achievable.** Don't say you want to earn a million dollars a year; most people don't. Set more achievable, specific goals, such as, "I want to buy my own house by the time I am 30."

◆ **Your goal should be worth what it will take to achieve it.** Becoming an astronaut or a brain surgeon takes years of training. Are you willing to spend that amount of time?

◆ **Your goal should include a time frame.** The goal "To earn a bachelor's degree in accounting" should include a date, for example.

◆ **Don't hesitate to change your goals as your life changes.** The birth of a child or the loss of a loved one may cause you to refocus your life.

Make the connection between college and life goals clear and explicit.

EXERCISE 3.1 **Examining Life Goals**

Directions   *Write a list of five to ten life goals. For each of your life goals, explain how attending college will help you achieve that goal.*

■ Organizing Your Life for Success in College

Organizing your life is essential to college success. Specifically, you need to organize space, courses, work, family, and finances.

Organize a Place to Study

Begin by assessing your living arrangements. Determine if they are conducive to study, and, if necessary, make changes. If you live on a floor of a dorm where parties occur frequently, then you are going to have difficulty studying. If you share an apartment or live at home, you may find studying at busy times nearly impossible. If you find your situation intolerable (your dorm roommate is entertaining friends in your room every evening, for example), then make a change as soon as possible. In the meantime, make temporary adjustments; alter the time or place you study. Consider alternatives such as the library, student lounge, or designated campus study areas.

It is usually beneficial to study in the same place each day, where all the materials you need (pens, computer, paper) are readily at hand. There is also a psychological advantage to studying in the same place each day: you build a mental association between an activity and the place where it occurs. If you become accustomed to studying at a particular desk, you will build up an association between the place (your desk) and the activity (reading and studying). Eventually, when you sit down at the desk, you expect to read or study. Be sure not to select a place you already associate with a different activity. Don't try to study in your TV chair or stretched out across your bed; you already have built associations with your chair and bed as places to relax or sleep. Assess your organizational skills by completing the questionnaire shown in Figure 3.1 on p. 54.

Organize Each Course

For each course you are taking, use the following strategies:

Become familiar with each textbook. Even though the lines in the bookstore may be long, purchase your textbooks as soon as possible in each new term. Be certain to buy new rather than used texts. Used textbooks that are already marked or underlined are distracting and make learning more difficult. You may not have an assignment right away, so spend time becoming familiar with each of your texts.

◆ **Read the preface or introduction and study the table of contents.**
◆ **Choose a chapter at random and examine its format.** What special features does it contain? How does the author emphasize what is important to learn? Does it contain review questions and vocabulary lists?
◆ **Check the end of the book.** Does it have an index, glossary (minidictionary of important words), bibliography, or appendix? If so, check to see what each contains. (The appendix often contains useful tables, charts, documents, or reference material to which you may frequently need to refer when using the text.)

When the first assignment is made, you will be able to put your texts to work for you immediately.

FIGURE 3.1
Rate Your Organizational and Time Management Skills

Respond to each of the following statements by checking "Always," "Sometimes," or "Never."

	Always	Sometimes	Never
1. Do you use a pocket calendar or assignment notebook to record due dates of assignments and exams?	❑	❑	❑
2. Do you study at your peak periods of concentration?	❑	❑	❑
3. Do you study difficult subjects first?	❑	❑	❑
4. Do you avoid studying in front of the TV?	❑	❑	❑
5. Do you use lists to keep organized?	❑	❑	❑
6. Do you assign priorities to your assignments?	❑	❑	❑
7. Do you give yourself deadlines or establish time limits by when assignments should be completed?	❑	❑	❑
8. Do you know when you are losing concentration and recognize when your attention span is weakening?	❑	❑	❑
9. Do you plan out what needs to be done each week?	❑	❑	❑
10. Do you plan to study at least two hours outside of class for every hour spent in class?	❑	❑	❑

If you answered "Sometimes" or "Never" to three or more of the questions, your time management skills need improvement.

Organize a notebook for each class.   Decide what type of notebook best suits each of your courses. For lecture classes with few or no supplementary materials, a spiral notebook works well. A loose-leaf notebook works best for courses in which numerous handouts, outlines, and supplementary materials are distributed. Date and organize these day-to-day class handouts, and place them next to the lecture notes with which they correspond. Handouts are important when studying and reviewing for an exam. Include all class homework assignments and returned quizzes, exams, and written assignments.

Use a pocket calendar or electronic calendar.   College professors frequently give long-term assignments and announce due dates for papers, assignments, and exams far in advance. Many do not feel that it is their responsibility to remind students as the dates approach. Consequently, you will need to organize a system for keeping track of what assignments need to be done and when each is due.

Use a pocket calendar or electronic calendar to record all your assignments as they are given. These allow you to see at a glance what assignments, tests, and quizzes are coming up.

Many Internet service providers, such as Google, Yahoo, and AOL, offer Web-based electronic calendars. These calendars provide daily, weekly, or monthly scheduling options in which you can enter your academic, work, and social activities. You can share your calendars and coordinate activities via e-mail with your friends and classmates; set repeating obligations (such as classes that meet on a regular basis) by only typing them in once; have meeting or appointment reminders sent to you via e-mail or cell phone; and even link activities to other Web sites or online documents. Because these calendars are Web-based, you can access them from just about any computer or most cell phones. A sample is shown in Figure 3.2.

Open a computer folder for each course.   Use it to keep files containing notes, assignments, syllabi, and all drafts and final copies of papers.

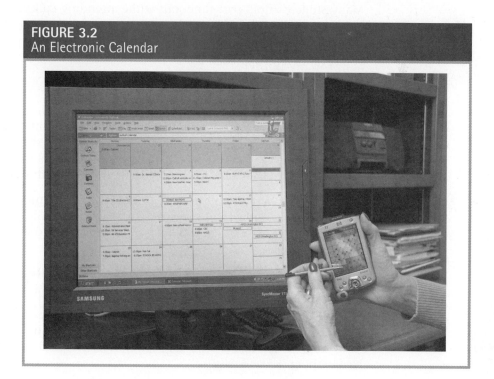

FIGURE 3.2
An Electronic Calendar

EXERCISE 3.2   ## Evaluating Your Organizational Skills

Directions   *Assess your organizational skills by answering each of the following questions.*

1. When an instructor makes an assignment during class, where do you record it?
2. Do you have a specific place to keep returned quizzes, completed homework, and graded papers for each course?
3. Are you familiar with each of your textbooks?
   a. Have you previewed each of your texts to learn if each contains a glossary, appendix, and answer key?
   b. Have you read the preface or introduction in each and studied the table of contents?
   c. Have you reviewed a random chapter in each text and become familiar with its format?
4. Have you chosen and organized a place to study? If you do not live on campus, have you found a place on campus to study during free hours?
5. Do you have a filing system (envelopes, folders) for keeping both college paperwork (transcripts, financial aid agreements) and everyday documents (car insurance, registrations, licenses, checking account statements)?

Organize Your Job to Work for You

Many students hold part-time jobs while attending college; others work full time and attend college part time. A job can be either a refreshing break from the routine of studying or a source of additional stress, depending upon how you organize and approach it.

Full-Time Students Should:

Keep work hours to a minimum.   The number of hours you work should not take needed time away from study. If you are unsure of how much time you will need for study, underestimate rather than overestimate the number of hours you can spend on the job. Many college-sponsored work-study programs limit students to a maximum of 15 hours per week; use this number as a guide.

Choose a job with a regular work schedule.   Unless you know in advance when and how long you will work each week, the job may turn your life into a nightmare of confused commitments, missed classes, and uncompleted assignments.

Make sure your employer understands your college commitments. If an employer or supervisor knows you are working toward a degree, he or she is often helpful and supportive.

Choose a job that provides a break or diversion from the task of studying.   A job that is physically active or involves working with people may be refreshing.

Part-Time Students Should:

Try to schedule class(es) early in the week.   You are more energetic at the beginning of the workweek than toward its end.

Plan to use part of your weekend for study.   Reserving a block of time on the weekend usually works better than trying to sandwich in study during the workweek.

Use spare time during the workweek to handle routine tasks and to get organized.   During the week, for example, you might reorganize a set of history lecture notes or prepare a set of vocabulary flash cards for biology.

Do not overload yourself with classes.   If you try carrying too many credit hours, you will feel overwhelmed and will not enjoy your classes. You run the risk, too, of not earning the grades you deserve.

Organize Your Family Responsibilities

If you are an adult returning to college, you may have family responsibilities in addition to those of college and a part-time or full-time job. Try the following suggestions to maintain a "happy" household as you start back to college.

Make sure family members understand how college will help you achieve your life goals.   Explain to everyone, including young children, why you are returning to school. Discuss how you may have less time for family activities, while reassuring everyone that spending less time does not mean that you care less about them.

Reserve special times for family members most affected by your decision.   Children are often most directly affected by your absence. They may also fail to understand why you must be alone to study. Designate a special time or activity each week that will be that child's exclusive time with you.

Make children part of the process.   Try to involve your children with your return to college. Take them for a brief campus visit so they can see where you attend classes. When studying at home, give them a job to do that will let them help. For example, one student asked her six-year-old to use a highlighter to color code vocabulary flash cards by chapter. Another gave her nine-year-old a list of words to check for correct spelling in a dictionary.

Redistribute household responsibilities.   Now that you are back in school, you probably do not have time to complete all the tasks you did previously. Assign responsibilities to other family members. Remember, your family wants to help you succeed in college, but often they do not know how to do so. Children, for example, depending on their age, can be asked to unpack groceries, put away dishes, vacuum, and mow the lawn.

Organize a message center.   Designate a place where family members should look for notes and messages.

Organize Your Finances

Organizing your finances, often for the first time in your life, is an important task. Worrying about money can be a major source of distraction and can interfere with your ability to concentrate on your course work. Budgeting, then, is essential; be sure to allow a "cushion" for hidden and unexpected expenses. These costs, especially if you are living away from home, may include local transportation, laundry and dry cleaning, cell phone bills, toiletries, and higher clothing costs in small college towns. Check with the college's financial aid office to be sure you are taking advantage of all sources of aid.

SKILLS IN ACTION

Organizing Your Life: A Case Study

Analyze the following situation, answer the questions below, and compare your responses with a classmate.

Shellie is a student returning to college after eight years of staying at home to raise her two children. Her children attend school from 8:15 to 3:00, and they have the following after-school activities: Coltan, in third grade, has soccer practice on Mondays, Wednesdays, and Fridays from 3:15 to 5:00. Sarah, a second grader, has joined a chorus that practices on Mondays from 4:30 to 5:30. She makes playdates about twice a week. Shellie's husband, Cyrus, works from 9:00 to 5:00 each weekday and is not available to take the children to their after-school activities. Shellie wants to figure out when she can take three courses this semester and put in the additional reading and study time required outside of class.

1. Evaluate the situation overall. What time management problems related to school and home is Shellie likely to face this semester? What suggestions would you give her for organizing now to prevent time management problems later?

2. Make a weekly schedule for Shellie to demonstrate when she can take classes and when she can devote three or four hours of uninterrupted time to study. Block out how she could spend her time each day.

3. Write a list of additional resources Shellie will need in order to succeed in her first semester back in college. Be creative in considering what kinds of help would be most beneficial.

4. Because Shellie is returning to college after eight years, she may not be aware of the alternatives to traditional classroom courses (that is, courses that take place between 9 a.m. and 3 p.m. on weekdays). What advice would you give her in this regard? Compare your advice with that of classmates.

REAL STUDENTS SPEAK

Nora Edge

St. John's College
Annapolis,
Maryland

Background: Nora is a junior at St. John's College and is taking a double major in literature and philosophy.

Goals: To join the Peace Corps right after graduating in order to apply what she has learned, gain work experience, and decide on her future plans.

Advice on Time Management: I find writing a schedule is the most useful way to deal with time management. I write it out on paper, carry it with me all the time, and check it constantly. When I have time between classes, I know what I'm doing. For example, I read ahead of time if there is no break between classes, and read for the next class when I do have a break. I find the best way to be successful is give myself time to breathe. I make sure I exercise three times a week and get 6–8 hours of sleep a night.

■ Analyzing Your Time Commitments

Effective time management can make the difference between being a mediocre student and being an excellent one. Your management of time can also determine whether you feel as if you should spend every waking moment studying or whether you are confident about your courses and know you can afford time for fun and relaxation.

A first step in managing your time more effectively is to analyze your commitments and determine the time each requires. In time management seminars sponsored by corporations, employees are first asked to identify required tasks and responsibilities—travel time, weekly meetings, reading and responding to memoranda, supervising subordinates, and so forth—and then to estimate the time each involves. You can profit from doing the same. To determine how much of your time is already committed, estimate the amount of time various activities require per week.

Apply the "2-for-1" Rule

To estimate study time, use the "2-for-1" rule. Most professors assume the 2-for-1 rule of student time management: Students should spent two hours studying outside of class for every hour spent in class. If you spend 12 hours per week attending classes, you should spend 24 hours outside class reading text assignments, doing research or experiments, studying for exams, or writing papers. This explains why carrying 12 credit hours is usually considered full-time study.

Depending on your familiarity and expertise in a given discipline, adjust the 2-for-1 rule. If you are an excellent math student, you may need less than two hours per class hour for math courses. On the other hand, if mathematics is a weak area, you may need to spend three or $3\frac{1}{2}$ hours of study per class hour.

Many students find it motivating to set their sights on a particular grade and to work toward earning it. Allot more time for study for higher grades. The 2-for-1 rule estimates the time the typical college student will need to earn an average passing grade (a C).

Consider each of your courses—its workload, your expertise in the field, and the grade toward which you are working—to estimate the amount of time per week each will require by completing the following chart:

Course Title	Desired Grade	Study Hours per Week

Determine If You Are Overcommitted

Many students take on extra work hours, make commitments to family and friends, or join sports, as the following case example shows.

Maria was majoring in accounting and had several difficult courses including business law and business management. Yet when her boss asked her to add Friday nights to her work schedule at TGI Friday's she agreed. Her best friend convinced her to join a ski club and her sister signed her up for an aerobics class. Without realizing it, Maria was overextended; she had more commitments than she could handle.

To find out if you are overcommitted, fill out the following Time Analysis chart.

Time Analysis

Activity	Hours per week
Classes and labs	_____
Study	_____
Sleep	_____
Breakfast, lunch, dinner	_____
Part-time job	_____
Transportation (driving, walking to class)	_____
Personal care (showering, dressing)	_____
Other commitments (sports, activities)	_____
Total	_____

After you have totaled your time commitments, subtract that total from 168, the number of hours in a week:

168 hours – (committed time) = _____.

The remainder represents the number of hours of uncommitted time you have available. If you find you have very little or no uncommitted time or if your total time commitment exceeds 168 hours, you are overextended. There are several possible solutions. You may need to revise your goals to settle for a B instead of an A in English composition, reduce the number of hours you work at your part-time job, or drop one or more activities. You can also become more efficient and spend less time completing required tasks by applying the principles of effective time management described in the following sections.

| EXERCISE 3.3 | **Analyzing Life Goals** |

Directions *Refer back to the life goals you developed in Exercise 3.1. Compare your time analysis and your life goals. Are you spending most of your time actively pursuing your goals? Use your comparison to decide how you wish to spend your time.*

■ Building a Study Plan

You have already estimated your total study hours per week and identified other weekly time commitments. The next step in successful time management is to display these commitments on a semester plan.

Develop a Semester/Term Schedule

Begin by blocking out class time and scheduled work hours. Also include other commitments that will remain unchanged throughout the semester or term. Sports team practice, regular babysitting on Tuesday evenings, and morning exercise routines are examples. Include your part-time job hours if they do not change from week to week. Use the blank schedule in Figure 3.3 as a worksheet. Alternatively, use an electronic calendar to develop a schedule. You will use this semester/term worksheet to develop a weekly study schedule.

Develop a Weekly Study Schedule

Once you have constructed a semester/term plan, the next step is to use the plan as a basis for developing a more specific, detailed weekly schedule. Print out or make enough copies of your semester plan so that you have one for each week of the semester. Before each week begins, preferably on Saturday or Sunday, review upcoming assignments, papers, and examinations. For each course, identify what needs to be done or reviewed; list specific chapters and pages along with assignments to complete. A sample list is shown in Figure 3.4 on p. 64.

Once you have constructed your weekly list, identify when you will accomplish these tasks, and write them on a copy of your semester/term plan. Use the following guidelines in selecting specific study times.

Use peak periods of concentration.   Everyone has high and low periods of concentration and attention. First, determine when these occur for you; then reserve peak times for intensive study and use less efficient times for more routine tasks such as researching information online. Use the lowest concentration times for nonacademic tasks: errands, laundry, phone calls, and so forth.

Study difficult subjects first.   While it is tempting to get easy tasks and short, little assignments out of the way first, do not give in to this approach. When you start studying, your mind is fresh and alert and you are at your peak of concentration. This is the time you are best equipped to handle difficult subjects. Thinking through complicated problems or studying complex ideas requires all the brainpower you have, and you are able to think most clearly at the beginning of a study session.

FIGURE 3.3
A Semester/Term Plan Worksheet

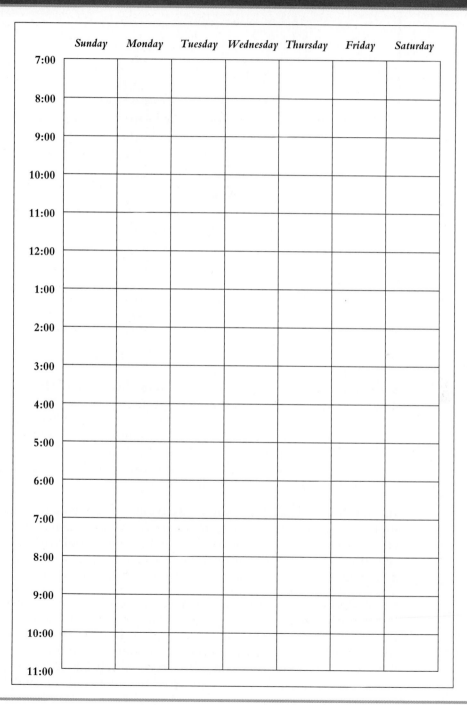

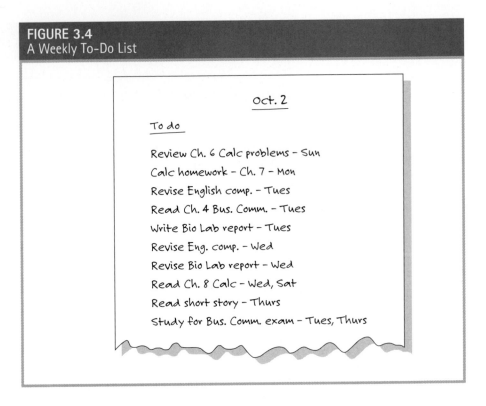

FIGURE 3.4
A Weekly To-Do List

Oct. 2

To do

Review Ch. 6 Calc problems – Sun
Calc homework – Ch. 7 – Mon
Revise English comp. – Tues
Read Ch. 4 Bus. Comm. – Tues
Write Bio Lab report – Tues
Revise Eng. comp. – Wed
Revise Bio Lab report – Wed
Read Ch. 8 Calc – Wed, Sat
Read short story – Thurs
Study for Bus. Comm. exam – Tues, Thurs

Schedule study for a particular course close to the time when you attend class.   Plan to study the evening before the class meets and soon after the class meeting. If a class meets on Tuesday and Thursday mornings, plan to study Monday evening and Tuesday afternoon or evening and again Wednesday. By studying close to class time, you will find it easier to see the connections between class lectures or discussions and what you are reading and studying, and so reinforce your learning.

Include short breaks in your study time.   Take a break before you begin studying each new subject. Your mind needs time to refocus—to switch from one set of facts, problems, and issues to another. Short breaks should also be included when you are working on just one assignment for a long period of time. A 10-minute break after 50 to 60 minutes of study is reasonable.

Use distributed learning and practice.   Learning occurs more effectively when it is divided and spaced over time, rather than done all at once. Distributed practice means that you should spread out your study sessions. For example, try to study a subject for an hour each of three nights rather than three hours in one evening. Distributed practice is effective for several reasons. First, research evidence suggests that after you stop studying, your mind continues to work on the material and learning continues for a brief time. If, then, you study over several blocks of time, this aftereffect occurs several times rather than once, as illustrated below. Second, distributed practice prevents mental fatigue and keeps you working at peak efficiency. Third, distributing the material over several sessions allows you to approach it in reasonable pieces that can be mastered more easily.

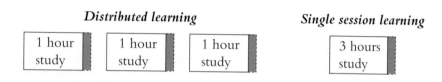

Distributed learning   *Single session learning*

| 1 hour study | 1 hour study | 1 hour study | | 3 hours study |

Be generous when estimating needed time.   It is better to overestimate than underestimate how much time you need to complete your study. If you overestimate, the free time you have left will function as a reward for hard work; however, if you underestimate you will feel pressured, rushed, and dissatisfied.

A computer science major designed a weekly plan using the worksheet shown in Figure 3.5 on p. 66. Since calculus was this student's most difficult course, he planned to devote nine hours per week to it. The class met Monday, Wednesday, and Friday; he decided to study the day before each class since the instructor spent most of the class reviewing difficult problems assigned as homework. He also planned to work on Saturday and Sunday afternoons, reviewing the week's assignment and reading new material. Because English was his strongest subject, he scheduled five hours weekly for English, but six hours each week for business communications and computer programming logic.

Planning Long-Term Assignments

When a term paper or semester project is assigned, draft a timetable for its completion. Since assignments such as these usually constitute a major portion of your final grade, you want to be certain to meet each deadline. It may be necessary to add additional hours to your weekly plan to work on such projects.

EXERCISE 3.4

Working Together

Building a Semester Plan

Directions   *Build a semester study plan, using the guidelines given above. Work with the plan for a week and then analyze its effectiveness. Revise it so it becomes more effective. Work with a classmate to identify problem areas in your schedules and discuss possible solutions.*

FIGURE 3.5
Sample Weekly Schedule

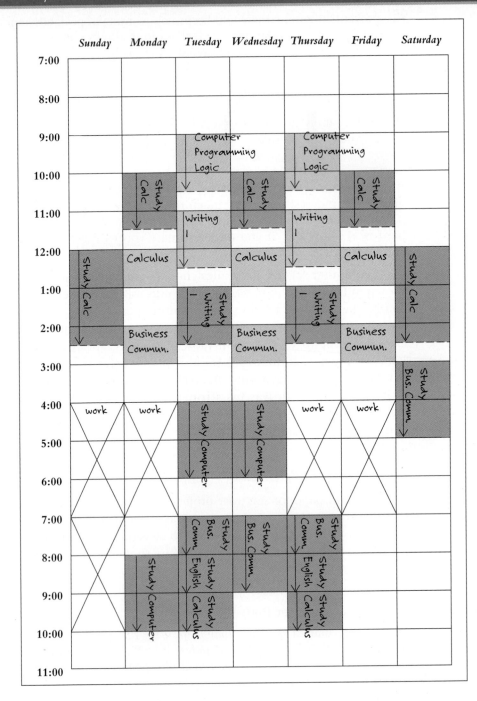

EXERCISE 3.5   **Preparing and Evaluating To-Do List**

Directions   *For each of the next several weeks, prepare a weekly to-do list. After each week, stop and analyze whether the list helped to improve your efficiency.*

■ Making Better Use of Time

Here are a few suggestions that will help you make the best use of your time.

1. **Assign priorities to your work.** There may be days or weeks when you cannot get every assignment done. Decide what is most important to complete immediately and which assignments could, if necessary, be completed later.

2. **Use lists to keep yourself organized and to save time.** A daily reminder list is helpful in keeping track of household tasks and errands as well as course assignments. As you think of things to be done, jot them down. Then, each morning, look over the list and figure out the best way to get everything done. You may find, for instance, that you can stop at the post office on the way to the bookstore, thus saving yourself a trip.

3. **Combine activities.** Most people think it is impossible to do two things at once, but busy students soon learn that they can combine some daily living chores with more routine kinds of class assignments. For example, you might outline a history chapter while waiting for your wash to finish at the laundromat. Or you might mentally review formulas for math and science courses or review vocabulary cards for a foreign language course while walking to class.

4. **Use spare moments.** Think of all the time that you spend waiting. You wait for a class to begin, for a ride, for a friend to call, for a take-out order to be ready. Although you should take advantage of some of these times to relax or take a break, other times you can use them to review a set of lecture notes, work on review questions at the end of a chapter, or review a set of problems. If you always carry with you something you can work on in empty moments, then you will always have a choice between relaxing and studying.

5. **Don't be afraid to admit you are trying to do too much.** If you find your life is becoming too hectic or that you are facing pressures beyond your ability to handle them, consider dropping a course. Don't be concerned that dropping a course will put you behind schedule for graduation; more than half of all college students take longer than the traditional four years to earn their degrees. (Do remember, however, to find out how dropping a course may affect your financial aid status.)

SKILLS IN ACTION

Examining Your Time Wasters

Many electronic time-savers, such as computers and cell phones, often become electronic time wasters. They become a form of entertainment and can be a constant source of interruption. Answer the following questions. Then compare your results with classmates.

1. How many text messages do I send and receive per day?_____ How many of these are "important"?_____ Do I stop what I am doing the second I get a text message?_____

2. How many e-mails do I send and receive per day?_____ How many of these are valuable in terms of communication?_____ How many are purely for entertainment or socializing?_____ How much time a day do I spend on e-mail that is not related to my college work?_____

3. How many calls do I receive on my cell phone each day?_____ Do I leave my cell phone "on" all the time, and do I answer it every time it rings, even when I'm reading, studying, or writing a paper?_____ Do I ever use my cell phone as a way to procrastinate?_____

4. How many hours a day do I spend surfing the Internet or socializing on MySpace or Facebook?_____ Does this socializing affect my studying, my concentration, and my grades? _____

5. How might the number of text messages, e-mails, and phone calls I make and receive and the amount of time I spend on the Internet affect my grades on exams and term papers?

■ Time Management Tips for Returning Adult Students

Returning adult students face unique time management problems. Younger students who move into dorms are beginning an entirely new lifestyle. Everything—where they eat, where they sleep, where they work—is different. They know they must adjust their habits to succeed in their new environment. Returning adults face a different challenge. They often do not realize that they, too, must adjust their lifestyle. Even a well-organized lifestyle usually must change. Here are some useful tips.

1. **Make a new schedule to reflect your new priorities.** Don't try to fit college into your old way of getting through the week; succeeding in college takes too much time for this to work well.

2. **Make a household schedule.** Just as you have planned a weekly study schedule, develop a weekly household schedule. Instead of hoping that

all jobs will get done, plan when you or a family member will tackle each. Designate specific times for laundry, shopping, errands, and so forth.

3. **Increase your efficiency by doing things at off-peak times.** Don't go to the grocery store or laundromat on a busy Saturday morning; instead choose a weekday early morning or later evening.

4. **Delegate jobs to others.** Because you are in college, you cannot possibly do everything you did before you returned. Don't hesitate to ask others for help.

5. **Use weekends for study.** Take care of household responsibilities during the week by "sandwiching" them in between work and school. This will free up larger blocks of time on the weekend for study.

6. **Consider remaining on or returning to campus to study.** Many adult students find their households too distracting for concentrated study and work better in the college library or at a local public library.

■ Time Management Tips for Commuters

Commuting to and from campus costs considerable time. Here's how to use your valuable time effectively.

1. **Use your commuting time.** If you are driving, listen to recordings of class lectures or mentally review material you studied recently. If you are riding, you may be able to read or complete routine assignments.

2. **Find a place on campus to study.** Most likely you will have open hours between classes. Find a quiet place on campus where you can use these hours for study; be sure to avoid the cafeteria and snack bar during study periods.

3. **Plan your next semester's schedule to cut down on commuting time.** Consider, for example, registering for both day and evening classes on three or four days, instead of driving to campus five days a week. Use your non-commuting day for assignments requiring concentrated blocks of time.

4. **Do not do things when everyone else does.** If you are spending valuable time hunting for a parking space, get to campus earlier. Use your early arrival time to get organized, review, and prepare for the day's classes. If you are wasting time standing in a cafeteria line, pack your lunch or plan to eat early or late to avoid crowds.

5. **Avoid the morning mad rush.** Your day begins earlier than most students, especially if you have an early class. Get organized the day and night before; fill your gas tank on the way home, select clothing, and pack your books and materials the night before.

6. **Buy a large backpack so you can comfortably carry books and notebooks.** Carry enough supplies (highlighters, index cards, etc.) so you can work between classes. Think of it as your portable desk away from home.

THINKING CRITICALLY
. . . About Procrastination

Procrastination is the tendency to postpone tasks that need to be done. If you know you should review your biology notes but decide to do something else instead, you are procrastinating. Many people tend to put off tasks that are difficult, dull, or unpleasant. Procrastination can serve as an early warning signal that something is going wrong in a course. For example, frequently putting off assigned math problems is a signal that you are having or will have trouble with your math course.

If you find yourself procrastinating in a particular course, ask yourself the following questions:

1. **What tasks am I avoiding?** Make a list of all the tasks you are avoiding.

2. **Why am I avoiding these tasks?** Think honestly about *why* you have avoided them. Perhaps they are boring, or too difficult.

3. **When, realistically, can I start each?** If you have avoided these tasks because they are dull, divide each task into manageable pieces and set up a schedule in which you do a small part each day. Dividing the task will make it seem less burdensome.

4. **Are the tasks too difficult?** If so, you should seek further information or assistance. You might:

    ◆ consult a classmate
    ◆ talk with your instructor
    ◆ get a tutor
    ◆ visit the academic skills center
    ◆ obtain a more basic text and read it first

■ Concentration Tips

Regardless of how effectively you plan your time, if you are not able to concentrate when you *do* study, you are not using your time efficiently.

Focus Your Attention

Concentration is focusing attention on the task at hand while shutting out external distractions such as noises, conversations, and interruptions.

Eliminate distractions.   Shut off your cell phone and disable instant messaging on your computer.

Vary your activities.   Avoid working on one type of activity for a long period of time; instead, alternate between several types of study. For example, you might plan your study schedule so that you read sociology for a while, then work on math problems, and finally switch to writing an English paper. This plan would be much more effective than doing all reading activities in the same study session. The change from one skill or mental process to another will be refreshing and make concentration easier.

Write and highlight as you read.   Have you ever read an entire page and then not remembered anything you had read? One way to solve this problem is to write or highlight. After reading a section, write or highlight what is important to remember. This activity forces you to think—to identify what is important, to see how ideas are related, and to evaluate their worth and importance.

Approach assignments critically.   Try to predict how the author's train of thought will develop. Make connections with what you have already learned about the subject, with what you have read previously in the course, and with what the instructor has said in class.

Challenge yourself with deadlines.   If you have difficulty maintaining concentration, try setting deadlines for completion of various tasks. Give yourself $1\frac{1}{2}$ hours maximum to draft a one-page English composition; allow only one hour for working on your biology lab report. Establishing a deadline will force you to stick with the assignment. You also will be motivating and conditioning yourself to work within time limits on exams.

End on a positive note.   When you stop working on a project or long-term assignment for an evening, stop at a point at which it will be easy to pick up again. If you end on a positive note, then you will be starting with that same positive note when you return to it.

Techniques for Self-Monitoring

An important part of strengthening your concentration is increasing your own awareness of your levels of concentration. Once you are aware of your concentration level and can recognize when your focus is beginning to blur, then you can take action to control and improve the situation. Here is some advice on how to monitor, or assess and control, your concentration.

Check your own concentration.   Keep track, for a half hour or so during a particular study session, of how many times you are distracted. Each time you think about something other than what you are studying, make a mark on a piece of paper. Total up your marks at the end of the specified time. You probably will be surprised to see how many times your concentration was broken. Work on decreasing the tally. Do not keep this tally every time you read or study anything. Instead, use it once a week or so as a check on your concentration.

Learn to read your symptoms of distractibility.   When you find that your concentration is broken, stop and analyze the situation. Why did you lose your concentration? Was it an external distraction? Did an idea in the text trigger your memory of something else? Look for patterns in loss of concentration: At what time of day are you most easily distracted? Where are you studying when distractions occur? What are you studying? Use this information to adjust your semester study plan.

Keep a list of distractions.   Often, as you are reading or studying, you will think of something you should remember to do. If, for example, you are trying to remember a dental appointment you have scheduled for the next afternoon, you will find that a reminder occasionally flashes through your mind. To prevent these mental reminders from disrupting your study, keep a distractions list on a separate sheet of paper. You will find that by writing this list, you will temporarily eliminate the distractions from your memory. Use the same paper to record other ideas and problems that distract you.

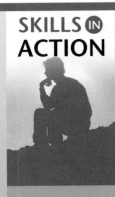

SKILLS IN ACTION

Using Self-Rewards

One way to motivate yourself to concentrate and meet your deadlines is to promise yourself small rewards when you accomplish key goals on the way to a major deadline. As an example, suppose you have to write a paper on schizophrenia for your psychology class. You might reward yourself as follows:

Accomplishment	Reward
1. Finish research →	See that movie I've been wanting to see
2. Complete first draft of paper →	Go to local coffeehouse and treat myself to a large hot chocolate
3. Revise paper, make corrections, and print out final draft →	Buy that new vampire novel that I have been waiting for

Think about a long-term project that you have in the pipeline. Put together a step-by-step plan for getting it done, as well as a reward schedule for yourself. Note that rewards do not have to be expensive or time-consuming to be effective! Also note that rewards work best if you indulge in them *only* after you have completed the required task. Working honestly with a reward system is the ultimate self-monitoring technique.

REVIEW: Five Key Points to Remember

1 **Get organized.** Organize a place to study. Organize each course by creating a notebook and keeping track of assignments and due dates.

2 **Manage your job and family responsibilities.** Get a commitment from your boss and family to help you attend college.

3 **Build a semester plan.** Include all your unchanging weekly commitments, including classes, work, and family.

4 **Develop weekly study schedules.** Use this to plan how and when you will complete all assignments and prepare for quizzes and exams.

5 **Build your concentration by focusing your attention.** Monitor your concentration and take action to improve it.

The Work Connection

Are you working a part-time job while you attend college? A part-time job can be more than just a way to earn money for tuition and books—it can also help you gain experience related to your career goals. For example, you can gain hands-on experience related to your classroom studies, get practical advice on career planning from on-the-job mentors, and even gain entrance to a company you'd like to work for after college. Here are two Web sites that allow you to search for part-time jobs:

Snag a Job (http://www.snagajob.com) allows you to search for part-time jobs and hourly employment by zip code.

Student Jobs (http://www.studentjobs.gov) provides information on both job searches and résumé preparation.

1. What would be an ideal part-time job for you based on your work or life goals? List at least three ways you could find such a job.

2. Visit one of the sites mentioned above, or your campus career resources center, and evaluate its usefulness to you in your part-time job search.

The Web Connection

1. Where Does Time Go?

    http://www.ucc.vt.edu/stdysk/TMInteractive.html

    Try this online inventory prepared by Virginia Polytechnic Institute and State University to find out how you spend your time each week. Compare your answers with your classmates'. What areas most commonly need improvement?

2. Study Environment Analysis

    http://www.ucc.vt.edu/stdysk/studydis.html

    Also from Virginia Tech, this site helps you evaluate the places where you study most often. Complete this analysis and write a plan for finding or creating the "perfect" study spot.

3. Seven-Day Procrastination Plan

    http://www.uiowa.edu/~shs/health_iowa/stress/procrastination.shtml

    From the Student Health Services at the University of Iowa, these tips will help you rid your life of procrastination. Pick one task that you have been putting off and follow these suggestions to get it done. Evaluate how well the tips worked for you. Is there anything you would change or add?

4 Managing Your Life and Coping with Stress

Do You Know?

How do you plan and manage your finances?

How do you maintain your health?

How do you make your job work for you?

How do you manage relationships?

How do you know if you're under stress?

How can you reduce stress?

College is a new experience; it creates new and different demands on your lifestyle. Your schedule is different than before you began college. You face new and more challenging academic requirements and expectations. You may have new living arrangements—a new apartment or dorm, for example. You are surrounded by new, unfamiliar people, both students and professors, and possibly roommates, as well. Because you have a new schedule, you may find yourself readjusting meal, work, exercise, and sleep habits. Your social life may change, too, as you meet new friends and lose touch with old ones. Many important aspects of your life, then, are affected by college. You can make these changes work for you, or you can let them pull you down and work against your college success. This chapter discusses four keys to a successful college lifestyle: finances, health, jobs, and relationships. The changes you face can be stressful; this chapter will also show you how to identify and cope with the stress these changes cause.

■ Finances: Planning and Managing Your Money

Money is always a problem; no one seems to have enough, and nearly everyone wants more. Money is a major worry for many students, and financial crises can destroy concentration and limit the ability to succeed. Time spent worrying about money is time that can be better spent studying or earning needed income. The keys to getting control of your finances are assessment and planning.

Assess Your Needs and Spending Patterns

The first step in money management is to assess your financial obligations and spending patterns. Use the following charts to find out how much money you need per semester or term and whether your current spending patterns are sensible and realistic. Estimate your costs for an entire semester or term. Be sure to list only essentials, not "would-like-to-buy" items.

EXPENSES PER SEMESTER/TERM	
Tuition and Fees	$_____
Housing (include utilities such as the heat, etc.)	$_____
Food	$_____
Books and Supplies	$_____
Insurance (health, car, etc.)	$_____
Transportation	$_____
Clothing/Personal Care Items	$_____
Other Essentials (child care, laundry, etc.)	$_____
Total	$_____

Now, estimate your sources of income, again for the entire semester or term. Be sure to include as savings money you earned in summer jobs.

SOURCES OF INCOME PER SEMESTER/TERM	
Savings	$_____
Part-Time Job	$_____
Scholarships/Grants	$_____
Student Loans	$_____
Parental Support	$_____
Total	$_____

If your total expenses exceed your total income, you have only two choices: you can either decrease your spending or increase your income.

Decrease Your Spending

Decreasing your spending may be easier than it sounds. Start by keeping track of everything you spend in a week, especially cash purchases. Be sure to include small items, as well as more costly ones. Keep track of parking meter fees, library fines, copying costs, coffee purchases, and vending machine snack purchases. At the end of the week draw a line through everything that was nonessential. Did you really need that one-dollar can of soda? Could you read the recent issue of your favorite magazine in the library or bookstore rather than purchase it?

Here are some other ways to reduce your spending:

1. **Do things yourself instead of paying others.** For example, do your laundry yourself instead of sending it out. Change the oil in your car yourself, or ask a friend to do it.

2. **Prepare your own food.** Make a pizza instead of ordering one. Pack your lunch instead of buying it.

3. **Use coupons; shop for sales.** Buy food and clothing when they're on sale.

4. **Reconsider your housing arrangements.** Can you move to a less expensive apartment, even if it is farther from campus? Consider finding a roommate to share living expenses. Offer to make repairs or do maintenance (painting, shoveling snow, etc.) in exchange for reduced rent.

5. **Walk instead of drive or ride.** Bus fares, cabs, and automobile operating expenses can add up. Walk to nearby destinations or consider carpooling. If you own a car, consider whether you can sell it and use public transportation.

6. **Seek free forms of entertainment.** Many campus activities are free, as are community-sponsored events.

EXERCISE 4.1

Working Together

Evaluating Your Finances

Directions   *Identify at least three ways you can reduce your spending. Compare your list with those of several classmates.*

Increase Your Income

The alternative to decreasing your spending is to increase your income. Here are a few sources to explore:

Student loans.   Check with the college's financial aid office to find out if you are eligible for student loans. Be sure to use them sparingly. You do not want excessive debt after graduation.

Student grants and scholarships.   Check to see if you are eligible for state, federal, or private grants and scholarships. Various social organizations, corporations, and fraternal organizations offer funding to eligible students. Check with a financial aid counselor to learn what is available.

Part-time jobs.   If you do not already have a part-time job, consider finding one. Many jobs are available on campus that allow you to schedule work hours around your class meeting times. If you already have a part-time job, consider finding a better paying one or adding additional weekend hours to your current job.

Check with your employer.   Many corporations offer tuition reimbursement programs or tuition assistance plans.

Develop a Budget

Once you have equalized income and expenses, develop a weekly budget to maintain your income/expense balance. Decide exactly how much you will spend on each category: clothing, food, entertainment, and so forth. In fact, some students find it helpful to create and label envelopes for each expense category. If you have allotted 20 dollars for entertainment per week, place a 20-dollar bill in an envelope marked "Entertainment." When you have spent the 20 dollars, do not borrow from other envelopes. Instead, seek free entertainment or postpone to the following week the activity you cannot afford.

Use Credit Cards Cautiously

Credit cards are the downfall of many students. Credit card companies make it easy for college students to obtain credit cards, and they offer generous lines of credit. They also have high finance charges and penalties for late payments. It is easy to overspend using credit cards. In fact some students find themselves hopelessly in debt after applying for and freely using numerous credit cards for a semester. Here is some advice:

1. **Apply for only one or two credit cards.** If you have more, you will be tempted to use them.
2. **Do not carry your credit card unless you plan to use it.** This strategy will prevent impulse buying or charging small items when you run out of cash.
3. **Pay your balance in full every month to avoid finance charges.** You can end up paying interest rates of 25 percent or higher if you do not pay the balance in full.
4. **Protect your credit rating by paying on time.** Your credit rating is valuable; a bad credit rating can seriously impact your ability to buy a home, finance a car, or obtain additional credit cards when needed.

SKILLS IN ACTION

Thinking About the Cost of Credit

Test your knowledge of credit cards by taking this brief quiz.

Case 1: You charge $1,000 on your credit card. The credit card charges 18 percent interest but says you only have to make a minimum payment of $10 per month.

1. Approximately how many years will it take you to pay off this debt if you make only the minimum payment per month?
   a. 2 years   b. 5 years   c. 10 years

2. If you make only the minimum payment per month, approximately how much *interest* will you have paid by the time the credit card is paid off?
   a. $140   b. $325   c. $800

Case 2: You decide to buy a new car with no money down. The cost of the car is $25,000 and you will pay off the loan (with an interest rate of 6 percent) in five years.

3. Approximately how much do you think your monthly payment on the car will be?
   a. $199   b. $275   c. $485

4. By the time your car loan is paid off, how much will you have paid in interest?
   a. $1,250   b. $2,675   c. $4,000

The answer to all four questions is *c.* Are you surprised by the answers? Discuss what these cases illustrate about credit card debt.

EXERCISE 4.2

Developing a Financial Plan

Directions   *Write a plan for improving your financial well-being. Include at least four actions you can take.*

■ Maintain Your Health

Your health is one of your most valuable assets, and you should strive to protect it. Because college requires a new schedule, it is easy to skip meals, munch too many snacks, and eat unhealthy fast foods. It is also easy to skip exercise and cut short your sleep time. Due to the pressures of college, some students get heavily involved with drugs and alcohol abuse, as well. This section of the chapter will offer suggestions for staying healthy.

Eat Sensibly

You are what you eat. This is an old saying, but it holds much truth. What you eat most directly influences how you feel and how healthy you are. Many students are unaware that their eating habits change upon beginning college. Some students who live on campus must get accustomed to cafeteria food. Others who live in apartments must begin cooking for themselves. Still others with no change in living arrangements find themselves just too busy to think about what they eat. Eating sensibly involves analyzing what you eat, choosing healthy foods, and avoiding unhealthy habits.

Analyze Your Eating Habits

To be sure that you are eating sensibly, analyze your eating habits. It is easy to forget how many handfuls of potato chips you grabbed on your way out the door or how many candy bars you consumed during a week. And then there are those cans of soda, that midnight pizza you ordered, and those french fries you could not resist ordering. Many students think they are eating sensibly until they actually start keeping track of what they eat.

Once you are well into your schedule for the semester or term, keep track of what you eat for a week. At the end of each day, write in a log everything you ate and the approximate time you ate it. Do not forget to include vending machine purchases, midday snacks, soft drinks, etc. At the end of the week, analyze your eating patterns and answer the following questions:

◆ When do you tend to snack?   _____
◆ Are your snack foods healthy or just crunchy?   _____
◆ What types of foods dominate your diet?   _____
◆ When do you eat the most?   _____
◆ How frequently do you eat?   _____
◆ Are certain types of foods absent from
   your diet (fruits, vegetables, for example)?   _____
◆ Do you tend to eat when you are stressed
   or when you are studying?   _____
◆ What portion of your diet is fast food?   _____
◆ Do you eat only when you are hungry?   _____
◆ Is eating usually a social activity?   _____
◆ Is eating often a nervous activity?   _____

Eat a Balanced Diet

Different nutrition experts offer different interpretations of what it means to eat a healthy diet. Most agree, however, that all the basic food groups should be represented, in varying proportions. The basic food groups are shown in the

FIGURE 4.1
The Food Guide Pyramid

MyPyramid
STEPS TO A HEALTHIER YOU
MyPyramid.gov

GRAINS	VEGETABLES	FRUITS	MILK	MEAT & BEANS
Make half your grains whole	Vary your veggies	Focus on fruits	Get your calcium-rich foods	Go lean with protein
Eat at least 3 oz. of whole-grain cereals, breads, crackers, rice, or pasta every day. 1 oz. is about 1 slice of bread, about 1 cup of breakfast cereal, or $\frac{1}{2}$ cup of cooked rice, cereal, or pasta.	Eat more dark-green veggies like broccoli, spinach, and other dark leafy greens. Eat more orange vegetables like carrots and sweetpotatoes. Eat more dry beans and peas like pinto beans, kidney beans, and lentils.	Eat a variety of fruit. Choose fresh, frozen, canned, or dried fruit. Go easy on fruit juices.	Go low-fat or fat-free when you choose milk, yogurt, and other milk products. If you don't or can't consume milk, choose lactose-free products or other calcium sources such as fortified foods and beverages.	Choose low-fat or lean meats and poultry. Bake it, broil it, or grill it. Vary your protein routine - choose more fish, beans, peas, nuts, and seeds.

food guide pyramid above. Developed by the U.S. Department of Agriculture, the pyramid indicates visually the recommended proportions of various food groups.

As you plan meals or select foods, keep the food pyramid in mind. If you are eating mostly fats and sweets, for example, you should consider making changes in your diet. Here are a few guidelines to follow in choosing a more healthy diet:

◆ Use sugar and salt sparingly or moderately.
◆ Choose foods low in saturated fats.
◆ Drink plenty of water.
◆ Include fiber in your diet.
◆ Avoid foods with empty calories.
◆ Avoid a fast-food diet.

Eat Regularly

Try not to skip meals. On those mornings that you have an early class, for example, take some healthy food with you, such as a granola bar and an apple, and eat them as you walk to class. Whenever possible, try to eat at the same time each day. Your body will begin to expect food at those times and you will avoid hunger pangs at other times. If you cannot develop a schedule that is the same each day of the week, then develop a separate plan for each day of the week.

Avoid Fads: Diets, Pills, and Programs

If you find yourself gaining weight, avoid fad diets. There are many diets that claim to help you shed pounds quickly. Many students find that the diets work for a while, but are not a substitute for developing new and healthy eating habits. Once dieters stop following the diet, they often begin regaining the weight they lost. Many diet pill products claim to facilitate weight loss, but their safety and effectiveness are questionable. Take diet pills only if they are prescribed and supervised by your medical doctor.

EXERCISE 4.3	**Evaluating Your Diet**

Directions   *Write an evaluation of your eating habits. What is healthy? What needs to change?*

Get Adequate Exercise; Focus on Physical Fitness

If you feel as if you need exercise, you probably do. Unfortunately, much of what is expected of you as a college student—attending classes, reading, writing, studying, doing homework, and researching on the Internet or in the library—requires low levels of physical activity.

Physical activity is important to your mental as well as your physical well-being. Exercise reduces the risks of heart disease and high blood pressure. It contributes to immunity from diseases and improves bone mass and weight control. Exercise has other benefits as well. It may help "burn off" stress, increase mental clarity, reduce tension, and improve self-esteem. Most experts agree that an exercise routine is one of the best ways to become and stay physically fit.

Analyze your limitations, likes, dislikes, and daily schedule of work, study, and classes. Consider your limitations. If you have weak ankles, avoid ice-skating, for instance. Consider your preferences. Don't join a volleyball team if you are not competitive or do not enjoy being part of a team. On the other hand, if being part of a team will motivate you to participate, then do consider team sports. Consider what is feasible and practical within your time limitations. Teams have regular practice times; if you do not want to add another commitment to your already busy life, then choose an activity that can be done at your own convenience.

Set fitness goals. Decide whether you want to improve your cardiovascular fitness, build strength and agility, or lose weight, for example.

Build an exercise program. The chart shown below provides guidelines for improving physical fitness through a variety of activity levels. Use it to get ideas of the level and types of exercise that are appropriate for you.

FIGURE 4.2
The Fitness Guide Pyramid

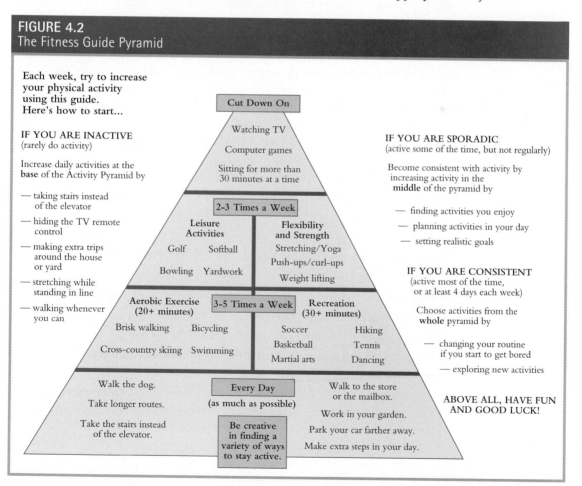

Each week, try to increase your physical activity using this guide. Here's how to start...

IF YOU ARE INACTIVE (rarely do activity)

Increase daily activities at the **base** of the Activity Pyramid by

— taking stairs instead of the elevator
— hiding the TV remote control
— making extra trips around the house or yard
— stretching while standing in line
— walking whenever you can

IF YOU ARE SPORADIC (active some of the time, but not regularly)

Become consistent with activity by increasing activity in the **middle** of the pyramid by

— finding activities you enjoy
— planning activities in your day
— setting realistic goals

IF YOU ARE CONSISTENT (active most of the time, or at least 4 days each week)

Choose activities from the **whole** pyramid by

— changing your routine if you start to get bored
— exploring new activities

ABOVE ALL, HAVE FUN AND GOOD LUCK!

Cut Down On
Watching TV
Computer games
Sitting for more than 30 minutes at a time

2-3 Times a Week
Leisure Activities
Golf   Softball
Bowling   Yardwork
Flexibility and Strength
Stretching/Yoga
Push-ups/curl-ups
Weight lifting

Aerobic Exercise (20+ minutes)
Brisk walking   Bicycling
Cross-country skiing   Swimming
3-5 Times a Week
Recreation (30+ minutes)
Soccer   Hiking
Basketball   Tennis
Martial arts   Dancing

Walk the dog.
Take longer routes.
Take the stairs instead of the elevator.
Every Day (as much as possible)
Be creative in finding a variety of ways to stay active.
Walk to the store or the mailbox.
Work in your garden.
Park your car farther away.
Make extra steps in your day.

Begin slowly and stick with your program. Many students make the mistake of undertaking a program that is too demanding and find themselves unable to keep up. It is best to start slowly and work up gradually to higher levels of performance. If you decide to start jogging, don't try to jog three miles the first day. Set a reasonable goal that you know you can achieve and gradually increase your distance each week. It will be helpful to choose a specific time to exercise each day, rather than to exercise whenever you have time or whenever you feel like it. If you have not chosen a team sport, try exercising with a friend; partners can motivate each other.

Get Enough Sleep

Lack of sleep is a common problem among college students. Sleep has two biological functions: it conserves energy so you can perform well when awake, and it restores the body by resupplying materials that were depleted during waking hours. If you do not get enough sleep, your body and your mind do not work well. If you are sleep deprived, you may decrease your ability to concentrate, learn and remember, solve problems, and think flexibly.

The amount of sleep needed varies among individuals. Some people need ten hours each night; others can function well on seven or eight hours per night. If you feel drowsy during class, doze during class, or fall asleep while studying, these are serious warning signals that you are sleep deprived. Take action immediately to get more sleep. If you feel tired, cranky, or irritable, or if you are having trouble concentrating, you may not be getting enough sleep. Try increasing your sleeping time, and see if you notice a difference.

Some students suffer from sleeplessness: they have difficulty falling asleep. Sleep insomnia—difficulty falling or staying asleep or waking too early—is common among many Americans. Here are a few suggestions to overcome insomnia:

1. **Avoid eating heavy meals late in the evening before bedtime.** An active digestive system may keep you awake.

2. **Don't drink alcohol or smoke before bedtime.** Both can keep you awake.

3. **Relax before retiring.** Watch TV, listen to music, or chat with friends, but do not study up until the minute you want to fall asleep.

4. **If you can't fall asleep, get up and do something.** If after a half hour or so you cannot fall asleep, get up. Return to bed a short time later.

5. **Get some exercise during the day.** Exercise may make you feel physically tired and may help you fall asleep. Do not exercise just before bedtime.

Avoid Substance Abuse and Addictions

Substance abuse refers to the overuse of drugs, alcohol, and tobacco. Substance abuse often leads to addictions. Addictions come in many forms, chemical or behavioral: there is drug addiction, alcohol addiction, Internet addiction, exercise addiction, money addiction (gambling, excessive shopping), and so forth. Addiction, broadly defined, is the continued involvement with a substance or activity despite negative effects. All types of addictions have four common characteristics: (1) the behavior is compulsive—an individual has an overwhelming need to perform it; (2) there is a lack of control, and the individual cannot judge when to stop; (3) the behavior always produces harmful, negative consequences such as bodily damage or academic problems; (4) the individual does not see that the behavior is responsible for the negative consequences.

Three common types of substance abuse and addictions among college students are the abuse of tobacco, drugs, and alcohol.

Tobacco.   Smoking cigarettes is harmful because it may cause lung cancer, heart disease, and other illnesses. Although smoking is banned in most public places, many students still smoke. If you smoke, analyze why you smoke. What does it do for you? Weigh the benefits versus the risks. If you decide to quit, seek help from a medical doctor who can offer assistance in overcoming the addiction.

Drugs.   Illegal drugs used by college students include marijuana, cocaine, heroin, club drugs, amphetamines, and LSD. Because drugs stimulate the brain's neurochemistry, including its pleasure centers, they often produce a temporary high, or feeling of elation or relaxation. Often the high is followed by a "low" which may lead to further drug use. Drugs are addictive, both physically and psychologically, and once you are dependent on a drug, it is very difficult to break the habit. Addiction has serious, long-term consequences including death from an overdose, arrest, academic failure, and broken relationships with friends and family.

The best way to avoid drug addiction is to stay away from drugs completely. Do not experiment or agree to try a drug once. Also avoid socializing with classmates who use drugs. They may encourage you to join them in substance abuse.

Alcohol.   Alcohol is a legal drug, but that does not mean it is not dangerous. It is important to use alcohol responsibly, if you use it at all. Binge drinking (having numerous drinks in a short period of time) or becoming intoxicated can lead to serious illness, even death. Before you decide to drink, understand the motivation behind it. If you do decide to drink, use the following suggestions to do so responsibly:

◆ **Be sure to eat before or while drinking.** Food slows the rate at which alcohol is absorbed into the circulatory system.

◆ **Get your own drinks.** That way you can be sure of what you are drinking, how strong your drinks are, and that no one has slipped a drug into your drink.

◆ **Do not drink if you are pregnant or think you may be pregnant.** Drinking may endanger the unborn baby and result in physical disabilities, learning problems, or intellectual impairment.

◆ **Avoid drinking games.** It is easy to lose track of how much you are drinking, and you may ingest alcohol at a rate faster than you are accustomed.

◆ **Know your limits.** Stop before you feel as if you have had too much.

◆ **Never drink and drive.** Choose a designated driver, and do not agree to ride with anyone who has been drinking.

THINKING CRITICALLY
. . . About Drinking

Easy, legal access to alcohol can lead to a casual attitude toward drinking. How can you know if you are drinking too much? The relatively safe use of alcohol, sometimes referred to as social drinking, can be defined as *the infrequent, planned use of a small amount of alcohol to enhance an already positive experience,* where "infrequent" means weekly or less and "small amount" means less than two to three 12-ounce beers or their equivalent.

If you drink more than "socially," consider stopping for one week (while continuing your usual activities where drinking occurs) as you think about the following questions:

1. **Do the people you drink with try to pressure you into drinking?** Alcohol promotes an artificial sense of familiarity or connection among people who may not have much in common besides the drinking.

2. **Do the activities and settings where you drink seem as interesting and attractive to you when you are sober as they do when you are drinking?** People can develop a reliance on alcohol to put them at ease in awkward situations.

3. **Do you have effective ways to manage your day-to-day emotions without using alcohol?** Since life has its ups and downs, using alcohol to feel better can lead to habitual use.

4. **Do you notice changes in your energy level, motivation, alertness, or clarity of thought?** The physical and mental effects of excessive alcohol use develop so gradually that many people don't notice the changes until it is too late.

SKILLS IN ACTION

Improving Health and Diet: A Case Study

Analyze the following situation and answer the questions that follow.

Shawn has never been physically active. In high school he didn't enjoy physical education classes because he didn't have the fitness level or skills needed for competitive activities like basketball or soccer. Now 20 years old and a sopho-more in college, Shawn typically drives his car to campus rather than walk 10 blocks from his apartment. His idea of a complete meal is a large pepperoni pizza delivered to his door, washed down with a large soda. To relax, he plays computer games. His motto is "Late to bed, late to rise." He routinely stays awake until 2 or 3 a.m. and prefers not to take morning classes so that he can sleep until 11 a.m. Recently Shawn heard about the adverse effects of a seden-tary lifestyle and he no longer wants to be a couch potato.[1]

1. Now that Shawn wants to have a more healthy and active lifestyle, how should he begin?

2. What types of activities should Shawn consider taking part in?

3. Make suggestions for improving Shawn's diet.

4. What might Shawn do to improve his sleep schedule?

EXERCISE 4.4   **Improving Your Health**

Directions   *Write a plan for improving your health. Include at least three strategies.*

■ Managing Your Part-Time Job

Many students hold part-time jobs while attending college, usually out of ne-cessity. They need the income to afford college. So the question is not whether you need to have a job. Instead you should ask: Do I have the right job? Is it a job that works for or against pursing a college degree? Is it a job that will be use-ful in obtaining a career position after graduation?

Evaluate Your Job

The following questionnaire can be used for your current job or for any job you are considering accepting. It will help you determine whether your job is an asset or a liability.

JOB QUESTIONNAIRE

1. **Do work hours fit easily with your class schedule?** If you find yourself hurrying from class to your job or worrying about being late for class because of your job, your job is creating added stress and pressure. Try to change your hours to create a less hectic schedule. If you are unable to do so, consider finding another job.
2. **Are your work hours the same each week?** It is helpful to have the same work schedule each week, just as you have a class schedule that does not change week to week. If you are working different hours each week, it is difficult to know when to study and how to arrange other commitments.
3. **Can you reduce your hours if needed with little difficulty?** If an important exam comes up or if you get behind because of the flu, for example, can you get someone to work for you? A job that is flexible enables you to pay more attention to academic priorities when necessary.
4. **Does your employer appreciate and support your college goals?** An employer who values college attendance is often more accommodating and supportive than one who does not.
5. **Is your job physically or mentally draining?** If you leave your job feeling physically tired, consider finding a job that is less demanding. A job performed in a loud, noisy, hectic environment may be more stressful than one that is not. A job in which you are constantly pressured to produce may leave you mentally exhausted. Evaluate your work environment and determine whether it is draining your energy. If it is, consider finding a job that is less taxing.
6. **Does your job cost you time in travel or preparation?** If you have to commute a distance to reach your part-time job, it is costing you time and money. Or if you have to launder uniforms, or perform other tasks in preparation for your job, then you must factor that time into your consideration of whether the job is workable for you. If your job is inconvenient, consider searching for one closer to where you live or closer to campus, or that requires less of your time in preparation.
7. **Are you working during peak study times?** Most people have a time of day or evening when they are most alert and can concentrate most easily. Are you wasting those precious hours working instead of studying? If so, try to rearrange your work hours.

Find a Job That Will Advance Your Career

Even though you may be working at a fast-food restaurant now, it probably is not something you plan to do for the rest of your life. It makes sense to hold part-time jobs that will help you land a job in the career for which you are preparing. If you plan to become a nurse, why not work in a hospital or a nursing home? You will learn a great deal about how a medical facility operates and have plenty of opportunities to observe nurses at work.

REAL STUDENTS SPEAK

Ebtisam Abusamak

Central Piedmont College

Charlotte, North Carolina

Background: Ebtisam graduated July 1, 2009, with a BSCA in Finance. She is currently working as a waitress and interning at Edward Jones.

Goal: To find a job as a financial analyst or asset manager.

Advice on Managing Stress: I found the key to managing stress was making sure I had a work/life balance, had enough time to eat healthy, sleep, workout, and being sure I had enough time to see family and friends. It's very hard! My boyfriend was really good for making sure I ate healthy and went to the gym. I would come back from the gym feeling really refreshed and ready to work. I also made sure I stopped every hour when I was studying to have something to eat, go for a walk, or watch TV for 5–10 minutes. If I worked a 2–3 hour stretch, I would take a 20–30 minute break and go for a walk."

To find a job related to your field of study, check with your college placement office, other students, and your professors. Also consider internships—supervised work experience in your field of study. Often, these are not well paying, but they are a definite asset when applying for a full-time job in your field.

EXERCISE 4.5

Working Together

Evaluating Your Job

Directions *Write an evaluation of your part-time job. Conclude with a sentence indicating whether it is beneficial in preparing you for your intended career. Share your evaluation with a classmate and discuss ways to learn useful skills for your intended careers.*

▪ Managing Relationships

College means new and changing relationships. You will develop new relationships with classmates, professors, and campus personnel. Your relationship with your family and existing friends may change as well. This section of the chapter offers advice on developing new friendships, improving your communication skills, managing conflict, and managing online relationships.

Seek New Friendships

College provides a wonderful opportunity to get to know people from new places and unknown cultures. One of the best ways to build new friendships is to get to know someone in each class. Another way is to participate in campus activities. Join a club, help out in a silent auction to support a local charity, or participate in a walkathon, for example.

Improve Your Communication Skills

Relationships depend on communication. Communication can occur through words, body language, gestures, posture, and so forth.

Pay attention to the emotional message, as well as to the intellectual one.   Observe how the speaker is feeling about what he or she is saying. If appropriate, respond with an emotional message. You might say, "That sounds so frustrating" or "You must have been very disappointed," for example, if you sense that the speaker is expressing frustration or disappointment.

Learn to share information about yourself with others.   To get along well with others and to develop new relationships, you have to be willing to share information about yourself with others. If you want to get to know another person, you have to allow him or her to get to know you. You certainly do not want to share your innermost beliefs and feelings with everyone immediately, but you can start slowly, first by sharing facts about yourself—family history, background, career goals, and so forth. As a relationship develops, trust builds, and you will feel more comfortable sharing more personal information.

Use "I" messages.   You can improve your communication with others by using "I" messages—messages that directly express your feelings. If a friend disappoints you, you may be tempted to say, "You disappointed me." It is more effective to use an "I" message—"I am disappointed." "You" messages place the listener on the defensive and make it seem as if you are blaming him or her. "I" messages, on the other hand, allow you to accept responsibility for your feelings. "I" messages should be specific and direct and, when appropriate, include reasons. Here is an example: If you are annoyed at a friend who is always late, you might say, "When you are late, I get upset because I end up wasting valuable time waiting."

Manage Online Relationships

The Internet has become an important part of our lives. It is a primary source of information, but it is also a way to communicate and develop new relationships. Here are a few tips for managing online relationships:

Don't reveal confidential information online.   It is sometimes possible for others to access your e-mail messages. As a general rule, do not write anything

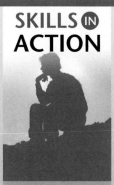

SKILLS IN ACTION

Fine-Tuning Your Communication Skills

The following are some situations in which you may find yourself. Complete each statement in a way that would maintain or preserve your relationship.

1. A friend asks you to lend him $100. You just got paid, so you have the money, but you really don't believe that your friend will pay you back. You say:

_____

_____

2. One of your closest friends invites you to a party that you know will be rather wild, with plenty of drinking and drug use. You don't want to go to the party, but you don't want to hurt your friend's feelings. You say:

_____

_____

3. You are leaving one of your classes when someone approaches you to ask for a date. You really are not interested in that person romantically, but you see each other regularly and you don't want to make the situation awkward. You say:

_____

_____

in an e-mail message or contribute anything to an online social network that you would not want published in your campus newspaper, for instance.

Be cautious about online friendships.   Some people falsely represent themselves. Although you may think you are communicating with a student on another college campus, you may actually be communicating with a young teenager, a criminal, or even a child. If you agree to meet someone you have met online, be sure to do so in a public place.

Do not use your employer's online account for personal e-mail. Some employers routinely screen e-mail, and it is not considered confidential.

Don't respond immediately to e-mail that angers you or is disturbing.   Take time to cool down. If you respond immediately, you may say things you later wish you had not said.

Manage Conflict

Conflicts occur when the behavior or intentions of one person interfere with those of another. A conflict may occur if a classmate dominates the discussion, not allowing other students to participate. A conflict may occur with a room-mate who leaves her clothes all over the floor, preventing the other roommate from being neat and organized. When individuals discuss a conflict, an argument may occur. Conflicts and arguments involve issues, but they also often involve emotions and feelings. Since conflicts can destroy relationships, use the following suggestions to deal with conflicts and arguments.

Avoid hasty reactions.   It is best to think through a conflict and approach the individual when you are calm and collected.

Allow the issues to become clear.   It is often wise to wait until a conflict is obvious, apparent, and recognized by both parties. Both are more likely to be willing to discuss the conflict and seek solutions when it is clear that there is a problem.

When you initiate a discussion to resolve a conflict, identify the issue.   Make it clear exactly what behaviors you want to discuss. Be as specific as possible about your criticisms.

Avoid angry, hostile outbursts.   If a discussion escalates to anger and hostility, stop the discussion. Postpone it until a later time.

If you have second thoughts about saying something, don't say it. You can never take back what you have said. It is better to wait than to be sorry.

■ Identifying Symptoms and Causes of Stress

Stress is a natural response to the expectations, demands, and challenges of life. When you are asked to perform more (or better) than you think you can, stress may result. For example, stress can occur when you don't have enough time to study for an upcoming exam (you are expected to study but you cannot find enough time). Stress occurs when your boss wants you to work for her on the weekend so she can take it off. (She expects you to work, but you cannot give up study time to work extra hours.)

Symptoms of Stress

A symptom is a sign or signal that stress exists, but it is not usually the cause of stress. Stress is an attitude that you are "losing it"—that you can't keep up. There are both emotional and physical symptoms of stress:

Emotional Symptoms:

◆ Feeling rushed or mentally exhausted
◆ Difficulty concentrating

- Short-temperedness
- Feeling listless, unfocused

Physical Symptoms:

- Headaches
- Fatigue
- Queasiness or indigestion
- Weight loss or weight gain

The Stress Questionnaire on page 94 will help you identify symptoms of stress you may be experiencing. Complete the questionnaire now before continuing with the chapter.

Causes of Stress

In order to reduce your stress, you need to identify situations that provoke a stressful response. In some cases, the situations are obvious. If so, write them on paper. Seeing them in print is the first step to making them manageable. Other times, however, you may be unable to point to specific situations. Following are some common stressors to consider.

Too many little things.   Any single event or situation by itself may not cause stress, but together they add up. For instance, getting a low grade on a biology lab report by itself may not be stressful, but if it occurs the same week during which your car "died," you argued with a close friend, and you discovered your checking account is overdrawn, you may experience stress.

Major life changes.   Every time you make a major change in your life you are susceptible to stress. Major changes include a new job, marriage, divorce, the birth of a child, or the death of someone close. Beginning college is one major life change. Try not to create multiple life changes, which multiply the potential for stress, especially during the semester.

Academic course work.   Your college classes may provoke stress, especially if you don't have enough time to prepare for each adequately. If you attend a class knowing you are not prepared or that you are underprepared, you are likely to experience stress.

Jobs.   Your job is important to you, and you feel pressure to perform well in order to keep it. Some jobs are more stressful than others. Those, for example, in which you work under constant time pressure tend to be stressful. Jobs that must be performed in loud, noisy, crowded, or unpleasant conditions—a hot kitchen, a noisy machine shop, and so forth—with co-workers who don't do their share can be stressful. Consider changing jobs if you are working in stressful conditions.

Stress Questionnaire

Respond to each of the following statements by checking "Yes," "No," or "Sometimes" in the boxes provided and then adding up the total for each column.

	Yes	No	Sometimes
1. I feel as if I don't have enough time in a week to get everything done.	❑	❑	❑
2. Having at least one healthy meal per day at which I can sit down and relax is unusual.	❑	❑	❑
3. I worry about money regularly.	❑	❑	❑
4. I have recently begun to smoke or use alcohol, or I have increased my use of either.	❑	❑	❑
5. I have more conflicts and disagreements with friends than I used to.	❑	❑	❑
6. I am having difficulty staying involved with social or religious activities.	❑	❑	❑
7. I seem to get colds and other minor illnesses (headaches, upset stomachs) more frequently.	❑	❑	❑
8. I find myself confused or listless more than usual.	❑	❑	❑
9. I resent the time I have to spend with routine chores.	❑	❑	❑
10. My usual level of physical activity or exercise has decreased.	❑	❑	❑
11. I am losing or gaining weight.	❑	❑	❑
12. I seldom get six to eight hours of sleep at night.	❑	❑	❑
13. I am having difficulty staying in contact with friends and family.	❑	❑	❑
14. I seldom find time to confide in friends.	❑	❑	❑
15. Small problems seem overwhelming.	❑	❑	❑
16. I seldom find time to do some fun things each week.	❑	❑	❑
17. I find myself unable to meet deadlines and am losing track of details (appointments, chores, promises to friends, and so on).	❑	❑	❑
18. I have difficulty concentrating on my assignments.	❑	❑	❑
19. I spend time worrying about grades.	❑	❑	❑
20. I am more short-tempered or more impatient than I used to be.	❑	❑	❑
Total	_____	_____	_____

If you answered "Yes" to more than four or five items, or "Sometimes" to more than six or seven items, you may be experiencing more stress than you realize. Evaluate the pattern of your responses. Look at the questions to which you answered "Yes" or "Sometimes." Some questions deal with physical habits; others focus on organizational skills. By checking your answers, you will get an idea of your own stress indicators.

Relationships.   Family, friends, and spouses can all be sources of stress if your relationship with them is troubled. Overly directive parents, self-centered or demanding friends, or insensitive spouses can all become sources of stress.

Financial problems.   Paying your tuition bill, meeting car payments, and paying rent and credit card bills create stress for many of us.

Lack of sleep.   Lack of sleep, usually caused by existing time pressures, can increase stress. Small problems may seem insurmountable when you are over-tired or suffering from long-term sleep deprivation.

Poor health, fitness, and nutrition.   Poor health or poor nutrition can increase existing stress and can produce additional stress. If you're not eating regular meals of healthy, nutritional foods, you are not providing your body with the fuel it needs to remain alert and active.

EXERCISE 4.6	**Analyzing Causes of Stress**

Directions   *Rate each of the following causes of stress as High, Medium, or Low for you.*

Source	Rating
Job	_____
Friends	_____
Family (spouse)	_____
Academic Course Work	_____
Health, Fitness, and Nutrition	_____
Financial Problems	_____
Sleep	_____

Compare your ratings with those of a classmate. Discuss means of eliminating or controlling each stressor.

■ Changing Your Thinking and Habits to Reduce Stress

While some people feel stress from a particular situation, others respond resourcefully to it. They don't feel daunted or overwhelmed by the challenge of getting things done. Instead, they feel motivated and even determined to suc-ceed. What makes the difference? The people who rise to the challenge think differently about the situation. *The situation is the same;* it is the individual's

REAL STUDENTS SPEAK

Corinne Roberts
———
Modesto
Junior College
Modesto, California

Background: Corinne has worked in her local public school system and as a day care provider. More recently she has been a stay-at-home mother of three. She is currently working and taking classes at Modesto Junior College. She plans to transfer to the university in her junior year.

Goal: To become a high school teacher.

Advice on Managing Stress: I choose a color for each class at the beginning of the semester. For example, English is blue. If the English syllabus is detailed, I write in all the dates of classes, tests, papers, in blue on a big desk calendar. When I have a big test coming up or I need some time to myself, I write "Mom needs space" on the Sunday of that week and the kids take care of themselves for a while.

There's a point in every semester where I begin to cry. You just have to remember tomorrow is around the corner. You either die with it or keep going. Think about whether college will make a big difference in your future. And it will, economically, for my family.

response that is different. For example, one student who has three midterm exams in one week may feel stressed, pressured, and anxious. Another student, however, faced with the same situation may regard it as a week of focused, intensive study that will leave her freer in following weeks to pursue other activities. You may not be able to change your environment in order to relieve stress, but you can always change how you think.

Modify Your Thinking

Accept responsibility.   People who are motivated by potentially stressful situations accept responsibility for completing a task—but only if the responsibility is actually theirs. Sometimes it isn't. To figure out whether you are responsible for a task, you can ask yourself these questions:

◆ Do I agree that this task is necessary?
◆ Am I the right person to perform this task?
◆ Do I have (or can I get) the resources I need to succeed at this task?

For example, suppose you are organizing a study group before final exams. Ask yourself:

◆ Is it necessary? *Yes, I want to do well on the exam and we all can benefit when we compare notes and exchange information.*

◆ Am I the right person? *Yes, I haven't organized a group this year although I've been invited to several.*

◆ Do I have the resources? *Yes, I can contact people during class. My living room is large enough for six people to work comfortably.*

When you can answer "yes" to all three of these questions, you have accepted responsibility for completing the task. If you answer "no" to any question, you can discuss your reservations with the person who assigned the task and figure out a solution. Or, as is sometimes the case, you may find that although the responsibility really isn't only yours, you agree to do the task anyway for various reasons: to preserve a relationship, to avoid potential complications or consequences, or to move on to more important things. That is, you come to understand that you are making a *personal choice* to take on the responsibility.

Focus on doing the best you can.   People who respond well to stressors focus on doing the best they can, not on how they might fail. Once you see success as possible, you can focus your attention on completing the task to the best of your ability. For example, instead of saying, "I cannot do this assignment on time," leave out the word "not." Ask yourself: "How *can* I finish this assignment on time?"

Visualize success.   Before beginning an assignment or before you walk into an exam room, stop, close your eyes, and imagine yourself beginning, successfully working on, and then completing the task. By visualizing success, you will give yourself a positive frame of mind in which to begin work. If you get discouraged midway through a task, stop and visualize yourself successfully completing the task. Sports psychologists encourage athletes to visualize themselves making successful plays, earning points, and winning the game. Use visualization to help you win the study game!

Focus on the benefits of achieving the goal.   People who handle stressors well focus on the benefits of achieving the goal, not the consequences of failing to achieve it. Instead of asking, "What's going to happen if I can't work this weekend? Will my boss be mad at me? Am I going to lose my job?" consider "What can I gain from working this weekend?" Sometimes the benefits will be for other people, as in "How will my co-worker benefit if I work this weekend while the boss is away?" Notice that by considering benefits, you focus on the positive consequences of completing the task.

EXERCISE 4.7	**Analyzing Your Response to Stress**

Directions   *Complete each of the following steps to analyze your response to stress.*

1. Choose a three-day period. At least one day should be a class day, and one a weekend day without classes.

2. Six or seven times throughout the day, stop and jot down hassles, annoyances, aggravations, conflicts, worries, and upsets that just occurred and the situations in which they occurred. Often, your answer may be "none." At other times, however, you will begin to identify stressors.

3. After the third day, look over your list for patterns. In what situations did you experience stress? You may, for example, discover that most stress occurred on the job, or that most stress occurred while studying or while attending classes.

4. Once you have identified your current stressors, choose one. Write brief answers to the following questions:

Do I accept responsibility for the task? Explain your thinking.

How can I focus on doing my best?

What are the benefits of achieving the goal?

Then think about how you will respond more effectively to a similar situation in the future.

EXERCISE 4.8

Working **Together**

Evaluating Stress Logs

Directions *Compare your three-day stress log described in Exercise 4.7 with that of a classmate. Exchange logs and look for patterns. What stressors do you share?*

Change Your Habits

It is possible to reduce stress by changing your habits. Experiment to discover which change will work for you.

Leave work problems at work.   Do not bring on-the-job problems home with you. If you bring a problem home with you it becomes part of your whole life and it tends to magnify in importance. Instead, discuss the problem with a co-worker or with your boss before you leave; then leave the problem at work. Face it again, if necessary, when you return.

Control your own time.   Take charge of your time; do not permit friends, roommates, or neighbors to consume it. Make clear when study times are planned, and don't allow interruptions. If people call or visit during those times, be brief and firm; insist that you must get back to work. Suggest an alternative time when you can fulfill their requests.

Getting control of your time will help you feel in control of your life. For more suggestions on time management, refer to Chapter 3.

Give yourself a break.   Constantly pushing yourself increases stress. Take a break; give yourself some downtime or personal space in which you can just be you. During your break you are not a student, not an employee, not a parent, not the one who cooks dinner. Just be yourself. Think of something you enjoy—a special song, a favorite place, a friend whom you miss. Your break can be brief: between one and five minutes is often sufficient to slow you down, provide relief from your routine, and reduce stress.

THINKING CRITICALLY
. . . About Accomplishing Tasks

When you feel overwhelmed about the number of tasks you have to accomplish, take five minutes to think through the following questions. Your responses will form a plan to eliminate the stress you are experiencing.

◆ How many different activities or concerns am I thinking about right now? If there are five or more, make a list of all your concerns. If there are four or fewer, just list them mentally.

◆ Which activities or tasks can be done later? Jot yourself a note to relieve your mind about these.

◆ Of the activities that need to be done now or today, which one is the most crucial to the priorities I have set for myself? (Your priorities may be for this week, this term, or your life goals. It depends on your situation.)

◆ How much time will this task take, approximately? Be generous in your estimate. Then take that much time to do the task.

Interact with others.   Sharing your concerns and problems with others and listening to their concerns will help you put your problems in perspective and realize that others experience similar problems. Problems seem smaller and more manageable once you talk about them. Sometimes just a brief phone call to a friend is all that is needed to help you to refocus.

Get some exercise.   Build an exercise routine into your weekly schedule. Exercise can reduce stress by enabling your body to release the hormone

norepinephrine, which promotes increased awareness, and endorphins, which give you a sense of well-being.

Help someone out.   If you spend all your time thinking about yourself and the amount of work you have, your problems will grow out of proportion. Refocus your attention occasionally on others. Spend time helping someone else when you can afford the time. You might shop for an elderly relative, tutor a classmate, or volunteer at a soup kitchen or animal shelter. Once your mind is off yourself and you see others with problems, your problems will seem more manageable.

Make fewer choices.   Stress tends to increase when you are responsible for making a large number of decisions. To reduce stress, eliminate some of the daily decisions that consume your time and energy. For example, instead of having to decide each evening what time to set your alarm clock for, get up at the same time each weekday. Instead of having to decide what to cook, eat, or order for dinner each night, decide on the menu for the whole week all at once. Alternatively, make every Monday pasta night, every Tuesday chicken night, and so forth. If you have fewer decisions to make, you'll feel less pressured and will have more time to think about important decisions you must make.

Reduce the clutter.   Get organized and keep everything in its place. You will feel as if you are more in control of your life and you won't waste time looking for misplaced objects or devoting hours to cleanup blitzes.

SKILLS IN ACTION

Coping with Stress: A Case Study

Analyze the following situation and answer the questions below.

> After being laid off due to a downturn in the local economy, a freshman business student, Robin, is returning to college after eight years of working full-time. She is taking the following courses: writing, mathematics, economics, and introduction to business. She has recently started her own business, a manicure shop, which is open two evenings a week and on weekends. She is the single parent of a five-year-old son who has just begun kindergarten and attends school only half the day. Robin is frustrated with college and feels constantly under stress. When she is working in her shop, she worries about her classes. When she studies, she finds herself thinking about how to get more clients for her shop. She feels guilty about not spending enough time with her son.

1. Analyze Robin's source(s) of stress.

2. Is Robin's return to college well timed? What advice would you offer her?

3. What time-management strategies should Robin use?

4. How can Robin reduce the stress she feels?

Change your study habits.   To reduce stress, you may need to change some of your study habits. For example, if you tend to go to classes unprepared—without having finished all the required reading, for example—you are creating stress for yourself. You will feel guilty and worry during class that the instructor may ask you a question you cannot answer. Make it a rule that you will always complete reading assignments before the class for which they are due.

Seek the help of others.   If you are unable to manage the stressors you face, seek the help of counselors in the campus counseling center. Often a skilled counselor can ask you the right questions to help you solve a stressful situation or help you examine a problem from a number of different perspectives.

REVIEW   Five Key Points to Remember

1   **Manage your finances.** Assess your needs and spending patterns; develop a budget to accommodate those needs; use credit cards cautiously.

2   **Maintain your health.** Focus on eating sensibly, getting enough exercise and sleep, and avoiding substance abuse.

3   **Relationships are key to college success.** Be sure to seek new friendships, improve your communication skills, manage conflict, and handle online relationships cautiously.

4   **Pay attention to the symptoms and causes of stress.** These may include both emotional and physical symptoms and have a wide variety of causes.

5   **Reduce stress by changing your thinking and your daily habits.** Accept responsibility, plan, organize, and focus outside yourself. Seek help, if needed.

Working Together

Working with a classmate, prepare individual plans for the next two weeks to identify the sources of stress you are most likely to encounter. Plan how you can respond more effectively to stressful situations. Your plan should include both changes to thinking and changes to habits. Then analyze each other's plans and offer suggestions for improvement.

The Work Connection

Employers find the ability to manage stress so important to job success that they have devised ways to measure this ability. One method is through different kinds of job interviews. Among the techniques used by human relations managers, two types are the *behavior interview* and the *stress interview*. The behavior interview involves asking the job candidate to describe how he or she has handled particular stressful situations in the past. The stress interview is designed to see how candidates handle an interviewer who deliberately creates a stress-provoking interaction. The first type focuses on how the potential employee has handled stress in the past, and the second on how the candidate handles stress in the present.[2]

1. Think about a stressful experience you handled well. Describe this experience as if talking to a potential employer to demonstrate your ability to manage stress.

2. Think about someone you know who seems particularly good at handling stressful situations. What strategies does he or she use to remain calm and reasonable? (If you're not sure, ask.) Make a list of at least three strategies you can develop.

The Web Connection

1. Success and Happiness Attributes Questionnaire

   http://www.csulb.edu/~tstevens/success/shaqCares.htm

   Try this online assessment from California State University, Long Beach. Use the results to make a basic plan for success in school, your Job, and life. Ask someone you know to complete the questionnaire too. Discuss your results.

2. Money Management

   http://moneymanagement.unt.edu/resources/downloads.html

   From the University of North Texas, this site offers downloadable materials to help you manage you money. Look over the various links to these files and pick one to explore further. Try creating a budget or following some of the tips. Evaluate your success and make a money management plan.

3. Top Ten Strategies for Wildly Effective Stress Management

   http://campushealth.unc.edu/index.php?option=com_content&task=view&id=464

   Read this list of tips for coping with stress from the University of North Carolina at Chapel Hill. Choose three of these and for each one, write some practical ways that you can implement the tip in your life.

5 Communication Skills for the Classroom

Do You Know?

How can you listen carefully and critically?

How can you participate effectively in class?

How can you ask and answer questions effectively?

What should you do to work productively with classmates on projects?

How can you make effective oral presentations?

Success in college depends on your ability to read, write, and think effectively, but it also depends on your ability to communicate with others. In many of your classes you participate by listening to and responding to classmates in class discussions. You must ask intelligent questions in class and be prepared to answer those asked by your instructor. You must also be able to communicate with classmates in both formal and informal situations. Finally, you must be able to make oral presentations. While each of these skills is important for college success, they are also important for career success. In most jobs, you must be able to express your ideas clearly, listen and respond to the ideas of co-workers and supervisors, and work productively in small groups, discussing problems and brainstorming solutions.

■ Listening Critically

As you listen to class lectures and class discussions, one task is to absorb and learn the information presented. See Chapter 12 for information on taking lecture notes and developing recall clues to learn them. However, another equally important task is to think critically about what your instructor presents and what other students say in class.

Common Pitfalls in Critical Listening

Avoid the following barriers to critical listening:

Avoid closed mindedness.   In college you will hear many ideas that you disagree with and you will meet people whose values differ from yours. What others may feel is right, wrong, or important in life may not be the same as what you feel. Avoid prejudging a speaker or his or her announced topic. Keep an open mind. Delay your judgment until the speaker has finished and you understand fully the speaker's message and intentions.

Avoid selective listening.   When listening to ideas with which they disagree, some listeners hear only what they want to hear. That is, they pay attention to ideas they agree with and may misinterpret or even ignore ideas with which they disagree. Selective listening often occurs when discussing ethnic, national, religious, or moral issues. To avoid selective listening, first recognize your own biases; be aware that you feel strongly about an issue. Make a deliberate effort to understand the speaker's viewpoint even though you disagree with it. Distract yourself from your feelings by taking notes or writing an outline.

Avoid oversimplifying difficult or complex ideas.   While it is tempting to ignore details or to simplify complicated ideas, try to get the full picture, including details, reasons, and supporting evidence. For example, if you were listening to an argument advocating the use of force to control world terrorism, the speaker's details would be extremely important. You would need to know when, why, how much, and by whom such force would be performed in order to evaluate the argument.

Avoid judging the speaker instead of the message.   Be sure to focus on the message, not the person delivering the message. Try not to be distracted by mannerisms, dress, or the method of delivery (pauses, tone of voice, grammatical errors, and so forth).

EXERCISE 5.1

Working **Together**

Identifying Topics

Directions   *Working with a classmate, identify at least three or four topics of class discussion for which it would be important to keep an open mind and avoid selective listening.*

Evaluate the Message

Use the following suggestions to evaluate a speaker's message:

- ◆ **Identify the speaker's main point or position on an issue.** The speaker may identify it by using key phrases such as "The issue is . . ." or "What I am trying to say is . . . ."

◆ Develop a mental outline of the speaker's message.

◆ Identify whether the speaker has supported his or her main point or position with reasons and evidence.

◆ Identify unanswered questions or opposing viewpoints.

<table>
<tr><td>EXERCISE 5.2</td><td></td></tr>
</table>

Preparing for a Class Discussion

Directions   *For a class discussion in one of your other courses, identify each of the following:*

a. Main point or issue

b. Reasons and evidence

c. Unanswered questions or opposing viewpoints

■ Participating in Class

Participating in class means more than being interested, prepared, and alert in class. To participate you must ask and answer questions and be involved in class discussions. Participating has a number of advantages. It will

◆ help you concentrate and stay focused

◆ make the instructor notice you and identify you as a serious, thoughtful student

◆ help you learn because you will remember concepts and ideas that you have spoken about

◆ give you practice in speaking before groups—a skill you definitely need in the workplace

Class participation requires planning and preparation as described next.

Prepare for Class Discussions

Preparing for a class discussion demands more time and effort than getting ready for a lecture class. In a lecture class, most of your work comes *after* the class, editing your notes and using the recall clue system to review them (see Chapter 12). The opposite is true for discussion courses, where most of your work is done *before* you go to class. You must spend considerable time reading, evaluating, and making notes.

Read the assignment.   Usually a class discussion is about a particular topic. Frequently, instructors give reading assignments that are intended to give you some background information. They are also meant to start you thinking about a topic, show you different points of a view about an issue, or indicate some aspects of a problem. Read carefully the material assigned. Do not just skim through it as you might for a lecture class. Instead, read the assignment with the purpose of learning all the material. Mark and highlight important ideas as you read.

Ask critical questions.   Class discussions focus on the application, analysis, and evaluation of ideas and information. To prepare for discussions, ask the following critical questions:

◆ How can I use this information? To what situations is it applicable?
◆ How does this information compare with other information I have read or learned on the same topic?
◆ What is the source of the material?
◆ Is the material fact or opinion?
◆ What is the author's purpose?
◆ Is the author biased?
◆ Is relevant and sufficient evidence provided?

These questions will provoke thought and provide a base of ideas to use in discussions.

Review, making notes for discussion.   After you have read the assignment, review it with the purpose of identifying and jotting down the following:

◆ **Ideas, concepts, or points of view you do not understand.** Keep a list of these; you can use the list as a guide to form questions during class.
◆ **Ideas and points with which you disagree or strongly agree.** By jotting these down, you will have some ideas to start with if your instructor asks you to react to the topic.
◆ **Good and poor examples.** Note examples that are particularly good or particularly poor. These will help you react to the topic.
◆ **Strong arguments and weak arguments.** As you read, try to follow the line of reasoning, and evaluate any arguments presented. Make notes on your evaluations; the notes will remind you of points you may want to make during the discussion.

Get Involved in Class Discussions

Discussion classes require greater, more active involvement and participation than do lecture classes. In lecture classes, your main concern is to listen carefully and to record notes accurately and completely. In discussion classes, your responsibility is much greater. Not only do you have to take notes, but you also have to participate in the discussion. The problem many students experience in getting involved in discussions is that they do not know what to say or when to say it. Here are a few instances when it might be appropriate to speak. Say something when

◆ you can ask a serious, thoughtful question
◆ someone asks a question that you can answer
◆ you have a comment or suggestion to make on what has already been said
◆ you can supply additional information that will clarify the topic under discussion
◆ you can correct an error or clarify a misunderstanding

To get further involved in the discussion, try the following suggestions:

1. **Even if you are reluctant to speak before a group, try to say something early in the discussion.** The longer you wait, the more difficult it becomes.

2. **Make your comments brief and to the point.** It is probably a mistake to say too much rather than too little. If your instructor feels you should say more, he or she will probably ask you to explain or elaborate further.

3. **Try to avoid getting involved in direct exchanges or disagreements with other class members.** Always speak to the group, not to individuals.

4. **Announce change of topics.** When you feel it is appropriate to introduce a new idea, clue your listeners that you are changing topics or introducing a new idea. You might say something like, "Another related question . . . ," or "Another point to consider is . . . ."

5. **Make notes.** If, as the discussion is going on, you think of comments or ideas that you want to make, jot them down. Then when you get a chance to speak, you will have your notes to refer to.

6. **Organize your remarks.** First, connect what you plan to say with what has already been said. Then state your ideas as clearly as possible. Next, develop or explain your ideas.

7. **Watch the group as you speak.** When making a point or offering a comment, watch both your instructor and others in the class. Their responses will show whether they understand you or need further information, whether they agree or disagree, and whether they are interested or uninterested. You can then decide, based on their responses, whether you made your point effectively or whether you need to explain or defend your argument more carefully.

Make Effective Contributions to the Discussion

Some students' participation in class can be distracting and disruptive. Use the following tips to be certain that you make a worthwhile contribution to the class discussion:

1. **Do not interrupt other speakers; wait until other speakers have finished.** Signal to your instructor that you would like to be recognized to speak, if necessary.

2. **Avoid talking privately with or making comments to another student while the discussion is going on.**

3. **Do not tell lengthy personal anecdotes.** Make sure that what you say is relevant to the ideas under discussion.

4. **Try not to monopolize the discussion.** Give others a chance to express their ideas.

5. **Be sensitive to the feelings and viewpoints of other class members.**

6. **Try not to be bullying, argumentative, or overly emotional.** These tactics detract from your effectiveness as a speaker.

■ Asking and Answering Questions

Asking clear, direct questions is a skill you can develop and improve. Framing clear, direct answers to questions asked by your instructors or by fellow students is also a skill worth developing. Effective questioning is important in college classes, but it is also an important workplace skill. Use the following suggestions to strengthen your questioning and answering skills.

1. **Conquer the fear of asking questions.** Many students are hesitant to ask or answer questions, often because they are concerned about how their classmates and instructors will respond. They fear that their questions may seem dumb or that their answer may be incorrect. Asking questions is often essential to a complete and thorough understanding, and you will find that once you've asked a question, other students will be glad you asked because they had the same question in mind. Answering questions posed by your instructor gives you an opportunity to evaluate how well you have learned or understood course content as well as to demonstrate your knowledge.

2. **To get started, as you read an assignment, jot down several questions that might clarify or explain it better.** Bring your list to class. Refer to your list as you speak, if necessary.

3. **When you ask a question, state it clearly and concisely.** Don't ramble or make excuses for asking.

4. **Remember, most instructors invite and respond favorably to questions.** If your question is a serious one, it will be received positively. Don't pose questions for the sake of asking a question. Class time is limited and valuable.

5. **In answering questions, think your responses through before you volunteer them.**

6. **Think of answering questions as a means of identifying yourself to the instructor as a serious, committed student, as well as a means of learning.**

EXERCISE 5.3

Working Together

Asking Questions

Directions   *Select a reading assignment from one of your other courses. Practice asking and answering questions with a student from that class. Take turns critiquing format, content, and delivery of both questions and answers.*

THINKING CRITICALLY
. . . About Meaningful Questions

Use the levels of thinking (Chapter 2, pp. 42–44) to ask meaningful questions. In general, avoid basic knowledge and comprehension questions, unless they pertain to complicated material you do not understand. Instead, ask questions that will lead you to a fuller understanding of the topic. Here are some sample questions to ask at each of the higher levels of thinking.

Applying: In what situations can this information be used?

Analyzing: How do ideas fit together?
How does it work?
what are its parts?

Evaluating: What standards or criteria exist?
Of what value is this information?

Creating: How can this idea be combined with related ideas?
What new and unique solutions or applications exist?

■ Working with Classmates: Group Projects

Many assignments and class activities involve working with a small group of classmates. For example, a sociology instructor might divide the class into groups and ask each group to brainstorm solutions to the economic or social problems of the elderly. Group projects are intended to enable students to learn from one another by viewing each other's thinking processes and by evaluating each other's ideas and approaches. Group activities also develop valuable skills in interpersonal communication that will be essential in your career.

Some students are reluctant to work in groups because they feel that they are not in control of the situation; they dislike having their grade depend on the performance of others as well as themselves. Use the following suggestions to help your group function effectively:

1. **Select alert, energetic classmates if you are permitted to choose group members.**

2. **Be an active, responsible participant.** Accept your share of the work and expect others to do the same. Approach the activity with a serious attitude, rather than joking or complaining about the assignment. This will establish a serious tone and cut down on wasted time.

3. **Consider a leadership role.** Because organization and direction are essential for productivity, every group needs a leader. Unless some other competent group member immediately assumes leadership, take a leadership role. While leadership may require more work, you will be in control. (Remember, too, that leadership roles are valuable experiences for your career.) As the group's leader, you will need to direct the group in analyzing the assignment, organizing a plan of action, distributing work assignments, planning, and, if the project is long-term, establishing deadlines.

4. **Suggest that specific tasks be assigned to each group member.** Be sure the group agrees upon task deadlines.

5. **Take advantage of individual strengths and weaknesses.** For instance, a person who seems indifferent or is easily distracted should not be assigned the task of recording the group's findings. The most organized, outgoing member might be assigned the task of making an oral report to the class.

TABLE 5.1 Improve Communication: Problems and Solutions

If a Group Member . . .	You May Want to Say . . .
Hasn't begun to do the work she's been assigned	"You've been given a difficult part of the project. How can we help you get started?"
Complains about the workload	"We all seem to have different amounts of work to do. Is there some way we might lessen your workload?"
Has missed meetings	"To ensure that we all meet regularly, would it be helpful if I called everyone the night before to confirm the day and time?"
Seems confused about the assignment	"This is an especially complicated assignment. Would it be useful to summarize each member's job?"
Is uncommunicative and doesn't share information	"Since we are all working from different angles, let's each make an outline of what we've done so far, so we can plan how to proceed from here."
Seems to be making you or other members do all the work	Make up a chart before the meeting with each member's responsibilities. Give each member a copy and ask, "Is there any part of your assignment that you have questions or concerns about? Would anyone like to change his or her completion date?" Be sure to get an answer from each member.

If your group is not functioning effectively or if one or more members are not doing their share, take action. Communicate directly, but try not to alienate or anger group members. Here are a few common complaints and possible solutions.

If these suggestions do not help you correct problems with a nonparticipating group member, discuss with your instructor how to drop the person from the group.

REAL STUDENTS SPEAK

Rachel Goodman

West Chester University
West Chester, Pennsylvania

Background: Rachel successfully completed an associate's degree at Middlesex County College in May 2005 and transferred to West Chester University in Pennsylvania.

Goal: To become an elementary school teacher.

Advice on Oral Presentations: I took an introduction to public speaking course. There are different kinds of speeches, like a persuasive speech, or one where you teach people something, or an informative speech, or an entertaining one. You have to be creative and know how to use visual aids. When you're persuasive, you have to work on tone and hand movements. I was very nervous in the beginning; it took me about two minutes to get started the first time, but I ended up getting an A in the course. I think the course would be very useful for lots of careers, like teaching.

EXERCISE 5.4

Working **Together**

Working Within a Group

Directions   *Suppose you are part of a five-member group that is preparing for a panel discussion on animal rights. One group member is very vocal and opinionated. You fear she is likely to dominate the discussion. Another group member is painfully shy and has volunteered to do double research if he doesn't have to speak much during the discussion. A third member appears uninterested and tends to sit back and watch as the group works and plans. How should the group respond to each of these individuals? List several possible solutions to each problem.*

■ Planning and Making Oral Presentations

Oral presentations may be done in groups or individually. Groups may be asked to report their findings, summarize their research, or describe a process or procedure. Individual presentations are often summaries of research papers, reviews or critiques, or interpretations of literary or artistic works. Use the following suggestions to make effective oral presentations:

1. **Understand the purpose of the assignment.** Analyze it carefully before beginning to work. Is the presentation intended to be informative? Are you to summarize, evaluate, or criticize?

2. **Research your topic thoroughly.**

3. **Collect and organize your information.**

4. **Prepare outline notes.** Use index cards (either 3 × 5 or 5 × 8) to record only key words and phrases.

5. **Consider the use of visual aids.** Depending on the type of assignment as well as on your topic, diagrams, photographs, or demonstrations may be appropriate and effective in maintaining audience interest.

6. **Anticipate questions your audience may ask.** Review and revise your notes to include answers.

7. **Practice delivery.** This will build your confidence and help you overcome nervousness. First, practice your presentation aloud several times by yourself. Time yourself to be sure you are within any limits. Then practice in front of friends and ask for criticism. Finally, record your presentation. Play it back, looking for ways to improve it.

8. **Deliver your presentation as effectively as possible.** Engage your audience's interest by maintaining eye contact; look directly at other students

as you speak. Make a deliberate effort to speak slowly; when you are nervous, your speech tends to speed up. Be enthusiastic and energetic.

If you need additional information or help with making oral presentations, consult your college's learning lab or obtain a guidebook on public speaking from your campus library.

As a variation on oral presentations, some instructors might ask each student (or group) to lead one class discussion or form panel discussions. As in oral presentations, organization is the essential ingredient for these activities. Plan ahead, outlining topics to be discussed, questions to be asked, or issues to confront.

Table 5.1 answers some commonly asked questions about making oral presentations.

TABLE 5.2 Questions and Answers About Oral Presentations

Questions	Answers
1. How can I overcome the fear of public speaking?	• Be sure to practice delivering your speech several times before you actually make your presentation in front of the class. Practice speaking slowly and distinctly, taking deep breaths, and pausing.
2. How can I make sure my presentation is interesting?	• Vary the content. For example, you could start off by telling an interesting story or engaging the class's attention by posing a thoughtful question. • Use visual aids such as the chalkboard, an overhead projector, or a chart that you've designed to help you maintain the interest of your audience.
3. What if, during my presentation, the instructor and/or the class starts to show signs of boredom?	• Change the tone or pitch of your voice. • Maintain your audience's interest by engagingthem in the presentation. Pose a question, for example. • Make eye contact with restless individuals.
4. What do I do if I "go blank"?	• Write notes on index cards. If you suddenly "go blank," all you need to do is look at your notes. • Ask whether there are any questions. Even if there aren't, this pause will give you time to think about what to say next.

SKILLS IN ACTION

Playing on Your Strengths

Assume that you are taking a course in which the instructor allows students to select from a menu of activities that earn points to determine their final grade. You must choose three of the following activities:

- ❑ Six quizzes
- ❑ One midterm and one final exam
- ❑ An oral report
- ❑ A group project
- ❑ A research paper
- ❑ A panel discusssion
- ❑ An interview with a community leader

- ❑ Serving as leader of a classroom discussion
- ❑ Doing volunteer work at a local charity
- ❑ Reading three additional books and writing a brief summary of each
- ❑ Keeping a daily journal
- ❑ Taking a two-day field trip to an out-of-town location

1. Explain your choices. Consider both your learning style and your communication skills.

2. What specific skills does each activity require?

3. Now think carefully about the choices you did *not* make. Would you avoid certain activities? Why? How might you go about improving your skills in those areas (because not all college professors will be so flexible about allowing you to choose what you will and won't do)?

Working Together

Five or six class members should volunteer to participate in a panel discussion on a current controversial issue. The panel members should convene to plan their panel discussion while the rest of the class forms groups of observers. The observers should critique the panel group's planning, efficiency, and interaction. Your instructor may plant "problem" panel members.

REVIEW | Five Key Points to Remember

1 **Be sure to listen, not just hear.** This involves listening critically—responding and reacting to what is said.

2 **Participate in class.** Prepare for class discussions; get involved in discussions.

3 **Do not hesitate to ask and answer question.** You will learn more if you are actively involved in the class.

4 **Work productively with classmates on group projects.** Do your share and diplomatically address problems with group members if they should occur.

5 **Make effective oral presentations.** Prepare thoroughly for presentation and practice your delivery.

The Work Connection

How will learning oral presentation skills aid you in the workplace? Writing in the "Job Market" column that appears in the *New York Times,* Sabra Chartrand reports that even in technical jobs, communication skills are highly valued. In job interviews, the interviewer may be seeking to find out whether the candidate can "clearly and eloquently express his goals" and answer questions about solving technical problems in a way that is "well expressed and easy to understand."[1] Working on group reports can also provide you with two other types of experiences that employers value: learning to work with a team and learning to take leadership roles within a group.

1. Which of your courses provide you with opportunities to give oral presentations? List four or five ways you learn the most from these experiences.

2. Aside from the course you are currently enrolled in, what other courses or campus activities would give you a chance to hone your oral presentation and team-building skills? Find and list about five different activities.

The Web Connection

1. Are You a Good Listener?

   http://www.effectivemeetings.com/productivity/communication/listener.asp

   Although this site is directed toward listening in meetings, it can also apply to the way students conduct themselves during class discussions and group work sessions. Try a variation of the exercise suggested—choose various points to monitor during your conversations and classes, not just interrupting.

2. Ten Tips for Public Speaking

   http://www.peachtreetm.org/publicspeakingtips

   Look here for some straightforward tips on handling yourself in a public speaking situation. Write a paragraph discussing how you feel about speaking in public. Which of these tips could be of use to you?

3. Making Your Voice Heard: Classroom Discussions and Participation

   http://www.studygs.net/intstudy.htm

   From the University of St. Thomas, this site provides valuable advice on contributing to discussions in your classes. Compare these tips with the reality of the classroom situation. In which of your classes can you reasonably implement these suggestions?

6 Thinking Critically and Solving Problems

Do You Know?

How can you make good decisions?

How can you specify a problem in a way that will help you solve it?

How do you analyze a problem?

Why should you identify a wide range of solutions to a problem?

How can you evaluate the possible solutions?

What factors should you consider in selecting a solution?

Each day as a college student you are faced with numerous decisions and problems. Some are more serious than others, and some are more difficult to solve than others. All require critical thinking—the careful analysis of the situation and ways to resolve it. Some of the decisions you face are academic—how to solve math problems, how to conclude an English composition, or which of two essay questions to answer. You also face nonacademic problems and decisions in day-to-day living—how to get to class if your car won't start or how to get that attractive person across the room to notice you. While these two types of decisions and problems seem quite different, the strategies for resolving them are very similar.

We have all made thousands of decisions and solved hundreds of problems in our lifetimes, but we may not have resolved them in the *best* possible ways. Nearly everyone can recall saying, "Why didn't I think of . . . ?" or "If only I had thought of . . . !" after the fact. The purpose of this chapter is to present systematic approaches to decision making and problem solving.

■ Thinking Critically About Decision Making

Decision making is a process of thinking critically about choices. Each of us makes numerous choices each day: what to wear, which way to walk to class, which assignment to work on first. Many are relatively unimportant—what to have for lunch, for example. Others, however, are of critical importance with far-reaching impact—what major to choose, for instance.

Decisions are different from hunches, wishes, or hopes. A decision means you will take a specific course of action. The statement "I would like to stop worrying about paying all my bills" is a wish. It is something you want to happen. To say, "I will develop a weekly budget to make sure I am able to pay all my bills," expresses a decision. Notice that it is action oriented. It points toward an outcome.

Types of Decisions

Let us consider several situations and analyze the type of decision making involved in each.

Situation 1:	You order a pizza with pepperoni and mushrooms.
Situation 2:	On a spring afternoon you and a group of friends, at the last minute, decide to cut class and take a ride to the lake.
Situation 3:	You decide to register for child psychology next semester because you've just finished introductory psychology and child psychology is required in your major.

While each of the situations involves choice, each involves very different types of thinking. In ordering a pizza, you make a *routine decision* involving little or no thought; you usually or always order it that way. The trip to the lake is a last-minute, *impulsive decision*. The decision to register for child psychology is a *reasoned decision* based on evidence.

Routine decisions are usually safe, habitual choices that make your life run smoothly. Impulsive decisions on social occasions, for example when everyone decides to go bowling at midnight, can be fun and interesting. However, in other situations, since they are not well thought out, they can cause or lead to problems. Suppose, for example, that the day you impulsively decide to cut class, the instructor gives an unannounced quiz.

In new or important situations, the best type of decision to make is a reasoned one, in which alternatives are identified and weighed and outcomes are predicted.

Make Reasoned Decisions

Suppose you are choosing courses to register for next semester. You have the option of (1) taking all required courses in your major, (2) deferring required courses and taking electives, and (3) registering for a mix of required and elective courses.

Weigh Your Options

Your first step is to weigh and compare your options. Factors you must consider include the workload involved in each course, their relative difficulty, the times they are offered, your family and work schedule, and so forth. Be sure to consider risks and predict future outcomes.

Examine Outcomes

An important part of decision making is to predict both short-term and long-term outcomes for each alternative. You may find that while an alternative seems most desirable in the present, it may pose problems or complications over a longer time period. For example, in choosing courses for next semester, suppose you decide against taking a public speaking course as an elective. You reason that it is not required, only recommended, and a mass media course would be more interesting. Your decision is reasonable for the short term. However, if you are considering a career in teaching, you may later find that a public speaking course would have been beneficial and that your decision was not effective in the long term. Use the following tips to make reasoned decisions.

TIPS FOR MAKING REASONED DECISIONS

1. **Recognize that not making a decision when one is called for is itself a decision.** If you make no decision to act, you have decided not to act. For example, by not deciding to make a doctor's appointment to have an injured ankle checked, you have decided to ignore it.

2. **Wait out a decision.** Some decisions benefit from the perspective of time. If an immediate decision is not necessary, consider letting the decision rest. Often, circumstances change and the right decision becomes clear.

3. **Focus on your life goals** (see Chapter 3). Decisions should move you closer to attaining your life goals—what you want out of life. Suppose you need to decide whether to rent a larger, more expensive apartment or to make do with the one you are currently renting. If one of your life goals is to be able to afford to attend law school, then renting a more expensive apartment will not help you achieve that goal.

4. **Talk with others.** Talking about the problem will help you define it, and you may hear yourself saying things you never before consciously realized.

5. **Play out the long-term consequences of a decision you are about to make.** Create a mental movie; imagine the various possible consequences of the decision at various stages—in one month, three months, one year, or three years, for instance.

SKILLS ACTION

Identifying Alternatives

The following situations are ones you may encounter in your college years. For each situation, consider the alternatives and determine which is likely to be the best course of action for you, based on the circumstances of your life. Also indicate what type of research you will need to do in order to assess the pros and cons of each alternative.

Situation	Possible Alternatives	Research Needed to Gather Information and Make the Decision
You want to play professional sports, but everyone keeps telling you how incredibly difficult it is to get picked up by a major sports team.		
The person you are dating tells you that he or she hopes to get married within a year and to start having children a year or so after that. You really like this person, but you want to focus more on your studies and hold off on getting married and having children until you have established a career.		
You graduate and are offered a terrific job. The problem is that you will have to move to another state for at least two years, leaving your friends and family behind.		

EXERCISE 6.1

Working Together

Comparing Important Decisions

Directions   *Make a list of important decisions that you face or will face in the next year. Compare your list with that of a classmate. You may discover that your lists contain similar items. Then discuss how you will reach each decision.*

■ Problem-Solving Strategies

While some people may have a natural aptitude for it, problem solving is a skill that you can and should develop. This means you must be willing to give up the comfort of such defenses or excuses as "I'm not good at problem solving" or "I'm not creative." It also means that you have to be willing to think in new ways, break old habits, and develop new approaches to solving problems.

The ability to solve problems is a valuable asset. It can make a substantial difference in your success in academic courses, in your future career, and in life. Many employers regard it as a necessary skill for holding positions of responsibility. Problem solving is a skill frequently assessed during a job interview. Questions that begin with "What would you do if . . . ?" or "Suppose you arrive at your desk one morning and you learn . . . " are designed to evaluate your problem-solving abilities.

A Model for Problem Solving

Put simply, a problem occurs when "what is" is not "what is desired." A problem exists when your grade in chemistry is not what you want it to be. A problem exists when you haven't finished your drawing for engineering, which is due tomorrow.

Let's call the "what is" your *present state* and the "what is desired" the *goal state*. Usually there are a number of ways to solve a problem, some more desirable than others. These various ways to solve a problem are called *solution paths*. A model for problem solving is shown in Figure 6.1.

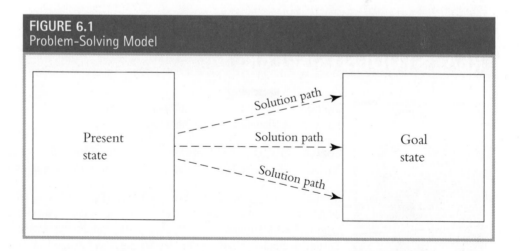

FIGURE 6.1
Problem-Solving Model

This model, when used as a basis for problem solving, forces you to identify existing circumstances (present state), the desired goal (goal state), and the various ways to achieve the goal (solution paths). On page 122 is an everyday situation that fits the problem-solving model:

Present State:	You have earned B− and C+ grades on your presentations for your public speaking course.
Desired State:	Solid B or A grades.
Solution Paths:	1. Practice your presentations with friends and ask them to critique your performance. 2. Ask your instructor for advice. 3. Spend more time organizing your presentations.

EXERCISE 6.2

Analyzing Problems

Directions *For each of the following situations, identify the present state and the goal state, and suggest several solution paths.*

1. You are scheduled to address your speech communication class when you suddenly realize you left your note cards on the desk in your room. The class begins in 10 minutes.
2. Your political science instructor has asked you to declare a topic for your term paper by Friday. When you go to the library to select a topic, you discover that all the sources you want to consult have been checked out by other students.
3. You find your assigned lab partner in biology to be irresponsible and careless, more intent on finishing and leaving early than on following procedures and discovering principles.

REAL STUDENTS SPEAK

Marlo Ricotta
––––––
**Niagara County
Community College
Niagara Falls, NY**

Background: Marlo is currently completing an associate's degree in business at Niagara County Community College.

Goals: To attend the State University of New York at Buffalo to obtain a bachelor's degree in labor relations and then pursue a degree in labor law.

Advice on Juggling School and Work: I prefer taking classes with adult students, so I take night classes and build my work schedule around school. I work 40 hours a week, 11-7, with Wednesdays and Sundays off. I study in the mornings and all day Wednesday. Sunday I take care of my house, do housework and laundry, and Sunday evening is for me. Don't bite off more than you can chew! Last semester I worked full-time and took four classes, and there were days I could hardly bear to open a book. This semester I took two classes.

■ Problem-Solving Processes

While some problems are solved easily with a burst of insight, most require deliberate, step-by-step analysis. It is easy to panic and let your mind run wild, jumping rapidly from one possible solution to another. However, this random approach to problem solving may create more problems than it solves. Here's a six-step approach to problem solving.

Step 1: Specify the Problem

A first step to solving a problem is to identify it as specifically as possible. For example, instead of saying, "My problem is my mass media course," try to pinpoint the problem: "My problem is the low grades I'm getting on the reaction papers" or "I don't understand what my professor is talking about in her lectures." Use the following suggestions to pinpoint a problem:

♦ **State the problem in a way that allows you to solve it successfully.** For example, if the library is only open during hours when you are in class or working, specify the problem in terms of your class and work schedule rather than in terms of the library's business hours. It is more likely that you will be able to adjust your schedule, use the Internet, or locate an alternative library than get the library to change its hours.

♦ **Express the problem verbally or in writing.** This process often helps to define and clarify the situation by eliminating extraneous information, focusing your attention, and triggering alternative perspectives.

♦ **Focus on language.** Often, language further clarifies the problem. For instance, if you approach a professor to change a grade, is your problem how to *argue* for a higher grade, how to *persuade* him or her, or how to *request* a reevaluation of your paper? The more specifically you can state the problem, the more likely it is that you will be able to identify workable solution paths.

Step 2: Analyze the Problem

Once you have specified the problem, the next step is to analyze it. Let us suppose you identified low grades on papers in mass media as your main problem with the course. You might begin by rereading each paper you have submitted and studying the professor's comments. Other possibilities include (1) arranging the papers from lowest to highest grades and analyzing the differences, (2) reading and comparing a friend's high-grade papers with yours, (3) asking a friend to criticize your papers, or (4) discussing the papers with your professor.

On occasion, in analyzing a problem, you may need to stretch your imagination and look beyond the obvious, surface situation for more creative options.

For example, a nursing student was having difficulty establishing a trusting rapport with patients. She and her clinical supervisor discussed various communication breakdowns, but none seemed to pinpoint the problem. Finally, after thinking about and discussing her problem with a lifelong friend, she understood her problem. She was working in a geriatrics ward, and both her elderly grandparents, with whom she had been very close, had recently died. She realized she was emotionally blocking the establishment of any rapport with an elderly person. She discussed the problem with her supervisor and then identified several solution paths.

In analyzing a problem, use the following suggestions:

◆ **Seek other perspectives.** Discuss problems with professors, parents, or friends. Be sure to consider how knowledgeable, familiar, experienced, and successful each person is in handling similar problems. Weigh their opinions accordingly.

◆ **Be flexible in your analysis.** Do not eliminate possibilities because they do not "sound like you" or seem likely.

◆ **Consider various strands of impact.** Although a problem may seem economic (for example, how to afford a car for transportation), don't ignore social or emotional aspects (have you failed to consider public transportation because your friends do not use it?).

◆ **Brainstorm about all possibilities and implications.** Spend three to five minutes listing anything you think of that remotely relates to your problem. Sort through the list later, preferably the next day. Most likely you will discover seeds of new ideas or new ways of looking at the problem.

◆ **Research problems for which you lack complete information.** Libraries and the Internet contain a wealth of information, and reading in related areas can trigger your mind and lead you to a solution. For example, a student having problems arranging for the care of her infant son discovered a Web site for new parents; it outlined procedures for locating and hiring babysitters. She learned that she needed to actively seek and advertise—rather than to passively follow up advertisements and references from friends.

| EXERCISE 6.3 | **Analyzing Problems** |

Directions   *Identify, as specifically as possible, the problem involved in each of the following situations, and suggest analyses.*

1. A friend says she plans to drop out of school for the year—she has morning classes and now she realizes that her seven-year-old son needs supervision while walking to school: he fights with his peers and is picked on by older children.
2. A two-year college student is enrolled in a computer-assisted drawing curriculum. He did not realize that the curriculum involves mathematics and technical skills. He wants to change his curriculum but doesn't know what area to transfer to.

Step 3: Formulate Possible Solution Paths

Once you have identified and analyzed the problem, you are ready to formulate possible solution paths. At this stage, your goal is to identify a wide range of possible solutions. Returning to the mass media problem, let's suppose that in analyzing your reaction papers you determined that your writing style and weak organization were causing low grades. Your ideas seemed adequate, but you were not expressing them in a manner acceptable to your professor. The next step is to identify all possible ways to correct the problem. You consider: (1) getting help from a classmate, (2) getting a tutor from the learning lab, (3) asking the mass media instructor for help, (4) visiting the writing lab on campus for tutoring, (5) having a friend who has superior English skills edit and proofread your papers, and (6) asking your English instructor to recommend a book on writing style.

When formulating possible solutions, use the following tips:

◆ **Try to think of all possible solutions.** For complicated problems, write down all possible solutions. At this stage, try not to evaluate a solution as you think of it. Just jot it down and continue thinking of others. Then reread your list; often it will help you think of alternative solutions.

◆ **Be creative.** Don't be afraid to think of crazy or outlandish solutions. Often, when wild solutions may in themselves be unacceptable, some aspect is workable or may trigger a solution that is.

◆ **Consider similar problems and how you have solved them.** You can learn from both your successes and your failures.

EXERCISE 6.4

Working Together

Identifying Solution Paths

Directions *For each of the problems described in Exercise 6.3, identify as many solution paths as possible. Then exchange your paper with a classmate. Can your classmate discover solution paths you did not think of?*

Step 4: Evaluate Possible Solution Paths

Once you have identified all possible solution paths, the next step is to weigh the advantages and disadvantages of each. To do so, you will need to think through each solution path in detail, considering how, when, and where you could accomplish each. Also consider whether you have the time, money, skills, knowledge, personal contacts, and so forth to pursue each solution path. Eliminate those that are impractical. For example, if you decided to get a tutor to help you write papers for the mass media course, you would need to consider practical details such as these:

◆ Do I have time to meet with a tutor?
◆ How will I feel working with a tutor?
◆ What will I do if I don't like my tutor?
◆ What if my tutor does not or cannot help me?

Consider both immediate and long-term results of each solution. For instance, for the mass media problem, having a friend edit and proofread your paper may be a workable solution to correct the immediate problem. In the long term, however, it may not be the best solution because you will not have improved your writing style and organizational skills.

For complex problems with numerous solution paths, the technique of *mapping* is often useful. Mapping is simply drawing a picture that connects details for each solution path. (See Chapter 14, p. 316.)

For example, suppose you are majoring in business and your advisor is encouraging you to consider a double major. She has suggested English, communications, or psychology, but you cannot decide which to choose. To evaluate each, you might draw a chart such as the one shown in Figure 6.2.

By studying the chart, you can more easily see the advantages of each alternative and make comparisons. While a map usually clarifies the situation, it seldom clearly identifies the best solution. Instead, the map enables you to evaluate each alternative logically and systematically.

FIGURE 6.2
Evaluating Solution Paths

	English	Communications	Psychology
Required credit hours outside major	0-16	24	0
Number of electives	24-48	35-45	64-74
Total credit hours in major	57	36	31
Graduation requirement	Thesis	No	Senior seminar
Foreign language requirement	Yes	No	No
Additional semester needed	Yes	No	No

In solving some problems, you may realize that you need more information before you can evaluate various solution paths. For the mass media course problem considered throughout this chapter, you may need to know whether tutoring can be arranged conveniently before you can evaluate it as an alternative. Or, in choosing a double major, you may find that you want more information than is provided in the college catalog. You might talk with your advisor or meet with the department chairperson or do research in your career guidance and placement center or library to get information on job opportunities.

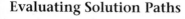

EXERCISE 6.5

**Working
Together**

Evaluating Solution Paths

Directions   *Working in small groups, evaluate each of the solution paths you devised for the problems listed in Exercise 6.3.*

THINKING CRITICALLY
. . . About Alternatives

An important step in both decision making and problem solving is weighing alternatives and selecting the one that is best for you. As you weigh decisions and possible solution paths, use the following questions to guide your thinking:

◆ What outcome is each alternative likely to produce, in both the short term and the long term?

◆ How easily can you accomplish each?

◆ What are the possible negative side effects of each?

◆ What risk, if any, is involved in each?

◆ Have I thought of all the alternatives?

◆ Which outcome will help me achieve my larger goals?

Working Together

Most students face financial hardships and experience money problems while attending college. Some students "max out" credit cards, others work as many as three part-time jobs. Working in groups of four or five students, select a real problem a group member faces or create a hypothetical financial problem that college students often face. Follow the first four steps in the problem-solving process to discover as many solution paths as possible.

Step 5: Choose a Solution

The fifth step in problem solving is the selection of one solution path. In weighing the various solution paths, there are three factors to consider.

◆ **Compatibility with your life goals and priorities.** In choosing a solution, you must match the solution with what you have identified as most important to you. In the case of the mass media course papers, if an immediate improvement in grades is more important than improving your writing skills, some solutions are better than others. In evaluating majors, you will need to decide how convenient spending an additional semester is and whether it fits within your short-term and long-term goals.

◆ **Amount of risk.** Some solutions involve more risk than others. For instance, working with a tutor from the learning lab may be a more reliable, controlled, and organized solution (and therefore less risky) than depending on the good nature of a classmate to help. The amount of risk you are willing to take depends on the seriousness of the problem and the consequences if the solution fails.

◆ **Practicality.** The most logical of solutions won't work if it is not practical. Regardless of how good a solution may seem, if you cannot carry it through, it is worthless. For instance, getting a tutor may seem the best solution to the mass media paper problem. However, if the tutor is only available at 8:00 in the morning and you know you'll have trouble keeping appointments at that time, then the solution is not practical.

Step 6: Evaluate Your Solution

Once you have chosen a solution path and have acted on it, check to be sure that it is working. Suppose you decided to work with a tutor to improve your grades on mass media assignments. If you get a higher grade on your next paper, you have evidence that your solution is working. If your grades are not improving, it is time to reconsider the problem and choose an alternative solution.

■ Keys to Problem Solving

Here are a few tips to make the problem-solving process work for you. Use them in conjunction with the problem-solving model just described.

1. **Think aloud or write.** Problem solving is a cognitive (mental) process. For complicated problems, many people find it useful to think aloud, talk to themselves, or write notes as they work through the problem-solving steps. Hearing or seeing yourself think, so to speak, seems to facilitate the process. Sometimes, especially when solving academic problems, by thinking aloud or writing you catch yourself using the wrong rule or formula, or saying something that is contradictory to what you have read.

2. **Allow time for incubation.** Archimedes, an ancient Greek, is said to have run naked through the streets shouting, "Eureka!" He was announcing that he had, while taking a bath, discovered the solution to a problem he had been studying for years, which is known today as Archimedes' principle. How and why was Archimedes able to arrive at a solution at a time when he wasn't even thinking about it? You may have similar experiences when all of a sudden during an exam you know an answer you couldn't think of 10 minutes ago, or a new solution to a problem you have been wrestling with for days flashes in your mind without warning.

   What happened to Archimedes, and what happens to you when you get sudden flashes of insight, illustrates a principle known as *incubation*. Just as chicken eggs are nurtured in the warmth and humidity of an incubator until ready to hatch, ideas, too, need incubation until they are ready to hatch or come together to solve a problem. Even though you may not be consciously thinking about a problem, it is still there, in the back of your mind.

   Time away from the problem allows ideas to gel or consolidate. It also provides a psychological distance and new perspective on the problem. The best advice, then, for when you cannot solve a problem is to wait. Give yourself time for the various solution paths to settle in. Distance from a problem also clears your mind, lessens the problem's importance, and often provides a fresh outlook.

3. **Talk about the problem.** If you describe the problem to someone else and talk about it, the problem often crystallizes, becoming clearer and more

defined, so that new solution paths sometimes surface. Talking to some-one else externalizes the problem (takes it outside of you) and provides a measure of psychological distance.

Analyzing Problems

Directions *Study the two problems listed below and apply the six-step problem-solving approach to each. Keep a written record of the process. Generate as many solutions as possible, and then state which solution you would select. Justify your choice.*

1. A major change has occurred recently in your family's financial situation, and you are not sure whether you will be able to afford to attend college next semester. Because it is near the end of the summer, you have heard that all of the college's financial aid funds have already been distributed for the next academic year.

2. It is the sixth week of a 15-week semester, and you have been hospitalized for complications resulting from bronchial pneumonia. Your doctor estimates you can return to classes in two to three weeks. You have already missed one week of classes.

SKILLS IN ACTION

Problem Solving: Case Study

Analyze the following situation and answer the questions below.

Deepak has completed his freshman year at a community college. When regis-tering in advance for his third semester, he realizes that a normal course load would put him within six credit hours of graduation. He is considering register-ing for a six-hour overload and graduating a semester early. As an accounting major, he has consistently earned high C and B grades. Upon graduation, he in-tends to get a full-time job and pursue a four-year degree part-time. One of his life goals is to become a CPA, or certified public accountant. He currently works part-time to earn living expenses.

1. What is the real problem that Deepak faces? What solution paths are available?

2. List the advantages and disadvantages of each solution path.

3. What factors should Deepak consider in evaluating various solution paths?

4. Project several different final outcomes, both short-term and long-term.

REVIEW: Five Key Points to Remember

1 **Problem solving is a process.** It involves moving from a present (undesired) state to a desired goal state. Various solution paths exist for moving from the present state to the desired state.

2 **State the problem as specifically as possible.** Analyze it in detail.

3 **Identify and evaluate possible solution paths.** Be flexible and creative.

4 **Choose a solution that suits your needs.** Consider your priorities, the amount of risk, and its practicality.

5 **Use problem-solving tools.** These include thinking aloud, writing, talking, and allowing for time for incubation.

The Work Connection

What do corporations look for in prospective employees? DeVry Institute of Technology conducted a survey to find out which skills and attitudes corporations value most highly. Here are the top ten employee capabilities for workplace success:

1. Excellent verbal and written skills

2. Hands-on ability (ability to apply concepts)

3. Ability to work in groups, including working with people of different backgrounds

4. Flexibility to adapt to and use "new structures, programs, procedures"

5. Critical thinking and problem-solving abilities

6. Creative thinking that leads to "breakthrough solutions"

7. Having a balanced life, including activities outside the workplace

8. Effective time management and dependability

9. In technical fields, the willingness to fail and then try again to find solutions

10. Personal commitment to team and corporate goals[1]

1. Divide the ten attributes listed above into two lists according to your current capabilities, one list for your strengths and another for weaker areas. Do this by considering specific examples from your school, work, and home life. Describe your strong points briefly as if talking to an interviewer. For your weak points, check through the table of contents of this book for suggestions.

2. Think about the courses you are enrolled in currently. What opportunities does each one present for you to become competent in the ten skills defined above? List at least three opportunities each presents.

3. What elective courses might help you improve these skills? List at least three courses and use the problem-solving model from this chapter to decide which ones to take.

The Web Connection

1. Are You a Good Decision Maker?

   http://www.sba.gov/smallbusinessplanner/manage/makedecisions/SERV_GOODD EC.html

   From the Online Women's Business Center at the Small Business Administration, this site offers decision-making tips, including useful "Common Decision-Making Mistakes." Pick a situation that is currently requiring you to make a decision. Use this site to work through the problem and possible solutions. Then evaluate the usefulness of the site for your purpose.

2. Universal Intellectual Standards

   http://www.criticalthinking.org/articles/universal–intellectual–standards.cfm

   Carefully read the standards on this Web site from the Foundation for Critical Thinking. Then find a newspaper or magazine article about a national issue. Write down specific questions you have about that issue based on these standards.

3. Decision Making Flowchart

   http://earthsys.ag.ohio–state.edu/Decision/DecisionFlowchart.pdf

   Print out this flowchart for decision making from Ohio State University. Use this method for solving a problem or situation with which you are currently dealing.

7 Learning Styles and Teaching Styles

Do You Know?

How can you discover your learning style?

How do you decide what you should learn?

How can awareness of your learning style help you study better?

How can you adapt to different teaching styles?

How can you evaluate your learning?

Learning from both textbooks and lectures may be the biggest challenge you face as a college student. Your success as a student depends almost entirely on your ability to learn. Often a student complains: "My instructor never tells us *how* to learn all this material!"

The reason instructors don't tell their students how to learn is simple. Students learn in many different ways. Advice offered to one student may not work for another. In this chapter you will discover how you learn best and then how to choose study methods that suit how you learn. You will also find out how to adapt your study methods to different teaching styles.

■ Analyzing Your Learning Style

Have you found some types of learning tasks easier than others? Perhaps writing a term paper is easier than solving calculus problems; taking lecture notes may be easier than reading and marking textbook chapters. Essay exams may be more difficult than objective exams. Or perhaps you have found one instructor easier to learn from than another. Have you also noticed that tasks that may be easy for you may be difficult for others? Each person has his or her own approach to taking in and processing information. For example, some students learn best visually, seeing charts, diagrams, or models. Others are auditory learners; they learn best by listening. Such students would learn more quickly from an instructor's lecture than from a textbook chapter on the same topic. Such variations in how people learn are known as *learning styles*.

To begin to understand learning style, think of everyday tasks and activities that you have learned to do easily and well. Think of others that are always troublesome. For example, is reading maps easy or difficult? Is drawing or sketching easy or difficult? Can you assemble items easily? Are activities that require physical coordination (such as racquetball) difficult? Can you easily remember the lyrics to popular songs? Just as some everyday tasks are easy and others are difficult, so are some academic tasks easy and others more challenging.

The following questionnaire is designed to assist you in analyzing your learning style. Complete and score the questionnaire now before continuing with the chapter.

Learning Style Questionnaire

Each item presents two alternatives. Select the alternative that best describes you. In cases in which neither choice suits you, select the one that is closer to your preference. Write the letter of your choice on the line to the left of each item.

Part One

_____ 1. For a grade in biology lab, I would prefer to
   a. work with a lab partner.
   b. work alone.

_____ 2. When faced with a difficult personal problem, I prefer to
   a. discuss it with others.
   b. resolve it myself.

_____ 3. Many instructors could improve their classes by
   a. including more discussion and group activities.
   b. allowing students to work on their own more frequently.

_____ 4. When listening to a lecture or speaker, I respond more to
   a. the person presenting the ideas.
   b. the ideas themselves.

_____ 5. When on a team project, I prefer to
   a. work with several team members.
   b. divide up tasks and complete those assigned to me.

_____ 6. I prefer to shop and do errands
   a. with friends.
   b. by myself.

_____ 7. A job in a busy office is
   a. more appealing than working alone.
   b. less appealing than working alone.

Part Two

_____ 1. To solve a math problem, I would prefer to
     a. draw or visualize the problem.
     b. study a sample problem and use it as a model.

_____ 2. To remember things best, I
     a. create a mental picture.
     b. write it down.

_____ 3. Assembling a bicycle from a diagram would be
     a. easy.
     b. challenging.

_____ 4. I prefer classes in which I
     a. handle equipment or work with models.
     b. participate in a class discussion.

_____ 5. To understand and remember how a machine works, I would
     a. draw a diagram.
     b. write notes.

_____ 6. I enjoy
     a. drawing or working with my hands.
     b. speaking, writing, and listening.

_____ 7. If I were trying to locate an office on an unfamiliar university campus, I would prefer a student to
     a. draw me a map.
     b. give me a set of written directions.

Part Three

_____ 1. I prefer to
     a. learn facts and details.
     b. construct theories and ideas.

_____ 2. I would prefer a job involving
     a. following specific instructions.
     b. reading, writing, and analyzing.

_____ 3. I prefer to
     a. solve math problems using a formula.
     b. discover why the formula works.

_____ 4. I would prefer to write a term paper explaining
     a. how a process works.
     b. a theory.

_____ 5. I prefer tasks that require me to follow
          a. careful, detailed instructions.
          b. reasoning and critical analysis.

_____ 6. For a criminal justice course I would prefer to
          a. discover how and when a law can be used.
          b. learn how and why it became law.

_____ 7. To learn more about the operation of a high-speed computer
          printer, I would prefer to
          a. work with several types of printers.
          b. understand the principles on which they operate.

Part Four

_____ 1. I would prefer to follow a set of
          a. oral directions.
          b. written directions.

_____ 2. I would prefer to
          a. attend a lecture given by a famous psychologist.
          b. read an article written by the psychologist.

_____ 3. I am better at remembering
          a. names.
          b. faces.

_____ 4. It is easier to learn new information using
          a. language (words).
          b. images (pictures).

_____ 5. I prefer classes in which the instructor
          a. lectures and answers questions.
          b. uses videos and PowerPoint presentations.

_____ 6. To obtain information about current events, I would prefer to
          a. listen to news on the radio.
          b. read the newspaper.

_____ 7. To learn how to operate a complicated machine, I would
          a. listen to a friend's explanation.
          b. watch a demonstration.

Part Five

_____ 1. To make decisions I rely on
          a. my experiences and "gut" feelings.
          b. facts and objective data.

———————— 2. To complete a task, I
  a. can use whatever is available to get the job done.
  b. must have everything I need at hand.

———————— 3. I prefer to express my ideas and feelings through
  a. music, song, or poetry.
  b. direct, concise language.

———————— 4. I prefer instructors who
  a. allow students to be guided by their own interests.
  b. make their expectations clear and explicit.

———————— 5. I tend to
  a. challenge and question what I hear and read.
  b. accept what I hear and read.

———————— 6. I prefer
  a. essay exams.
  b. objective (multiple-choice, true/false) exams.

———————— 7. In completing an assignment I prefer to
  a. figure out my own approach.
  b. be told exactly what to do.

To score your questionnaire, record the total number of choice *a*'s and the total number of choice *b*'s for each part of the questionnaire. Record your totals in the scoring grid provided below.

SCORING GRID		
Parts	**Total Number of Choice A**	**Total Number of Choice B**
Part One	————————	————————
	Social	Independent
Part Two	————————	————————
	Spatial	Verbal
Part Three	————————	————————
	Applied	Conceptual
Part Four	————————	————————
	Auditory	Visual
Part Five	————————	————————
	Creative	Pragmatic

Now, circle your higher score for each part of the questionnaire. The word below the score you circled indicates a dominant aspect of your learning style. The next section explains how to interpret your scores and describes these aspects.

■ Interpreting Your Scores

The questionnaire was divided into five parts; each part identifies one aspect of your learning style. Each of these five aspects is explained below.

Part One—Social or Independent Learners

This score reveals your preferred level of interaction with other people in the learning process. If you are a social learner, you prefer to work with others—both peers and instructors—closely and directly. Social learners tend to be people oriented and enjoy personal interaction. If you are an independent learner, you prefer to work and study alone. You tend to be self-directed or self-motivated, and you are often goal oriented.

Part Two—Spatial or Verbal Learners

This score reveals your ability to work with spatial relationships. Spatial learners are able to visualize or mentally see how things work or how they are positioned in space. Their strengths may include drawing, assembling things, or repairing. Verbal learners tend to rely on verbal or language skills, rather than positioning things in space.

Part Three—Applied or Conceptual Learners

This score describes the types of learning tasks and learning situations you prefer and find easiest to handle. If you are an applied learner, you prefer tasks that involve real objects and situations. Practical, real-life learning situations are ideal for you. Examples will often make an idea clear and understandable. If you are a conceptual learner, you prefer to work with language and ideas; practical applications are not necessary for understanding. You may enjoy working with theories and concepts and tend to work from rule to example.

Part Four—Auditory or Visual Learners

This score indicates through which sensory mode you prefer to process information. Auditory learners tend to learn more effectively through listening, while visual learners process information by seeing it in print or other visual modes including video, picture, or diagram. If you have a higher score on auditory than visual, you tend to be an auditory learner. That is, you tend to learn more easily by hearing than by reading. A higher score on visual suggests strengths with visual modes of learning.

Part Five—Creative or Pragmatic Learners

This score describes the approach you prefer to take toward learning tasks. Creative learners are imaginative and innovative. They prefer to learn through discovery or experimentation. They are comfortable taking risks and following hunches. Pragmatic learners are practical, logical, and systematic. They seek order and are comfortable following rules.

Evaluate Your Results

By responding to the questionnaire and analyzing the results, you should have discovered more about yourself as a learner. However, several words of caution are in order.

The questionnaire is an informal indicator of your learning style. Other more formal and more accurate measures of learning style are available. These include *Kolb's Learning Style Inventory* and *Myers-Briggs Type Indicator*. These tests may be available through your college's counseling, testing, or academic skills center.

Learning style has many more aspects than those identified through the questionnaire in this chapter. To learn more about other factors, one or both of the tests listed above would be useful.

REAL STUDENTS SPEAK

Michael Archer

Greenfield
Community College
Greenfield,
Massachusetts

Background: Michel is currently in his second year of studying fine arts at Greenfield Community College.

Goals: To transfer to a four-year college and complete a bachelor's degree in fine arts, majoring in sculpture.

Advice on Learning Styles: I found out how visual I am through school and taking classes with different teachers. I had success in science and math classes that used a lot of visual aids and visual explanations and did not do as well in English. Now I use words to create an image that I can remember. In art history, for example, when I read about a painting, I look for what I've just read about in the painting and then when I see the picture again I can remember what I learned about it. The words come first and then I make connections to the painting and the information sticks. So, if you find a learning style that works for you, you should develop that skill and make it work for you in other parts of your learning experience.

Learning style is *not* a fixed, unchanging quality.   Just as personalities can change and develop, so can learning styles change and develop through exposure, instruction, or practice. For example, as you experience more college lectures, your skill as an auditory learner may be strengthened.

People are not necessarily clearly strong or weak in each aspect. Some students, for example, may be able to learn equally well spatially or verbally. If there was very little difference between your two scores on one or more parts of the questionnaire, then you may have strengths in both areas.

When most students discover the features of their learning style, they recognize themselves.   A frequent comment is "Yep, that's me." If, for some reason, you feel the description of yourself as a learner is incorrect, then do not make changes in your learning strategies based on the information. Instead, discuss your style with your instructor, or consider taking one of the tests listed above.

| EXERCISE 7.1 | ### Evaluating the Learning Style Questionnaire |

Directions   *Evaluate the results of the learning style questionnaire by answering the following questions.*

1. How accurately do you think the results describe you? Identify aspects that you agree and disagree with. Explain why you disagree.
2. Evaluate your current study methods in light of the questionnaire's results. What are you doing that is effective? What changes are needed?

Working Together

Each class member should bring a week's worth of lecture notes for any course. Exchange your lecture notes with another student. Each of you should take about ten minutes to study the notes your classmate prepared. You are looking for evidence to indicate whether your partner is (1) a spatial or verbal learner, and (2) an applied or conceptual learner. Keep track of the evidence that you notice for each of these two aspects of your partner's learning style. When the study time is over, discuss your findings with your partner. Then your partner can share the results of his or her learning style questionnaire with you. Were you right on each count? Discuss what each of you, when taking lecture notes, can do differently to highlight the strengths of your particular learning style or to improve weaker areas.

■ Deciding What to Learn

Before you begin an assignment you should decide how you will approach it. Will you highlight it, outline it, prepare index cards, or record it? Your decision depends on two factors: what you need to learn and your learning style.

Research on how people learn has clearly established that we remember only what we *intend* to remember. For example, take a moment to sketch the face of a dollar bill. Or draw the keypad on a telephone, indicating which letters correspond with each number.

Why did you have difficulty with each of these tasks? You certainly have seen each of these items many times. Most likely, you could not recall the needed information because you never *intentionally* learned it. This principle of intention strongly influences and controls your learning. Unless you select a given piece of information as important, and then consciously work on storing it in your memory, you will quickly forget it. Learning, then, is a sifting and sorting process in which you identify what is necessary and important to learn and remember. Here are a few suggestions on deciding what to learn:

1. **Follow your instructor's emphases.** Notice the topics the instructor emphasizes in lectures, spends a great deal of time discussing, or seems interested in or excited about; these are likely to be important.

2. **Review previous exams and quizzes.** They indicate the type of information to learn.

3. **Use the structure and organization of your text to identify key ideas and concepts.** Use the table of contents, chapter introductions, headings, summaries, and review questions as guides.

4. **Use chapter objectives.** These usually indicate the most important topics in the chapter.

5. **Use the end-of-chapter review questions.** These questions usually suggest what is important.

6. **Talk with other students who have taken the course.** They may be able to tell you what kinds of information your instructor emphasizes.

EXERCISE 7.2

Analyzing a Textbook Assignment

Directions   *For a textbook reading assignment given by one of your instructors, use the suggestions given above to write a list of what you need to learn as you read the chapter.*

THINKING CRITICALLY
. . . About the Intent to Learn

Intending to learn a piece of information is the first step in actually learning it. Two different meanings of the word *intention* can help you figure out ways to increase and heighten your intent to learn: (1) a plan of action, and (2) an aim or purpose to guide an action. Think about these definitions while answering the following questions:

◆ What actions can you take to strengthen your intent to learn?

◆ What personal purposes or reasons do you have for learning the course material?

◆ What do you aim to do with this material later that makes you want to learn it now?

The more specific your questions and answers are, the better you will be able to focus on your intent to learn.

■ Using Learning Style to Choose a Study Method

Once you have analyzed a learning task, you are ready to select the best techniques to accomplish it. Many students just jump into an assignment, only to find out midway through it that a different approach would have produced better results and saved valuable time. Here is an example:

> Sarah, a spatial, social learner, was preparing for a midterm examination in human anatomy and physiology. As soon as the exam was announced, she began to prepare detailed outlines of each chapter. The day of the exam, in comparing notes with a classmate, she discovered that a system of testing herself by drawing and labeling diagrams and making tables and function charts would have been a more active means of learning. She also realized that studying with a classmate and testing each other would have been more effective.

Suppose you are faced with the task of reviewing several chapters in your mass media and communications text in preparation for an essay exam. What strategy would you use to learn and remember as much as possible? Some students would use the same strategy they use for every other reading assignment: reread and highlight. A better approach is to choose a strategy that fits your learning style as well as the nature of the material to be read and the type of

FIGURE 7.1
Differing Learning Strategies

Course:	Anatomy and Physiology	
Type of Exam:	Multiple Choice	
	Student A	**Student B**
Learning Style:	Social, spatial, applied	Independent, verbal, conceptual
Learning Strategies:	1. study with classmate(s)	1. study alone
	2. draw diagrams, sketches	2. prepare index cards
	3. prepare charts	3. use summary sheets
	4. associate with practical situations	4. reorganize the information

exam you anticipate. For example, you might predict possible essay questions and organize information to answer each.

Use your learning style to decide how best to study. What is best for you may not be best for a classmate. In fact, two students with differing learning styles may study for the same exam in the same class in very different ways, as shown in Figure 7.1.

Figure 7.2 (p. 144) provides examples of learning methods that are suitable for each aspect of learning style in the learning style questionnaire. To use this chart, first go through and circle or highlight the five aspects of your learning style as identified in the scoring grid on p. 137 and then study the corresponding suggestions.

Here are a few suggestions to use in deciding how to approach an assignment:

1. **Define the characteristics or nature of the task.** State as explicitly as possible what you are expected to accomplish.

2. **Identify your options.** What strategies can you use? You will be able to answer this question more explicitly later, after you have worked through all the chapters of this book.

3. **Try to match the strategy to the material.** As you will see in later chapters, not all learning strategies are equally effective in all situations. To find the best match, ask yourself questions such as these: (1) What types of thinking and learning are required? For example, is the task primarily one of problem solving, or does it require creative thought? (2) What level of recall is required (facts and details or just major concepts)? (3) Am I expected to make applications? (4) Am I expected to evaluate and criticize? Review Table 2.2, "Levels of Thinking," on p. 43 to think of other useful questions.

FIGURE 7.2
Learning Strategies for Various Learning Styles

Social
1. Interact with instructor.
2. Find a study partner.
3. Form a study group.
4. Take courses involving class discussion.
5. Work with a tutor.

Spatial
1. Draw diagrams, make charts and sketches.
2. Use outlining.
3. Use visualization.
4. Use mapping (see Chapter 14).

Applied
1. Associate ideas with their application.
2. Take courses with a lab or practicum.
3. Think of practical situations to which learning applies.
4. Use case studies, examples, and applications to cue your learning.

Auditory
1. Record review notes.
2. Discuss/study with friends.
3. Talk aloud when studying.
4. Record lectures.

Creative
1. Take courses that involve exploration, experimentation, or discussion.
2. Use annotation to record impressions and reactions.
3. Ask questions about chapter content and answer them.

Independent
1. Use computer-assisted instruction if available.
2. Enroll in courses using traditional lecture-exam format.
3. Consider independent study courses.
4. Purchase review books and study guides, if available.

Verbal
1. Record steps, processes, procedures in words.
2. Write summaries.
3. Translate diagrams and drawings into language.
4. Write your interpretation next to textbook drawings, maps, graphics.

Conceptual
1. Use outlining.
2. Focus on thought patterns (see Chapter 11).
3. Organize materials into rules and examples.

Visual
1. Use mapping (see Chapter 14).
2. Use visualization.
3. Use computer-assisted instruction if available.
4. Use videos when available.
5. Draw diagrams, charts, and maps.

Pragmatic
1. Write lists of steps, processes, and procedures.
2. Write summaries and outlines.
3. Use a structured study environment.
4. Focus on problem-solving logical sequence.

EXERCISE 7.3

Working Together

Identifying Learning Strategies

Directions   *Discuss with a classmate what learning strategies might be effective for each of the following students in each of the following situations.*

Student A: strong visual, spatial learning style

Student B: strong social, applied learning style

Student C: strong auditory, conceptual learning style

Situation 1:   Attending a city court trial as an assignment for a criminal justice class to learn about criminal trial procedures

Situation 2:   Reading a chapter assignment in a book titled *The Intelligence Controversy* for a psychology course. The instructor plans a class discussion of the assignment.

Situation 3:   Reading an assigned research report on North–South wage differences in the *American Economics Review* about which the student must write a synopsis

Situation 4:   Watching a class demonstration in psychology designed to explain various forms of conditioning

EXERCISE 7.4   ### Selecting Learning Strategies

Directions   *For the assignment you chose in Exercise 7.2, write a list of the learning strategies you intend to use as you read and study the chapter.*

■ Adapting to Various Teaching Styles

Just as each student has his or her own learning style, each instructor has his or her own teaching style. Some instructors, for example, have a teaching style that promotes social interaction among students. An instructor may organize small group activities, encourage class participation, or require students to work in pairs or teams to complete a specific task. Other instructors offer little or no opportunity for social interaction. A lecture class is an example.

Some instructors are very applied; they teach by example. Others are more conceptual; they focus on presenting ideas, rules, theories, and so forth. In fact, the same five categories of learning styles identified on pp. 138–139 can be applied to teaching styles as well.

To an extent, of course, the subject matter also dictates how the instructor teaches. A biology instructor, for instance, has a large body of factual information to present and may feel he or she has little time to schedule group interaction.

Compare Learning and Teaching Styles

Most likely you can learn better from one instructor than another and you feel more comfortable in certain instructors' classes than others. When aspects of your learning style match aspects of your instructor's teaching style, you are on the same "wavelength," so to speak: the instructor is teaching the way you learn. On the other hand, when your learning style does not correspond to an instructor's teaching style, you may not be as comfortable, and learning will be more of a challenge. You may have to work harder in that class by taking extra steps to reorganize or reformat the material into a form in which you can learn it better. The following discussion of the five categories of learning-teaching styles includes suggestions for how you might make changes in how you study to accommodate each.

Social-Independent

If your instructor organizes numerous in-class group activities and you tend to be an independent learner, then you will need to spend time alone after class reviewing the class activity, making notes, perhaps even repeating the activity by yourself to make it more meaningful. If your instructor seldom uses in-class group activities and you tend to be a social learner, try to arrange to study regularly with a classmate or create or join a study group.

Spatial-Verbal

If you are a spatial learner and your instructor has a verbal teaching style (he or she lectures and writes notes on the board), then you will need to draw diagrams, charts, and pictures to learn the material. On the other hand, if you are a verbal learner and your instructor is spatial (he or she frequently uses diagrams, flowcharts, and so forth), then you may need to translate the diagrams and flowcharts into words in order to learn them more easily.

Applied-Conceptual

If your instructor seldom uses examples, models, or case studies and you are an applied learner, you need to think of your own examples to make the course material real and memorable to you. Leave space in your class notes to add examples. Add them during class if they come to mind; if not, take time as you review your notes to add examples. If your instructor uses numerous demonstrations and examples and you are a conceptual learner, you may need to leave space in your class notes to write in rules or generalizations that state what the examples are intended to prove.

Auditory-Visual

If your instructor announces essential course information (such as paper assignments, class projects, or descriptions of upcoming exams) orally and you are a visual learner, you should be sure to record as much information as possible in your notes. If your instructor relies on lectures to present new material not included in your textbook, taking complete lecture notes is especially important. If your instructor uses numerous visual aids and you tend to be an auditory learner, consider recording summaries of these visual aids.

Creative-Pragmatic

Suppose your instructor is very systematic and organized in his or her lectures, and, as a creative learner, you prefer to discover ideas through experimentation and free-flowing discussion. Then you should consider creating a column in your class notes to record your responses and creative thoughts or reserving the bottom quarter of each page for such annotations. If your instructor is creative and tends to use a loose or free-flowing class format, and you tend to be a pragmatic learner, you may need to rewrite and restructure class notes. If he or she fails to give you specific guidelines for completing activities or assignments, you should talk with your instructor or ask for more information.

EXERCISE 7.5

Analying Teaching Styles

Directions   *Analyze your instructors' teaching styles by completing the following chart for the courses you are taking this semester. List as many teaching characteristics as you can, but do not try to cover every aspect of each instructor's teaching style.*

Course	Instructor's Name	Teaching Style Characteristics
1.		
2.		
3.		
4.		
5.		
6.		

EXERCISE 7.6   **Comparing Teaching and Learning Styles**

Directions   *After you have completed the chart in Exercise 7.5, select one of your instructors whose teaching style does not match your learning style. Write a paragraph describing the differences in your styles. Explain how you will change your study methods to make up for these differences.*

▮ Evaluating Your Learning

You maintain an awareness or check on how well you are performing many daily activities. In sports such as hockey, baseball, or bowling, you know if you are playing a poor game; you actually keep score and deliberately try to correct errors and improve your performance. When preparing a favorite food, you often taste it to be assured it will turn out as expected. You know whether your car is clean after taking it through the car wash.

A similar type of checking should occur as you learn and study. You should be aware of, or *monitor,* your performance. You need to keep track of whether the study method you have chosen is working. Here are a few questions that will help you decide whether you have chosen an effective study method.

1. **At what pace am I working?** If you are working extremely rapidly, you may not be spending enough time with the material. Consider adding additional steps to your chosen method. For example, if you have chosen to read and highlight, consider adding annotations or the preparation of flash cards. If your pace is so slow that you are inefficient, consider dropping a step. For example, perhaps you do not need to both highlight and outline a chapter.

2. **How much do I remember?** For textbook chapters, use the headings to test your recall. Turn each heading into a question and then answer it.

Heading	Question
Evaluating Storage and Retrieval Costs	How are storage and retrieval costs evaluated?
Multiple Uses of Stored Data	What are the uses of stored data?
The Database Concept	What is the database concept, and how is it used?

Since a heading announces the subject of the section that follows it, questions based on the heading will test your recall of the key ideas presented about that subject.

The best time to pose and answer these questions is *while you are reading*. As you finish each section, stop and take a moment to glance at the heading and recall the main points the section presented.

3. **How does this information fit with other material I have learned?** If you can draw connections between current and prior learning, your study method is working. If you can answer the following questions, you are probably on the right track.

   ◆ What does this topic have to do with topics discussed earlier in the chapter?
   ◆ How does this reading assignment fit with the topics of this week's class lectures?
   ◆ What does this chapter have to do with the chapter assigned last week?
   ◆ What principle do these problems illustrate?

These questions enable you to determine whether your learning is meaningful. They will help you check whether you are simply taking in information without much thought or whether you are thinking critically about the information and fitting it into the scheme of the course. The best times to ask connection questions are before you begin and after you finish the chapter or each major section.

EXERCISE 7.7

Asking Questions

Directions   *What questions would you ask when reading an economics textbook chapter titled "The Distribution of Income"?[1] The major headings of two sections are*

Income Distribution in the United States
Historical Changes in Adjusted Income
Age Distribution and Income
Rags to Riches: Mobility

> **Some Characteristics of Income Distribution**
> Family Income Characteristics
> Poverty
> Poverty During Recession
> Race and Sex Discrimination: Wages
> Programs to Alleviate Poverty

As you evaluate your learning, you may, at times, find that a particular strategy is not working as well as it did in the past. You may find that an assignment is taking too long, that you do not seem to be making the right connections, or that you are not mastering the material as well as you feel you should. Perhaps the best way to describe this situation is to say that nothing has "clicked." It is best to stop, assess the situation, and modify your approach.

Often, a tried-and-true strategy that has always worked in the past fails when applied to a new type of learning. At first, the strategy may seem to be working as well as usual because you are so comfortable with it. Only later, when assessing your progress, do you realize that the strategy was not effective. For example, a student taking her first philosophy course approached the course by focusing on facts, as she had always done in other courses. She learned names and dates but found very few facts to learn. Eventually she realized her focus was too specific—she needed to focus on larger issues, theories, worldviews, and so forth.

SKILLS IN ACTION

Evaluating Your Learning Through Self-Monitoring

Students often get so wrapped up in their day-to-day assignments that they do not step back to look at the big picture and take the time to understand how well they are mastering the subjects they are studying. Create and complete a table using the following headings for the courses you are taking this semester.

Course Name	What I Am Enjoying About This Course	Key Things I Have Learned	How I Might Improve My Grade, My Comprehension, or My Engagement with the Material

The key to modifying your approach is to determine how the current situation differs from others in which you have used the strategy successfully. That difference pinpoints the problem. Next, you must alter your approach to accommodate that difference. Identify alternative approaches that are consistent with your learning style, evaluate each, and select the one most likely to work. It is also helpful to check with students who are doing well in the class to find out what learning strategies they are using.

EXERCISE 7.8   **Evaluating Your Learning**

Directions   *Complete the assignment you chose in Exercise 7.2. As you work, evaluate your learning, using one or more of the questions given on p. 149.*

REVIEW: Five Key Points to Remember

1 **Use your learning style.** Understanding your learning style can help you choose the best way to study and learn.

2 **Study effectively.** Deciding what you need to learn before you begin an assignment will increase your study efficiency.

3 **Be aware of teaching styles.** Be aware of your instructors' teaching styles. Make changes in how you approach your classes based on both your learning style and your instructors' teaching styles.

4 **Keep track of your learning.** Monitor how effectively you are learning by keeping track of your pace and the amount of material you can recall.

5 **Connect new and prior learning.** Drawing connections between current assignments and previous ones will make what you learn more meaningful and, therefore, easier to remember.

The Work Connection

Your learning style is closely related to how you think and solve problems. As you approach a task or problem, you may tend to view it a certain way and overlook other ways that may lead to workable approaches and solutions. Pragmatic learners, for example, may tend to focus only on logical and systematic methods; applied learners may try to recall other practical situations in which a similar problem is solved. You can expand your ability to learn and thrive—at work, at school, and in your career—by broadening your perspective on a problem by asking all of these questions: "*Why* (should I know/do this)?" "*What* (do I need to know/do)?" "*How* (is it done/does it work)?" and "*What if* (x, y, or z happened)?" Seeking answers to all four of these questions, particularly in new or difficult situations, will stimulate your curiosity and help you find new solutions that may not have occurred to you if you had thought about a problem from only your usual perspective.

1. Think of a recent problem or challenge at work, home, or school. Write four complete questions using the samples above to broaden your thinking about this situation.

2. Answer as many of the questions as you can. For any you can't answer, what further information would you need to answer them? Write down the questions that would help you gather this information.

The Web Connection

1. Teaching Styles

   http://www.ntlf.com/html/lib/faq/ts-indiana.htm

   From the National Teaching and Learning Forum, this site identifies five typical teaching styles and their advantages and disadvantages. Make a list of your instructors and indicate which style or styles they exhibit. Give examples.

2. Best Teacher Description

   http://humanities.byu.edu/elc/teacher/bestteacher.html

   Compiled by a Brigham Young University faculty member, this site lists the characteristics of good teachers as described by students. Print this Web page and use it as a checklist to evaluate your instructors. Highlight the qualities that are most important to you.

3. Index of Learning Styles Questionnaire

   http://www.engr.ncsu.edu/learningstyles/ilsweb.html

   Try another learning style assessment at this site from North Carolina State University. Compare your results with those from the assessment in this book. How do online tests differ from those on paper? Which do you prefer? Is this a result of your learning style?

8 Learning and Memory

Do You Know?

How do learning and memory work?

What are the three stages of remembering?

How can you improve your ability to learn?

Let's assume you have just finished reading a chapter in a data processing text; you read carefully and underlined important ideas. How much of that chapter are you likely to remember tomorrow? How much will you recall next week? The answers are surprising! Research evidence suggests that:

◆ within one day, you will have forgotten more than half of what you read
◆ within a week, your recall will have dropped to less than 30 percent

These statistics have serious implications for you as a learner in college as well as later in your career. The rate of forgetting is rapid and dramatic *unless* you take specific steps to prevent it. This chapter briefly describes how learning and memory work. Once you become familiar with the learning process, you will learn numerous strategies for improving storage and retrieval of information and for overcoming forgetting.

■ How Learning and Memory Work

A popular but incorrect notion of memory is that it is a vast storage tank or a huge repository where information is deposited and retained. Rather, memory is a three-stage process.

1. **Encoding is a process of acquiring information.** Suppose you are unable to answer the question on a business exam, "Define a capital account." If you have never heard of a capital account, you never acquired the information.

FIGURE 8.1
A Model of Memory

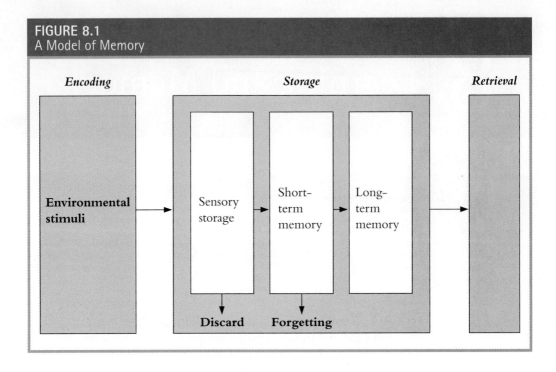

2. **Storage involves placement of information in your memory.** If you once knew the term *capital account* and now cannot recall it, the memory may have faded or decayed.

3. **Retrieval is the process of getting at and using information held in storage.** Another reason for your inability to remember the definition of capital account may be retrieval failure. Although the information is stored, you are unable to retrieve it.

Figure 8.1 is a visual model of verbal learning and memory processes. Refer to it frequently as you read the sections below that explain each stage.

Stage 1: Encoding

Every waking moment your mind is bombarded with information and impressions of what is going on around you. Your five senses—hearing, sight, touch, taste, and smell—provide information about the world around you and your interaction with it. Think for a moment of all the signals your brain receives at a given moment. If you are reading, your eyes transmit not only the visual patterns of the words, but also information about the size and color of the print. You may hear a door slamming, a clock ticking, a dog barking. You may smell perfume or food cooking, your sense of touch and feeling may signal that the pen you are using to highlight will soon run out of ink or that the room is chilly. When you listen to a classroom lecture, you are constantly receiving stimuli—from the professor, from the lecture hall, from students around you. All these environmental stimuli are transmitted to your brain for a very brief period of *sensory storage*.

Stage 2: Storage
Sensory Storage

Information received from your sense organs is transmitted through the nervous system to the brain, which accepts and interprets it. The information lingers briefly in the nervous system for your brain to interpret it. This lingering is known as **sensory storage**.

How does your mind handle this barrage of information from the senses? Thanks to *selective attention*, or *selective perception*, your brain automatically sorts out the more important signals from the trivial ones. Trivial signals, such as insignificant noises around you, are ignored or discarded.

Although your sensory storage accepts all information, information is kept there only briefly, usually less than a few seconds. The function of sensory storage then is to retain information long enough for you to selectively attend to it and transmit it to your short-term memory.

Short-Term Memory

Short-term memory holds the information acquired from your sensory storage system. It is used to store information you wish to retain for only a few seconds. A telephone number, for example, is stored in your short-term memory until you dial it. A lecturer's words are retained until you can record them in your notes. Most researchers agree that short-term memory lasts much less than one minute, perhaps 20 seconds or less. Information can be kept or maintained longer if you practice or rehearse the information (repeating a phone number, for example). When you are introduced to someone, then, unless you repeat or rehearse his or her name at the time of introduction, you will not be able to remember it. New incoming information will force it out of your short-term memory.

Your short-term memory is limited in capacity as well as in time span. Research conducted by George Miller, a psychologist who studied memory, suggests that we have room in our short-term memory to store from five to nine chunks (or pieces) of information at a time, or, on the average, seven.[1] Known as the Number Seven Theory, this finding has direct implications in both daily and academic situations. When you read a textbook chapter or listen to a lecture, for example, your short-term memory is unable to retain each piece of information you are receiving. To retain information beyond the limitations of short-term memory, it must be transferred to your long-term memory for more permanent storage.

| EXERCISE 8.1 | **Understanding the Memory Process** |

Directions   *Answer the following items using your knowledge of the memory process.*

1. Observe and analyze the area in which you are sitting. What sensory impressions (sights, sounds, touch sensations) have you been ignoring due to selective attention?

2. Can you remember what you ate for lunch last Tuesday? If not, why not?

3. Why are dashes placed in your Social Security number after the third and fifth numbers?

4. Explain why two people are able to carry on a deep conversation at a crowded, noisy party.

5. Explain why someone who looked up a phone number and then walked into another room to dial it forgot the number.

Learning: The Transfer from Short- to Long-Term Memory

To retain information beyond the brief moment you acquire it, you must transfer it to long-term memory for permanent storage. Three processes can help you store information in long-term memory: rote learning, rehearsal, and recoding.

◆ **Rote learning.** Rote learning involves repetition of information. Learning the spelling of a word, memorizing the exact definition of a word, or repeating a formula until you can remember it are examples. Material learned through this means is often learned in a fixed order. Rote learning is usually an inefficient means to store information because, as you will see later, it is difficult to retrieve.

◆ **Elaborative rehearsal.** Elaborative rehearsal is a thinking process. It involves connecting new material to be learned with already learned material, asking questions, and making associations. It is a process of making the information meaningful and fitting it together with what you already know. This form of rehearsal is discussed in more detail later.

◆ **Recoding.** Recoding is a process of rearranging, changing, or grouping information so that it becomes more meaningful and easier to recall. For example, you could recode the following shopping list into three, easier to remember groups:

> eggs, carrots, bleach, oranges, laundry soap, milk, onions, yogurt, cheese, plums, ammonia

Dairy	Produce	Cleaning supplies
eggs, milk, cheese, yogurt	carrots, onions, oranges, plums	laundry soap, ammonia, bleach

You could recode information from a reading assignment by outlining it. Taking notes from lectures is also a form of recoding.

Rehearsal and recoding are the underlying principles on which many learning strategies presented later in this book are based. Chapter 14, for example, discusses textbook highlighting and marking. Highlighting is actually a form of elaborative rehearsal. When you decide which information to highlight, you are reviewing the information and sorting the important from the unimportant. When you make marginal notes, you are recoding the information by classifying, organizing, labeling, or summarizing it.

EXERCISE 8.2

Understanding the Memory Process

Directions   *Answer the following questions using your knowledge of the memory process.*

1. On many campuses, weekly recitations or discussions are scheduled for small groups to review material presented in large lecture classes. What learning function do these recitation sections provide?

2. A literature instructor showed her class a film based on a short story that she had assigned. What learning function(s) did the video provide?

3. Why might a text that contains pictures and diagrams be easier to learn from than one without them?

4. Two groups of students read the same textbook chapter. One group highlighted key ideas on each page. The second group paraphrased and recorded the important ideas from each page. Explain why the second group received higher scores on a test based on the chapter than did the first group.

Long-Term Memory

Long-term memory is your permanent store of information. Unlike short-term memory, your long-term memory is nearly unlimited in both span and capacity. It contains hundreds of thousands of facts, details, impressions, and experiences that you have accumulated throughout your life.

Information is stored in long-term memory in three ways: (1) linguistic (language), (2) imaginal (mental or visual images), and (3) motor (physical). The linguistic method, which deals with words, is the most important in academic learning. Ideas, concepts, and facts are encoded and often stored using language. Activities such as taking lecture notes, highlighting texts, and writing outlines are examples. The imaginal method involves creation of mental or visual images. Drawing a diagram of a process or sketching the human ear in order to learn its parts are examples. The third method, motor, refers primarily to physical activities such as riding a bicycle, driving a car, or hitting a baseball. Significant research evidence suggests that using two methods produces better recall than if only one is used.

Stage 3: Retrieval

Think of retrieval as pulling stored information from your memory. You use retrieval when you solve math or science problems, take quizzes or exams, and write papers. Retrieval is closely tied to storage. The manner in which information is stored in your memory affects how well you can retrieve it. For example, suppose you have studied a topic but find that on an exam you are unable to remember much about it. There are several possible explanations: (1) you never completely learned (stored) the information at all, (2) you did not study (store) the information in the right way, (3) you are not asking the right questions or using the right means to retrieve it, or (4) you have forgotten it.

EXERCISE 8.3

Working Together

Applying Principles of Memory

Directions   *Working with a classmate, use the principles of memory discussed so far in this chapter to explain each of the following situations.*

1. A student does well on multiple-choice items on a test but has difficulty with easy questions. What does this indicate about how he stored the information?

2. A student spends more time than anyone else in the class preparing for the midterm exam, yet she cannot remember important definitions and concepts at the time of the exam. Offer several possibilities that may explain her problem.

3. What method of storage does each of the following situations involve?
   a. Replacing the cartridge in your printer
   b. Drawing a blood sample from a patient's arm
   c. Plotting a graph to include in a term paper that shows the relationships among median income, sex, and educational level
   d. Interpreting a map
   e. Solving a problem in business math

4. You cannot state the sixth number of your Social Security number without repeating the first five.

EXERCISE 8.4

Understanding the Memory Process

Directions   *Identify the encoding, storage, and retrieval stages in each of the following tasks.*

1. Learning to read a patient's chart
2. Learning the lyrics to a popular song
3. Learning to drive a stick shift car
4. Learning to program a DVD-R (DVD-Recordable)

Forgetting

Despite the vast capacity of human long-term memory, not all information remains there indefinitely. Forgetting does occur, and for newly learned material, it can occur at a dramatic rate. Table 8.1 summarizes the results of a research study[2] designed to measure the rate at which subjects forget previously learned verbal material.

This study has serious implications for you as a learner. It indicates that you will quickly forget a large portion of information you have learned *unless you take action to prevent it.*

Numerous theories have been offered to explain why forgetting occurs. One argues that the learned information fades from disuse, much as handwriting on a piece of paper fades over time. Another, more popular theory suggests that interference with competing information causes forgetting. Two types of interference—proactive and retroactive—have been identified, as shown in Figure 8.2.

TABLE 8.1 Rate of Forgetting	
Time Lapse from Initial Learning	Amount of Material Remembered
1 day	54%
7 days	35%
14 days	21%
21 days	18%
28 days	19%
63 days	17%

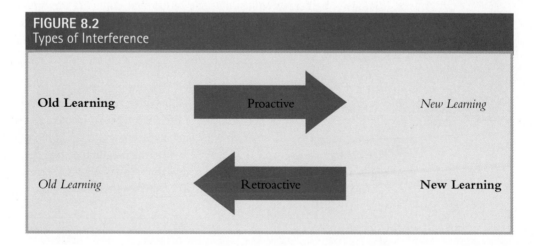

FIGURE 8.2
Types of Interference

Old Learning   Proactive   *New Learning*

Old Learning   Retroactive   **New Learning**

Proactive Interference

This situation occurs when old knowledge interferes with the recall of new, recently acquired knowledge. For example, you may have difficulty remembering a new formula in math if it is very similar to one you had learned last week. To combat this type of interference, make a conscious effort to examine similarities and differences between old and new learning.

Retroactive Interference

New learning sometimes interferes with the recall of old learning. You may be unable to recall a lecture from two weeks ago because the content of this week's lecture is blocking it. To overcome this type of interference, be certain to review previously learned material frequently, as well as to keep current with new material.

SKILLS IN ACTION

Memory and College Vocabulary

Following are some terms you may encounter in your courses. What techniques or tricks can you use to help you remember the meanings of these terms?

1. (Literature): *Alliteration* is the use of multiple words beginning with the same letter, as in the sentence "Bob bought bunches of begonias for Betty." How can you learn the meaning of this term?_____

   _____

2. (Biology): The *corpus callosum* is the tissue that connects the right and left sides of the brain. The term means "firm body" in Latin. How does knowing the meaning of the Latin phrase help you remember what the corpus callosum is? _____

   _____

3. (Psychology): *Locus of control* refers to a person's perception of his or her own ability to control his or her behavior or life. Two types of locus of control are *internal* and *external*. What do you think an *internal locus of control* means? An *external locus of control?* How does knowing the meaning of two common words, *internal* and *external*, combined with the psychological term *locus of control*, help you remember the definitions of these terms? _____

   _____

EXERCISE 8.5	**Understanding the Memory Process**

Directions   *Answer the following questions using your knowledge of memory and forgetting.*

1. Someone who memorized a follow-up appointment date and time before he left a doctor's appointment is unable to recall it the next day. Why?

2. A victim of a robbery is unable to give a detailed, accurate description of the criminal to a police artist the morning after the robbery. What could the victim have done to improve his or her recall?

3. A student is taking an introductory course in Spanish and, at the same time, is completing several years of study of Hebrew as part of his religious training. What learning problems might he expect?

4. What learning problems would you expect if you were taking a British literature and an American literature course during the same semester?

■ Strategies for Improving Encoding, Storage, and Retrieval

Using the following strategies will increase the effectiveness of your memory processes and retard forgetting.

Strategies for Improving Encoding

Use the following suggestions to improve encoding, which is the process of taking in information.

1. **Exclude competing stimuli.** Consciously exclude everything that does not relate to what you want to encode. For instance, if you are reading, do not sit where there are other competing visual stimuli, such as television.

2. **Use various sensory modes.** Use as many senses as possible to take in information. When listening to a lecture, for example, pay attention to visual clues the lecturer provides as well as to what he or she says.

3. **Carefully and specifically define your purpose.** Know clearly and specifically what types of information you need. If you are reading reference material for a research paper, pay attention to facts and statistics. If you are reading material to prepare for a class discussion, focus on controversial issues.

4. **Use previewing.** Since encoding involves accepting an incoming message, it is helpful to anticipate both the content and structure of that message. Preview-ing, discussed in Chapter 13, provides this preliminary information.

Strategies for Improving Storage

Use the following suggestions to improve how efficiently you store information.

1. **Use immediate review.** After working on a chapter for several hours (with frequent breaks) it is tempting, when you finish, to close the book and move on to something else. To quit, however, without taking five to ten minutes to review what you have read is a serious mistake. Since you have already invested several hours of time and effort, it is worthwhile to spend a few more minutes insuring that investment. Reviewing *immediately* following reading is an effective way of storing information and facilitating retrieval. A review of your notes immediately following a lecture is also effective.

   Immediate review is effective because it allows you to begin to see the big picture, to discover how individual portions of the chapter fit together and how they relate to prior learning.

   To review a chapter you have just read, follow these seven steps:

   ◆ **Begin as soon as you have finished reading the chapter.**

   ◆ **Go back to the beginning of the chapter and review all the boldfaced text or major headings.**

   ◆ **For each heading, form a question.** If a heading is "Causes of Hormonal Imbalance," ask, "What are the causes of hormonal imbalance?" For the heading "Treating Hormonal Imbalance," ask, "What are the treatments for hormonal imbalance?"

   ◆ **Then look away from the page, or cover it up with a sheet of paper, and try to answer each question.** Try to recall the causes of hormonal imbalance and its treatment. You can answer mentally, aloud, or on paper.

   ◆ **Check to see if you have answered the question completely by referring back to the text.** If you could not answer your question or only partially recalled information, check to see what you have missed and then retest your recall.

   ◆ **Continue through the chapter in this manner, heading by heading.**

   ◆ **When you have finished, stop and think.** Try to recall how the chapter was organized and how it progressed from idea to idea. Try to identify five to ten key points it discussed. Reread the chapter summary, if available, to verify these points.

   Substantial research evidence supports the value of immediate review. Students who use immediate review consistently experience higher retention than those who do not review.

2. **Use numerous sensory channels to store information.** Learning can be enhanced by using sight, sound, and touch. If you can incorporate writing, listening, drawing or diagramming, and recitation or discussion into your study habits, storage will be more effective.

3. **Organize or recode information to be stored.** Remembering a large number of individual facts or pieces of information is often a difficult,

frustrating task. **Recoding** is a primary means of storing information in your long-term memory. Recoding involves grouping information into sets or chunks. Instead of overloading your memory with numerous individual facts, you work with a set of information that is stored as one chunk rather than numerous individual facts. Retrieval, then, is easier, too, because a chunk is retrieved as one piece and related information stays together. For example, a physics student used the chunking strategy to organize and connect the topics of speed, velocity, and acceleration into one topic, motion. A business student studying the differences among consumer markets used chunking to group the differences into three categories: geographic, demographic, and income differences.

To organize information, keep the following suggestions in mind:

◆ Discover how the material you are studying is connected. Search for some organizing principle.

◆ Look for similarities and differences.

◆ Look for sequences and for obvious divisions or breaking points within the sequences.

| EXERCISE 8.6 | **Using Recoding** |

Working Together

Directions   *Working with a classmate, decide how you could organize or recode each of the following types of information for most effective storage.*

a. The problems two-career families face

b. The effects of terrorism

c. The reasons for recycling garbage

d. Ecological problems of the future

4. **Use elaboration.** Studying a chapter by rereading it is not effective. Instead you must think about, or *elaborate* upon, the material—ask questions, make associations and inferences, think of practical applications, and create mental images. For example, a mechanical engineering student was studying the first law of thermodynamics: Whenever heat is added to a system, it transforms into an equal amount of some other form of energy. The student began by being certain she understood the law, so she expressed it in writing using her own words. She wrote: "Heat added = increase in internal energy and/or external work done by the system." Then she began to think of situations in which she had observed the law, in a steam engine's operation, for instance. She asked herself: What happens in the atmosphere when a body of air is heated? What external work is done?

5. **Connect new learning with previous learning.** Isolated, unrelated pieces of information are difficult to store and also difficult to retrieve. If, however, you can link new learning to already stored information, it will be easier to store and retrieve since you have an established memory slot

REAL STUDENTS SPEAK

Lauren Croce

University of
Massachusetts

Amherst,
Massachusetts

Background: Lauren is a teaching assistant at Deerfield Elementary School and a senior at UMass, Amherst, pursuing her degree through the University Without Walls. She will graduate in July 2010 with a bachelor's degree focusing on elementary education.

Goals: She plans to continue her education and obtain a master's degree in special education.

Advice on Connecting New and Previous Learning: I'm a person who makes connections between what I learn and my life experiences. When I read a textbook or listen to a lecture, I create concrete examples in my mind. For example, if I'm learning about how prisms break up light, I remember making rainbows with preschool children. Right now, I'm reading an anthropology text about religion as part of culture, so I think about examples I know, like how specific religious groups connect to the political process. The idea is that when I learn new information, I relate it to something else I have read or heard. That's how I remember it.

in which to hold it. For example, an economics student associated the factors influencing the supply and demand curves with practical instances from his family's retail florist business.

EXERCISE 8.7

Working Together

Identifying Techniques to Improve Storage

Directions   *Working in pairs, discuss techniques that might improve storage in the following tasks.*

1. Learning to identify and distinguish various types of figurative language used in literature

2. Learning various bacterial forms and characteristics

3. Learning the environmental factors that affect entry of a product into a foreign market for a business marketing course

4. Learning the process of federal budget preparation for an American government course

Strategies for Improving Retrieval

Your ability to retrieve information is the true test of how accurately and completely you have stored it. The following strategies will improve your ability to retrieve information.

1. **Use visualization.** Try to visualize, or create a mental picture of, what you need to learn. Your picture or image should be sufficiently detailed

to include as much related information as possible. A student of anatomy and physiology found visualizations an effective way to learn the parts of the skeletal system. She would first draw it on paper and then visualize, or mentally draw, the system.

Visualization makes retrieval easier because the information is stored in one unified piece, and, if you can recall any part of the mental picture, then you will be able to retrieve the whole picture.

2. **Develop retrieval clues.** Think of your memory as having slots or compartments in which information is stored. If you can name or label what is in the slot, you will know where to look to find information that fits that slot. Think of memory slots as similar to the way kitchen cupboards are often organized, with specific items in specific places. If you need a knife to cut a pizza, you look in the silverware and utensils drawer. Similarly, if you have a memory slot labeled "environmental problems" in which you store information related to pollution—its problems, causes, and solutions—you can retrieve information on air pollution by calling up the appropriate retrieval clue. To develop retrieval clues, select a word or phrase that summarizes or categorizes several pieces of information. For example, you

THINKING CRITICALLY
. . . About Learning Strategies

Some of the strategies in this chapter will work better for you than others; a few may not work for you at all. Some may work for one course but not for another. The key to making information in this chapter work for you is to try to *critically evaluate* each strategy.

Begin by selecting two or three strategies that appeal to you. Decide which ones you will use for which course. Use them for a week. At the end of the week, do a preliminary evaluation. Rate the strategy as "very useful," "somewhat useful," or "not useful," and record your evaluation in the chart shown on p. 166.

Use the following questions to help you in rating each strategy:

1. Did the strategy seem to make a difference in how easily I was able to learn?

2. Was it easy to use or was it time-consuming?

3. Did it help me see the information in a new way?

4. Did it improve my understanding of the material?

The next week, choose two or three more strategies to concentrate on and evaluate.

A word of caution: Some strategies may take a little time to get used to. If a strategy seems to have potential but does not work right away, stick with it for a longer period of time.

might use the phrase *motivation theories* to organize information for a psychology course on instinct, drive, cognition, arousal, and opponent-process theories and the major proponents of each.

3. **Simulate test conditions.** Practice retrieving learned information by simulating (practicing) test conditions. If you are studying for a math exam, prepare by solving problems. If you know your exam in a law enforcement course will consist of three essay questions, then prepare by anticipating possible essay questions and drafting an answer to each.

4. **Learn beyond mastery.** It is tempting to stop studying as soon as you feel you have learned a given body of information. However, to ensure complete, thorough learning, it is best to conduct a few more reviews. When you learned to drive a car, you did not stop practicing parallel parking after the first time you accomplished it correctly. Similarly, for a botany course you should not, at the moment you feel you have mastered it, stop reviewing the process of photosynthesis and its place within the carbon cycle. Instead, use additional review to make the material stick and to prevent interference from subsequent learning.

EVALUATING LEARNING STRATEGIES

Strategies	Very Useful	Rating Somewhat Useful	Not Useful
Encoding			
Exclude competing stimuli	❑	❑	❑
Use various sensory modes	❑	❑	❑
Define your purpose	❑	❑	❑
Use previewing	❑	❑	❑
Storage			
Use immediate review	❑	❑	❑
Use numerous sensory channels	❑	❑	❑
Recode information	❑	❑	❑
Use elaboration	❑	❑	❑
Connect new to previous learning	❑	❑	❑
Retrieval			
Use visualization	❑	❑	❑
Develop retrieval clues	❑	❑	❑
Simulate test conditions	❑	❑	❑
Learn beyond mastery	❑	❑	❑

SKILLS IN ACTION

Creating an Environment for Learning and Remembering

Suppose you will be taking your psychology midterm examination in two weeks. You decide to begin studying early because there is a lot to remember: the textbook readings, several journal articles, and your classroom notes. Indicate whether each of the following behaviors is conducive (helpful) or detrimental (harmful) to learning. For those behaviors that are detrimental, indicate how you should adjust your behavior.

Behavior or Activity	Conducive to Learning	Detrimental to Learning	Corrective Action
1. Playing rock music in the background while you reread chapters from your psychology textbook			
2. Listening to a recorded lecture on your iPod while you are walking in the park to get some exercise or to relax			
3. Making flash cards of key vocabulary terms and working with another student to test each other			
4. Using a highlighter to highlight large chunks of material in the textbook			
5. Working with a study group that has several funny people in it who keep you entertained and laughing			

EXERCISE 8.8   Identifying Learning Strategies

Directions   *What strategies would you use to learn (encode, store, and retrieve) each of the following types of information most efficiently?*

1. Vocabulary words for a Spanish I course
2. The process of leaf development in plants for a botany course
3. A comparison between the Bill of Rights at the time it was written and in today's political and social climate
4. Types of nonverbal communication and their uses in communicating with an audience

Working Together

Form groups of four or five students and discuss causes of and solutions to each of the following situations:

1. A student frequently misplaces his car keys and wastes valuable time looking for them.

2. A friend has difficulty remembering names of new people he meets at a party.

3. An American history student is studying the major world wars. First he studies World War I and, later, studies World War II. He is having difficulty remembering the major causes of World War II, having already learned those of World War I.

REVIEW Five Key Points to Remember

1 **Understand the memory process.** The memory process involves three steps: encoding, storage, and retrieval. Learning involves moving information from your short- to your long-term memory.

2 **Improve your encoding skills.** Exclude competing stimuli, use various sensory modes, define your purpose, and use previewing.

3 **Store information effectively.** Rote learning, elaborative rehearsal, and recoding are ways to store information in long-term memory. Immediate review, using numerous sensory channels, recoding, elaboration, and connecting new information to previously learned material are useful strategies for storing information more effectively.

4 **Use retrieval strategies.** Use visualization, retrieval clues, test simulation, and learning beyond mastery to improve retrieval of information.

5 **Prevent forgetting.** Forgetting occurs rapidly unless you encode, store, and retrieve information properly.

The Work Connection

Read the following information and respond to the questions below:

If you are a student returning to college to learn new skills and attitudes that will help you succeed in today's high-performance workplace, congratulations! If you are just beginning to prepare for your first career, consider that you may need to refocus, retrain, or even change careers over the course of a lifetime. Plan never to stop learning. A commitment to life-long learning is becoming a prerequisite for sound career planning in an ever-changing work environment. Indeed, a phrase that describes the attitudes of lifelong learners has been coined: *career self-reliance*. Career self-reliance means taking responsibility for your own career: continually updating your skills, always seeking to improve your performance, and understanding how your skills are marketable both within and outside of your current company and industry. Lifelong learning is the "path to job security and career health."[3]

1. How will knowledge of the learning and memory processes help you become more self-reliant in college courses?

2. How do you think the skills and strategies taught in this chapter would help you refocus, retrain, or change careers, should it become necessary?

3. Rate your current level of self-reliance as a student. Give two examples that explain or justify your rating.

The Web Connection

1. Try these online memory experiments:

   http://www.dcity.org/braingames/pennies/
   http://www.essex.ac.uk/psychology/experiments/memtask.html
   http://www.exploratorium.edu/brain_explorer/memory.html

   Write a paragraph about your experiences with these sites. Were you surprised by your performances?

2. Improving Your Memory

   http://www.ctl.ua.edu/CTLStudyAids/StudySkillsFlyers/MemorySkills/improving
   memory.htm

   From the University of Alabama, this informative Web site discusses the "Four R's of Remembering." Use this technique once this week while you are studying. Make notes about what works and what does not work for you.

3. Remembering

   http://www.ucc.vt.edu/stdysk/remember.html

   This Virginia Tech site provides memory information specifically geared to college students. Look over the tips for memorization. Print them out and ask people you know what techniques they use for memorization. Mark the responses that appear on the Web site. Add any new tips that you receive. Do you see any patterns or find that one technique is used more than others?

9 Study Strategies for Academic Disciplines

Do You Know?

How can you get off to a good start in an unfamiliar field of study?

What are the characteristics of each academic discipline?

How should you adapt your reading and study strategies for each discipline?

What particular thought patterns can you expect in each discipline?

How should you take lecture notes for each discipline?

Each academic discipline is a unique system of study; each takes a specialized approach to the study of the world around us. To illustrate, let's choose as an example human beings—and consider how various disciplines might approach their study.[1]

◆ An artist might consider a human as an object of beauty and record a person's fluid, flexible muscular structure and meaningful facial expressions on canvas.

◆ A psychologist might study what human needs are fulfilled by various behaviours.

◆ A historian might research the historical importance of human decisions—their decisions to enter wars or form alliances with other countries.

◆ An anthropologist might trace the evolution of the human race.

◆ A mathematician might calculate human life expectancies based on lifestyle, gender, race.

◆ An economist might focus on the supply of and demand for essential human goods (food, clothing transportation) and the amount of business that they generate.

◆ A biologist would categorize humans as *Homo sapiens*.

◆ A physiologist would be concerned with the human bodily functions (breathing, heart rate, temperature).

Each academic discipline, then, approaches a given object or event with a different focus or perspective. Each has its own special purposes and interests that define the scope of the discipline. You will find that each discipline has its own method of studying the topics with which it is concerned. Because each discipline is unique, each requires somewhat different study and learning strategies.

■ Approaching New Fields of Study

In your first few years of college, you are likely to encounter disciplines with which you have had no prior experience. Anthropology, political science, or organic chemistry may be new to you. In the beginning, these new fields of study may seem unfamiliar or foreign. One student described this feeling as "being on the outside looking in," watching other students participate in the class but being unable to do so himself. At first, you may feel lost, confused, or frustrated in such courses. You may be unfamiliar with the specialized language of the discipline, with what types of learning and thinking are expected, and with conventions, approaches, and methodology of the discipline.

When approaching a new field of study, try the following:

1. **Spend more time than usual reading and studying.** You are doing more than reading and studying: You are learning how to learn as well.

2. **Since you do not know how you will eventually use it, organize the same information in several different ways.** For example, in an anthropology course, you might learn events and discoveries chronologically (according to occurrence in time) as well as comparatively (according to similarities and differences among various discoveries). In an accounting course, you might organize information by procedures as well as by controlling principles.

3. **Use several methods of learning.** Since you are not sure which will be most effective for the types of learning and thinking that are required, try several methods at once. For example, you might highlight textbook information (to promote factual recall) as well as write outlines and summaries (to interpret and consolidate ideas). You might also draw diagrams that map the relationships between concepts and ideas (see Chapter 14).

4. **Look for similarities between the new subject matter and other academic fields that are familiar to you.** If similarities exist, you may be able to modify or adapt existing learning approaches and strategies to fit your new field of study.

5. **Establish an overview of the field.** Spend time studying the table of contents of your textbook; it provides an outline of the course. Look for patterns, progression of ideas, and recurring themes, approaches, or problems.

6. **Obtain additional reference materials, if necessary.** Some college texts delve into a subject immediately, providing only a brief introduction or overview in the first chapter. If your text does this, spend an hour or so online or in the library getting a more comprehensive overview of the field.

SKILLS IN ACTION

Coping with a Challenging Course

Sooner or later, it happens to every student: you encounter a course you just do not like or are not "good" at. You probably had your most-disliked courses in high school, and you will have them in college as well.

Take a minute to think about a current or past class that you disliked and/or one in which you got a low grade. Answer the following questions:

1. Which class or subject was it?

2. Why, exactly, did you dislike the course or do poorly in it? Offer specific reasons rather than vague generalities.

3. Which of the tips in this section would have been helpful in that class? Which can you apply right now, and to which of your courses?

◆ Read or skim several online encyclopedia entries in your field of study, taking notes if necessary.
◆ Check the library's online catalog to see how the subject is divided.
◆ Locate two or three introductory texts in the field. Study the table of contents of each and skim the first chapter.

■ The Social Sciences and History

The social sciences are concerned with the study of people, their development, and how they function together and interact. Included are psychology, anthropology, sociology, political science, and economics. They deal with political, economic, social, cultural, and behavioral aspects of human beings. The term "science" is appropriate because each discipline concentrates on defining problems; observing, gathering, and interpreting information; and reporting measurable results. Some social science courses are required in most degree programs.

What to Expect

Courses in the social sciences tend to have the following characteristics:

◆ **They are highly factual.** Especially in introductory courses, an instructor's first task is to acquaint you with what is already known—principles, rules, and facts—so that you can subsequently use them in approaching new problems and unique situations.
◆ **They introduce a vast number of new terms.**
◆ **They require large amounts of reading.**

◆ **They make use of graphics (maps, charts, tables, graphs).**
◆ **They are research oriented.** Many texts describe or report research studies as supporting evidence. In introductory courses, the outcome of the research and what it proves or suggests are usually most important.
◆ **They emphasize theories, and often the social scientists who developed them.**

How to Read and Study the Social Sciences

It is easy to get lost in detail and to lose sight of the general topics with which a social science is concerned. Use the following guidelines when reading social science materials:

1. **Keep up with assignments, reading a chapter section or two each day.**

2. **Be certain to develop a course master file to record and learn new terminology (refer to Chapter 10).**

3. **Maintain a focus on large ideas: concepts, trends, and patterns.** Previewing before and reviewing after reading will help establish this focus.

What Thought Patterns to Anticipate

Three thought patterns predominate in the social sciences: listing, comparison and contrast, and cause and effect. Table 9.1 describes their uses and includes several examples from specific disciplines.

TABLE 9.1 Thought Patterns* in the Social Sciences

Pattern	Uses	Examples

Listing	Presenting facts, illustrations, findings, or examples; listing research	Sociology
		    Types of white-collar crime
		    Examples of institutional racism
		    Environmental abuses

Comparison and contrast	Evaluating two sides of an issue; comparing and contrasting theories, groups, behaviors, events	Political science
		    A comparison of ethnic groups' political power
		    A study of various urban development strategies
		    A discussion of types of consumer
		        representation groups

Cause and effect	Studing behavior and motivation; examining connections among events, actions, behaviors	Psychology
		    Sources of stress and how the body reacts
		        to it
		    The underlying causes of aggressive behavior
		    Means of controlling and treating phobias

*See Chapter 11.

Taking Lecture Notes

Use the following suggestions to improve your note taking in social science courses:

◆ **Take notes.** Regardless of whether the lecture supplements or covers material identical to your textbook, take thorough, complete notes. Recording information you have already read or will read in your text will reinforce your learning. Later, after checking the corresponding text closely, you may shorten and reorganize your notes to best fit with text material.

◆ **Summarize cases or examples.** Especially in sociology, psychology, and anthropology classes, a lecturer may use case studies (descriptions of a particular person, action, or problem) to illustrate a concept presented in the text. In your notes, try to summarize the key information of the case study, recording enough facts to bring the example to mind again when you review.

◆ **Edit your notes.** In history lectures, editing your notes is particularly essential. Often an instructor will discuss numerous events, people, and laws simultaneously. Other instructors seem to switch between historical periods, discussing various trends or issues. As you edit, try to indicate the chronological sequence of events. Also, try to collect all facts about a particular person, event, or issue in one place.

EXERCISE 9.1

Working Together

Analyzing an Assignment

Directions *Working in a small group, analyze the following situation and answer the questions.*

A psychology student has been assigned a 1,000-word paper on the founders of the field of psychology.

1. Analyze the purpose of the assignment.
2. How should the student approach the assignment?
3. Is research necessary? If so, what sources might he or she begin with?
4. What thought pattern(s) could he or she use to organize the paper?

SKILLS IN ACTION

Thinking Like a Social Scientist

The following is an excerpt from a psychology textbook. Read it and answer the questions that follow.

Researchers have looked at the relationship between adolescent drug use and psychological health (Shedler & Block, 1990). Participants in this investigation were 18-year-olds who had been under study since they were three years old. Based on their level of drug use, they were divided into one of three groups: (1) *abstainers* (N = 29), who had never tried any drug; (2) *experimenters* (N = 36), who had used marijuana "once or twice, or a few times" and who had tried no more than one other drug; and (3) *frequent users* (N = 20), who used marijuana frequently and had tried at least one other drug. There were no socioeconomic or IQ differences among the groups.

The researchers found that *frequent users* were generally maladjusted, alienated, deficient in impulse control, and "manifestly" distressed. The *abstainers* were overly anxious, "emotionally constricted," and lacking in social skills. These same results were apparent when the researchers examined records from when the same subjects were 7 and 11 years old. Generally, the *experimenters* were better adjusted and psychologically "healthier" than either of the other two groups. The authors of this study are concerned that their data may be misinterpreted—that their data might be taken to indicate "that drug use might somehow improve an adolescent's psychological health." Clearly this interpretation would be in error. You recognize these as correlational data from which no conclusion regarding cause and effect is justified.

While drug use among adolescents is a matter of great concern, there is evidence that we need not get hysterical about infrequent drug use among teenagers.[2]

—Gerow, *Psychology: An Introduction,* pp. 305–306

Though only three short paragraphs, this passage is packed with information. Practice the skills you have learned thus far in this chapter by answering these questions.

1. What thought pattern does the passage use?

2. What were the names of the people who conducted this study? In what year was it conducted?

3. How many 18-year-olds, in total, were used as the subjects of this study?

4. What other disciplines would find this research and these results useful? Which discipline's methods were used in the study? (Hint: Though you may not have taken a course in this topic, these experimenters definitely used *statistics* to report on their results.)

5. It is easy to read a passage and simply skip over terms that are unfamiliar. What do you think "manifestly distressed" means? What does "emotionally constricted" mean? What are "correlational data"?

6. Based on this passage, is it safe to assume that parents should encourage their children to try drugs occasionally, but not to get addicted to them?

■ The Life and Physical Sciences

Life sciences refers to the study of living organisms: anatomy and physiology, zoology, botany, and biology. The **physical sciences** are concerned with the function, structure, and composition of energy, matter, and substance in our environment and include physics, chemistry, and physical geology. Sometimes called the natural sciences, both types are primarily concerned with two questions: "Why?" and "How?" Scientists constantly ask these two questions and conduct experiments and research to learn the answers.

To work effectively in a science course, adopt a scientific way of thinking. The usual concerns, such as "What is important to learn?" and "How much supporting information do I need to learn?" may be of only secondary importance. Instead, to be most successful, you must adopt a scientific mind-set—you need to become comfortable with asking literal questions and seeking answers, or analyzing problems and seeking solutions or explanations.

To benefit most from your learning, ask practical questions. For example, if you are a nursing student studying organic chemistry, the question you must always keep in the back of your mind is "How does what I am learning apply to the field of nursing?"

Some students of science become too involved with fact and detail and fail to step back and look at the larger picture. Often, they fail to recognize connections and relationships between the subject matter at hand and its applications to various concerns and professions.

What to Expect

Scientific and technical material, both in lecture and in textbooks, has special characteristics:

◆ **Unfamiliar subject matter.** Scientific topics are unfamiliar to many of us. For example, few of us have a background of everyday experience with molecular structure, mutant genes, or radioactive isotopes. Because topics are unfamiliar, learning does not occur as easily as in other subjects. Consequently, all science courses require extra study time, perhaps even twice as much.

◆ **A requirement of active participation.** Many science courses require a weekly laboratory in addition to class lectures. Here the purpose is to test, apply, experiment with, or demonstrate the principles presented in lectures. Labs are important: Look for applications of lecture content.

◆ **Factual density.** The pure sciences are even more factual than the social sciences. Introductory science courses leave little room for interpretation, debate, opinion, or conjecture. Texts and lectures appear formal, straightforward, and regimented (and to students who thrive on interaction and controversy—uninteresting).

How to Read and Study Scientific Material

Use the following suggestions when reading and studying scientific material:

1. **Preview assignments.** Because scientific material is often unfamiliar, previewing the chapter before you give it a thorough reading is essential. Also preview the problems at the end of the chapter. These problems provide clues about important principles emphasized in the chapter. Preview the vocabulary list to identify terms you will need to learn.

2. **Do not skip anything.** Unlike with other, more familiar subjects, you cannot afford to skip anything. Never try to read quickly or settle for getting the gist of the meaning. Facts and details are important, as are the connections among them.

3. **Read carefully and thoughtfully.** Some students find it effective to read each section of a chapter at least twice: The first reading is intended to acquaint them with key ideas; the second reading is to fill in the details and grasp specific, detailed concepts.

4. **Be alert for gaps in information.** Because information in a science course is presented sequentially and understanding depends on mastering earlier information, you may find that you lack background or specific information on a topic. It is your responsibility, if you should identify such a gap, to fill it through reading, researching, locating online sources, using a scientific encyclopedia, or checking with your instructor.

5. **Focus on applications.** Though science courses contain a great deal of abstract theory and fact, they are also very concerned with applications. The end-of-chapter problems often focus on the use and application of information learned.

6. **Make everyday connections.** To make the subject matter less abstract and easier to learn, try to relate facts, ideas, and principles to things with which you are familiar. In a human anatomy and physiology course, for example, when studying the bones in the skeletal system, try to feel your own bones. In chemistry, when studying various types of solutions, think of everyday liquids that are representative of each type.

7. **Ask questions.** Do not look for facts—look for answers. Keep in mind constantly the questions "Why?" "How?" and "Under what conditions?" For each occurrence, be sure you understand how and why it happens.

8. **Learn the notation system.** Each field uses its own version of shorthand, a series of signs, symbols, and characters that have become standard

abbreviations or notations. To work within a given field, then, a first step is to learn its notation system. Make these notations a part of your course master file (see Chapter 10).

9. **Translate formulas into words.** Most scientific fields express key relationships in abbreviated formulas. To be certain that you understand the relationship, try to express it in your own words. This will establish verbal connections and make storage and retrieval easier.

10. **Develop a vocabulary master file.** The vocabulary of the sciences is exact and precise. In many of the sciences, learning depends on mastering a great deal of new terminology. Fortunately, the sciences rely more heavily on a common base of prefixes, roots, and suffixes than do most other disciplines. It is especially worthwhile, then, to develop a master file of word parts and learn them as soon as possible (see Chapter 10).

What Thought Patterns to Anticipate

The three most commonly used thought patterns (see Chapter 11) in scientific courses are cause and effect, process, and problem-solution. As you will see on the next page, these three patterns often intertwine. Uses and examples of these patterns are shown in Table 9.2.

TABLE 9.2 Thought Patterns* in the Sciences

Pattern	Uses	Examples
Cause and effect	Explaining why natural phenomena occur	**Biology** Why trees shed their leaves Why plant cells divide (mitosis) The conditions under which plant fossil formation occurs
Process	Describing how events occur; presenting steps in experimental procedures	**Anatomy and physiology** How the liver functions How white blood cells function in the immune system Transmittal of genetic code from parents to child
Problem-solution	Solving practical problems; studying currently unexplained phenomena	**Physics** How sound waves transfer energy How refraction of light produces mirages Practical problems, such as estimating the time needed for an 850W coffeemaker to prepare 10 cups of coffee when the water used is 55°F

*See Chapter 11.

Taking Lecture Notes

Use the following guidelines to polish your lecture note taking in the sciences:

◆ **Don't get lost in detail.** Lectures in the life and natural sciences may involve experiments, demonstrations, or solving sample problems. It is easy to get lost in recording details, thus losing sight of the principles each is intended to emphasize. Do not try to record all the details of each step in a demonstration or experiment; instead, focus on key processes and procedures. For sample problems, record what the instructor writes on the board, leaving plenty of blank space. Then, as you edit your notes after the lecture, try to describe and fill in what occurred at each step.

◆ **Make quick sketches.** Diagrams and charts are often used as illustrations. When these are presented, draw a quick sketch, not a careful copy. You can redraw it later during editing, or a similar drawing may appear in your text. Concentrate on the process or point the diagram is intended to show. Label the steps if possible; if time is insufficient, simply number the steps in the process. Later, as you edit your lecture notes, write out the steps.

◆ **Outline or summarize each day's notes.** This will help you gain a perspective on key ideas and will force you to organize the details.

◆ **Use scientific notation.** Learn the scientific notation system and use it as you take notes. It is a shorthand system that will speed up your note taking significantly. At first, to help yourself get started, keep a list of common symbols and abbreviations close at hand for fast reference. As you edit your notes, build the habit of using symbols: look for places where you could have used a sign or symbol instead of a word, and make corrections.

When You Are Having Difficulty

If the sciences are typically a difficult field of study for you, or if you suddenly find yourself not doing well in a science course, try the following survival tactics:

1. **Make changes in your learning strategies.** Many students mistakenly think they will get by in their one or two required science courses using the same reading, study, and thinking strategies that work in other fields. Plan on making the changes already described in this section. You cannot be even minimally successful unless you make them.

2. **Learn from classmates.** Talk with and observe the strategies of students who are doing well in the course. You are likely to pick up new and useful procedures.

3. **Obtain a tutor.** Many academic-skills centers offer peer tutors for specific courses.

REAL STUDENTS SPEAK

Ben Howard
———
**Brown University
Providence, Rhode
Island**

Background: Ben is a senior at Brown where he is majoring in mechanical engineering.

Goals: To take a year off after graduating and/or to attend graduate school. He would like to apply his skills in mechanical engineering to video technology.

Advice on Synthesizing Sources: For math and science, for me, it's more like playing a violin than memorizing. It's a different process from studying for history, for example; it's less memorizing and more learning a process. When I study for engineering, I do every single homework, because if you miss even one piece of the process you're lost later. I always make an equation sheet, regardless of whether I can bring it into the test. In many engineering classes the professor will provide a sheet with equations for the test, but you should still be very familiar with them beforehand. Even if you can bring them into a test, the more familiar you are with them the better.

4. **Learn the metric system.** If the metric system is used, and you have not learned it, spend the time and effort needed to learn it. It is essential to most scientific fields.

5. **Double your study time.** If you are having trouble with a course, first (if you have not done so already) make a commitment to spend more time and work harder. Use this added time to revise and try out new strategies. Never waste time on a strategy that is not working.

6. **Purchase a review book, student practice manual, or other learning aid and use it regularly.** Use online resources that may accompany your textbook.

7. **Pull the course together:**
   ◆ Review your notes and text assignments; discover how they work together and where they seem to be headed.
   ◆ As you review, make lists of topics you do understand and those you do not.
   ◆ Decide whether you are experiencing difficulty due to gaps in your scientific background. Ask yourself whether the instructor assumes you know things when you do not. If so, consider obtaining a tutor. Check with your college's learning assistance center on the availability of tutorial services.

| EXERCISE 9.2 | **Analyzing a Course Requirement** |

Directions   *Analyze the following situation and answer the questions below.*

An English major is taking a required chemistry course to fulfill a general education requirement. A weekly three-hour laboratory is required, for which he must perform a series of experiments and submit a two-page report. The student complains about the lab: If he can find out the results of each experiment by looking them up in a book or by reading his text, he wants to know, why spend the three hours performing experiments for which the results are already known? He also complains about the lab's required format, since it allows no creativity or self-expression.

1. What could you explain to this student to overcome his objections?
2. What does he fail to understand about science?
3. Evaluate the quality of his thinking about his chemistry course.

■ Mathematics

Mathematics follows a prescribed order of events. Problems are solved using specified step-by-step procedures. Theorems are derived in a tightly logical, sequential order. Much of what you learn is dependent on skills that preceded it. Mathematics, then, is cumulative—skills build upon one another. For example, you cannot solve bank interest problems in financial accounting if you do not know how to work with percentages.

What to Expect

Mathematics is a discipline that requires regular, consistent, day-to-day study. Here are a few things you should expect in a mathematics course:

◆ **Expect every class to count.** Class attendance and participation are essential for learning math. Even if there is a "cut" policy, don't cut class. Because math learning is sequential, if you miss one specific skill, that gap in your understanding and competence may cause problems all semester.

◆ **Expect regular homework assignments.** Whether or not an instructor collects or grades homework, be sure to complete all assignments by their due date. Practice is essential. Never let yourself get behind or skip assignments. Because today's assignment will be used in the next section or chapter, skipping an assignment will interfere with your ability to complete future assignments.

◆ **Accuracy and precision are important.** Many students, accustomed to flexible approaches to learning, have difficulty adjusting to the precise nature of mathematics. In particular, they are disturbed that "close does not count" and that knowledge of technique is not sufficient; rather, the technique must be precisely and accurately applied in order to be considered correct. Develop the habit of checking your work and focusing on accuracy.

How to Read and Study Mathematics Texts

Use the following guidelines for reading and studying mathematics:

1. **Plan on spending more time.** Studying a mathematics textbook takes more time than reading textbooks in most other disciplines. As is also true of life and physical sciences, mathematics is concise and factually dense. Nearly everything is important.

2. **Focus on process and procedure.** Be certain to understand *why* and *how* various procedures are used.

3. **Pay attention to sample problems.** Usually, a textbook section that explains a procedure step-by-step is followed by a sample problem. The best way to read a section is to read a sentence or two and then refer to the sample problem to see how the information is applied. Then return to the text and read the explanation of the next step, and then refer to the sample problem again. The process of alternating between text and problem may seem confusing at first, but remember that your purpose is to see *how* the problem illustrates the process being described. Then practice solving the problem without referring to the text.

4. **Learn to read mathematical language.** Mathematics, through use of notations, symbols, and formulas, expresses complicated relationships in a very brief, concise form. For example, the mathematical equation $c^2 = a^2 + b^2$ says that the square of the hypotenuse of a right triangle is equal to the sum of the squares of the two remaining sides. A large amount of information is packed into the smallest unit of mathematical language.

5. **Study daily.** Never let your work pile up until the weekend. The principle of distributed learning (see p. 64) is especially important in mathematics.

6. **Learn to solve problems.** Quizzes and exams are made up almost exclusively of problems to solve. Here are a few tips to follow in solving mathematical problems:

   ◆ Be certain you understand what the problem is saying and what it is asking for. Try to express the problem in your own words.
   ◆ Identify the relevant information that is provided to solve the problem. (Some math problems may provide irrelevant or distracting information that is not useful in solving the problem.) Highlight or circle essential information.
   ◆ Recall the formulas you have learned that relate to the problem at hand, and select which you will work with.
   ◆ If you do not know or are unsure of how to solve a problem, look for similarities between it and sample problems you have studied.

◆ Be sure to check your work. Many students lose points, or sometimes full credit, due to arithmetic errors.

7. **Study and practice variations of problems.** Explore the different forms in which a problem can be expressed, and identify variations of the same type of problem.

What Thought Patterns to Anticipate

Three thought patterns (see Chapter 11) predominate in the study of mathematics: process, problem-solution, and comparison and contrast, as shown in Table 9.3 below.

Taking Class Notes

Mathematics instructors seldom present formal lectures. Instead, they work through and explain procedures and problems. Here are a few suggestions for improving your note-taking skills in mathematics classes:

1. **Focus on concepts and procedures.** Concentrate on understanding the concept or procedure the instructor is explaining. Then, once you understand it, write it down.

2. **Record processes.** As you edit your notes, try to identify and describe the steps followed in solving problems.

3. **Study the text before class.** Many instructors follow the textbook closely; consequently, it is useful to become familiar with the chapter before attending class.

TABLE 9.3 Thought Patterns* in Mathematics

Pattern	Uses	Examples
Process	Describing steps to follow in solving problems or proving theorems	Algebra Solving quadratic equations
Problem-solution	Solving sample problems; homework problems	Business math Computing the interest on a $5,000 car loan at 5.5% add-on rate with monthly payments
Comparison and contrast	Recognizing how new problems are different from sample problems, how problem types differ; determining what operations are used in several types of problems	Basic mathematics Similarities between ratios and percentages

*See Chapter 11.

Ask questions. Most instructors are open to, and encourage students to ask, questions. Do not hesitate to ask a question; often several other people in the class have the same question but are reluctant to ask it.

EXERCISE 9.3

Working Together

Offering Advice

Directions *Working with a classmate, analyze the following situation and decide what advice you would offer this student.*

A theater arts student is failing a required mathematics course. He has identified two difficulties.

1. He has trouble thinking in signs and symbols; the symbols and notations remain foreign and unfamiliar despite repeated attempts to memorize them.

2. Although he knows how to solve sample problems and those done in class, he cannot solve similar problems when they appear on an exam.

■ Literature and the Arts

Literature and the arts concentrate on the search for reasons, values, and interpretations in all areas of human interest and experience. Often, their focus is on subjective evaluation and interpretation of ideas expressed through literary or artistic works. Arts and humanities cover the full range of human experience. Many vehicles of expression are used to interpret the broad variety of topics covered: music, sculpture, painting, essays, poems, novels, and the body of information known as **criticism** that discusses, interprets, and evaluates each.

What to Expect

Courses in the arts and humanities are unique in the following ways:

They do not focus on a given body of information, sets of theories, facts, or principles to learn. Instead, the focus is on ideas or their expression through various literary or artistic modes.

♦ **Most arts and humanities courses require and depend heavily on writing skills.** Analyses, interpretations, critiques, or reviews of critical essays (essays written about a given literary or artistic work) are often required and determine grades.

♦ **Often, there is no right answer or single, correct interpretation.** A literary work or philosophical theory can be interpreted in numerous ways. The interpretation, however, must be reasoned, logical, and consistent.

♦ **The instructor's own values, opinions, and perspective on life are necessarily revealed as he or she interprets and discusses a particular work.** Many students find this disturbing and mistakenly assume that they are forced to accept a given set of beliefs and attitudes. Actually, you are never forced to accept—but merely to understand and react to—a given philosophy.

◆ **To analyze and interpret art and literature, you must activate your feelings and imagination as well as your critical reasoning skills.** You must also define your values and hold them up for comparison with those expressed in various works and those of your instructor and your classmates.

How to Read and Analyze Literature

You will encounter two basic types of reading in the field of literature and criticism. *Original works* refers to literary pieces themselves: poems, articles, essays, philosophical treatises, short stories, plays, and novels. *Criticism* refers to all that has been written *about* a given original work and its author (book reviews, essays, biographies). In most introductory courses, the primary emphasis is on reading and interpreting original works. However, completing a paper or assignment sometimes requires you to consult secondary sources, to read what someone else thinks of the work you are studying. The suggestions listed below apply to reading original works.

1. **Read slowly, carefully, and more than once.** Read a work the first time simply to establish its overall content and literal meaning: What is it about, or who is doing what, when, and where? Establish the main characters, basic plot, and setting. On your second reading, focus on interpretation. Find the writer's message and think about your reactions to the work.

2. **Annotate as you read.** Jot down your reactions, hunches, insights, feelings, and questions. Mark or underline sections you feel are important—insightful statements by characters, or sections that provide clues to meaning. Circle repeated words or images, mark where characters are described, and look for unusual techniques or style. Table 9.4 (p. 186) lists features that often provide important clues to meaning.

3. **Look for themes and patterns.** After you have read and annotated, inventory your annotations, looking for themes and patterns. Try to discover how ideas work together to suggest themes. Here are some possible themes in literature:

   ◆ **Questions, issues, problems raised by the story:** moral, political, philosophical, religious
   ◆ **Abstract ideas:** love, death, heroism, escapism
   ◆ **Conflicting situations:** appearance versus reality, freedom versus restraint, poverty versus wealth
   ◆ **Common literary topics:** self-realization, the inescapability of death, fall from innocence, search for the meaning of life

What Thought Patterns to Anticipate

In original works, the predominant thought patterns include chronological order, process, comparison and contrast, and cause and effect, as shown in Table 9.5 (p. 186).

TABLE 9.4 Literary Clues to Meaning

Features of Language

Symbolism (objects or events that can be interpreted on several different levels)
Descriptive words (words that create a mental picture)
Emotionally charged words
Words and phrases with multiple meanings
Similes and metaphors (words that define by drawing a comparison)
Unusual or striking words
Repetition of words or phrases
Sarcastic or ironic statements (those that say one thing but mean another)

Characterization

What the characters say about their own thoughts, actions, motives
What the characters say about actions, motives of others (their perceptions of other characters)
What the characters actually do (compare this with what they say they do—often a character is self-deceived or naïve)
Contradictions or inconsistencies
How the writer describes the characters (to detect his or her attitude toward them)

Organization and Structure

How the work begins, including clues about what will happen next (foreshadowing)
The setting and how it changes
The mood (feeling) the writer creates
How the mood and setting relate to the characters' actions
Complications or conflicts that arise
Resolution of these conflicts
Who is telling the story (narrator) and what he or she knows or does not know about the characters and their motives and actions
Whether the narrator is objective or biased

TABLE 9.5 Thought Patterns* in Literature and the Arts

Pattern	Uses	Examples
Chronological order	Sequencing events in fictional works; noting the development of various artistic or literary periods	Sequence of events in Crane's "The Open Boat"
Process	Studying the process through which a writer or artist achieved his or her effect	Development of character in Thurber's "The Catbird Seat"
Comparison and contrast	Studying two or more artists, works, writers, or schools of thought	Comparing Steinbeck's and Hawthorne's use of symbolism
Cause and effect	Examining character motivation, studying effects of various literary and artistic techniques	Evaluating Hemingway's use of tone

*See Chapter 11.

THINKING CRITICALLY
. . . About Literature

Literature often makes use of imaginative or creative language to express meaning. Try to think critically and creatively in order to grasp the full meaning intended by the writer. Here are a few questions to ask that will focus your attention on the use of creative expressions in literature:

1. **Does the writer use descriptive language?** If so, what impact does it make? Descriptive language uses words that create a sensory impression or response. It is intended to help you create a mental picture of what the writer is describing. For example, to describe a stormy evening, a poet may write this:

   Under the thunder-dark cloud, the storm mounts, flashes, and resounds.

   These words give you a vivid picture of the storm and help you imagine its strength. When reading descriptive language, read slowly, allowing time for sensory impressions to register and for you to react to them.

2. **Does the writer use connotative language?** Connotative language suggests meanings beyond a word's primary, dictionary meaning. For example, the words *crowd, mob, gang,* and *audience* all mean a group of assembled people, but their connotative meanings are quite different. A crowd implies large numbers, a mob implies unruly or disorganized behavior, and so forth. Writers select words with particular connotative meanings to create a particular feeling or to evoke a particular response. Be sure to critically analyze a writer's use of connotative language to determine what effect he or she intends.

3. **What figurative expressions are used?** Figurative language is a way of describing something that makes sense on an imaginative or creative level but not on a literal or factual level. For example, Ezra Pound's poetic lines

   A sea
   Harsher than granite

   do not mean that the sea was a rock. Instead, they suggest that the sea shares some characteristics of granite: hardness, coldness, immutability. Two common types of figurative expressions are *similes* and *metaphors.* A simile makes a direct comparison by using the words *like* or *as* (her lips were as red as a rose). A metaphor makes a comparison by directly equating the two objects (her lips were a rose).

How to Study and Analyze Art

Art is primarily a visual form of expression (with the exception of music). As is true in the study of literature, there are two main sources of study: the original work and criticism that discusses form, process, and style.

As you study and analyze original art forms, keep the following guidelines in mind.[2]

1. **Establish a first impression of and reaction to the work.**
2. **Learn what background information is available.** Where and when was the work created? What is known about the artist? Where was the work originally shown?
3. **Identify, if possible, the purpose of the work.** Is it intended to portray a person, show respect, display a dilemma, make a religious statement, express feelings?
4. **Study the title and determine how it relates to the work.**
5. **Examine the subject matter and the characteristics of the medium used and evaluate the techniques.** In drawing and painting, for example, you would consider such factors as composition (color, lines, shape), depth, and scale (relative size).
6. **After carefully studying the work, ask yourself three questions:**

◆ What is the artist trying to accomplish?
◆ Why did he or she do what was done? This type of question will force you to examine each feature of the work closely. *Examples:* In Michelangelo's *The Creation of Adam,* why is the creator's arm stretched toward Adam's? Why is the creator's body diagonal? Why is Adam's left leg supporting his arm?
◆ What is my response to this work and why do I feel that way? *Examples:* Why do I feel sorry for the child in the photograph? Why does the portrait seem depressing? Why does that landscape seem inviting and relaxing?

How to Read Criticism

Criticism refers to written materials that discuss, interpret, and evaluate a particular work. Some students wrongly think that criticism is negative or limited to finding fault with a work. Actually, its primary purpose is to analyze and interpret. Criticism may include both positive and negative aspects. Film and book reviews are examples of criticism. Criticism also includes scholarly works that carefully research or examine a particular aspect, theme, or approach. Often, in order to complete a term paper, you will be required to consult several critical sources. In using these sources, follow these guidelines:

1. **Read and study the original work carefully and thoroughly before you consult critical sources.**
2. **Make a preliminary interpretation of the work before reading criticism.** Decide what you think the work means and why it was produced. Record these ideas in note form. If you consult sources before forming your own impressions, your judgment will be colored by what you read, and

you will have difficulty separating your ideas from those you encountered as you read.

3. **Recognize that not all critics agree.** You may encounter three critics who present three different interpretations of Leonardo's *Mona Lisa*.

4. **Although it is perfectly acceptable to revise your own interpretations based on your reading, do not immediately discard your own interpretation as soon as you encounter one that differs.**

SKILLS IN ACTION

Reading Literary Criticism

Sometimes the term *literary criticism* has a connotation of being intellectual or theoretical. However, any response to a written work, even in the form of informal reviews, can be considered criticism.

One interesting public forum for criticism is Amazon.com, which not only sells books online but also allows readers to post their reviews of the books they've read. Go to http://www.amazon.com and look up a book you have read recently or in the past. You will likely find many reviews written by all types of readers. Read the first page of reviews. Did they give you any additional insight into the book? Did you find elements that you agreed or disagreed with? Which reviews did you take seriously, and why? Which ones did you dismiss as useless, and why?

Taking Lecture Notes

Lectures in literature and fine arts classes are primarily intended to guide and direct you in your interpretation of original works. Instructors provide essential background information and discuss the various themes, conventions, and characteristics of the particular art form. When taking notes, use the following suggestions:

◆ **Make notes directly on the page where the poem, story, or art reproduction is printed.** When an instructor discusses and interprets a poem, for example, the easiest way to record notes is to jot them in the margin next to the line or section of the poem to which they refer.

◆ **After the lecture, try to summarize the instructor's main points.** Include the outstanding features of the work, various literary or artistic devices used, and predominant theme(s) identified.

EXERCISE 9.4	**Analyzing a Required Course**

Directions   *Analyze the following situation and answer the questions that follow.*

An engineering student at the State University of New York at Buffalo is taking a required composition and literature course. He dislikes the course because he feels it has nothing to do with his major and the readings do not address current issues. He feels uncomfortable in the course because he is not sure what he should learn. He has not submitted several papers, each of which required him to explore a dominant theme in a specific literary work. He read each work several times but could not identify anything to write about.

1. What does this student fail to understand about literature?
2. What should he do to feel more comfortable and confident about the course?
3. What steps should the student take to solve his problem with writing assigned papers?

■ Career Fields

Career fields include many applied, currently popular fields such as criminal justice, physical therapy, accounting, nursing, and technologies/engineering. Career fields are usually highly technical and specialized. They most closely resemble the life and physical sciences, and much of the advice given in the section on life and physical sciences (pp. 176–181) applies here. This section will present *only* information to supplement that contained in the earlier section.

What to Expect

Career fields differ from pure sciences primarily in focus. While the emphasis in life and physical sciences is knowledge and theoretical problem solving, most career fields are concerned with direct, practical application of knowledge and skill. Expect the following:

◆ **An emphasis on process and procedure.**

◆ **More practical applications, in both textbook and lecture, of material taught.**

◆ **Labs, practicums, clinical, or on-site work experience as an integral part of the course.**

◆ **Grading and evaluation to be performance based.** Your grade in an introductory accounting course, for example, will be based on your ability to balance a ledger.

◆ **Exactness and precision.** Develop systems of methodically performing tasks so you do not miss or overlook steps.

How to Study Career Fields

In studying career fields, use the following suggestions:

1. **Learn the language of the field.** Be certain to learn the specialized terminology and incorporate it into your own speech and writing. To communicate effectively on the job, you will need to speak the language of your field (see Chapter 10).

2. **Maintain a practical focus.** Whenever you learn new information or procedures, ask, "How and when will I use this information?"

3. **Note applications of what you are learning.** Since exams often test your ability to apply and use what is learned, as you read, make marginal notes indicating situations or circumstances in which the information would be useful.

What Thought Patterns to Anticipate

Process and problem-solution are the two predominant thought patterns (see Chapter 11) evident in many career fields, as shown in Table 9.6.

Taking Lecture Notes

Use the following suggestions to take notes most effectively:

◆ **Lectures often involve practical demonstrations.** Focus on the demonstration itself, not on taking notes. Afterward, record the purpose of the demonstration and the points it was intended to emphasize.

TABLE 9.6 Thought Patterns* in the Career Fields

Pattern	Uses	Examples
Process	Learning and describing procedures	**Nursing** Obtaining a radial pulse Passing a nasogastric tube
Problem-solution	Practical applications; clinical or field situations	**Computer science** Modifying a program to suit job specifications Detecting a bug

*See Chapter 11.

◆ Emphasize process and procedure in your notes.
◆ Pay attention to clues your instructor provides about the use and application of information presented.

| EXERCISE 9.5 | ### Analyzing a Learning Situation |

Directions *Analyze the following situation and answer the questions below.*

A nursing student is earning A or high B grades in Nursing I and required courses in English composition, anatomy and physiology, and psychology. However, she is failing a clinical practicum that focuses on basic procedures of patient care. She is evaluated in this course on performing procedures, such as taking a blood sample from models in the clinic under close scrutiny by her clinical instructor. Although she memorizes each procedure, step-by-step, she can't recall them in practical situations. She says she gets nervous and freezes up during clinical evaluations.

1. How should this student revise her learning strategies for the clinical course?

2. What can she do to avoid freezing up during evaluations?

Working Together

Groups of four to six students should each select one of the following topics and identify how various academic disciplines might approach and study it:

1. Stem cell research

2. Television commercials

3. Drug abuse

REVIEW   Five Key Points to Remember

1 **Recognize that new fields of study require extra work.** Because they are unfamiliar, be sure to spend time learning about the discipline and figuring out how best to learn and study it.

2 **For social sciences, determine the significance, importance, and connections between facts.** Observe how facts shape concepts, theories, and patterns.

3 **For the life and physical sciences and career fields, plan on using unique reading and study strategies.** Focus on facts, principles, and procedures.

4 **For mathematics, develop a daily study plan.** Concentrate on and practice problem solving; learn mathematical language.

5 **For literature and the arts, focus on ideas and interpretation.** Analyze, annotate, and look for themes and patterns.

The Work Connection

How does learning about new fields of study increase your ability to find a career you will enjoy? As you study new disciplines, you have an opportunity to figure out which types of thinking and learning you most enjoy. You can use this information to help choose a career that's right for you. Consider how you can combine your goals, your strengths, and your abilities with your interest in a particular academic field to choose a career that will allow you to stay flexible and employable in a changing economy.

1. Of the different subjects that you have studied so far, which ones do you enjoy the most? For each, list three or four particular aspects you find interesting.

2. When you envision your life five years from now, what do you see? Imagine that you are looking at yourself enjoying an ideal day at work. Are the aspects you wrote about in question 1 present in your ideal image of your future work life? If so, which ones?

The Web Connection

1. Examples of everyday item equivalencies for metric units of length, mass, volume, and temperature

   http://lamar.colostate.edu/~hillger/frame.htm

   Visit this site from the U.S. Metric Association to see visual comparisons of the metric system with the U.S. system of measurement. Pick two units and create your own visual example. Share these with your classmates.

2. American Mathematical Society

   http://e-math.ams.org/

   In exploring the AMS's site, you will discover how a field of study's professional society can lead a new student to important information about that subject. Make a list of what you learned about the world of mathematicians from this site.

3. Nature News

   For up-to-date news on the environment, genetics, astronomy and more, see the Web site for Nature Magazine's news stories at:

   http://www.nature.com/news/index.html

   Find reports that correspond with what you are learning in your classes. Discuss some of these latest developments in science with your classmates.

10 Learning Specialized and Technical Vocabulary

Do You Know?

How is terminology a key to course mastery?

How do you use mapping to learn new terminology?

Why are core prefixes, roots, and suffixes important in learning new terminology?

What are course master files, and how can you create them?

Have you noticed that each sport and hobby has its own language—a specialized set of words with specific meanings? Baseball players and fans talk about slides, home runs, errors, and runs batted in. Wine enthusiasts may discuss a wine's tannin, nose, bouquet, and finish. Each academic discipline also has its own language. For each course you take, you encounter an extensive set of words and terms that are used in a particular way in that subject area.

■ Terminology: The Key to Course Mastery

One of the first tasks you face in a new course is to learn the specialized language of that course. This task is especially important in introductory courses in which the subject is new and unfamiliar. In an introductory computer science course, for instance, you often start by learning how a computer functions. From that point, many new terms are introduced: *bit, byte, field, numeric characters, character positions, statements, coding, format,* and so forth.

Specialized Terminology in Class Lectures

Often, the first few class lectures in a course are devoted to acquainting students with the nature and scope of the field and introducing them to its specialized language.

You can see, then, that many disciplines devote considerable time to presenting the language of the course carefully and explicitly. Be sure to record accurately each new term for later review and study. Good lecturers give students clues to what terms and definitions are important to record. They may

- write new words on the chalkboard, as a means of emphasis
- slow down, almost dictating so that you can record definitions
- repeat a word and its definition several times or offer several variations of meaning

As a part of your note-taking system (see Chapter 12), develop a consistent way of easily identifying new terms and definitions recorded in your notes. You might circle or draw a box around each new term; or, as you edit your notes, highlight each new term; or write "def." in the margin each time a definition is included. The particular mark or symbol you use is a matter of preference; the important thing is to find some way to mark definitions for further study.

| EXERCISE 10.1 | ### Identifying New Terms |

Directions *Estimate the number of new terms that each of your instructors introduced during the first several weeks for each of your courses. Now, check the accuracy of your estimates by reviewing the first two weeks of your class notes for each course you are taking. How many new terms and definitions were included for each course?*

Specialized Terminology in Textbooks

The first few chapters within a textbook are often introductory. They are written to familiarize you with the subject of study and acquaint you with its specialized language. In one particular economics textbook, 34 new terms were introduced in the first two chapters (40 pages). In the first two chapters (28 pages) of a chemistry book, 56 specialized words were introduced. A sample of the words introduced in each text is given below. Some of the words are words of common, everyday usage that take on a specialized meaning; others are technical terms used only in the subject area.

New terms: Economics text	New terms: Chemistry text
capital	matter
ownership	element
opportunity cost	halogen
distribution	isotope
productive contribution	allotropic form
durable goods	nonmetal
economic system	group (family)
barter	burning
commodity money	toxicity

Textbook authors use various means to emphasize and define new terminology within chapters:

◆ italics, boldfaced type, or colored print
◆ marginal annotations
◆ "New Terminology" or "Vocabulary" lists that appear at the beginning or end of each chapter

A text's **glossary** is a comprehensive list of terms and meanings introduced throughout the text that is found at the back of the text. The glossary is particularly useful at the end of the course when you have covered all or most of the chapters. Use it to test your recall of terminology: read an entry, cover up the meaning, and try to remember it; then check to see if you were correct.

EXERCISE 10.2

Analyzing Terminology in Textbooks

Directions   *Review the first chapter from two of your texts and then answer the following questions.*

1. How many new terms are introduced in each?
2. If your text contains a glossary, is each of these new terms listed?
3. Are most new words technical terms, or are they words from everyday usage to which a specialized meaning is attached?
4. How does each textbook author call your attention to these new terms?

Learning New Terminology

The following is a demonstration that makes an important point about learning new terminology. Follow the directions as listed.

Step 1

Read the following paragraphs from a computer science textbook; you will be able to refer back to the passage when completing the remaining steps.

7.4.1 Hash Functions

The hash function takes an element to be stored in a table and transforms it into a location in the table. If this transformation makes certain table locations more likely to occur than others, the chance of collision is increased and the efficiency of searches and insertions is decreased. The phenomenon of some table locations being more likely is called primary clustering. The ideal hash function spreads the elements uniformly throughout the table—that is, does not exhibit primary clustering. In fact, we would really like a hash function that, given any z, chooses a random location in the table in which to store z; this would minimize primary clustering. This is, of course, impossible, since the function h cannot be probabilistic but must be deterministic, yielding the same location every time it is applied to the same element (otherwise, how would we ever find an element after it was inserted?!). The achievable ideal is to design hash functions that exhibit pseudorandom behavior—behavior that appears random but that is reproducible.

Unfortunately, there are no hard and fast rules for constructing hash functions. We will examine four basic techniques that can be used individually or in combination. The properties of any particular hash function are hard to determine because they depend so heavily on the set of elements that will be encountered in practice. Thus the construction of a good hash function from these basic techniques is more an art than anything amenable to analysis, but we will present general principles that usually prove successful, pointing out their pitfalls as well.[1]

Step 2

Complete Quiz 1, referring to the passage as needed.

Quiz 1

1. Into what form does a hash function transform an element?
2. Define the term *primary clustering.*
3. Describe an ideal hash function.
4. Why are the properties of a hash function difficult to determine?
5. What is "pseudorandom" behavior?

Step 3

Check your answers using the Answer Key on p. 210. No doubt you did quite well. But did you really *understand* what you read? Let's find out.

Step 4

Complete Quiz 2, referring to the passage as needed.

Quiz 2

1. Give an example of an element to be stored in a table.
2. Define the term *transformation.*
3. Define *z* and *h.*
4. In what situations might "primary clustering" be important?

Unless you have already taken courses in computer programming, you probably could not answer these questions. Why not? You did well with Quiz 1;

how is Quiz 2 different? Quiz 2 tested your *understanding* of the terms used in the passage. Quiz 1 only asked you to locate information in the passage; it measured your ability to find answers—not to understand their meaning.

The differences between Quiz 1 and Quiz 2 illustrate the difference between merely manipulating new terminology and really understanding it. Many students fall into the trap of convincing themselves that they have learned new terminology when, actually, all they have learned is how to find answers. Often, the answers lack real meaning to such students. You will know you have really mastered the terminology of a particular course when you begin to *think,* as well as speak and write, using those terms.

EXERCISE 10.3 **Learning New Terminology**

Directions   *Select a beginning chapter that you have already read from one of your textbooks. Make a list of ten new terms it introduces. Without reference to the text, test your understanding of each by expressing its meaning in your own words. Whenever possible, include an example of how the term is used. Then check your understanding by examining the chapter again.*

Working Together

Work with a partner for this activity. Each of you should take one chapter that your class has already covered in this book and do the following: Write a quiz of five questions that will test your classmate's understanding of the chapter's important terms. Make sure that your classmate will need to do more than merely repeat the definitions of the terms to get the right answers. Exchange questions. Take the other person's quiz. Then evaluate and discuss your results.

Using Subject Area Dictionaries

Many academic fields have specialized dictionaries that list most of the important words used in that discipline. These dictionaries list specialized meanings for words and suggest how and when to use the words. The field of nursing, for instance, has *Taber's Cyclopedic Medical Dictionary.* Other subject area dictionaries include *A Dictionary of Anthropology, The New Grove Dictionary of Music and Musicians,* and *A Dictionary of Economics.*

Find out whether there are subject area dictionaries for the disciplines you are studying. Most libraries have copies of specialized dictionaries in the reference section, and you can also access numerous subject area dictionaries online.

REAL STUDENTS SPEAK

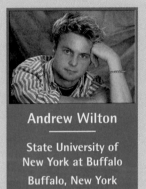

Andrew Wilton

State University of
New York at Buffalo

Buffalo, New York

Background: Andrew is a senior at SUNY, where he is pursuing a degree in sociology, works part-time in a grocery store, and is interning at a family counseling center.

Goals: To attend the SUNY School of Social Work, starting in September 2010, to obtain a master's degree in social work. He is considering several career options including working in non-profit administration, providing counseling services, and working as a medical social worker.

Advice on Learning Specialized Vocabulary: In introductory classes you often get a list of terms you need to know for the course. You need to pay attention to this, learn the terms, and relate them to each other. Reading through the list helps, but I think it's most useful to see how they relate to each other. When you take notes, get down the basic definitions of terms. If you can, use other terms you are already familiar with, so you build a web of related terms, rather than learning all of the definitions separately. In more advanced classes, integrate new terms and vocabulary with what you have learned in previous classes. If you use terms you've learned in previous classes to define new terms, it helps you to relate concepts and ideas and remember what you have learned.

EXERCISE 10.4

Locating Subject Area Dictionaries

Directions   *For each of the courses you are taking, find out if there is a subject area dictionary available. If so, record its title. Then determine whether or not your library has a copy or whether you can access it on the Internet. For each dictionary you can locate, be ready to share its call number or Internet address with your classmates.*

■ Mapping Related Terminology

In most disciplines, you will be learning related groups of terms rather than separate, isolated words. For example, in a criminal justice course, you will learn a cluster of terms that describe the judicial process. In business marketing, you learn terms that describe marketing management: *market diversification, market-focus objective, opportunity forecasts,* and so forth. Mapping is an

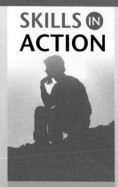

SKILLS IN ACTION

Adapting Vocabulary Learning to Teaching Style

Analyze the following situation and answer the questions below.

A well-respected biology professor teaches her class from the first day using the terminology of her field extensively. Rarely does she explain or define a term. Some students say they are easily confused. Others complain among themselves, saying, "She assumes we know everything already; if we did, we wouldn't be taking the course!"

1. Do you agree or disagree with the students' complaints? Why?
2. Why do you think the professor chooses this approach?
3. How does this teaching style facilitate active thinking and learning?
4. What might students in this class do to prepare for the professor's lecture?
5. How should students structure their note-taking techniques to account for this lecture style?
6. Do a Google search for an online glossary of biology terms. Did you find any useful Web sites to aid in your studying and learning?
7. Do a search on Amazon.com for a printed subject area dictionary for the field of biology. Which one looks most interesting and helpful? Why?

effective method to use when learning such related sets or clusters of words. Mapping, as discussed in Chapter 14, involves drawing a chart or diagram that maps or shows the connections among various terms.

A map can organize terminology to be learned by grouping related terms together and making them more meaningful by showing connections and relationships. Figure 10.1 (p. 202) shows a map that might be useful in organizing the terminology introduced in the first chapter of a physics text. It relates the various states and physical properties of matter. This map makes it easy to visualize how matter is classified and to understand the various external and internal properties used to describe matter.

Mapping can help you avoid the pitfall, described earlier, of using terms but not really understanding their meaning. Mapping forces you to think—to analyze how terms are related; by thinking, you are actively learning.

FIGURE 10.1
A Map of New Terminology

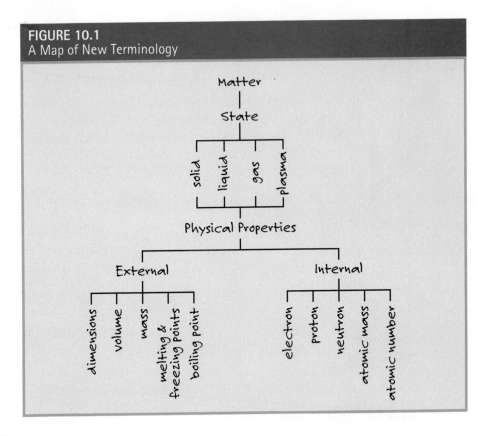

EXERCISE 10.5

Drawing a Map

Directions   *Read the following paragraph from the first chapter of a business advertising text and draw a map relating the key terms introduced.*

> Economists take a somewhat different approach, looking at marketing in terms of benefits to buyers. They suggest that consumers buy goods because they feel the goods will provide satisfaction, or utility. Economists identify four types of utility. *Form utility* is created when a producer manufactures, mines and refines, or grows and harvests a product. In addition to form utility you also buy *place utility:* you pay for the product being in a local store instead of in the producer's warehouse. You also buy *time utility:* you pay retailers to have swimwear and Christmas gifts in stock when you want to buy. Finally, you buy *possession utility:* you pay, as part of a sales, lease, or rental transaction, to have possession of a product transferred to you. Because the last three utilities are provided by marketing, marketing might be defined in terms of buyer benefits as the creation of time, place, and possession utilities.[2]

EXERCISE 10.6

Drawing a Map

Directions   *Select a section of the first chapter from one of your textbooks and draw a map relating the key terms introduced in that section.*

THINKING CRITICALLY
. . . About Vocabulary

As you learn new terminology for each of your courses, make sure you understand each new term. Use the following questions to evaluate your learning:

1. Can you explain a term in your *own* words, not those of the textbook author?
2. Can you explain a new term to a friend or classmate so that they understand it?
3. Can you explain differences between similar terms?
4. Can you think of examples or situations in which the term can be used?
5. Can you use newly learned terms in your speech, note taking, and writing?
6. Do you see terms as related sets of information, rather than individual pieces of information? Use mapping (pp. 200–201) to help you organize sets of information.

■ Learning Core Prefixes, Roots, and Suffixes

Many words in the English language are made up of word parts called prefixes, roots, and suffixes, or beginnings, middles, and endings of words. These word parts have specific meanings and when added together can provide strong clues to the meanings of a particular word. Particular academic disciplines often use a core of common prefixes, roots, and suffixes. For example, in the field of human anatomy and physiology, the prefix *endo-* means "inner," and the root *derma* refers to "skin." Thus the word *endoderm* refers to the inner layer of cells in the skin. Numerous other words are formed using this root in conjunction with a suffix:

Root	Suffix	Example	Meaning
derma (skin)	*-itis* (inflammation)	*dermatitis*	inflammation of skin
	-osis (abnormal or diseased condition)	*dermatosis*	skin disease
	-logy (study of)	*dermatology*	branch of medicine that deals with the skin

As you are learning new terminology for each course, make a point of noticing recurring prefixes, roots, and suffixes. Compile a list of these and their meanings, along with several examples of each. You will find these common word parts useful in learning other new terms that contain them. A sample list for the field of psychology is given below.

Prefixes	Meaning	Example
psych(o)-	mind or mental processes	*psychoanalysis*
neur(o)-	pertaining to nerves or nervous system	*neurosis*
super-	above, over, outside	*superego*

Roots	Meaning	Example
somat(o)	pertaining to the body	*psychosomatic illness*
phobia	intense fear	*claustrophobia*
patho	indicates disease or suffering	*pathological*

Suffixes	Meaning	Example
-osis	disorder or abnormal condition	*neurosis*
-ic	pertaining to	*neurotic*
-ism	indicates theory or principle of	*behaviorism*

For courses involving scientific measurement, be sure to learn prefixes that refer to the metric system.

EXERCISE 10.7

Identifying Word Parts

Directions   *For one of your courses, identify five commonly used prefixes, roots, and suffixes. If you have difficulty, review the glossary of the text to discover commonly used word parts.*

SKILLS IN ACTION

Using Word Parts to Decipher Meaning

The roots, prefixes, and suffixes listed above provide only a small sample of the hundreds of word parts that you can combine to increase your understanding of college-level vocabulary. Try developing your skills with these exercises.

1. The Greek word for the marketplace is *agora*. So what does an *agoraphobic* person fear?

2. Based on the table above, what do you suppose *pathology* means? What is a *psychopath*?

3. *Thromb* means "clotting" in Latin. So what medical condition do you think *coronary thrombosis* refers to?

■ Developing a Course Master File

For each course you are taking, set up a master file in which you include new terminology to be learned and a list of essential prefixes, roots, and suffixes you have identified as important. Also include lists of frequently used signs, abbreviations, symbols, and their meanings. In the sciences, numerous symbols are used in formulas. Some students resist making a special effort to learn the symbols; they assume that they will learn them eventually. This is a mistake because, until you do learn them, you will feel uncomfortable with the course and have trouble actively participating.

You can construct and organize your master file in a number of ways:

Index cards.   Using a separate card for each entry, write the term (or symbol, abbreviation, etc.) on the front and the meaning on the back. Create separate packets of cards for prefixes, roots, and suffixes, new terms, abbreviations, and so forth.

Notebook sections.   Divide a small (6" x 9") spiral notebook into sections and create running lists of terms and meanings.

Computer files.   The computer's word processing capabilities allow you to add to, rearrange, and delete items easily. Using the cut-and-paste or copy functions, you can group similar terms for more effective study. A biology student, for example, grouped terms together according to the following categories: energy and life cells, biological processes, reproduction, biological systems, brain and behavior, and environmental structure issues.

An abbreviated version of a course master file for a nursing course in which students were studying laboratory assessment of blood is shown in Table 10.1 on p. 206.

Because each course deals with very different subject matter, your course master file will differ for each course you are taking. Table 10.2 (p. 206) lists tips for individualizing your course file to suit the requirements of particular academic disciplines. Check with your college's learning assistance center; it may offer lists of common prefixes and roots.

| EXERCISE 10.8 | Developing a Master File |

Directions   *Begin preparing a master file for one of your courses. Use both your text and corresponding lecture notes. Begin with the first chapter, and list new terms, prefixes, roots, and suffixes as well as symbols and abbreviations.*

TABLE 10.1   Sample Course Master File

New Terminology

plasma—blood from which cellular material has been removed
platelets—photoplasmic disks; promote coagulation
bilirubin—orange-yellowish pigmentation in bile carried to the liver by the blood

Prefixes, Roots, and Suffixes

Prefixes	Meaning	Example
trans-	across	transfusion
electro-	indicates electricity	electrophoresis
hyper-	abnormal, excessive	hyperthyroidism

Roots	Meaning	Example
hem	blood	hematology
thromb	clot	thrombus
cardi	heart	cardiodynamics

Suffixes	Meaning	Example
-lysis	dissolution or decomposition	hydrolysis
-lyte	substance that can be decomposed by a particular process	electrolyte
-stasis	slowing or stoppage	hemostasis

Symbols and Abbreviations

CBC	complete blood count
WBC	white blood count
RBC	red blood count
HbF	hemoglobin, fetal
ESR	erythrocyte sedimentation rate

TABLE 10.2   Tips for Learning Specialized Vocabulary in Various Fields of Study

Sciences	
	Learn standard symbols.
	ex: F = force
	W = work
	Learn the metric system.
	ex: *deci* = tenth
	Learn notation systems.
	ex: $HNO_2 \nrightarrow N_2O_2 + H_2O$
	Consult data books and handbooks.
	ex: *Biology Data Book*
	Merck Index
	Handbook of Chemistry & Physics
	Van Nostrand's Scientific Encyclopedia

Mathematics	Learn words as well as the process they imply.
	    ex: *average* (add, then divide)
	        product (multiply)
	Learn symbols.
	    ex: >, <, Σ, ∫
	Learn abbreviations.
	    ex: *quad., vol.*
	Consult: *Encyclopedia Dictionary of Mathematics*

Literature	Learn terms used to describe various features of literature.
	    ex: *tone, mood, iambic pentameter*
	Learn terms that describe various styles of writing.
	    ex: *informal, graphic, verbose*
	Learn terms that refer to particular parts of literary works.
	    ex: *drama, interlude, finale, denouement*
	Learn terms that refer to techniques.
	    ex: *flashback, monologue, soliloquy*
	Learn legendary/mythological figures.
	    ex: *Midas, Venus*
	Consult: *Handbook of Literary Terms*
	    A Dictionary of World Mythology

Arts	Learn terms that describe qualities, impressions, techniques. Learn terms that refer to mode of expression. ex: *design, form, structure* Consult: *The Thames and Hudson Dictionary of Art and Artists*
Applied Sciences, Technical Courses, Computer Science	
	Learn terms that denote process; concentrate on steps in the process. Develop a working knowledge of the terminology; use the terminology in your speaking and writing. Draw diagrams to get the big picture and to show overall relationships. Connect terminology and processes with everyday experience, observable occurrences. Consult: *McGraw-Hill Dictionary of Scientific and Technical Terms*

Business	Learn terms that describe organization.
	    ex: *conglomerate, franchise*
	Learn abbreviations.
	    ex: *OTC, IBF, APR*
	Learn processes and procedures.
	    ex: *price, control, time study*
	Consult: *Dictionary of Business, Finance, and Banking*

(continues)

Social Sciences	Learn words that describe general behaviors.
	ex: *aggression, assimilation*
	Learn stages and processes.
	ex: *oral stage, displacement*
	Learn laws, principles, theories.
	ex: *late selection theory, Sapir-Whorf Hypothesis*
	Learn important researchers, theorists.
	ex: *Maslow, Keynes*
	Consult: *International Encyclopedia of the Social Sciences*
History	Learn important historical figures.
	ex: *Napoleon, Mao Zedong*
	Learn places of historical significance.
	ex: *Sparta, Babylonia, Prussia*
	Consult: *Encyclopedia of World History*

REVIEW Five Key Points to Remember

1 **Pay attention to new terminology in both lectures and textbooks.** Develop a system for recording and marking new terms.

2 **Use a subject area dictionary in your major field of study.** These provide in-depth definitions and discuss usage.

3 **Use mapping to group terminology.** Develop sets or clusters of words that you learn together.

4 **Learn core prefixes, roots, and suffixes.** These will unlock the meanings of many more words than memorizing single word meanings.

5 **Create a course master file.** Use it to record terms, signs, abbreviations, symbols, and their meanings.

The Work Connection

How is learning new terminology linked to your career success? Forecasts of work in the digital age (the era of computers) suggest that many workers will do "knowledge work, . . . handl[ing] information rather than physical things."[3] In his book *The Work of Nations* (1991), former Secretary of Labor Robert Reich called those who do knowledge work "symbolic analysts." Their jobs consist of identifying and solving problems through manipulating symbols: words, numbers, images."[4] As the workforce shifts to knowledge- and information-based work, your ability to learn new terminology will help you stay competitive.

1. In the current workforce, about 20 percent of employed people are knowledge workers.[5] List four or five types of work that you would consider to be primarily about handling information.

2. Consider the careers you may want. What aspects of these careers have to do with manipulating words, numbers, or images? List at least two or three ideas for each possible career.

The Web Connection

1. Vocabulary: An Ongoing Process

   http://www.ucc.vt.edu/stdysk/vocabula.html

   Virginia Tech offers some simple tips for increasing your vocabulary. Read today's newspaper. Write down any words that are unfamiliar to you and look them up in a dictionary. Try to use them during the week.

2. Vocabulary Quizzes

   http://webster.commnet.edu/grammar/vocabulary.htm#quizzes

   Pick a few of these vocabulary quizzes from Capital Community College to complete online. Use a dictionary if necessary. Evaluate your performance. Choose some words from the quizzes to learn using techniques from this chapter.

3. A Word a Day

   http://www.wordsmith.org/awad/index.html

   Sign up to receive a word a day in your e-mail or read a newsletter about words at this interesting site for language lovers. Use the new words in your writing and speech.

Answers to Quiz #1, p. 198

1. A hash function transforms an element to a location in a table.

2. Primary clustering refers to the situation in which some table locations are more likely than others.

3. An ideal hash function spreads the elements uniformly throughout the table.

4. The properties of a hash function are difficult to determine because they depend on the set of elements that will be encountered in the practice.

5. Pseudorandom behavior is behavior that appears to be random but is actually reproducible.

The College Student's
TROUBLESHOOTING GUIDE

To become a successful student you must take charge of your learning. Success also entails recognizing difficult situations when they arise and actively looking for solutions. You can use this troubleshooting guide when you find yourself facing unexpected challenges. You may be surprised to know that most of these problems are extremely common, so you're not alone! To find a solution to a problem you are facing, scan through the following outline of topics and then locate the section that deals with your problem.

Troubleshooting Guide Index

1. SETTING GOALS AND PRIORITIES

PROBLEM	POSSIBLE SOLUTIONS
1a. Problems with Drifting or Aimlessness: You wonder what you should be accomplishing in your first year of college. (For more information, see Chapter 3, "Establishing Goals and Managing Your Time.")	• *Recognize that you are not alone.* Many other students are feeling the same way, because the transition from high school to college is also the transition from childhood to adulthood. For older or returning students, returning to college often requires a major restructuring of life patterns and time commitments. • *Develop a positive relationship with your advisor*, who will help you navigate the complexities of the curriculum and required courses, and may be able to help you choose a major or career path. • *Use your freshman year to explore different avenues and different interests* to help you discover what you want to do and who you want to be. • *Approach each new experience with an open mind.* College is all about expanding your horizons. • *Keep your eye on your goals.* Develop a sense of what you want to accomplish and think of every class, every grade, and every project as moving you closer to that goal. • *Pursue extracurricular activities.* Join clubs and/or sports teams to develop your social network, which can help you find your place in the campus social scene while also helping you discover your talents and interests.
1b. Coping with Required Courses: You have to take a course, and you don't know why.	• *Understand that college has two goals:* (1) to provide you with a well-rounded education, and (2) to help you develop expertise in a chosen area (major). • *Develop the proper mind-set:* Required courses may seem irrelevant to you, but keep an open mind. Ask how the material being taught can apply to your life or to your major. Remain open to new ideas. • *Recognize that the curriculum for your major has been carefully developed to give you the skills and knowledge you need to succeed in that field.* For example, psychology majors must take statistics. They might not like the course, but understanding statistics is essential to success in the field.

1c. Choosing a Major: You haven't chosen a major or think you might have chosen the wrong one.	• *Take some time to read through the college's course catalog.* Read the course descriptions in each discipline and look for the courses that spur your interest. If you can find three or four courses in a particular discipline that really grab you, you may have found your major. • *Take aptitude tests* (often available in the counseling center) to determine your strengths and the fields/careers/majors best suited to your personality. • *Find the balance between your major and a career.* Many students worry about whether their major will help them get a good job. Students who are passionate about their chosen field and do well in their courses are almost certain to find a job and a career in which they will excel. • *Consider choosing a minor to broaden your horizons even further and to increase your employability upon graduation.* Students with minors often have more career paths open to them than students who took majors without minors.

2. TEXTBOOK READING ASSIGNMENTS

PROBLEM	POSSIBLE SOLUTIONS
2a. Rereading: You have to keep rereading the textbook, but you still don't understand everything.	• *Slow down.* You may be reading too fast. Textbook reading requires a slower pace than other reading materials, such as magazines and newspapers. • *Take breaks.* Don't overwhelm yourself with information. Read in chunks, and take a break between major headings of each chapter. • *Use your textbook features to help with the "big picture."* Look for marginal definitions, chapter summaries, and other helpful material. • *Ask questions in class.* Prepare your questions in advance so that they are as specific as possible.
2b. Highlighting: You're not sure what to highlight. Sometimes everything seems important, and sometimes nothing seems important. (For more information, see Chapter 14, "Organizing and Synthesizing Course Content.")	• *Look for clues that tell you what's important.* These include words in **boldface** or *italics*. Often the key term is followed by an example. Highlight the definition and use a marginal annotation, such as a star, to indicate something you need to remember. • *Highlight only the results of research studies.* This is the material you will most likely be tested on.

	• *Look for topic sentences and highlight key parts of them.* Many times a topic sentence will contain the main idea of a paragraph or longer passage. Identifying main ideas will help you build a framework of knowledge.
	• *For each section you read, highlight only those areas that will help you review for an exam.* Focus on the big picture.
2c. Understanding: Your instructor assumes you understand the material, but you don't.	• *Understand your instructor's expectations.* These are often spelled out in the syllabus. Be sure you have fulfilled the necessary prerequisites so that you don't find yourself in over your head.
	• *Spend more time reading and studying.* College reading requires intense concentration. Get rid of distractions (for example, your cell phone) and focus on your reading.
	• *Explore "discovery learning."* This teaching technique is purposefully challenging, requiring students to do more research and reading on their own to understand the lecture. Do not accept a lack of understanding; work to change it.
	• *Visit your instructor during office hours,* ask questions of the TA (teaching assistant), or get tutoring.
	• *Join a study group* in which all members help one another better understand the material.
2d. Deadlines: You just do not have enough time to get your assignments done. (For more information, see Chapter 3, "Establishing Goals and Managing Your Time.")	• *Eliminate socializing or unnecessary activities* to add more time to your schedule.
	• *Don't procrastinate.* It is counterproductive and very stress-inducing.
	• *Keep a master calendar of due dates,* and monitor your progress toward meeting each individual deadline.
	• *Use a "buddy system":* Ask a friend or classmate to help you stay on top of deadlines. Return the favor. In other words, spur each other on toward achievement.
	• *Reward yourself when you have met a deadline.*
	• *Understand the ramifications of missed assignments:* lower grades, more stress, perhaps even failing the course and having to repeat it.

3. NOTE TAKING

PROBLEM	POSSIBLE SOLUTIONS
3a. Focus: Your mind wanders and you get bored.	• *Sit in the front of the room.* • *Be certain to preview assignments.* • *Pose questions you expect to be answered in the lecture.*
3b. Instructor Speed: Your instructor talks too fast.	• *Develop a shorthand system;* use abbreviations. Leave blanks and fill them in later. • *Compare notes after class with a classmate.*
3c. Instructor Focus: Your instructor rambles.	• *Review correlating text assignments to determine organizing principles.*
3d. Organization: Some ideas don't seem to fit anywhere.	• *Record these ideas in the margin or in parentheses in your notes.* Go back and reassess them later during editing (see p. 261).
3e. Understanding: Everything seems important, or nothing seems important.	• *You have not identified key concepts or may lack necessary background knowledge.* Locate a more basic textbook or reference work that discusses the topic to get up to speed. • *Use the textbook headings as cues for what to listen for, and what to take notes on, during lectures.*
3f. Vocabulary: You don't understand or can't spell all the new technical terms.	• *Record the terms phonetically, the way they sound;* fill in correct spellings during editing (see p. 261). • *For terms that are still unfamiliar, look in your textbook glossary or discipline dictionary.*

For more information on taking notes, see Chapter 12, "Note Taking for Class Lectures."

4. GRADES AND TAKING TESTS

PROBLEM	POSSIBLE SOLUTIONS
4a. Problems with Test Grades: You thought you were well prepared for the exam, but you got a C.	• *Look for a pattern of errors in the questions you got wrong.* Do the errors indicate difficulty with a certain topic? • *Learn better test-taking skills.* For more information, see Chapters 16–18 of this book. • *Spend more time studying for the exam, and start studying earlier.* Cramming the night before an exam is usually ineffective. Reviewing a little each night for a week before the exam is a much more effective method. • *Learn from your first exam.* Study your instructor's questioning techniques and determine what is important to him or her. Then adjust your study habits accordingly for the second exam. • *If you truly believe your instructor has made an error in grading, approach him or her after class to ask for a corrected grade.* • *If you are displeased with your grade, politely discuss the problem with your instructor.*
4b. Problems with Your GPA: You are getting a lot of C's, but you want A's and B's.	• *Alter your ways of thinking and studying.* You may be bringing a high-school way of studying to college, which requires a different set of studying and thinking skills. • *Adjust your schedule so that you can give more time to your studies.* Recognize that sacrifices and trade-offs must be made to improve your grades. • *College grades are a direct result of the amount of effort you put into each class.* The more you study, the better your grade is likely to be. • *Balance your courses each term between difficult, medium, and easy.* If you have to take a difficult course for your major, balance it out with an "easy" phys ed course to help keep your GPA healthy. • *Take action early in the term if your grades are not what you want them to be.* If you receive a C on your first assignment or exam, take immediate steps to discover the source of the problem and take corrective action. You may not end up with an A in the course, but with effort you can end up with a B.
4c. Taking Exams: You run out of time and get lower grades because of it.	• *Plan your time better by previewing the entire exam first,* seeing how many points each section is worth, and then allocating your time properly. For more details, see Chapter 17, "Reasoning Skills for Objective Exams."

5. WRITING SKILLS

PROBLEM	POSSIBLE SOLUTIONS
5a. Problems with Writing: You need to improve your writing, but you don't know how to go about it.	• *Take a course in college writing or technical writing.* • *Make use of your campus writing center or get one-on-one tutoring.* • *Take brush-up or developmental courses in writing and grammar if you feel your skills are not up to par.*
5b. Problems with Term Papers: You have no idea how to write a term paper.	• *To write a good term paper, you must completely understand the assignment given by your instructor.* Read each assignment very carefully and provide what your instructor has asked for. • *Learn good research methods and proper documentation for your sources.* Most college writing courses teach you these skills, so take a writing course in your first year of college. • *Understand the most basic skill of writing an effective paper: making a point and providing examples to support it.* • *Ask friends or classmates to read your paper before you submit it.* Listen to their suggestions and revise your paper to improve it. • *Use the spell-check and grammar-check functions of your word processing program before turning in your paper.*
5c. Problems with Essay Exams: You do not tend to do well on essay exams.	• *Learn the skills required to ace an essay exam.* For more details, see Chapter 18, "Taking Essay Exams."

6. TECHNOLOGY

PROBLEM	POSSIBLE SOLUTIONS
6a. The Technology Blues: You are not computer savvy, but everyone thinks you should be.	• *Learn the most commonly used programs: Microsoft Word and Excel.* Learn enough about computer hardware to know how to use a CD-ROM drive, how to boot up and shut down, and how to access programs. • *Bookstores are filled with hundreds of step-by-step workbooks to help you learn computer basics.* Ask someone in the computer center for recommendations.

6b. Problems with Course Management Systems: Your instructor conducts much of the course online, but you don't understand the system.	• *The home page of the course management system (such as Blackboard, WebCT, Moodle, or Sakai) is the "dashboard" from which you navigate to your various assignments.* Become familiar with the home page and check it daily. Immediately read any announcements from your instructor, and respond accordingly. • *Quizzes and tests are often given in course management systems, and the same test-taking tips apply to computer testing as to regular testing.* For more details on how to take tests, see Part Five of this book, "Exams: Thinking Under Pressure."
6c. Getting Computer Time: The computer labs are always crowded or inaccessible.	• *Most computer labs have sign-up sheets.* Learn when the sheets are put out so that you can be one of the first to choose your desired time. • *Do not miss your scheduled appointments for computer time;* crowded labs can make it impossible for you to get a computer, especially during midterms and final exams. • *Do not expect that available computer times will necessarily be convenient for you.* You may need to rearrange your schedule. • *Do not wait until the last minute to begin a computer project.* Unexpected hardware, software, or network problems can cause your project to be late and your grade to be lower. • *If you don't have a home computer, save your money to purchase an inexpensive laptop.* Ask your advisor if the college makes any scholarship money available to students to purchase computers.

7. INTERPERSONAL CONFLICTS

PROBLEM	POSSIBLE SOLUTIONS
7a. Conflicts with Classmates or Other Students (For more information, see Chapter 4, "Managing Your Life and Coping with Stress.")	• *Use the avoidance technique.* Simply avoid the other person. If you're in the same class, sit on the other side of the room and time your comings and goings so they don't coincide. • *Try to resolve the situation by talking.* Speak calmly about the problem and see if a compromise can be reached. In the best-case scenario, the problem is solved. In the worst-case scenario, you can "agree to disagree" and act civilly toward each other. • *Make a peace offering.* If you feel at fault or wish to apologize, write a note or offer some token of apology. Clear the air and get on with your studies!

7b. Conflicts with Instructors: You don't like your instructor.	• *If you dislike your instructor instantly, transfer out of the class as soon as possible.* Take the same course with a different instructor. • *If you cannot avoid the instructor, make a virtue of necessity.* Work hard to focus on the ideas being taught and not on the instructor's personality. • *Don't let your dislike show.* Your instructor will most likely notice, making a bad situation worse. • *Just get through it.* Within ten or 15 weeks, the course will be over, and you may never have to deal with that instructor again.
7c. Problems with Instructors: Your professors aren't available or approachable.	• *Attempt to see your instructor during office hours.* If your professor isn't there, leave a polite note. • *E-mail your professor in advance* asking for an appointment at a convenient day or time. • *Stay after class to talk with your professor.* Many instructors appreciate students who talk to them after class. • *If you feel intimidated by your professor, remember that your professor at one time probably felt intimidated by his or her instructors.* Most people respond well to polite, respectful questions and requests for help. Be sure your request is legitimate; do not ask your instructor for extensions or make-up exams unless you have very serious (e.g., medical or family) reasons for doing so.

8. SAFETY AND SECURITY

PROBLEM	POSSIBLE SOLUTIONS
8a. Safety: Another student is acting strangely or in a way that makes you uncomfortable.	• *Trust your instincts.* Remove yourself from the situation if possible. • *Tell someone you trust—your advisor, an instructor, the dean—about your concerns.* Remember that you may be doing the campus a favor by making administrators aware of a potential problem. • *When reporting on another person's behavior, be as specific as possible.* Explain exactly what happened, where, and when.

8b. Security: You don't feel safe on campus at night or in particular areas.	• *Report suspicious activity to your campus security office.* • *Arrange with a friend or classmate to travel to and from buildings or public transportation together.* Walk in groups whenever possible. • *Take a self-defense course, and/or carry a small can of mace or pepper spray with you.* • *Do check-ins with friends:* Call a friend to let him or her know you have arrived home safely. Always carry identification with you, as well as some cash for emergencies.

9. LIVING AND COMMUTING ARRANGEMENTS

PROBLEM	POSSIBLE SOLUTIONS
9a. Problems with Roommates	• *Communication is key.* Talk with your roommate(s) about the sources of conflict and try to come up with compromises. • *Write up a set of "house rules" to which all roommates agree,* and post these in a conspicuous location. • *Share the workload and pay your portion of the bills on time.* Be respectful of others' needs for space, peace, and quiet. • *If you live in a dorm, talk to your residence supervisor about the problem.* He or she may have good advice. • *If you have truly irreconcilable differences with roommates, find another place to live.* • *Seek different living arrangements with another person whose schedule is the opposite of yours.* For example, if you expect to be home at night, find a roommate who works nights.
9b. Problems with Family Members	• *Arrange a time and place to have a serious but civil conversation about your differences.* Focus on your family bonds and look for a solution that will work for both of you. • *Work out a give-and-take arrangement.* When a family member does a favor for you (such as watch your children while you are in class), try to return the favor or offer a small token of your thanks. • *If your college studies force you to be away from home more than your family would like, find a way to devote "quality time" each month to the people who miss you.* Set aside a day or time when family will come first. In return, ask your family to understand the major demands that college makes on your time. • *Sometimes time spent apart can help people better appreciate one another.* If you have a particularly strong conflict with a family member, try spending some time apart. You may find you miss each other.

9c. Commuting Difficulties	• *Build extra time into your schedule to allow for unexpected events,* such as traffic, slow buses, or trains that don't arrive on time. Nothing is more stressful than arriving "just in time" for a class or an exam.
	• *Plan to arrive a minimum of ten minutes early for every appointment, which will give you a margin for error.* If you arrive to class early, use the time to review your notes or textbook for the upcoming lecture.
	• *Don't cut your schedule too tight.* For example, scheduling a class on the other side of a large campus may require you to take a bus; and the bus may be unreliable. If the bus shows up late, you'll be late for class.
	• *Minimize your time commuting to and from campus by clustering your schedule* so that your classes are clumped at certain times or on certain days. This has the added benefit of maximizing your study time (because you're spending less time getting to and from campus).
	• *Always have a back-up plan.* Know the bus schedule in case your car breaks down, and the train schedule in case the bus breaks down. When possible, carpool with roommates to save on commuting expenses.
	• Parking is a problem on many campuses. *To get parking, arrive as early in the day as you can.* Even if you arrive two hours before your first class, you can spend those two hours in the library reading and studying.

10. WELLNESS ISSUES

PROBLEM	POSSIBLE SOLUTIONS
10a. Isolation: You feel like one tiny person on a huge campus.	• *Campus bulletin boards are filled with flyers for campus organizations, clubs, and activities.* Read the bulletin boards and attend meetings that you think will interest you.
	• *Most colleges have a free counseling center;* make an appointment to talk with a counselor.
	• *Take courses in which teamwork is required* (such as science labs or communication courses). As you get deeper into your major, you'll find yourself taking courses with the many of the same people.

10b. "Party" Issues: You want to study, but it seems that everyone around you just wants to have a good time.	• *If you are serious about your studies, make the library your second home.* It will be quiet and conducive to study, and many libraries now have computer centers that will allow you to work on your computer. • *It's never easy to study for an exam when you'd rather be out having fun with your friends or be home with your family.* Think about your decisions in terms of the future benefits of your college education.
10c. Timing Issues: You are considering taking a semester or term off from college.	• *You should attend courses only when you can give them the time and attention they need.* Different students need different amounts of time to complete their education. Don't work with an artificial timetable; instead, look closely at your life and determine how long it will take you to complete your degree. • *Remember to pursue course options that may help you better manage your time.* Many schools offer courses at night and on weekends, as well as online courses. Interim sessions (between terms) are extremely intensive courses that get you the credits you need but require you to give up almost everything else to complete them successfully.

11 Thought Patterns of Academic Disciplines

Do You Know?

What are thought patterns?

How can recognition of thought patterns help you master your courses?

What are six common academic thought patterns?

How can these thought patterns improve your memory and learning?

This semester or term you are probably taking courses in several disciplines simultaneously. You may study English composition, biology, psychology, and philosophy all in one semester. During one day you may write a descriptive essay, learn how cells divide, and study early schools of psychology. Consequently, you are forced to shift gears for each course, developing new approaches and strategies.

What few students realize is that a biologist and a psychologist, for example, think about and approach their subject matter in similar ways. While their subject matter and their vocabulary differ, they think the same way. Regardless of their field of expertise, then, researchers, textbook authors, and your professors all use standard patterns of thought to organize and express their ideas.

You might think of these patterns as learning blueprints. We have hundreds of blueprints, or preestablished operating instructions, that enable us to perform numerous everyday activities. These are sometimes referred to as *schema*. You may have a blueprint for riding a bicycle, swimming the crawl stroke, tying a shoelace, making pizza, or ironing a shirt. You have numerous academic blueprints as well: solving algebra problems, completing a biology lab, or writing an English composition. These blueprints enable you to complete a task without analyzing it or rediscovering the best way to do it each time.

■ Thought Patterns: Guides to Learning

Familiarity with these basic thought patterns will enable you to approach all your courses more easily and effectively. Following are four reasons why textbook chapters are easier to read if you can identify the thought pattern(s) by which they are organized.

REAL STUDENTS SPEAK

Noah Klugman
___
Kalamazoo College
Kalamazoo, Michigan

Background: Noah is a junior at Kalamazoo College where he is pursuing a 2/3 degree; he will receive a bachelor's degree in physics and computer science in three years and then transfer into a university and obtain a bachelor's in computer engineering in two years. In the summer of 2009, Noah was awarded a space grant and worked at the NASA/Caltech Jet Propulsion Lab in Pasadena, California.

Goals: To work full-time at the Jet Propulsion Lab on the Mars Rover program.

Advice on Using Thought Patterns to Get the Most Out of a Class: I made a point when I was starting out of spending time with my professors, finding out what they were interested in and attempting to understand their thought patterns and approach to their disciplines. This helped me understand how they organized their lectures, so I understood them better. It also helped if I got an assignment that was vague, because it gave me a starting point for approaching the assignment, I knew what was an adequate amount of work to put in, and how to impress my professor.

1. **Recognizing patterns will enable you to anticipate the author's or speaker's thought development.** For example, from a heading or topic sentence alone, you often can predict the pattern of thought the section or paragraph will follow. Suppose you read the following topic sentence:

   > When you are viewing an online computer system in action, it is as if you are watching a science fiction movie.

   Here, you would anticipate a comparison-contrast between the system and the movie. If a speaker announced, "Today we'll consider the impact of stress upon health," you could anticipate the speaker will focus on effects.

2. **Patterns improve your understanding.** Thought patterns indicate how ideas are organized. If, for example, you establish that a lecturer intends to contrast two forms of media advertising, then the lecture will be easier to follow.

3. **Patterns facilitate storage and retrieval of information in memory.** Information that is grouped, chunked, or organized is easier to store than single, unrelated bits of information. Also, the manner in which information is stored in memory influences the ease with which it is retrieved. Patterns provide a vehicle for organizing information and function as retrieval clues for later recall.

ACADEMIC THOUGHT PATTERNS

Here are the commonly used thought patterns:

- Order or sequence
- Comparison and contrast
- Cause and effect
- Classification
- Definition
- Listing

In later chapters, you will see how these patterns are useful in taking lecture notes, reading textbooks, writing papers, and preparing for and taking exams.

---

4. **Patterns provide a means of analyzing assignments.** Often, an assignment seems difficult or confusing until you understand its function. Patterns provide a vehicle for organizing and expressing your ideas in a coherent, comprehensible form. As you write essay exam answers, class assignments, or term papers, patterns provide a base or structure around which you can effectively express your thoughts.

■ Order or Sequence

If you were asked to summarize the plot of a film, you would mention key events in the order in which they occurred. In describing how to solve a math problem, you would detail the process step-by-step. If asked to list what you feel are your accomplishments so far this week, you might present them in order of importance, listing your most important accomplishment first, and so forth. In describing a building, you might detail the front, then the sides, then the roof. In each case, you present information in a particular sequence or order. Each of the above examples, then, illustrates a thought pattern known as order or sequence. Each form is described briefly below.

Chronology

Chronological order refers to the sequence in which events occur in time. This pattern is used in the academic disciplines concerned with the interpretation of events in the past. History, government, and anthropology are prime examples. In literature, chronological order is evident in novels, short stories, and narrative essays.

Speakers and writers often provide transitional words and phrases that signal that this thought pattern is being used. These signals may occur within single sentences or as transitions or connections between sentences. Several examples of these transitional clues follow. (Transitional words that occur in phrases are italicized here to help you spot them.)

CHRONOLOGY AND PROCESS PATTERN TRANSITIONAL WORDS/PHRASES

In-sentence clues	*in* ancient times *at* the start of the battle *on* September 12 the *first* Homo sapiens *later* efforts
Between-sentence transitions	*then, later, first, before, during, by the time, while, afterward, as, after, thereafter, meanwhile, at that point*

Process

Process explains how to do something and is used in disciplines that focus on procedures, steps, or stages. These include mathematics, natural and life sciences, computer science, and engineering. The pattern is similar to chronology in that steps or stages follow each other in time.

Transitional words and phrases often used in conjunction with this pattern are similar to those used for chronological order.

Order of Importance

Order of importance shows order of priority or preference. Ideas are arranged in one of two ways: from most important to least important, or from least to most important. Here are some commonly used transitions that suggest this pattern.

ORDER OF IMPORTANCE PATTERNS TRANSITIONAL WORDS/PHRASES

In-sentence clues	is *less* essential than . . . *more* revealing is . . . of *primary* interest
Between-sentence transitions	*first, next, last, most important, primarily, secondarily*

Spatial Order

Information organized according to its physical location or position or order in space uses a pattern that is known as **spatial order**. It is used in numerous technical fields, engineering, and the biological sciences.

Transitional words and phrases that indicate spatial order include the following:

SPATIAL ORDER PATTERN TRANSITIONAL WORDS/PHRASES	
In-sentence clues	the *center* the *lower* portion the *outside* area *beneath* the surface
Between-sentence transitions	*next to, beside, to the left, in the center, externally*

EXERCISE 11.1

Working Together

Identifying Order and Sequence

Directions   *Working in pairs, read each of the following opening sentences from a textbook reading assignment and anticipate whether the material will be developed using chronology, process, order of importance, or spatial order.*

1. The rise of organizations of women both preceded and postdated the civil rights movements.[1]
2. As is common with all other cells, the neuron has a nucleus, a cell body, and a cell membrane, which encloses the whole cell.
3. As people move away from denial (they can no longer reject the fact that they are ill because their symptoms are growing so acute), anger (being angry is not helping symptoms), and bargaining (also ineffective; they are becoming worse, not better), they eventually arrive at a stage of really admitting to themselves that they are ill.[2]
4. Short fibers, dendrites, branch out around the cell body and a single long fiber, the axon, extends from the cell body.
5. The basic technique for input loop control involves using a flag to signal when the EOF record has been read.[3]
6. The battle for women's suffrage was fought mostly in the last years of the 19th and first years of the 20th century.[4]
7. A newborn needs careful assessment to be certain that his musculoskeletal and neurological systems are intact.
8. The key consideration in determining whether a college education is a good investment is the opportunity cost, the cost of choosing college over other alternatives.

■ Comparison and Contrast

The **comparison pattern** is used to emphasize or discuss *similarities* between or among ideas, theories, concepts, or events, while the **contrast pattern** emphasizes *differences*. When a speaker or writer is concerned with both similarities and differences, a combination pattern is used. Comparison and contrast are widely used in the social sciences, where different groups, societies, cultures, or behaviors are studied. Literature courses may require comparisons among poets, among several literary works, or among stylistic features. A business course may examine various management styles, compare organizational structures, or contrast retailing plans.

A speaker or writer may be concerned with similarities, differences, or both similarities and differences. For example, suppose a professor of American literature is comparing two American poets, Whitman and Frost. Each of the following organizations is possible:

◆ Compare and contrast the two; that is, discuss their similarities, then their differences.

◆ Discuss characteristics of Whitman, then discuss characteristics of Frost, then summarize their similarities and differences.

◆ Discuss by characteristic. For example, first discuss the two poets' use of metaphor, then their use of rhyme, and then their common themes.

◆ Words and phrases that reflect these patterns are listed below:

COMPARISON AND CONTRAST PATTERN TRANSITIONAL WORDS/PHRASES

	Contrast		Comparison
Within-sentence clues	*unlike* Bush, Obama . . . *less* rigid than . . . *contrasted* with *differs* from	**Within-sentence clues**	. . . *similarities between* is *as* powerful *as* . . . *like* Bush, Obama . . . *both* Bush and Obama . . . Obama *resembles* Bush *in that* . . .
Between-sentence transitions	*in contrast* *however* *on the other hand* *as opposed to*	**Between-sentence transitions**	*in a like manner* *similarly* *likewise* *correspondingly* *in the same way*

| EXERCISE 11.2 | **Identifying Comparison and Contrast** |

Directions   *Read each of the following opening sentences from textbook reading assignments and anticipate whether a comparison, contrast, or combination pattern will be used.*

1. Black Muslim religious practices closely follow those of Islam, a major religion of the Middle East and North Africa.
2. The majority of Americans will be better off in the year 2025 than we are today.
3. Two recent research reports have come to opposing conclusions about the dangers of hazardous waste pollution to the area's water table.
4. Both Werner (2008) and Waible (2009) focus on variability of genetic traces in pinpointing causes of cancer.
5. In the few areas on which they agree, the two authors dispute the credibility of each other's sources.

■ Cause and Effect

The **cause and effect pattern** expresses a relationship between two or more actions, events, or occurrences that are connected in time. The relationship differs, however, from chronological order in that one event leads to another by causing it. Information that is organized using the cause and effect pattern may

◆ explain causes, sources, reasons, motives, and action
◆ explain the effects, results, or consequences of a particular action
◆ explain both causes and effects

The cause and effect pattern is used in all disciplines that ask the question "why," all that involve research, and all that search for explanations. It predominates in science, technology, and social science.

In its simplest form, cause and effect is straightforward and direct. In other situations, causes and effects, or reasons and consequences, although not directly stated, can be inferred. For example, consider the following sentence:

Because wages are decreasing, the pace of inflation is slowing.

Decreasing wages is the cause or reason, and the slowing of inflation is the result or consequence. Notice, however, that the relationship is not directly stated, only implied.

Many statements expressing cause and effect relationships appear in direct order, with the cause stated first and the effect following.

I couldn't find my keys, so I was late for class.

However, reverse order is sometimes used, as in the following statement:

I was late for class because I couldn't find my keys.

EXERCISE 11.3 **Identifying Causes and Effects**

Directions *Identify the cause and the effect in each of the following statements.*

1. Your buying decisions influence the prices farmers receive for their products.
2. A computer program is easy or difficult to run, depending on the software system you use.
3. Recently, the Justice Department investigated charges that some banks made predatory loans.
4. Computer users suffer when they use poorly designed antivirus software.
5. The threat of nuclear war has been with us for so long—nearly three generations—that we are in serious danger of forgetting the real dangers it poses.

The cause and effect pattern may express multiple causes, or multiple effects, or both multiple causes and multiple effects. For example, both slippery road conditions and your excessive speed (causes) may contribute to your car's sliding into the ditch (effect). In other instances, a chain of causes or effects may occur. For instance, missing the bus may force you to miss your 8:00 a.m. class, which in turn may cause you to not turn in your term paper on time, which may result in a penalty grade.

Transitional words or phrases that suggest the cause and effect pattern include the following:

CAUSE AND EFFECT PATTERN
TRANSITIONAL WORDS/PHRASES

Within-sentence clues	Emotional outbursts *create* . . .
	Heart disease *stems from* . . .
	Lack of sleep *leads to* . . .
	Hypertension *causes* . . .
	An interest rate increase resulted in . . .
Between-sentence transitions	*therefore, consequently, hence, for this reason, since*

EXERCISE 11.4 **Identifying Causes and Effects**

Directions *For each of the following statements, determine whether it expresses single or multiple causes and single or multiple effects.*

1. Acute stress may lead to an inability to think clearly, to organize, and to make decisions.
2. A mild stimulant, such as caffeine, appears to change a person's ability to maintain attention and concentration on relevant stimuli at hand.

3. Many people consider large families a blessing, or have religious objections to birth control, or are culturally ill-suited to the regular use of birth control methods.[5]
4. Regional conflict, then, is at the base of the huge military bill of the Third World, together with ideological competition, and sometimes revolution, between Western-oriented governments and Socialist movements.[6]
5. Geography and territorial position are among the most enduring determinants of national power and national defense.

■ Classification

Suppose you are discussing the kind of movies you enjoy. It would be helpful to identify movies by type: horror, comedy, documentary, and so forth. By dividing a topic and discussing each of its components, you are using the **classification pattern**.

This pattern is widely used in many academic subjects. For example, a psychology text might explain human needs by classifying them into two categories: primary and secondary. Or, in a chemistry textbook, various compounds may be grouped and discussed according to common characteristics, such as the presence of hydrogen or oxygen. The classification pattern divides a topic into parts, grouping them by common or shared characteristics.

Here are a few examples of topics and the classifications or categories into which each might be divided:

Cars: sports, luxury, hybrid

Energy: kinetic, potential

Diseases: communicable, noncommunicable

Transitional words and phrases that indicate the classification pattern are as follows:

CLASSIFICATION PATTERN TRANSITIONAL WORDS/PHRASES	
Within-sentence clues	There are several *kinds* of . . . There are numerous *types* of . . . can be *classified* as . . . is *composed* of . . . *comprises* . . .
Between-sentence transitions	*finally, another, one type of* . . .

| EXERCISE 11.5 | **Creating Categories** |

Working Together

Directions *Working in pairs, divide each of the topics listed below into several categories.*

1. Emotions
2. Music
3. Discrimination
4. Laws
5. Literature

■ Definition

The **definition pattern** approaches a topic by explaining what it is. Suppose you were asked to define the word *comedian* for someone unfamiliar with the term. First, you would probably say that a comedian is a person who entertains. Then you might distinguish a comedian from other types of entertainers by saying that a comedian is an entertainer who tells jokes and makes others laugh. Finally, you might mention, by way of example, the names of several well-known comedians who have appeared on television. Although you may have presented it informally, your definition would have followed the standard, classic pattern. The first part of your definition tells what general class or group the term belongs to (entertainers). The second part tells what distinguishes the term from other items in the same class or category. The third part includes further explanation, characteristics, examples, or application.

Here are a few additional examples:

	General Class	**Distinguishing Characteristics**
Opossum	animal	ratlike tail
		nocturnal habits
Prejudice	emotional attitude	involving a tendency to respond negatively to certain identifiable groups or group members

Transitional words and phrases that indicate the definition pattern are as follows:

DEFINITION PATTERN TRANSITIONAL WORDS/PHRASES

nepotism *is . . .*
classical conditioning *refers to . . .*
acceleration *can be defined as . . .*
empathy *means . . .*

Other transitional words/phrases are:

consists of, is a term that, involves, is called, is characterized by, that is, occurs when, exists when, are those that, entails, corresponds to, is literally

| EXERCISE 11.6 | **Writing Definitions** |

Directions   *Using the pattern described above, write a definition for each of the following.*

1. Athlete
2. Cheating
3. Music
4. Internet
5. Discrimination

■ Listing

If asked to describe an exam you just took, you might mention its length, its difficulty, the topics it covered, and the types of questions it contained. These details about the exam could be arranged in any order; each detail provides further information about the exam, but each has no specific relationship to any other. This arrangement of ideas is known as **listing**, the presentation of pieces of information on a given topic by stating them one after the other.

This pattern is widely used in college textbooks in most academic disciplines. The listing pattern is the least structured pattern because it is often a list of items: factors that influence light emission, characteristics of a particular poet, a description of an atom, a list of characteristics that define poverty, for example. Listing may also be used to explain, support, or provide evidence. Support may be in the form of facts, statistics, or examples. For instance, the statement "The newest sexually transmitted disease to come to public awareness, AIDS, was first documented in 1981 and has spread rapidly since that time" would be followed by details about its discovery and statistics documenting its spread.

The words or phrases used for this pattern include the following:

LISTING PATTERN TRANSITIONAL WORDS/PHRASES	
Within-sentence clues	the second . . . . . . and . . . also there are several . . . (1) . . . , (2) . . . , and (3) . . . (a) . . . , (b) . . . , (c) . . .
Between-sentence transitions	*In addition,* *first, second, third* *finally* *another*

| EXERCISE 11.7 | **Using the Listing Pattern** |

Directions   *Identify the topics listed below that might be developed using the listing pattern.*

1. Sources of Drug Information
2. Types of Electronic Media
3. Problem-Solving Techniques
4. Two Famous Twentieth-Century Composers
5. Obstacles to Creative Thought

■ Mixed Patterns

Patterns are often combined. In describing a process, a writer may also give reasons why each step must be followed in the prescribed order. A lecturer may define a concept by comparing it to something similar or familiar. Let's suppose your political science professor opens a lecture by stating that the distinction between *power* and *power potential* is an important one in considering balance of power. You might expect a definition pattern, in which the two terms are defined, but you might also anticipate the difference or "distinction" between the two terms to be discussed using a contrast pattern.

THINKING CRITICALLY
. . . About Patterns

When you learn to identify patterns, you see the ideas in a piece of writing or a lecture as a coherent set rather than as unconnected facts. Patterns focus your attention on concepts, larger ideas, and issues rather than on small, individual details.

Patterns, then, help you decide what is important and what is not. Here's a list of patterns and what they emphasize:

Pattern	What Is Important
Chronology	• dates and events
Process	• steps or procedures
Importance	• priorities
Spatial	• physical location
Comparison	• similarities
Contrast	• differences
Cause and effect	• sequence, actions, relationships, consequences, motives
Classification	• characteristics and distinguishing features
Definition	• terminology, examples

| EXERCISE 11.8 | ## Anticipating Patterns |

Directions   *For each of the following topic sentences, anticipate two patterns that are likely to be evident in the paragraph.*

1. On balance, then, here appear to be four discernible reasons for nuclear weapons development: security, prestige, regional dominance or equilibrium, and reification of modern scientific development.[7]
2. Before examining the components of the balance of power, it will be useful to clarify five features about the international system that apply regardless of historical era or structural form.[8]
3. Industry, the second and more modern form of production, displaced feudalism.[9]
4. Like reinforcement, punishment comes in two varieties, positive and negative.[10]
5. The reasons for this huge increase in military expenditure in the Third World are many, and they go considerably beyond reasons of national grandeur. Perhaps most important is the degree to which the developing nations remain of interest to the superpowers.[11]

| EXERCISE 11.9 | ## Anticipating Patterns |

Directions   *For each of the following lecture topics, anticipate and discuss what pattern(s) the lecture is likely to exhibit.*

1. Conducting an Interview
2. Why Computers Use Binary-Coded Information
3. Functions of Money
4. Classical Versus Instrumental Conditioning
5. Narrowing a Research Paper Topic
6. Assigning Data to a Two-Level Table
7. Adolescence: The Failure to Cope
8. Cures for Inflation
9. Phillips Curves: Hypothetical and Actual
10. Apartheid: Tradition or Discrimination?

| EXERCISE 11.10 | ## Anticipating Patterns |

Directions   *For each of the following topic sentences, anticipate what pattern(s) that paragraph is likely to exhibit.*

1. Oil field development has been shown to have negative environmental impacts.
2. Unlike Japan and the Western European countries, Canada has been relatively removed from the balance of terror.
3. The term *society* refers to people who share a common culture and live in the same geographic area.
4. Large numbers of European immigrants first began to arrive in the United States in the 1920s.
5. Short fibers, called dendrites, branch out around the cell body and a single, long fiber, the axon, extends from the cell body.
6. Throughout the nuclear era much attention has been given to the various types of unintended nuclear war—war initiated by accident, error, or terrorist activity.

7. With the Doppler technique, high-frequency sound waves are "bounced off" body tissue; the rate and pitch at which they return demonstrate the movement and density of the underlying tissue.

8. The sections of a comprehensive medical history are introduction, chief concern, history of present illness, past medical history, family medical history, and review of systems.

9. In addition to nuclear devices and missiles and weapons for land, sea, and air warfare, arms designers have created a variety of weapons less well known but equally horrifying.[12]

10. Behaviorists see the individual as essentially passive, while cognitive psychologists maintain that the individual actively interacts with the environment.

Working Together

While the thought patterns presented in this chapter are widely used in academic thinking, writing, and speaking, they also are important and frequent in our everyday lives. In groups of five or six, brainstorm a list of as many daily activities or decisions as you can that involve one (or more) of the six thought patterns discussed in this chapter.

SKILLS IN ACTION

Using Thought Patterns

Analyze the following situation and answer the questions below:

A student attending the University of Toronto is given an assignment in art history class to write an essay discussing two paintings, one by Renoir, the other by Daumier. She has spent considerable time studying each painting, but she has no idea of how to begin the assignment. Although the paintings are obviously very different, she cannot seem to find an organizing principle on which to base her essay.

Feeling as if she is making no progress, she calls several friends and asks advice. One friend advises her to read some general background information on each artist. Another advises her to focus on her first impression of each painting and write about those impressions.

1. Evaluate the advice given by each friend.

2. What advice would you offer that would help the student complete this assignment?

3. What thought patterns would help this student organize her paper?

REVIEW   Five Key Points to Remember

1 Use the **order and sequence pattern** to organize information that follows a prescribed series of events. Use the list pattern if there is no prescribed sequence.

2 Use the **comparison and contrast pattern** to emphasize or discuss similarities and differences.

3 Use the **cause and effect pattern** to show relationships between two or more actions, events, or occurrences.

4 Use the **classification pattern** to show how a subject can be divided into parts or types.

5 Use the **definition pattern** to explain a term by giving its general class and distinguishing characteristics.

The Work Connection

The thought patterns you use in speech and writing will affect how your listener or reader thinks about a topic and about you, the speaker or writer. This is particularly true in that important work document, the résumé. Because your résumé needs to clearly highlight your best qualifications for a job, it's worth taking the time to think about how best to organize it. There are two basic patterns for successful résumés. The *chronological pattern* provides a list of your previous positions and accomplishments in reverse order (that is, the most recent job first). It is most useful when your job history shows progress and you are staying in the same career field. The *functional pattern,* similar to classification in this chapter, emphasizes the particular skills and abilities you have developed and downplays when you developed them. It is most useful when you want to emphasize skills you haven't used in recent jobs, when you are changing careers or reentering the job market, or when you want to show experience gained through courses or volunteer work.

1. Consider your own work and education history. Do you think a chronological or functional résumé would be more to your advantage? Why?

2. Imagine you have spent the last ten years raising your children and running your household. What skills and abilities from your experience could you add to your functional résumé?

The Web Connection

1. Meet Melvil Dewey

   http://www.thrall.org/dewey/dewbio.htm

   The Dewey Decimal System is one of the most famous classification systems. Read about the man who created it at this site from the Middletown Thrall Library in New York State. Determine what kind of classification system your library uses. Find out the general call numbers for the subjects you are studying.

2. The Amazing Rube Goldberg

   http://www.rubegoldberg.com/

   The machines in Rube Goldberg's cartoons depict cause and effect in a mechanical and humorous way. See some of his drawings as well as real inventions inspired by his imagination at this site dedicated to Goldberg. Draw or create your own Rube Goldberg machine.

3. Storyboarding

   http://westernreservepublicmedia.org/producer/vid2sb1.htm

   Filmmakers use storyboarding to lay out a sequence of shots. This site from Western Reserve Public Media shows an example of the use of storyboarding. Create a storyboard for a brief story of your own or for part of your day.

12 Note Taking for Class Lectures

Do You Know?

Why should you learn systematic approaches for effective listening and note taking in lectures?

What techniques can you develop to record the content and organization of lectures?

What are the various lecture styles, and how can you recognize them?

How can you identify and use instructors' thought patterns to take good notes?

How should you edit and review your notes?

Your instructor's lectures are a primary source of information. Think of them as his or her personalized explanation of course content. Note taking is your way of recording this important explanation. This chapter discusses listening and note-taking techniques, describes various lecture styles, demonstrates how to anticipate and identify lecturers' thought patterns, and presents systems for editing and reviewing your notes.

■ Sharpening Your Listening Skills

During college lectures, listening is your primary means of taking in information. Listening is also an essential skill in most careers. It is estimated that between 35 and 40 percent of a white-collar worker's day is spent listening. Yet research indicates that most adult students or employees do not listen efficiently. Rate the effectiveness of your listening skills by completing the questionnaire shown in Figure 12.1 on p. 241.

The Distinction Between Hearing and Listening

Have you ever found yourself not listening to a friend who is talking to you? Instead, perhaps you are thinking about something else entirely or about what

FIGURE 12.1
Rate Your Learning and Note-Taking Skills

Respond to each of the following questions by checking "Always," "Sometimes," or "Never."

	Always	*Sometimes*	*Never*
1. Do you tune in to a lecture before it begins by rereading previous notes orassigned material?	❏	❏	❏
2. Do you pay attention to the speaker's gestures, tone of voice, and bodylanguage?	❏	❏	❏
3. Do you reread and revise your notes after you have taken them?	❏	❏	❏
4. Do you use abbreviations instead of writing out long or frequently usedwords?	❏	❏	❏
5. Are you able to stay alert and focused throughout a lecture?	❏	❏	❏
6. Do you try to record only what is important in the lecture?	❏	❏	❏
7. Before attending the lecture, do you read the textbook assignment that isrelated to the lecture?	❏	❏	❏
8. Are you able to take notes on material that is boring, technical, or overlycomplicated?	❏	❏	❏
9. Do your notes reflect the lecturer's organization?	❏	❏	❏
10. Do you review your notes periodically to keep the content fresh in your mind?	❏	❏	❏

If you answered "Sometimes" or "Never" to more than one or two questions listed above, your note-taking skills need improvement.

you'll say next. Have you ever found yourself not listening to an instructor during class? In each case, the speaker's voice was loud and clear; you could *hear* but you were not *listening*. Hearing is a passive process in which sound waves are automatically received by the ear. In contrast, listening is an intellectual activity that involves comprehension and interpretation of incoming information. Listening is intentional—something you do deliberately and purposefully. It requires your attention and your concentration.

Tips for Effective Listening

Use the following suggestions to sharpen your listening skills:

◆ **Tune in.** Focus your attention on the lecture or presentation before it begins. Recall what you know about the topic. Review related reading assignments while you are waiting for the lecture to begin.

◆ **Listen carefully to the speaker's opening comments.** As your mind refocuses from prior tasks and problems, it is easy to miss the speaker's opening remarks, which may be among the most important. Here the speaker may establish connections with prior lectures, identify his or her purpose, or describe the lecture's content or organization.

◆ **Attempt to understand the lecturer's purpose.** If it is not stated explicitly, try to reason it out. Is the purpose to present facts, discuss and raise questions, demonstrate a trend or pattern, or present a technique or procedure?

◆ **Maintain eye contact with the lecturer.** Eye contact improves communication; you will feel more involved and find it easier to stay interested in the lecture.

◆ **Stay active by asking mental questions.** Questions will keep your attention focused. Ask: What key point is the lecturer making? How does it fit with previously discussed key points? How is the lecture organized? How will the lecturer prove the point?

◆ **Anticipate what is to follow.** A good lecturer provides clues about his or her organization. Try to predict or anticipate what the lecturer is leading up to or what topics will follow.

◆ **Stick with the lecture.** When a lecture becomes confusing, complicated, or technical, it is tempting to tune out, telling yourself you'll figure it out later by reading your textbook. Resist this temptation by taking detailed notes. These notes, when reviewed after the lecture, will be valuable as you try to straighten out your confusion.

◆ **Avoid emotional involvement.** If the lecture is on a controversial issue or the lecturer mentions a topic or word that has emotional meaning for you, it is easy to become emotionally involved. When this occurs, your listening sometimes becomes selective—you hear what you want to hear. Instead, try to remain objective and open-minded. Force yourself to concentrate on the speaker's position, not your own.

♦ **Focus on content, not delivery.** It is easy to become so annoyed, upset, charmed by, or engaged with the lecturer as a person that you fail to comprehend the message he or she is conveying. Force yourself to focus on the message and disregard personal characteristics such as an annoying laugh or overused expressions.

♦ **Focus on ideas, not facts.** If you concentrate on recording and remembering separate, unconnected facts, you may miss key concepts, trends, and patterns.

♦ **Fill the gap between rate of speech and rate of thinking.** The rate of speech is much slower than the speed of thought. To listen most effectively in class, use this gap to think about the lecture. Anticipate what is to follow, think of situations where the information may be applied, pose questions, or make the information fit with your prior knowledge and experience.

■ How to Start with an Advantage

Here are a few suggestions that will enable you to approach lectures confidently and efficiently—with distinct advantages over students who just appear in class with a pen.

Get Organized

Use the following tips to approach note taking in an organized, systematic manner:

♦ **Organize a notebook for each course.** Use standard size, $8\frac{1}{2} \times 11$ inches. Not enough information fits on a page in smaller notebooks, making review more difficult. Either spiral or loose-leaf notebooks are acceptable; loose-leaf types allow you to add class handouts, review sheets, and quizzes beside the notes to which they pertain.

♦ **Use ink.** Pencil tends to smear.

♦ **Date your notes for later reference.**

♦ **Get used to sitting in the same place, preferably near the front of the room.** You will feel more comfortable and less distracted if you have your own seat. Sitting near the front is especially important in large lecture halls. You will feel as if you are in more direct contact with the instructor and will be able to see as well as hear emphasis as you observe his or her facial expressions and gestures.

♦ **Make it a point to attend all lectures, even if attendance is not mandatory.** Borrowing and copying a classmate's notes is not a substitute for attending the lecture, since it does not involve the key learning processes of identifying, organizing, and condensing information. If it is absolutely necessary to miss a class, be certain to borrow and photocopy several students' notes. Then, after you have reviewed each set, write your own set of notes. Doing so forces you to think about, compare, and decide what is important.

Be Thoroughly Prepared for Each Lecture

Lecture note taking will be easier and you will understand and remember more if you prepare in advance by reading related text assignments. It is tempting to delay reading an assignment until after the lecture because a text assignment seems easier once you have heard the lecture on the same topic. However, reading the text in advance will improve your comprehension of the lecture.

If you are unable to read an assignment completely before a particular lecture, preview it using the procedure described in Chapter 13 to obtain a basic familiarity, and plan to read it after the lecture.

Overcoming Common Problems

Instructors present lectures differently, use various lecture styles, and organize their subjects in different ways. Therefore, it is common to experience difficulty taking notes in one or more courses. Table 12.1 identifies common problems associated with lecture note taking and offers possible solutions.

TABLE 12.1   Common Note-Taking Problems

Problem	Solution
"My mind wanders and I get bored."	Sit in the front of the room. Be certain to preview assignments. Pose questions you expect to be answered in the lecture.
"The instructor talks too fast."	Develop a shorthand system; use abbreviations. Leave blanks and fill them in later.
"The lecturer rambles."	Preview correlating text assignments to determine organizing principles.
"Some ideas don't seem to fit anywhere."	Record them in the margin or in parentheses within your notes for reassessment later during editing (see p. 263).
"Everything seems important." "Nothing seems important."	You have not identified key concepts and may lack necessary or background knowledge. Locate a more basic textbook that discusses the topic.
"I can't spell all the new technical terms."	Record them phonetically, the way they sound; fill in correct spellings during editing (see p. 264).

SKILLS IN ACTION

Starting with an Advantage: Case Study

Consider the following case study:

> Jan shows up for her math class 15 minutes late because she couldn't find her calculator, which she never did find. She sneaks into the back of the room so that her professor won't notice; then she has to squint because she can't see the blackboard or the equations her instructor is writing on it. Fortunately, one of her classmates lets her copy the worked-out equations from his notebook. But all she has is a red pen, and she keeps having to scratch things out and rewrite them. She's feeling frustrated because the material shouldn't be this difficult, which was why she didn't bother to read the textbook assignment before class—she thought she understood the material enough to skip the assignment. One of the instructor's calculations makes no sense to her at all, but she doesn't want to raise her hand and interrupt her instructor, or call attention to the fact that she was late.

Make a list of at least five mistakes Jan has made that put her at a disadvantage right from the beginning. What can and should she do to avoid repeating these mistakes and instead enter the class with an advantage?

■ Recording Appropriate Content and Organization

The worst mistake you can make when taking notes is to try to record everything the instructor says. If you are constantly writing, you have little time to think—to understand, assimilate, or react to what is being said. The following sections offer some general suggestions on recording and organizing key information.

Identify Main Ideas

The main ideas of a lecture are the points your instructor emphasizes. They are the major ideas that the details, explanations, examples, and general discussion support. Frequently, instructors give clues such as the following to show what is important in a lecture.

◆ **Points repeated.** When an instructor repeats a statement, he or she is indicating to you that the idea or concept is important. Look for signals such as "This, you will recall . . ." or "As we saw last week in a different framework . . . ."

REAL STUDENTS SPEAK

Tony Chatila
———
Miami-Dade
Community College
Miami, Florida

Background: Tony is a freshman at Miami-Dade Community College where he is pursuing an associate's degree in liberal arts.

Goals: To transfer to the University of Miami and obtain a bachelor's degree. He is considering long term of goals of working in sports medicine or as a pediatrician.

Advice on Taking Notes in Lecture: I don't like to take too many notes. I focus on the main points and anything I don't understand. I use abbreviations and write down key words, like Pearl Harbor, December 7, 1941. If the teacher is talking about things I've already learned, I don't write it down, but if I don't know the information or it's interesting or if I don't understand it, then I write it down. Later I'll check it out. I always take notes on anything written on the board, and I always review my notes before a test to make sure I remember everything. Always keep a focus in class, don't fool around, and try not to write too much.

◆ **Change in voice.** Some lecturers change the tone or pitch of their voices when they are trying to emphasize major points. A speaker's voice may get louder or softer or higher or lower as he or she presents important ideas.

◆ **Change in rate of speech.** Speakers may slow down as they discuss important concepts. Sometimes a speaker goes so slowly that he or she seems to be dictating information. If, for example, a speaker giving a definition pauses slightly between each word or phrase, it is a way of telling you that the definition is important and you should write it down.

◆ **Listing and numbering points.** Lecturers often directly state that there are "three important causes" or "four significant effects" or "five possible situations" as they begin discussing a topic. These expressions are clues to the material's importance.

◆ **Writing on the chalkboard or using PowerPoint.** Some lecturers write or project key words or outlines of major ideas as they speak. Although not all important ideas are presented in written form, you can be sure that what is written is important.

◆ **Direct announcement.** Occasionally, an instructor will announce straightforwardly that a particular concept or idea is especially important. He or she may begin by saying, "Particularly important to remember is . . ." or

"One important fact that you must keep in mind is . . . ." The instructor may even hint that such information would make a good exam question. Be sure to mark hints like these in your notes. Emphasize these items with an asterisk or write "exam?" in the margin.

♦ **Nonverbal clues.** Many speakers provide clues to what they feel is important through their movements and actions as well as their words. Some lecturers walk toward their audience as they make a major point. Others may use hand gestures, pound the table, or pace back and forth as they present key ideas. While each speaker is different, most speakers use some type of nonverbal clues.

At the beginning of each course, be sure to analyze each professor's means of emphasis. Think of this analysis as a means of tuning in or getting on the same wavelength as your professor.

| EXERCISE 12.1 | **Analyzing an Instructor's Lecture Technique** |

Directions *Analyze the lecture technique of one of your instructors. Attend one lecture, and as you take notes, try to be particularly aware of how he or she lets you know what is important. After the lecture, analyze your instructor's lecture technique, using the following questions.*

1. How does he or she emphasize what is important?
2. What nonverbal clues are evident?

Then analyze your note-taking skills.

1. What note-taking problems did you encounter?
2. What can be done to overcome these problems?

Record Details and Examples

A difficult part of taking notes is deciding how much detail to include. You cannot record everything because the normal speed of speech greatly exceeds the normal speed of writing. As a rule of thumb, record a brief phrase to summarize each major supporting detail.

If an instructor gives you several examples of a particular law, situation, or problem, be sure to write down in summary form at least one example. Record more than one if you have time. While at the time of the lecture it may seem that you completely understand what is being discussed, you will find that a few weeks later you really do need examples to help you recall the lecture.

Reflect the Lecture's Organization

As you record the main ideas and details, organize them so that you can easily see how the lecture was organized and recall the relative importance of ideas. A simple way to show a lecture's organization is to use a system of indentation. Retain a regular margin on your paper. Start your notes on the most important of the topics at the left margin. For less important main ideas, indent your notes slightly. For major details, indent slightly farther. Indent even farther for examples and other details. The rule of thumb to follow is this: The less important the idea, the farther it should be indented. Use bullets or dashes to make your indentations easily distinguishable. Your notes might be organized like this:

Sample Informal Outline

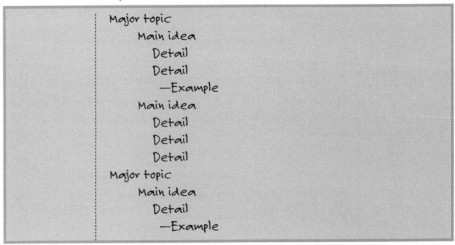

Notice that the sample looks like an outline but is missing the roman numerals (I, II, III), capital letters (A, B, C), and Arabic numerals (1, 2, 3) that usually enumerate an outline. This system of note taking accomplishes the same goal as an outline—it stratifies information to show, at a glance, the relative importance of the various facts or ideas listed. If the organization of a lecture is obvious, use a number or letter system in addition to indenting.

Since not all instructors' lectures follow a tightly organized pattern, it is not always possible to develop an outline. Try not to spend too much time during the lecture thinking about the outline format. Be primarily concerned with recording ideas; you can always reorganize your notes after the lecture.

The notes in Figures 12.2 and 12.3 (pp. 249–250) were taken by two students on the same lecture. The notes in Figure 12.2 clearly indicate main ideas, important details, and examples and reflect the lecture's organization. The notes in Figure 12.3 are lengthy and do not emphasize key ideas. Read and evaluate each set of notes.

FIGURE 12.2
An Effective Note-Taking Style

Marketing 101

Consumer Behavior

How Buyers Buy
2 factors involved:
   defs
    1. product adoption = consumer's decision to buy
    2. product diffusion = rate of adoption by
        consumers throughout market
prod w/ quick diffusion = good chance of success
  " " slow   "   must sustain loss
                 until diff. increases
A. Types of Adopters – 5 classes, based on
      speed of adoption
  1. innovators – 1st to buy   young, bit eccentric
    rely on printed info rather than salespeople
  2. early adopters – socially, financially well-to-do.
    if this group doesn't buy – product will fail
  3. early majority adopters – careful, cautious
    – most influenced by salespeople, ads
  4. late majority adopters – opinion followers
    rely heavily on friends, family
  5. Laggards – fearful of new, older people, less
    educated peers are primary source of info
B. Factors affecting Diffusion

Take Notes More Efficiently

If you record main ideas, details, and examples, using the indentation system to show the lecture's organization, you will take adequate notes. However, the following tips can help you make note taking easier, make your notes more complete, and make study and review easier.

- ◆ **Leave blank spaces.** To make your notes more readable and to make it easier to see the organization of ideas, leave plenty of blank space. If you know you missed a detail or definition, leave additional blank space. Fill it in later by checking with a friend or referring to your text.

FIGURE 12.3
An Ineffective Note-Taking Style

<u>Marketing 101</u>

What Makes Buyers Buy What They Do

There are two factors involved: product adoption and product diffusion. Adoption – decision to buy. Diffusion means adoption throughout the market.

There are 5 classes of buyers

Innovators are the first to buy. They are young and eccentric and rely on printed information rather than salespeople. People who are socially and financially well off are early adopters. If this group doesn't buy the product will fail. Early majority adopters are most influenced by salespeople & ads.

Late majority adopters are opinion followers who rely heavily on information from friends and family. Laggards are older people who are less educated and are the last to buy. Their peers are their primary source.

There are several factors that affect diffusion.

◆ **Mark assignments.** Occasionally, an instructor will announce an assignment or test in the middle of a lecture. As you jot it down, write "Assignment" or "Test Date" in the margin so that you can find it easily and transfer it to your assignment notebook.

◆ **Mark ideas that are unclear.** If an instructor presents a fact or idea that is unclear, put a question mark in the margin. Later, ask your instructor or a classmate for clarification.

◆ **Don't plan to recopy your notes.** Some students recopy their notes each evening. They feel that recopying helps them review the information and think it is a good way to study. Actually, recopying often becomes a mechanical process that takes a lot of time but very little thought. Time spent recopying can be better spent reorganizing them or reviewing the notes in a manner that will be suggested later in this chapter (see p. 261).

◆ **Consider recording lectures in special situations.** Students who lack confidence in their note-taking ability find it reassuring to record lectures until they are certain they are able to take accurate and complete notes. Other students record lectures from a particularly difficult course. Also, students who must spend large amounts of time commuting to campus listen to lectures recorded on their laptops during this time.

Because you spend at least an additional hour in listening for every hour spent in class, recording is usually time-consuming and inefficient in terms of the time spent relative to the amount of learning that occurs.

Generally, recording is not recommended. However, there are obvious exceptions. Students for whom English is not their first language often find the process valuable. If you do decide to record a lecture, be certain to obtain the permission of your instructor.

◆ **Try not to write complete sentences.** Use as few words as possible. You will be able to record more information, and review will be easier.

◆ **Use abbreviations.** To save time, try to use abbreviations instead of writing out long or frequently used words. If you are taking a course in psychology, you would not want to write out p-s-y-c-h-o-l-o-g-y each time the word is used. It is much faster to use the abbreviation "psych." Try to develop abbreviations for each subject area you are studying. The following abbreviations, devised by a student in business management, will give you an idea of the possibilities and choices you have. Notice that both common words and specialized words are abbreviated.

Common Words	Abbreviation	Specialized Words	Abbreviation
and	+	organization	org.
with	w/	management	man.
compare, comparison	comp.	data bank	D.B.
importance	imp't.	structure	str.
advantage	adv.	evaluation	eval.
introduction	intro.	management by objectives	MBO
continued	cont'd.	management information system	MIS
		organizational development	OD
		communication	comm.
		simulation	sim.

Develop Creative Note-Taking Systems

Do not hesitate to create variations of the traditional lecture note-taking format. Here are a few possibilities; do not try to use them all in each course. Instead, choose those that fit your learning style and the individual courses you are taking.

◆ **Consider using color.** Either during the lecture or after it, use different colored pens or highlighters to distinguish particular types of information. For example, in psychology you might record or mark definitions in green and use blue to identify important research studies.

◆ **Create a response column.** Use it to record your own thoughts and reactions to the lecture.

◆ **Leave space for a summary.** Some students find it beneficial to write a brief summary at the end of each lecture.

◆ **Leave space for maps.** Especially if you are a spatial learner, you may find it helpful to draw or see diagrams or maps (see Chapter 14) that translate ideas from words to pictures.

◆ **Add an application column.** Consider adding a column or section of your notes in which you can add examples that illustrate lecture content. You might add these during the lecture as they come to mind, or do so later as you review your notes.

■ Taking Notes on Your Laptop

Some students bring their laptop to class and use them to take notes during class. There are both advantages and disadvantages, as well as do's and don'ts, for taking notes using a computer.

The Advantages

◆ Your notes are clear, legible, and easy to review.
◆ You can share notes with classmates easily.
◆ You can quickly improve your notes by reorganizing and editing (see p. 261)
◆ You can integrate notes you take from textbook reading with lecture notes.
◆ By cutting and pasting, you can pull together related notes on a topic when studying for exams.

The Disadvantages

◆ Carrying a laptop can be cumbersome, and you have to worry about its security.

- ◆ If you haven't tried computer note taking before, it may be distracting. You may find yourself concentrating on the mechanics of taking notes rather than on lecture content.
- ◆ Because you can only see a screen full of content at a time, you may not be able to see connections and logical progressions of ideas. You may end up printing your notes for study and review.

Do's and Don'ts

If you decide to take notes electronically, use the following tips to make the process work for you:

- ◆ Do make sure you can plug in your laptop or that you have sufficient battery power.
- ◆ Do set up a folder for each course. Create a separate file for each day's notes; include the date of the lecture in the name of the file.
- ◆ Do save your document frequently, so you don't lose anything.
- ◆ Do keep a pen and paper handy to record diagrams, drawings, and figures.
- ◆ Don't allow distracting programs such as e-mail and instant messaging compete for your attention.
- ◆ Don't risk interrupting class with annoying beeps and buzzes. Turn the sound off.

■ Working with Various Lecture Formats

Not all instructors lecture in the same way or for the same purpose. In fact, two instructors teaching the same course who use the same text may use very different lecture formats. Lectures may differ in focus, purpose, and organization, as well as content. There are four general lecture formats: factual, conceptual, analytical, and discussion.

The Factual Lecture Format

The **factual lecture format** centers around a straightforward presentation of information: facts, definitions, historical events, rules, principles, processes, and procedures. Many introductory-level course lectures fall into this category. The primary purpose of this type of lecture is to present and explain. You must acquire a base of knowledge as you begin to study a new discipline. As one psychology instructor tells his students: "You have to learn about psychology before you can think about and work within it." Here are a few examples of lecture topics using the factual style:

Course	Lecture Topic
Public speaking	Analyzing Your Audience
American government	The Structure of American Elections
Nursing	Fluid and Electrolyte Balance
Business communication	Strategies for Interviewing

Here are a few suggestions for taking notes from factual lectures:

◆ Be as accurate and complete as possible.
◆ If you have difficulty recording all the needed information, leave blank spaces and fill in the information later. Check with a classmate, if necessary.
◆ Don't waste time rewriting information that duplicates what is contained in your text; jot down the topic and a page reference.

The notes shown in Figure 12.2 on p. 249 were taken from a factual lecture.

THINKING CRITICALLY
. . . About Lectures

Although listening to a lecture is demanding, try to *think about* the lecture as well as take notes on it. Here are a few questions to ask:

Before the Lecture

1. What content and focus do you anticipate?
2. How does the lecture topic fit with the previous lecture?

During the Lecture

1. What are the most important ideas and concepts?
2. What examples from your own experience come to mind?
3. What information is unclear, if any?

After the Lecture

1. What did you learn from the lecture?
2. What levels of thinking does the lecture require? Focus especially on applying, analyzing, evaluating, and creating.

The Conceptual Lecture Format

The **conceptual lecture format** focuses on the analysis and interpretation of information. It is concerned with ideas, trends, and concepts. Although factual information may provide the basis of this type of lecture, the focus is often on issues, policies, problems, and perspectives. This format is common in philosophy, special-issue classes such as "Environmental Problems," sociology, and economics. Here are a few examples of lecture topics that employ a conceptual format:

Course	Lecture Topic
Social problems	Welfare: Myths and Realities
Ecology	Solving the World Food Shortage
Marketing and advertising	Controlling Consumer Behavior

Use the following tips for taking notes on conceptual lectures:

◆ **Focus on concepts, or broad, organizing ideas.** For example, it is much more important to record the concept that "impressionism, as an art form, dominated the last 20 years of the 19th century" than it is to record every fact your instructor gives you about impressionism.

◆ **Record only as much detail as you need to understand and recall the concept.** Choose the most vivid details or those that provide the strongest evidence.

◆ **Record key details on which your instructor spends the most time.** A sample set of notes from a conceptual lecture is shown in Figure 12.4 (p. 256).

The Analytical Lecture Format

The **analytical lecture format** is used in courses that examine literary or artistic works, social issues, mathematical or scientific problems, and philosophical, moral, or religious issues. This style is evident in literature, art, mathematics, science, and philosophy courses, as well as in seminars that focus on a particular social issue, historical or literary period, or art form. In analytical lectures, close study is usually followed by interpretation. Personal reaction is often important, as is assessment of value, worth, and aesthetic qualities. A search for reasons and interpretation of actions or published works is often involved.

FIGURE 12.4
Conceptual Style Notes

<u>Nuclear Arms Race & Third World Countries</u>

basic attitude is one of resentment

1. 3rd world countries are the poor getting poorer while watching rich countries get richer
   ∴ they deplore the expenditure of valuable economic & natural resources on "war games"
2. 3rd world knows that the US and S. Union have spent trillions on the arms race
   ∴ resent claims by these 2 countries that they lack eco. capability to assist them fight poverty
3. Superpowers attempt to establish influence in 3rd world countries
   ∴ 3rd world countries feel "used" and suspicious of offers of "friendship"

Here are a few topics of lectures that use the analytical format:

Course	Lecture Topic
Literature	Steinbeck's Use of Symbolism
Philosophy	Mill's Theory of Utilitarianism
Business law	Antitrust Litigation: Three Illustrative Cases

To take notes on analytical lectures, use the following suggestions.

◆ Record themes, essential characteristics, theories, the significance of related events, and important facts.
◆ When analyzing a case, poem, story, or painting, make notes in the margin of your textbook as it is discussed.
◆ Focus on the significance or importance of the work being analyzed.

Figure 12.5 shows a sample portion of notes taken on the analysis of Keats's poem "Ode on a Grecian Urn."

FIGURE 12.5
Analytical Style Notes

John Keats (1795–1821)

theme of permanence
figures on urn never change

Ode on a Grecian Urn — 2 interpretations

1820

refers to urn

1. *as yet*

Thou still unravished bride of quietness, 2. *motionless*
    Thou foster-child of silence and slow time,
Sylvan historian, who canst thus express

rustic
woodland
scene   A flowery tale more sweetly than our rhyme:
What leaf-fringed legend haunts about thy shape *Tempe— beautiful rural* 5
    Of deities or mortals, or of both, *valley in Greece*
        In Tempe or the dales of Arcady — *Valleys of Arcadia—*
    What men or gods are these? What maidens loth? *often symbolize pastoral*
What mad pursuit? What struggle to escape? *ideal*

feeling
of lack   What pipes and timbrels? What wild ecstasy? 10

Heard melodies are sweet, but those unheard *words don't quite express*
    Are sweeter; therefore, ye soft pipes, play on; *thought, what is imagined is*
Not to the sensual° ear, but, more endeared, *better than what is expressed*
    Pipe to the spirit ditties of no tone: — *imagined sounds* *physical*
Fair youth, beneath the trees, thou canst not leave 15
    Thy song, nor ever can those trees be bare; *nothing will change*
        Bold Lover, never, never canst thou kiss,
Though winning near the goal–yet, do not grieve; *yet never will*
        She cannot fade, though thou hast not thy bliss, *achieve the goal*
permanence
    For ever wilt thou love, and she be fair! . . . 20

The Discussion Format

This form cannot be called a lecture format since the emphasis is not on the presentation of ideas but on their exchange. The purpose of **class discussion** is to involve students in thinking about, reacting to, and evaluating the topic at hand. Discussion-style classes are common in disciplines that involve controversial issues or subjective evaluation.

For discussion classes, advance preparation is the key. In fact, you need to spend more time preparing for a discussion than you do studying your notes afterward. Plan to spend considerable time reading, making notes, and organizing your thinking about the topic. Make lists of questions, points with which you agree or disagree, good or poor examples, and strong or weak arguments. These lists will provide a basis for your input into the discussion.

When participating in class discussion, students often neglect to take notes. While careful, detailed note taking may not be as critical for class discussions as for lectures, try to keep a record of key points in the discussion. Not only will the notes be valuable for later review, they are also useful for immediate reaction and response during the discussion. If you have recorded someone's argument or objection, you are better prepared to defend or criticize it than if you do so purely from memory.

You might also use your notes to outline or sketch a response before you present it. Writing is a vehicle that clarifies your thinking. By informally outlining or jotting down the points you intend to make, you will organize and focus your thoughts, thus improving your contribution.

Discussion notes are much less detailed and reflect less organization than lecture notes. Think of them as a chronological record of the discussion, a list of ideas and topics discussed. After class, it is especially important to reread and edit discussion notes (see p. 261).

EXERCISE 12.2

Working Together

Identifying Patterns

Directions   *Each student should bring notebooks from two courses he or she is currently taking. Students should exchange notebooks and identify the predominant format used in several lectures.*

SKILLS IN ACTION

Analyzing Your Current Courses

Analyze each of the classes you attend next week, and draw a table using the following format. For lecture format, indicate whether that particular class followed the *factual format, conceptual format, analytical format,* or *discussion format.* (Note that for each course, your instructor may follow different formats on different days.) In the "Takeaway" column, write a brief summary (no more than two sentences) of the key idea(s) you took away from that particular class, or the progress you made.

Course Name	Date	Class Topic*	Lecture Format	Takeaway

*Note that the class topic is often directly presented in the course syllabus, so you should always keep your course syllabus handy for each course you take.

■ Note Taking and Learning Style

Refresh your memory of your learning style by reviewing the results on pp. 134–137. Your learning style influences your listening skills and your note-taking ability. Certain lecture formats, too, may be easier for you to work with due to your learning style. Auditory learners, of course, are well suited to listening and note taking, while visual learners are less inclined to learn by listening. Verbal learners find the lecture mode more appropriate than do spatial learners, who prefer a more concrete mode of presentation. Table 12.2 offers suggestions for adapting your listening and note-taking abilities for various aspects of your learning style.

TABLE 12.2   Adapting Note Taking to Your Learning Style

Learning Characteristic	Note-Taking Strategy
Auditory	Take advantage of your advantage! Take thorough and complete notes.
Visual	Work on note-taking skills; practice by recording a lecture; analyze and revise your notes.
Creative	Annotate your notes, recording impressions, reactions, spin-off ideas, related ideas.
Pragmatic	Reorganize notes during editing. Pay attention to the lecturer's organization.
Social	Review and edit notes with a classmate. Compare notes with others.
Independent	Choose seating in close contact with the instructor; avoid distracting groups of students.
Applied	Think of applications (record as annotations). Write questions in the margin about applications.
Conceptual	Discover idea relationships. Watch for patterns.
Spatial	Add diagrams, maps during editing.
Verbal	Record the lecturer's diagrams, drawings—but translate into words during editing.

■ Using the Lecturer's Thought Patterns

If you approach lectures simply as a means of acquiring information, you are missing an important learning opportunity. Lectures reveal how the instructor thinks: how he or she processes, organizes, and approaches the material. Understanding the lecturer's thought patterns will show you what to record and help you follow the lecturer's organization.

Anticipating and Identifying Patterns in Lectures

The most common thought patterns used in lectures are those discussed in Chapter 11: order or sequence, comparison and contrast, cause and effect, classification, definition, and listing. Lecturers often use various devices to make their pattern of organization apparent.

◆ **Organizing statements.** At the beginning of a lecture, instructors frequently announce the topic and provide clues to their approach. For instance, a psychology instructor may open a lecture by saying:

> This morning we will define behaviorism by studying two of its leading advocates—
> B. F. Skinner and Watson. Both believed that . . .

From this statement you can predict a comparison and perhaps contrast pattern between Skinner and Watson, as well as discussion of the characteristics of behaviorism (definition pattern).

◆ **Transitions.** Good speakers and lecturers use transitions to assist their audiences in anticipating and following their train of thought. As they move from point to point, they often use a transitional word or phrase to signal the change. These transitions are similar to those used in writing, except that they tend to be more direct and frequent than in written language. If, for example, a lecturer says, "Consequently, we have . . . ," you can anticipate a cause and effect pattern.

◆ **Lecture format.** A lecturer's thought patterns are, to some extent, reflected in the format of lecture used. An instructor who uses a discussion format is more likely to employ the cause and effect or comparison or contrast patterns than to follow listing or order/sequence patterns. For example, a political science class discussion on Third World countries might involve such topics as reasons for their growing importance or their effects on other countries.

Patterns as an Aid to Organizing Your Notes

Once you have identified a lecturer's predominant pattern, you can use that knowledge to organize your lecture notes. Note-taking tips for each pattern are presented in Table 12.3.

TABLE 12.3   Using Patterns in Lecture Note Taking

Pattern	Note-Taking Tips
Order or sequence	Record dates; focus on order and sequence; use timeline for historical events; draw diagrams; record in order of importance; outline events or steps in a process.
Comparison and contrast	Record similarities, differences, and basis of comparison; use two columns or make a chart.
Cause and effect	Distinguish causes from effects; use diagrams.
Classification	Use outline form; list characteristics and distinguishing features.
Definition	Record general group or class; list distinguishing characteristics; include several examples.
Listing	Record in list or outline form; record order of presentation.

EXERCISE 12.3

Predicting Patterns

Directions   *For each lecture topic, predict what pattern(s) might be used.*

Course	Lecture Title/Topics
American government	The Bill of Rights—Then and Now
Speech communications	Ways to Research Your Topic
Nursing	Transfusion Reactions
Human sexuality	Components of Interpersonal Intimacy
Engineering/technology	The Rationale for the Use of Standard Parts

EXERCISE 12.4

Identifying Patterns

Directions   *Review your notes from each class lecture you attended last week, and identify the predominant patterns used in each lecture. Substantiate your answers.*

■ Editing and Reviewing Your Notes

You should not assume that your lecture notes are accurate and complete or that simply by taking notes you have learned the information the notes record. Two more steps are necessary: (1) you must edit your notes, making them thorough and accurate, and (2) you need to develop and use a system for study and review.

Edit Lecture Notes

Even experienced note takers find that they often miss some information and are unable to record as many details or examples as they would like during a lecture. Fortunately, the solution is simple. Do not plan on taking a final and complete set of notes during the lecture. Instead, record just enough during the lecture to help you remember a main idea, detail, or example. Leave plenty of blank space; then, as soon as possible after class, review the notes. Fill in the missing information and expand the notes, adding any details or examples. The process of revising notes to make them more complete and accurate is called *editing*.

Editing notes for a one-hour lecture should take no more than five or ten minutes. Some students find editing is easier when working with groups of two or three classmates. Group interaction and discussion provide a focus on the lectures, and one person may have recorded information that others did not.

The longer the time lapse between the note taking and the editing, the more facts and examples you will be unable to recall and fill in.

The sample lecture notes in Figure 12.6 have been edited. The notes taken during the lecture are in dark print; the additions and changes made during the editing are in the shaded areas. Read the notes, noticing the types of information added during editing.

Use the Recall Clue System (The Cornell System)

The recall clue system helps make the review and study of lecture notes easier and more effective. It involves the following steps:

◆ **Leave a two-inch margin at the left side of each page of notes.**
◆ **Keep the margin blank while you are taking notes.**
◆ **After you have edited your notes, fill in the left margin with words and phrases that briefly summarize the notes.** These *recall clues* should be words that will trigger your memory and help you recall the complete information in your notes.

These clues function as memory tags. They help you retrieve information that is labeled with these tags. Figure 12.7 (p. 264) shows a sample of notes in which the recall clue system has been used.

To study your notes using the recall clues:

1. **Cover up the notes with a sheet of paper, exposing only the recall clues in the left margin.**

2. **Read the first recall clue and try to remember the information in the portion of the notes beside it.**

3. **Slide the paper down and check that portion to see if you remembered all the important facts.** If you remembered only part of the information, cover up that portion of your notes and again check your recall.

4. **Continue checking until you are satisfied that you can remember all the important facts.**

5. **Move on to the next recall clue on the page, testing and checking again.**

FIGURE 12.6
Sample Edited Notes

Econ. 102   Unemployment
A. Unempl ^oyment Rate
  -calculated by gov't
  →uses labor force as base rate = % of ^labor force
  not working
  This stat misleading-
  1. Counts part-time workers ←   ex., teenager working in family business is counted
  labor force = all 16 yr olds & older who are employed or unemployed but actively seeking work
  2. Counts only those actively seeking work
    - many are unemployed but have given up trying to find a job
      ∴unemp. rate may be under slated
B. Types of Unemployment
  1. frictional - 5-6%
  def.- unempl. due to movm't from job job or entering ^labor market
      for 1st time
    - This type is desirable - suggests healthy economy
  2. cyclical -
    - depression   ← - is usually high during
  def.- associated w/ cycles of the economy
  ? - greatest in industries producing durable goods
      ex. autos, appliances
  ? - less severe in non-durable goods ex. clothing, food.

A variation on the recall clue system that students have found effective is to write questions rather than summary words and phrases in the margin. The questions trigger your memory and enable you to recall the information that answers your question. With the questions you can test yourself, thereby simulating an exam. They also force you to think and actively respond to course content.

FIGURE 12.7
Recall Clue System

4 factors affecting comm.	Bus. Comm.
	Flow of communication ↔
	- regardless of flow – must be concerned
	w/ 1)accuracy, 2)completeness, 3)lack of bias,
	4)proper transmission of the message
3 directions of comm.	A. Downward Comm. ↓
	- sending info. to employees at lower level of
	company
downward comm.	- usually communicating policies, orders, directives,
	goals
	- usually no response expected or received
adv. and disadv upward comm.	B. Upward Comm. ↑
	- sending info to someone above you in the organiz.
	Often perceived as risky, -can have positive effects
	if done well—ex-promotion, new assignment
	C. Horizontal ↔
uses of horizontal comm.	- information exchanged w/ employee at same level
	- usually verbal
	- exchanging ideas or working out technical problems
	- usually found at lower levels of company

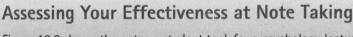

SKILLS IN ACTION

Assessing Your Effectiveness at Note Taking

Figure 12.8 shows the notes a student took for a psychology lecture on stress. Review the notes and then critique them using the checklist in Table 12.4.

FIGURE 12.8
Notes from a Psychology Class

Coping with stress is a problem solving activity done by direct action –
    behavior that masters it. Palliation – way of addressing symptoms of
    stress
    stress and your ability to cope are affected by cognitive appraisal –
    also by sympathetic support –

Predictability –
    – more stress if unpredictable advance notice helps

Control affects the intensity of stress
    experiment by Brady showed monkeys more stressed by control than
    non-control
    – used "executive monkey"

Relaxation involves muscle tension control
    – headaches, hypertension, insomnia
    – at least 30 minutes/day progressive relaxation

TABLE 12.4 Note-Taking Checklist	Yes	No
1. Notes are titled and dated.	❏	❏
2. A separate line is used for each key idea.	❏	❏
3. Less important ideas are indented.	❏	❏
4. Abbreviations and symbols are used.	❏	❏
5. The organization of the lecture is apparent.	❏	❏
6. Words and phrases (not entire sentences) are recorded.	❏	❏
7. Examples and illustrations are included.	❏	❏
8. Sufficient explanation and detail are included.	❏	❏
9. Adequate space is left for editing.	❏	❏
10. Marginal space is available for recall clues.	❏	❏

REVIEW   Five Key Points To Remember

1   **Be sure you are listening actively in lectures, not just hearing the instructor speak.** This means you have to think, react, respond, and write.

2   **Be prepared for class lectures.** Do so by reading assignments in advance.

3   **Take effective notes.** This involves recording main ideas, key details, and examples, as well as reflecting the lecture's organization. Be creative in developing new note-taking systems. Use thought patterns to guide you.

4   **Identify the lecture format: factual, conceptual, analytical, or discussion.** Adapt your note-taking strategies to reflect the lecture format. Also consider your learning style.

5   **Develop a system of editing and reviewing your notes.** After a lecture, write marginal recall clues, and test yourself using these recall clues (the Cornell System).

Working Together

Activity I

Reading and listening are both receptive communication skills. Working in groups of three or four students, discuss how reading and listening are similar and how they differ. Consider factors such as purpose, process, types of thinking, interference, recall, and retention. One student should record each group's findings and report them to the class. After each group has reported, the class should consider this question: Are some people better listeners than readers, and vice versa? Discuss why this may be true.

Activity II

Each student should bring to class a notebook or a set of notes from a recent lecture. Working in small groups, students should exchange and evaluate one another's notes, using the checklist shown in Table 12.4.

The Work Connection

Learning by listening carefully and taking good notes can be a valuable skill not only in your education but also as you explore different careers by conducting *informational interviews.* When you interview people who have jobs that interest you, you can gain insight into whether you might like to have such a job. Listening closely as someone describes the career field, the organization, and his or her own career path can provide you with details about what it would be like to work at a similar job. The same basic guidelines for understanding class lectures also apply to learning from informational interviews:

◆ Use the tips for effective listening (p. 242).
◆ Prepare for the interview by writing down questions you want to ask.
◆ Take notes of main ideas, important details, and important issues in the field.
◆ Review your notes immediately after the interview and fill in any missing information so you won't forget it.

1. List five people who have jobs that seem interesting. Choose one to interview. Contact the person to ask for a 10–15-minute interview.

2. Before the interview, write down questions about that person's career, typical careers in the field, and the types of skills needed to do the job. Leave blank spaces to fill in brief answers during the interview.

The Web Connection

1. Note-Taking Systems

   http://www.sas.calpoly.edu/asc/ssl/notetaking.systems.html

   This site from Caltech, San Luis Obispo, describes five major note-taking systems along with information on when to use them and advantages and disadvantages of each. Write a paragraph about your note-taking style. Does it fit into any of these five categories?

2. Taking Notes for Someone Else

   http://www.dartmouth.edu/~acskills/docs/taking_notes_for_others.doc

   You might need to take notes for a classmate one day. The Academic Skills Center at Dartmouth College prepared this helpful Web site with tips for this situation. Print out this document and mark the suggestions that could be applied to any type of note taking. Explain which items are especially important when you are taking notes for someone else.

3. Abbreviations in Note Taking

http://gettingstarted.und.edu/learningservices/pdf/NOTETAKING%20Abbreviations.pdf

Look over this list of abbreviations you can use in your note taking from the University of North Dakota, Grand Forks. Print the list out and highlight the abbreviations you already use. Identify the new ones that could be of use to you. Jot down any additional abbreviations that you currently use.

13 Learning from Textbooks, Graphics, and Online Sources

Do You Know?

What textbook features aid learning?

What are previewing techniques, and how are they useful?

How do you use the SQ3R reading/study system?

How should you read graphic material to understand its meaning?

How can you choose a method for reading nontextbook reading assignments?

How do you read and evaluate Internet sources?

Each semester you will spend hours reading, reviewing, and studying textbooks and other information sources. The course textbook is often the focal point of a college course. Class lectures are often coordinated with reading assignments in the course text, written assignments require you to apply or evaluate ideas and concepts presented in the textbook, and term papers explore topics introduced in the text.

This chapter presents strategies for using textbooks as efficiently as possible. It discusses the organization of the textbook; describes its unique features; demonstrates how to preview textbook reading assignments; discusses the SQ3R reading/study system; presents strategies for studying graphs, tables, and diagrams; addresses how to handle nontextbook reading assignments; and teaches you to read and evaluate Internet sources.

■ Features of Textbooks

College textbooks are written by college professors who are experienced teachers. They know their subject matter, but they also know their students. Having taught the material, textbook writers know topics you may have difficulty understanding and know the best way to explain them. Because textbooks are written by teachers, they contain numerous features to help you learn.

Keys to Overall Textbook Organization

Textbooks are highly organized, well-structured sources of information. They contain the following parts:

Preface.   Traditionally, a textbook begins with an opening statement, called a *preface,* in which the author describes some or all of the following:

◆ Author's reasons for writing the text
◆ Intended audience
◆ Major points of emphasis
◆ Special learning features
◆ Structure or organization of the book
◆ Distinctive features
◆ Suggestions on how to use the text
◆ Author's qualifications
◆ References or authorities consulted

Reading the preface gives you a firsthand impression of the author and his or her attitudes toward the text. Think of it as a chance to get a glimpse of the author as a person.

Some authors include, instead of or in addition to a preface, an introduction titled "To the Student." Written specifically for you, it contains information similar to that of a preface. The author may include an introduction "To the Instructor" as well. Although this section often may be quite technical, discussing teaching methodologies and theoretical issues, it may contain information of interest to students as well.

EXERCISE 13.1   ### Analyzing Textbooks

Directions   *Read or reread the preface or introduction to the student in this book* and *in one of your other textbooks. Using the list above as a guide, identify the types of information each provides.*

Table of contents.   The table of contents is an outline of the textbook's main topics and subtopics. It shows the organization of the text and indicates the interrelations among the topics. Often, it reveals thought patterns used throughout the text.

Besides using the table of contents to preview a text's overall content and organization, be sure to refer to it before reading particular chapters. Although chapters are organized as separate units, they are interrelated. To understand a given chapter, note what topics immediately precede and follow it.

Many textbooks also include a brief table of contents, listing only unit and chapter titles, followed by a complete table of contents that lists subheadings and various learning aids contained within each chapter. The brief table of contents is most useful for assessing the overall content and structure of the entire text, while the complete one is more helpful when studying individual chapters.

Predicting Patterns

Directions   *Turn to the table of contents of one of your textbooks. Choose a unit or part that you have not read. Use the table of contents to predict the thought pattern(s) for each chapter.*

Appendix.   The appendix of a textbook contains supplementary information that does not fit within the framework of the chapters. Often, the appendix offers valuable aids. For example, an American government text contains three appendixes:

Appendix 1	The Declaration of Independence
Appendix 2	The Constitution of the United States of America
Appendix 3	Beyond the Call of Duty: Data and Documents

The textbook includes Appendixes 1 and 2 for the readers' convenience, since the text refers to each frequently. Appendix 3 lists and explains additional sources of information for each chapter.

Glossary.   The glossary is a minidictionary of specialized vocabulary used throughout the text. Uses of the glossary are discussed in Chapter 10.

Index.   At the very end of many texts, you will find an alphabetical subject index, listing topics covered in the text along with page references. Although its primary function is to allow you to locate information on a specific topic, it also can be used as a study aid for final exams. If you have covered most or all of the chapters in the text, then you should be familiar with each topic indexed. For example, suppose the index of an accounting textbook listed the following:

> Purchases
>   determining the cost of, 169–170
>   of equipment for cash, 17–18, 36–37, 200
>   of merchandise for cash, 201–202
>   of merchandise on credit, 163–168

To review for an exam, look at each entry and test your recall. In the accounting textbook example, you would ask yourself: How is the cost of purchases determined? How are equipment purchases using cash recorded? What are the procedures for purchases of merchandise on credit?

Some texts also include a name index that allows you to locate references to individuals mentioned in the text.

The checklist in Figure 13.1 (p. 272) is provided to help you quickly assess a textbook's content and organization.

FIGURE 13.1
Assessing Your Textbook's Learning Features

Check "Yes" or "No" after each of the following statements.

	Yes	No
Preface		
The purpose of the text is stated.	☐	☐
The intended audience is indicated.	☐	☐
The preface explains how the book is organized.	☐	☐
The author's credentials are included.	☐	☐
Distinctive features are described.	☐	☐
Major points of emphasis are discussed.	☐	☐
Aids to learning are described.	☐	☐
Table of Contents		
Brief table of contents is included.	☐	☐
The chapters are grouped into parts or sections.	☐	☐
Thought pattern(s) throughout the text are evident.	☐	☐
Appendix		
Useful tables and charts are included.	☐	☐
Supplementary documents are included.	☐	☐
Background or reference material is included.	☐	☐
Glossary		
The text contains a glossary.	☐	☐
Word pronunciation and meaning are provided.	☐	☐
Index		
A subject index is included.	☐	☐
A name index is included.	☐	☐

EXERCISE 13.3 **Analyzing a Textbook**

Directions   *Use the checklist in Figure 13.1 to analyze the content and organization of one of your textbooks.*

Learning Aids in Textbooks

In addition to its useful organizational features, a textbook contains numerous learning aids: chapter previews, marginal notes, special-interest boxes or inserts, review questions, lists of key terms, summaries, and references. A textbook is a guide to learning, a source that directs your attention, shows you what is important, and leads you to apply your knowledge. Learning will be easier if you use the textbook's learning aids to your best advantage.

Chapter preview/Overview.   Research indicates that if readers have some knowledge of the content and organization of material *before* they begin to read it, their comprehension and recall increase. Consequently, numerous textbooks begin each chapter with some kind of preview. Previews take several common forms.

> **Chapter objectives.** In some texts, the objectives of each chapter are listed beneath its title. Objectives may appear as statements such as "To explain photosynthesis," or as questions, as in this book. The objectives are intended to focus your attention on important ideas and concepts. They are usually listed in the order in which the topics appear in the chapter, presenting an abbreviated outline of the main topics.

> **Chapter outline.** Other texts provide a brief outline of each chapter's contents. Formed from the headings and subheadings used throughout the chapter, the outline reflects both the content and organization of the chapter. As you study a chapter outline, pay attention to the sequence and progression of topics and look for thought patterns.

> **Chapter overview.** Some textbook authors provide a preview paragraph in which they state what the chapter is about, discuss why certain topics are important, focus the reader's attention on important issues, or indicate how the chapter relates to other chapters in the book. Overviews may be labeled "Chapter Preview," "Overview," or a less obvious title such as "Memo."

> Each type of preview can be used to activate and monitor your learning before, during, and after reading the chapter.

Before reading

◆ Use the chapter preview to activate your prior knowledge of the subject. Recall what you already know about the subject by trying to anticipate the chapter's main points.
◆ Use chapter previews to predict the predominant thought patterns.
◆ Use previews to anticipate which portions or sections of the chapter will be most difficult or challenging.

While reading

◆ Use the preview as a guide to what is important to learn.
◆ Mark or underline key information mentioned in the preview.

After reading

◆ Use the preview to monitor the effectiveness of your reading.

◆ Test your ability to recall the key information.

◆ Review immediately any material you were unable to recall.

Marginal notations.   Textbooks used to have wide, empty margins, useful to students for jotting notes. Now, textbook authors take advantage of this available space to offer commentary on the text; pose questions based on the text; provide illustrations, examples, and drawings; or identify key vocabulary. Figure 13.2, excerpted from a psychology text, illustrates one type of marginal notation. In the excerpt, brief definitions of key terms are given in the margin next to the sentence in which each term is first introduced.

The best way to approach marginal notes is to refer to them once you have read the text to which they correspond. Often marginal notes can be used to review and check your recall. If the marginal notes are in the form of questions, go through the chapter, section by section, answering each question. Test your ability to define each key term in your own words.

Special-interest inserts.   Many textbooks may contain, at various points within or at the end of the chapters, brief articles, essays, or commentaries that provide a practical perspective or an application of the topic under discussion. Usually these inserts are set apart from the text using boxes or shaded or colored print. Usually, too, the inserts are consistently titled throughout

---

FIGURE 13.2
Marginal Notations

There are other biases that lead us to make incorrect attributions about ourselves or others. One is called the **just world hypothesis,** in which people believe that we live in a world where good things happen only to good people and bad things happen only to bad people (Lerner, 1965, 1980). It's a sort of "everybody gets what they deserve" mentality. We see this bias (or fallacy) when we hear people claim that victims of rape often "ask for it by the way they dress and act." In fact, even the victims of rape sometimes engage in self-blame in an attempt to explain why in the world they were singled out for a crime in which they were the victim quite by chance (Janoff-Bulman, 1979; McCaul et al., 1990).

Another bias that affects our attributions is the **self-serving bias.** It occurs when we attribute successes or positive outcomes to personal, internal sources and failures or negative outcomes to situational, external sources (Harvey & Weary, 1984; Miller & Ross, 1975). We tend to think that when we do well it is because we're able, talented, and work hard, whereas when we do poorly it is the fault of someone or something else.

just world hypothesis
the belief that the world is just and that people get what they deserve

self-serving bias *the tendency to attribute our successes to our own effort and abilities, and our failures to situational, external sources*

Gerow, *Psychology: An Introduction*

the text, often suggesting their function, such as "Focus," "Counterpoint," or "Today's Problems." In a sociology textbook, in a chapter on drug abuse, a vivid narrative of the life of a drug addict may be included. Or, in an economics text, specific situations that apply key concepts may be included.

Make use of article inserts in the following ways:

◆ Read the insert *after* you have read the text material on the page.
◆ Determine the purpose of the insert and mark in the margin the concept or principle to which the insert refers.
◆ When reviewing for exams, especially essay exams, quickly review the chapter inserts, especially if your instructor has emphasized them.

EXERCISE 13.4   ## Analyzing a Textbook Insert

Directions   *Read the box insert in Figure 13.3, which is taken from a marketing text chapter on investment opportunities. Then answer the following questions.*

1. What marketing principle does this special-interest box illustrate?
2. How useful do you feel this insert would be in preparing for an exam?
3. Do you feel the example of the Bic Corporation will make the concept presented here come alive and seem real? Give reasons for your answer.

FIGURE 13.3
A Special-Interest Insert

MARKETING IN ACTION

Bic Corporation Sets Objectives

"Without a clear, concise statement of objectives, there can be no viable strategy," states Donald M. Wilchek, a marketing manager at the Bic Corporation. "At Bic, specific objectives are set before a project is undertaken." This is just as true for small projects such as the development of a selling sheet as it is for the major launch of a new product. The corporate philosophy is that if money is spent, the firm must know what it hopes to achieve by the expenditure. This has been true at Bic since the company first began with the introduction of simple stick pens.

The disposable "crystal" stick pen, still Bic's largest seller, was regionally launched in 1959 and nationally launched with a retail price of 19 cents in 1964. The company's objective was clear and concise—dominate the ballpoint pen market. Utilizing a straightforward strategy of producing a product that draws a line as well or better than anything on the market, pricing it significantly lower than the competition, making it almost universally available, and letting consumers know about it, Bic has clearly succeeded in achieving its objective. Today, Bic accounts for about two of every three ballpoint pens sold at retail.

Kinnear, Bernhardt, and Krentler,
Principles of Marketing

Questions for review. Many textbook chapters conclude with a set of review questions. Read through these questions *before* you read the chapter. They serve as a list of what is important in the chapter. Usually the questions are listed in the order in which the topics appear in the chapter, forming an outline.

As you read and locate answers in the text, be sure to highlight or mark them. Review questions are a useful but by no means a sufficient review. These questions often test only factual recall of specific information. They seldom require you to pull together ideas, compare, assess causes, or react to the information presented.

Lists of key terms. A list of key terms is often found at the end of each chapter. Usually, only specialized terms that are introduced for the first time in that chapter are included. Glancing through the list before reading the chapter will familiarize you with them and make reading go more smoothly.

Chapter summaries. Reading the end-of-chapter summary is useful both *before* and *after* you read a chapter. Before reading, the summary will familiarize you with the chapter's basic organization and content. After the chapter, it provides an excellent review and helps you tie together, or consolidate, the major points covered in the chapter.

Suggested readings or references. Many textbook authors provide a list of suggested readings at the end of each chapter or section. This list refers you to additional sources, both books and periodicals, that provide more information on topics discussed in the chapter. References given in this list provide a useful starting point when researching a topic discussed in the chapter.

The evaluation list shown in Table 13.1 will enable you to quickly assess the learning aids a chapter provides.

<table>
<tr><td>**EXERCISE 13.5**</td><td>**Identifying Learning Aids**</td></tr>
</table>

Directions   *Use the evaluation list shown in Table 13.1 to analyze how the author of one of your current textbooks guides your learning.*

Working Together

Each student should bring two textbooks to class. Working in groups of three, students should complete each of the following activities.

1. Students should exchange texts and review each text using the list on p. 272. Then each student should identify the text that provides the strongest learning aids and justify his or her choice to the group. Collectively the group should agree on the "best" textbook.

2. Each group should appoint a group spokesperson who will present and describe the group's choice to the class. Depending on class size, the class might also identify the text with the strongest learning aids from among those chosen by each group.

TABLE 13.1 Evaluation of Learning Aids

Chapter preview
What preview format is used?
What is its primary purpose?
What thought patterns are evident?
How can you use it for review?

Marginal notations
What format is used?
How can you use them for study and review?

Special-interest inserts
How do they relate to chapter content?
How much importance should you place on them?

Review questions
Do the questions provide an outline of chapter content? (Compare them with chapter headings.)
What types of thinking do they require? Are they primarily factual, or do they require critical thinking?

Key terminology
How many, if any, words are already familiar?
How difficult do you predict the chapter will be?

Chapter summary
Does it list the main topics the chapter will cover?
Is a thought pattern evident?

Suggested readings
What types of sources are listed?
To which topics do they refer?

■ Previewing Your Textbooks

Familiarity with a task enhances your ability to perform it effectively. If you are familiar with a large city, driving to a destination there is relatively simple. Similarly, if you are familiar with a reading or class assignment before you begin, you will find that you can read or complete it more easily and retain more information. You can become familiar with your reading assignments by focusing on those features that convey the major ideas and how they are organized. *Previewing* provides a means of familiarizing yourself quickly with the content and organization of an assignment before you begin.

How to Preview Textbook Reading Assignments

Think of previewing as getting a sneak preview of what a chapter will be about. Use the following steps:

1. **Read the title and subtitle.** The title provides the overall topic of the article or chapter; the subtitle suggests the specific focus, aspect, or approach toward the overall topic.

2. **Read the introduction or the first paragraph.** The introduction or first paragraph serves as a lead-in to the chapter, establishing the overall subject and suggesting how it will be developed.

3. **Read each boldfaced (or colored) heading.** Headings label the contents of each section, announcing the major topic of the section.

4. **Read the first sentence under each heading.** The first sentence often states the central thought of the section. If the first sentence seems introductory, read the last sentence; often this sentence states or restates the central thought.

5. **Note any typographical aids.** Italics emphasize important terminology and definitions by using slanted (*italic*) type to distinguish them from the rest of the passage. Notice any material that is numbered 1, 2, 3; lettered a, b, c; or presented in list form.

6. **Note any graphic aids.** Graphs, charts, photographs, and tables often suggest what is important in the chapter. Be sure to read the captions for photographs and the legends for graphs, charts, or tables.

7. **Read the last paragraph or summary.** This provides a condensed view of the chapter, often outlining the key points in the chapter.

8. **Read quickly any end-of-article or end-of-chapter material.** This might include references, study questions, discussion questions, chapter outlines, or vocabulary lists. If there are study questions, read them through quickly since they will indicate what is important to remember in the chapter. If a vocabulary list is included, rapidly skim through it to identify terms that you will need to learn as you read.

Figure 13.4 illustrates how previewing is done. A section of a business communications textbook chapter discussing job application letters is reprinted there; the portions to focus on when previewing are shaded. Read only those portions. After you have finished, test the effectiveness of your previewing by answering the questions in Exercise 13.6.

FIGURE 13.4
Demonstration of Previewing

The Unsolicited Letter

Ambitious job seekers don't limit their search to advertised openings. The unsolicited, or "prospecting" letter is a good way of uncovering other possibilities. Such letters have advantages and disadvantages.

Disadvantages. The unsolicited approach does have two drawbacks: (1) You may waste time writing letters to organizations that simply have no openings, (2) Because you don't know what the opening is (if there is one), you can't tailor your letter to specific requirements as James Calvin did in his solicited letter.

Advantages. This cold-canvassing approach does have one important advantage: for an advertised opening, you will compete with legions of qualified applicants, whereas your unsolicited letter might arrive just when an opening has materialized. If it does, your application will receive immediate attention, and you just might get the job. Even when there is no immediate opening, companies usually file an impressive application until an opening does occur. Or the application may be passed along to a company that has an opening. Therefore, unsolicited letters generally are a sound investment if your targets are well chosen and your expectations realistic.

The Aggressive Approach to Unsolicited Letters. If you've thoroughly researched a company and its needs, you might find that your specific qualifications can benefit a company. (For further discussion on how to research a company, see the following chapter, "Interviews.") Your unsolicited letter then becomes the means to achieve your end—getting a particular job with a particular company. Thorough research is the key, for, in effect, you ideally create your own position by showing a personnel director or executive how your particular qualifications, skills, and aptitudes match that company's needs. Even if you don't convince them that they need you for the position you want, they may consider you for another—or refer you to another company looking for a person such as yourself. After all, you have demonstrated your initiative and desire to accept responsibility. Employers actively seek candidates with such qualities.

Reader Interest. Because your unsolicited letter is unexpected, attract your reader's attention early and make him or her want to read further. Don't begin: "I am writing to inquire about the possibility of obtaining a position with your company." By now, your reader is asleep. If you can't establish a direct connection through a mutual acquaintance, use an interesting opening, such as:

> Does your hotel chain have a place for a junior manager with a college degree in hospitality management, a proven commitment to quality service, and customer-relations experience that extends beyond textbooks? If so, please consider my application for a position.

Unlike the usual, time-worn, and cliched opening, this approach gets through to your reader.

The Prototype

Most of your letters, whether solicited to unsolicited, can be versions of your one model, the prototype. Thus, your prototype must represent you and your goals in the best possible light. As you approach your job search, give yourself plenty of time to compose a model letter and résumé. Employers will regard the quality of your application as an indication of the quality of your work.

Above all, your letter and résumé must be visually appealing and free of errors. One or two spelling or grammatical errors might seem minor. But look at these documents from the employer's point of view. An employer expects you to present yourself in the most favorable way. A candidate who doesn't take the

(continues)

FIGURE 13.4

time to proofread carefully doesn't project the qualities employers want. After all, if you aren't conscientious about such important documents as your own application letter and résumé, how conscientious will you be with the employer's documents? Businesses incur a good deal of expense projecting favorable images. The image you project must measure up to their standards.

Your Dossier

Your dossier is a folder containing your credentials, college transcripts, letters of recommendation, and any other items (such as a notice of scholarship award or letter of commendation) that testify to your accomplishments. In your letter and résumé, you talk about yourself; in your dossier, others talk about you. An employer impressed by what you've said will want to read what others think about you and will request a copy of your dossier.

If your college has a placement office, it will keep your dossier on file and send copies to employers who request them. In any case, keep your own copy on file. Then, if an employer writes to request your dossier, you can make a photocopy and mail it, advising your reader that the placement office copy is on the way. This isn't needless repetition! Most employers establish a specific timetable for (1) advertising an opening, (2) reading letters and résumés, (3) requesting and reviewing dossiers, (4) holding interviews, and (5) making job offers. Obviously, if your letter and résumé don't arrive until the screening process is at step 3, you're out of luck. The same holds true if your dossier arrives when the screening process is at the end of step 4. Timing, then, is crucial. Too often, dossier requests from employers sit and gather dust in some "incoming" box on a desk in the placement office. Sometimes, one or two weeks will pass before your dossier is mailed out. The only loser is you.

Dumont and Lannon, *Business Communication*

EXERCISE 13.6   ## Checking Your Recall

Directions   *Without referring back to Figure 13.4, answer the following questions.*

1. What is an unsolicited letter?
2. What are its advantages?
3. What is one disadvantage?
4. What is a prototype?
5. What is a dossier?

Most likely, you were able to answer all or most of the questions correctly. Previewing, then, does provide you with a great deal of information. Now, suppose you were to return to Figure 13.4 and read the entire section. You would find it to be an easier task than it would have been if you had not previewed it.

Why Is Previewing Effective?

Previewing helps you make decisions.   Just as a film preview helps you make decisions about whether you want to see a film, previewing helps you make decisions about how you will approach the material in a book. Based on what you

THINKING CRITICALLY
. . . About Previewing

While previewing a reading assignment, you can make predictions about its content and organization. Specifically, you can anticipate what an assignment will contain and how it will be presented. Ask the following questions to sharpen your critical thinking–previewing skills:

◆ How difficult is the material?

◆ How is it organized?

◆ What is the overall subject and how is it approached?

◆ What type of material is it (practical, theoretical, historical background, or a case study)?

◆ Where are the logical breaking points where you might divide the assignment into portions, perhaps reserving a portion for a later study session?

◆ At what points should you stop and review?

◆ How does this material connect to class lectures?

discover about the text's organization and content, you can determine which reasoning and thinking strategies will be necessary for learning the material.

Previewing activates your thought processes.   It puts your mind in gear and initiates your thoughts on the subject.

Previewing activates your prior knowledge of the subject.   It helps you connect new material with what you already know.

Previewing gives you a mental outline of the chapter's content.   It enables you to see how ideas are connected, and since you know where the author is headed, reading will be easier than if you had not previewed.

EXERCISE 13.7   Previewing a Textbook Chapter

Directions   *Select a chapter in one of your textbooks that you have not read and preview it using the procedure described in this section. When you have finished, answer the following questions.*

1. What is its overall subject?
2. What topics (aspects of the subject) does the chapter discuss? List as many as you can recall.
3. How difficult do you expect the chapter to be?
4. How is the subject approached? That is, is the material practical, theoretical, historical, research oriented, procedural?

■ Using the SQ3R Reading/Study System

The SQ3R system has been used successfully for many years and has proved effective in increasing retention of information. It is especially useful for textbooks and other highly factual, well-organized materials. Basically, SQ3R is a way of learning as you read. Its name is taken from the first letter of each step.

The SQ3R Steps

1. **Survey.** Become familiar with the overall content and organization of the material. You already have learned this technique and know it as previewing.

2. **Question.** Formulate questions about the material that you expect to be able to answer as you read. As you read each successive heading, turn it into a question.

3. **Read.** As you read each section, actively search for the answers to your guide questions. When you find the answers, underline or mark the portions of the text that concisely state the information.

4. **Recite.** Probably the most important part of the system, "recite" means that after each section or after each major heading, you should stop, look away from the page, and try to remember the answer to your question. If you are unable to remember, look back at the page and reread the material. Then test yourself again by looking away from the page and "reciting" the answer to your question. This step is a form of comprehension and retention assessment that enables you to catch and correct weak or incomplete comprehension or recall. Here, you are operating primarily at the knowledge and understanding levels of thinking.

5. **Review.** Immediately after you have finished reading, go back through the material again, reading titles, introductions, summaries, headings, and graphic material. As you read each heading, recall your question and test yourself to see whether you still can remember the answer. If you cannot, reread that section. Once you are satisfied that you have understood and recalled key information, move toward the higher-level thinking skills. Try to apply, analyze, and evaluate the material. Ask questions. Some students like to add a fourth "R" step—for "React."

Applying SQ3R

Now, to get a clear picture of how the steps in the SQ3R method work together to produce an efficient approach to reading/study, let's apply the method to a textbook reading. Suppose you have been assigned in a communication class

REAL STUDENTS SPEAK

Lishai Goldstein

McGill University
Montreal, Canada

Background: Lishai is a freshman at McGill. She has not chosen a major yet.

Goals: To complete a degree, probably in political science, to work abroad, and maybe to attend graduate school.

Advice on Reading textbooks: An organized table of contents that connects information is very useful. Having a very detailed table of contents in my political science textbook helped me understand the information, and it was very useful for studying because it provided an outline of all the important points. I read the footnotes written by different authors, which were helpful in providing more detail. Sometimes it's helpful to find terminology in bold or italics, because definitions can get lost in the text otherwise.

the article in Figure 13.5 on p. 284 on nonverbal communication. Follow each of the SQ3R steps in reading this section.

Survey.   Preview the article, noting introductions, headings, first sentences, and typographical clues. From this prereading, you should have a good idea of what information this textbook excerpt will convey and should know the general conclusions the authors draw about the subject.

Question.   Now, using the headings as a starting point, develop several questions to which you expect to find answers in the article. Think of these as guide questions. You might ask such questions as:

What are the major types of nonverbal cues?

What are spatial cues?

What messages are communicated at each of the four distances?

Read.   Now read the selection through. Keep your questions in mind. Stop at the end of each major section and proceed to the next step.

Recite.   After each section, stop reading and check to see whether you can recall the answer to the corresponding question.

Review.   When you have finished reading the entire article, take a few minutes to reread the headings, recall your questions, and write answers to your questions to see how well you can remember the answers.

FIGURE 13.5
Demonstration of SQ3R

Types of Nonverbal Cues[1]

You now have a definition of nonverbal communication, you know how much nonverbal communication counts, you understand the characteristics most nonverbal cues share, and you know the functions and forms, so it is time to examine the types of nonverbal cues. In this section, spatial cues, visual cues, vocal cues, touch, time, and silence will be discussed.

Spatial Cues

Spatial cues are the distances we choose to stand or sit from others. Each of us carries with us something called informal space. We might think of this as a bubble; we occupy the center of the bubble. This bubble expands or contracts depending on varying conditions and circumstances such as these:

◆ Age and sex of those involved.
◆ Cultural and ethnic background of the participants.
◆ Topic or subject matter.
◆ Setting for the interaction.
◆ Physical characteristics of the participants (size or shape).
◆ Attitudinal and emotional orientation of partners.
◆ Characteristics of the interpersonal relationship (like friendship).
◆ Personality characteristics of those involved.

In this book *The Silent Language*, Edward T. Hall, a cultural anthropologist, identifies the distances that people assume when they talk with others. He calls these distances intimate, personal, social, and public. In many cases, the adjustments that occur in these distances result from some of the factors listed above.

Intimate distance. At an **intimate distance** (0 to 18 inches), you often use a soft or barely audible whisper to share intimate or confidential information. Physical contact becomes easy at this distance. This is the distance we use for physical comforting, lovemaking, and physical fighting, among other things.

Personal distance. Hall identified the range of 18 inches to 4 feet as **personal distance**. When you disclose yourself to someone, you are likely to do it within this distance. The topics you discuss at this range may be somewhat confidential and usually are personal and mutually involving. At personal distance you are still able to touch another if you want to. This is likely to be the distance between people conversing at a party, between classmates in a casual conversation, or within many work relationships. This distance assumes a well-established acquaintanceship. It is probably the most comfortable distance for free exchange of feedback.

Social distance. When you are talking at a normal level with another person, sharing concerns that are not of a personal nature, you usually use the **social distance** (4 to 12 feet). Many of your on-the-job conversations take place at this distance. Seating arrangements in living rooms may be based on "conversation groups" of chairs placed at a distance of 4 to 7 feet from each other. Hall calls 4 to 7 feet the close phase of social distance; from 7 to 12 feet is the far phase of social distance.

The greater the distance, the more formal the business or social discourse conducted is likely to be. Often, the desks of important people are broad enough to hold visitors at a distance of 7 to 12 feet. Eye contact at this distance becomes more important to the flow of communication; without visual contact one party is likely to feel shut out and the conversation may come to a halt.

Public distance. **Public distance** (12 feet and farther) is well outside the range for close involvement with another person. It is impractical for interpersonal communication. You are limited to what you can see and hear at that distance; topics for conversation are relatively impersonal and formal; and most of the communication that occurs is in the public-speaking style, with subjects planned in advance and limited opportunities for feedback . . . .

Weaver, Understanding Interpersonal Communication

How SQ3R Helps You Learn

The SQ3R system helps you learn in three ways.

1. **Your comprehension will increase.** By surveying or previewing, you acquire an overview of the material that serves as an outline to follow as you read. In the Question step, you are focusing your attention and identifying what is important to look for as you read.

2. **Your recall of the material will improve.** By testing yourself while reading and immediately after you finish, you build a systematic review pattern that provides the repetition needed to promote learning and recall.

3. **You will save time later when you are ready to study the material for an exam.** Since you already have learned the material through recitation and review, you will find that you need much less time to prepare for an exam.

Adapting the SQ3R System

To make the best use of SQ3R, you must adapt the procedure to fit the material you are studying and your learning style.

Adapting SQ3R to suit the material.   Your texts and other required readings vary greatly from course to course. To accommodate this variation, use the SQ3R system as a base or model. Then add, vary, or rearrange the steps to fit the material.

For example, when working with a mathematics text, you might add a Study the Sample Problems step in which you analyze the problem-solving process. When reading an essay, short story, or poem for a literature class, add a React step in which you analyze various features of the writing, including the writer's style, tone, purpose, and point of view. For textbooks with a great deal of factual information to learn, you might add Highlight, Take Notes, or Outline steps.

Adapting SQ3R to suit your learning style.   Throughout your school experience, you probably have found that some learning techniques work better for you than others. Just as everyone's personality is unique, so is everyone's learning style. Refer to the Learning Style Questionnaire discussed in Chapter 7, p. 134.

Use knowledge of your learning style to develop your own reading/study system. Experiment with various study methods and adapt the SQ3R system accordingly. For instance, if writing outlines helps you recall information, then replace the Recite step with an Outline step, or make the Review step a Review and Outline step. Or if you have discovered that you learn well by listening, replace the Recite and Review steps with Record and Listen steps, in which you dictate and record information to be learned and review by listening to the recording. Test variations until you find the most effective system.

EXERCISE 13.8	## Modifying the SQ3R System

Working Together

Directions   *Get together with other students taking the same course (or courses within the same discipline or department). Discuss and prepare a list of modifications to the SQ3R system that would be appropriate for your course's content and learning requirements.*

EXERCISE 13.9	## Applying SQ3R

Directions   *Apply the SQ3R system to a chapter in one of your other textbooks. List your questions on a separate sheet, and underline the answers in your textbook. Evaluate the effectiveness of your approach and decide on any modifications needed.*

■ Learning from Graphs, Tables, and Diagrams

Many textbooks use graphics to illustrate, explain, or summarize information. These graphics present a visual picture of a given situation and present a great deal of information in a relatively small space.

It is tempting to skip over graphs, tables, and diagrams; stopping to study a graph takes time and seems to break your flow. Because they do not present information in verbal form (there are no statements to highlight or remember), some students think they are unimportant. Actually, graphics are often *more* important than the paragraphs that surround them. Graphics require time and effort to prepare and are expensive to include in a text. Consequently, graphics often indicate what the author thinks is important.

How to Read Graphics

Here are some general suggestions for reading graphics:

1. **Read the title or caption.** The title often tells you what situation or relationship is being described.

2. **Determine how the graphic is organized.** If you are working with a table, note the column headings. For a graph, notice what is marked on the vertical and horizontal axes.

3. **Note any symbols and abbreviations used.**

4. **Determine the scale or unit of measurement.** Note how the variables are measured. For example, does a graph show expenditures in dollars, thousands of dollars, or millions of dollars?

5. **Identify the trend(s) or pattern(s) the graph is intended to show.** The following sections will discuss this step in greater detail.

6. **Read any footnotes.** Footnotes printed at the bottom of a graph or chart indicate how the data were collected, explain what certain numbers or headings mean, or describe statistical procedures.

7. **Check the source.** The source of data is usually cited at the bottom of the graph or chart. Unless the information was collected by the author, you are likely to find a research journal or publication listed from which the data were taken. Identifying the source is helpful in assessing the reliability of the data.

Identifying Thought Patterns in Graphics

All graphics describe some type of relationship. Not coincidentally, these relationships correspond to the thought patterns studied earlier, in Chapter 11.

Tables: Comparison and Classification of Information

Sociologists, psychologists, economists, and business analysts frequently use tables to organize and present statistical evidence. A table is an organized display of factual information, usually numbers or statistics. Its purpose is to classify information so that comparisons can be made between or among data.

Take a few minutes now to study the table in Figure 13.6 (p. 288), using the suggestions listed above. Then analyze the table, using the following steps.

◆ **Determine how the data are classified or divided.** This table compares U.S. advertising spending for six media for the years 2006–2010.

◆ **Make comparisons and look for trends.** This step involves surveying the media categories and noting changes across time. For example, by looking at newspaper advertising, you can see a steady and significant decline across the time period. The category network and cable television, on the other hand, remain strong with only a slight decline in the most recent years. Be certain to make comparisons between and among the various media, noting upward and downward trends.

◆ **Draw conclusions.** The final step is to decide what the data presented are intended to show. You can conclude from Figure 13.6 that there has been a steady decline in the use of print sources (newspapers, consumer magazines, and yellow pages) for advertising. Visual and audio sources

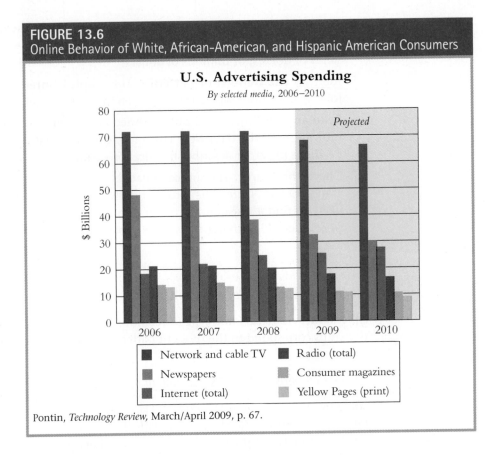

FIGURE 13.6
Online Behavior of White, African-American, and Hispanic American Consumers

U.S. Advertising Spending
By selected media, 2006–2010

Legend:
- Network and cable TV
- Newspapers
- Internet (total)
- Radio (total)
- Consumer magazines
- Yellow Pages (print)

Pontin, *Technology Review,* March/April 2009, p. 67.

(television and radio) are relatively stable sources of advertising, and the Internet is the only medium that has shown an increase as a source of advertising. Often, you will find clues, or sometimes direct statements, in the paragraphs that correspond to the table. The portion of the text that refers you to the table often makes a general statement about what the table is intended to show.

Once you have drawn your conclusions, be sure to stop, think, and react. For example, you might consider what the data in Figure 13.6 suggest about the changes in methods of communication or leisure activities.

EXERCISE 13.10

Analyzing a Table

Directions *Study the table shown in Figure 13.7 and answer the following questions.*

1. What change of direction or focus has community health nursing taken?
2. How has the service emphasis changed?
3. What thought patterns are evident in this table?

FIGURE 13.7
Table

Development of Community Health Nursing

Stages	Focus	Nursing Orientation	Service Emphasis	Institutional Base (Agencies)
District nursing (1860–1900)	Sick poor	Individual	Curative: beginning of preventive	Voluntary: some government
Public health nursing (1900–1970)	Needy public	Family	Curative: preventive	Government: some voluntary
Emergence of community health nursing (1970–present)	Total community	Population	Health promotion: illness prevention	Many kinds: some independent practice

Graphs: Relationships Among Variables

Graphs show the relation between two or more variables, such as price and demand or expenditures over time. They are pictures of relationships between two or more sets of information. The basic types of graphics are: *linear, circle,* and *bar.*

◆ **Linear graphs.** For linear graphs, information is plotted along a vertical and a horizontal axis, with one or more variables plotted on each. The resulting graph allows easy comparison between the variables. A sample linear graph is shown in Figure 13.8 on p. 290. The line graph displays the numbers of marriages and divorces from 1890 to 2010. It enables you to observe increases and decreases in marriage and divorce.

In addition to comparison by decades, the graph also allows you to determine the general trend or pattern between the variables. Generally, this graph shows a steady increase in both marriage and divorce. You can see that in years when the marriage rate declined, the divorce rate also declined.

◆ **Circle graphs.** A circle graph, also called a pie chart, is used to show whole-part relationships, or to show how given parts of a unit have been divided or classified. Figure 13.9 (p. 290) shows a series of three circle graphs that present the population of the United States for 2000, 2025, and 2050. Each of these graphs is divided or classified by racial or ethnic group. Circle graphs often are used to emphasize proportions or to show relative size or importance of various parts.

FIGURE 13.8
A Linear Graph

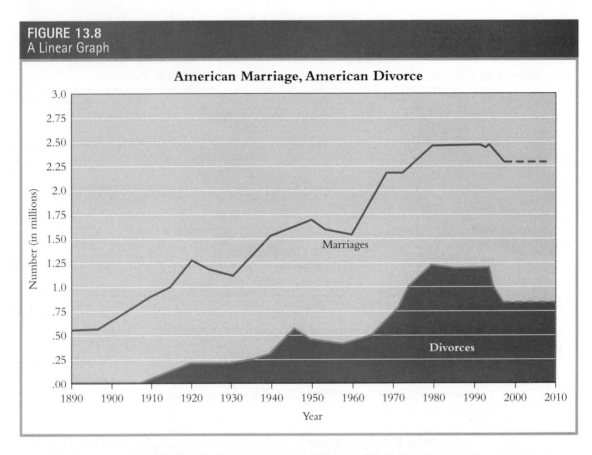

American Marriage, American Divorce

FIGURE 13.9
Circle Graphs

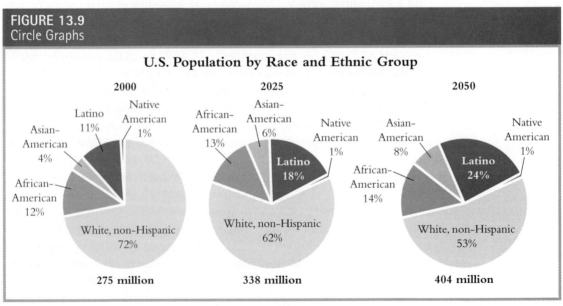

U.S. Population by Race and Ethnic Group

FIGURE 13.10
Bar Graphs

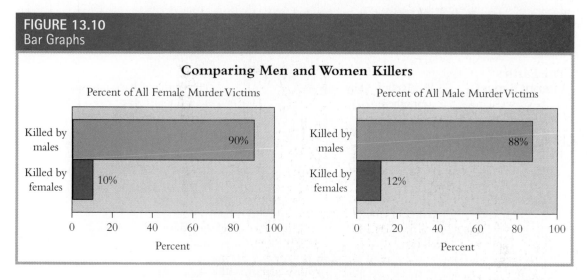

Bar graphs. A bar graph is often used to make comparisons between quantities or amounts. Figure 13.10 presents bar graphs that compare the gender of murderers for both male and female victims.

Diagrams: Explanations of Process

Diagrams are often included in technical and scientific as well as business and economics texts to explain processes. Diagrams are intended to help you visualize, see relationships between parts, and understand sequence. Figure 13.11 on p. 292, taken from a biology text, demonstrates how a portion of the sun's energy is used to heat the earth.

Reading diagrams differs from reading other types of graphics in that diagrams often correspond to fairly large segments of text, requiring you to switch back and forth frequently between the text and the diagram, determining to which part of the process each paragraph refers.

Often, the text presents an overview of the diagram, as in Figure 13.11. The underlined sentence summarizes what the diagram is intended to demonstrate. The text may also offer more detail about the process shown. The second paragraph, for example, explains the work accomplished by the 50 percent of solar energy that reaches earth.

Because diagrams of process and the corresponding text are often difficult, complicated, or highly technical, plan on reading these sections more than once. Use the first reading to grasp the overall process. In subsequent readings, focus on the details of the process, examining each step and understanding its progression.

One of the best ways to study a diagram is to redraw it without referring to the original, including as much detail as possible. Or test your understanding and recall of the process explained in a diagram by explaining it, step-by-step in writing, using your own words.

FIGURE 13.11
A Process Diagram and Corresponding Text

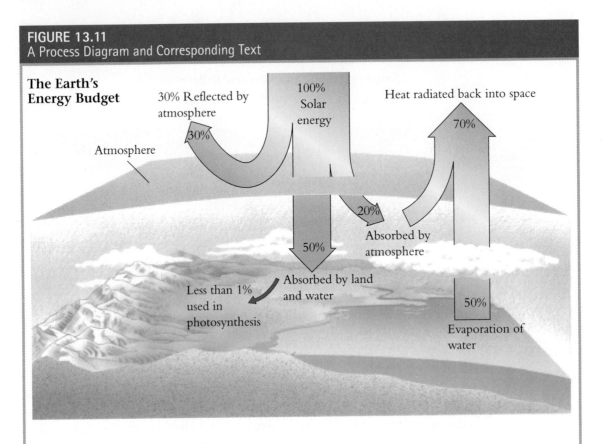

The Earth's Energy Budget

30% Reflected by atmosphere

100% Solar energy

Heat radiated back into space

30%

70%

Atmosphere

20%

50%

Absorbed by atmosphere

Less than 1% used in photosynthesis

Absorbed by land and water

50%

Evaporation of water

The relative constancy of conditions in the biosphere depends ultimately on an equilibrium between energy entering and energy leaving. Most of the absorbed energy reenters the atmosphere through evaporation from the earth's water. The thin arrow represents energy released by organisms.

SOLAR ENERGY

For the most part, the surface of the earth is heated by solar energy, energy from the sun. Only about half of the incoming solar energy ever actually reaches the earth's surface; about 30% is reflected back into space, while 20% is absorbed by the atmosphere. The 50% that does reach earth is absorbed by the land and waters, from which it radiates back into the atmosphere as heat. However, a great deal of work is accomplished during the time it interacts with the biosphere.

You are aware, of course (if all is going well), that photosynthesis drives much of the activity of life by enabling the energy of sunlight to be captured in the molecules of food manufactured by plants. However, you may be surprised to hear that on this green planet, less than 1% of incoming solar energy is used in photosynthesis. Actually, most of the solar energy reaching the earth is used to shuffle water around in the **hydrologic cycle,** which is the evaporation and condensation of the earth's waters. This cycle, of course, is responsible for the earth's rainfall pattern. In addition to distributing water more equitably over the earth's surface, the cycle redistributes heat.

Ferl, Wallace, and Sanders, *Biology: The Realm of Life*

EXERCISE 13.11   **Analyzing a Diagram**

Directions   *Study Figure 13.12. Then answer the following questions.*

1. What is the purpose of the diagram?
2. What control does the executive branch exert over the judicial branch?

FIGURE 13.12
A Conceptual Diagram

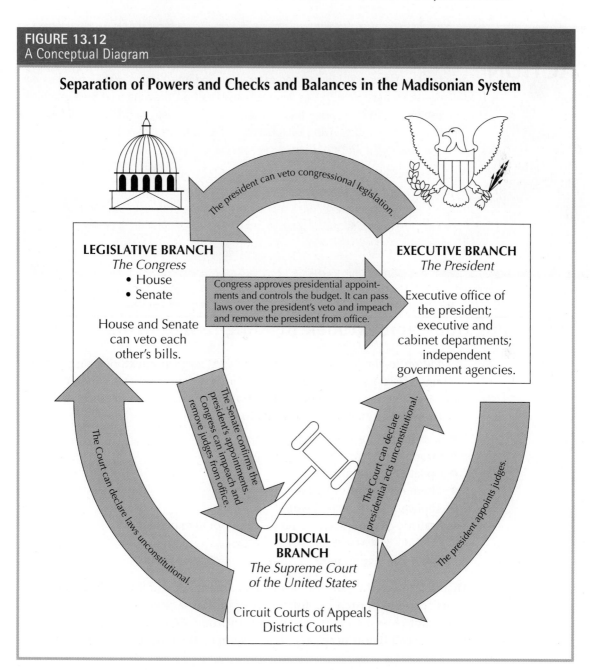

Separation of Powers and Checks and Balances in the Madisonian System

The president can veto congressional legislation.

LEGISLATIVE BRANCH
The Congress
• House
• Senate

House and Senate can veto each other's bills.

Congress approves presidential appointments and controls the budget. It can pass laws over the president's veto and impeach and remove the president from office.

EXECUTIVE BRANCH
The President

Executive office of the president; executive and cabinet departments; independent government agencies.

The Senate confirms the president's appointments. Congress can impeach and remove judges from office.

The Court can declare presidential acts unconstitutional.

The Court can declare laws unconstitutional.

The president appoints judges.

JUDICIAL BRANCH
The Supreme Court of the United States

Circuit Courts of Appeals
District Courts

3. How does the judicial branch influence the legislative branch?
4. If a president were convicted of a criminal act, what branch would handle his or her removal from office?
5. Now test your knowledge of the procedure by drawing your own diagram without referring to the original.

SKILLS IN ACTION

Making Your Own Graphics

This section of the text has focused on reading and interpreting graphics and using them as study aids. However, as you may have realized, drawing your own graphics can also be an effective study tool. These need not be fancy or professional looking; the simple act of drawing even boxes, circles, and arrows will help you better learn and memorize information.

Choose a class you are currently taking and look through your notebook. Have you drawn any figures to help you remember the material? Using the textbook for that course, draw any type of graphic that will help you learn the material. This might be a circle graph, a process diagram, a table summarizing a classification, and so on.

■ Learning from Nontextbook Reading Assignments

In addition to the textbook, many professors assign nontextbook supplemental readings. These assignments are drawn from a variety of sources: other textbooks, paperbacks, newspapers, periodicals, scholarly journals, and reference books.

These assignments may be given to present

◆ New topics not covered in your text
◆ Information not covered in the text
◆ Updated information
◆ Alternative points of view
◆ Applications or related issues
◆ Realistic examples, case studies, or personal experiences

Analyzing the Assignment

First determine the purpose of the assignment: How does it relate to existing course content? Listen carefully as your professor announces the assignment; important clues are often provided at this time. Next, determine the type and level of recall that is necessary. If, for example, the purpose of an assignment is

TABLE 13.2 Strategies for Nontextbook Readings

Assignment	Purpose	Reading Strategies	Study Strategies
Historical novel (American history course)	To acquaint you with living conditions of the historical period	Read rapidly, noting trends, patterns, characteristics; skip highly detailed descriptive portions	Write a brief synopsis of the basic plot; make notes (including some examples) of lifestyle, living conditions (social, religious, political, as well as economic)
Essay on exchange in Moroccan bazaars for economics course	To describe a system of barter	Read for main points, noting process, procedures, and principles	Highlight key points
Article titled "What Teens Know About Birth Control" assigned in a maternal care nursing course	To reveal attitudes toward and lack of information about birth control	Read to locate topics of information, misinformation, and lack of information; skip details and examples	Prepare a three-column list: information, misinformation, and lack of information

to present new, important topics not covered in your text, then a high level of recall is required. If, on the other hand, an assignment's purpose is to expose you to alternative points of view on a controversial issue, then key ideas are needed, but highly factual recall is not. Or, if an assignment is given to help you understand real-life experiences, key ideas may be all that are necessary.

Choosing Reading and Study Strategies

Depending upon the purpose of the assignment and the necessary level and type of recall, you may need to read one assignment quite differently from another. Your choices range from a careful, thorough reading to skimming to obtain an overview of the key ideas presented. Before you begin, select a study strategy to enable you to retain and recall the information. Table 13.2 lists examples of nontextbook assignments and their purposes and suggests possible reading and study approaches for each. The table demonstrates that strategies vary widely to suit the material and the purpose for which it was assigned.

■ Reading Internet Sources

Many instructors use the Internet and require their students to do so. It is important to develop effective ways of reading the wide range of Internet sources available to you.

Developing New Ways of Thinking and Reading

Reading electronic text is different than reading print text. A print source is linear—it goes in a straight line from idea to idea. Electronic sources, however, tend to be multidirectional. Using links, you can follow numerous paths. (See Figure 13.13).

Reading electronic sources demands a different type of thinking than reading print sources. Using electronic text also requires new reading strategies. Use the following suggestions to change and adapt how you read.

1. **Focus on your purpose.** Focus clearly on your purpose for visiting the site. What information do you need? Because you must create your own path through the site, fix in your mind what you are looking for. If you do not, you may wander aimlessly, waste valuable time, or even become lost, following numerous links that lead you farther and farther away from the site at which you began.

2. **Get used to the site's design and layout.** Each Web site has unique features and arranges information differently. Use the following suggestions to help you get used to a site's design and layout.

   ◆ **When you reach a new site, spend a few minutes getting used to it and discovering how it is organized.** Scroll through it quickly to determine how it is organized and what information is available. Especially on large and complex sites, you will have a number of different choices for locating the information you need.

   ◆ **Consider both the focus of and limitations of your learning style.** Are you a spatial learner? If so, you may have a tendency to focus too heavily on the graphic elements of the screen. If, on the other hand, you

FIGURE 13.13
The Differences Between Print and Electronic Sources

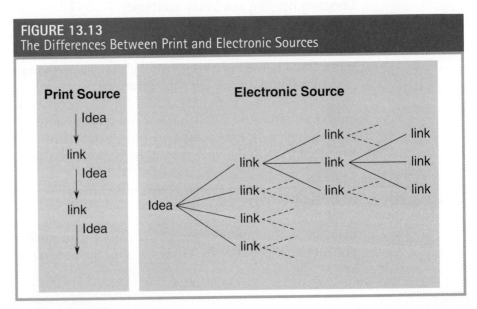

tend to focus on words, you may ignore important visual elements or signals. If you focus *only* on the words and ignore color and graphics on a particular screen, you probably will miss information or may not move through the site in the most efficient way.

3. **Pay attention to how information is organized.** Because you can navigate through a Web site in many different ways, it is important to have the right expectations and to make several decisions before you begin.

   ◆ **Use the site map, if provided, to discover what information is available and how it is organized.** A sample site map for the Consumer Reports Web site, http://www.consumerreports.org, is shown in Figure 13.14. Notice that the links are categorized according to the types of information (ratings, subscription information, products, etc.) a consumer may need.

   ◆ **Consider the order in which you want to take in information.** Choose an order in which to explore links; avoid randomly clicking on link buttons. Doing so is somewhat like randomly choosing pages to

FIGURE 13.14
The Site Map of the Consumer Reports Web Site (http://www.consumerreports.org)

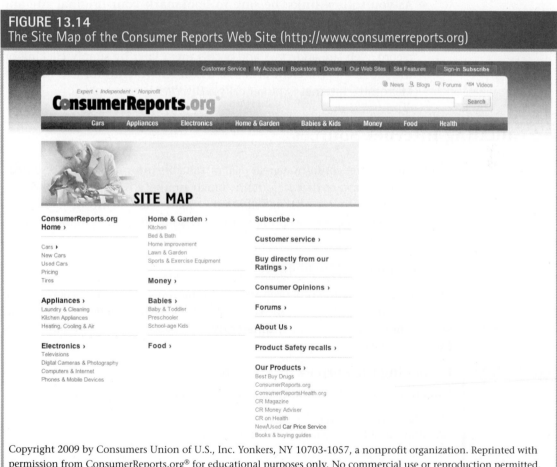

read out of a reference book. Do you need definitions first? Do you want historical background first?

◆ **Expect shorter, less detailed sentences and paragraphs.** Much online communication tends to be briefer and more concise than in traditional sources. As a result, you may have to mentally fill in transitions and make inferences about the relationships among ideas. For example, you may have to infer similarities and differences or recognize cause-and-effect connections on your own.

4. **Use links to find the information you need.** Links are unique to electronic text. The suggestions below will help you use links to find the information you need.

◆ **Plan on exploring links to find complete and detailed information.** Both remote links (those that take you to another site) and related links (within a site) are intended to provide more detailed information on topics introduced on the home page.

◆ **As you follow links, be sure to bookmark your original site and other useful sites you come across so you can find them again.** Bookmarking is a feature on your Internet browser that allows you to record Web site addresses and access them later by simply clicking on the site name. Different browsers use different terms for this function. Microsoft's Internet Explorer calls it *Favorites* for example.

■ Evaluating Internet Sources

While the Internet contains a great deal of valuable information and resources, you need to be aware that it contains much rumor, gossip, hoaxes, and misinformation. In other words, not all Internet sources are trustworthy. You must evaluate a source before accepting it. Here are some guidelines to follow when evaluating Internet sources.

Evaluating the Purpose of a Web Site

There are five basic types of Web sites: informational, news, advocacy, personal, and commercial. As you can see in Table 13.3, each has a different purpose, so you should approach each differently. The following sections summarize these differences.

| EXERCISE 13.12 | **Evaluating the Purpose of Web Sites** |

Directions   *Visit each of the following Web sites and identify the purpose of each.*

1. http://levysheetmusic.msc.jhu.edu/
2. http://jurist.law.pitt.edu/paperchase/
3. http://www.scorecard.org/
4. http://myhome.spu.edu/sigafoes/
5. http://www.skylineexhibits.com/

TABLE 13.3 Types of Web Sites			
Type	Purpose	Description	URL Suffix
Informational	To present facts, information, and research data	May contain reports, statistical data, results of research studies, and reference materials	.edu or .gov
News	To provide current information on local, national, and international news	Often supplements print newspapers, periodicals, and television news programs	.com
Advocacy	To promote a particular cause or point of view	May be concerned with a controversial issue; often sponsored by nonprofit groups	.org
Personal	To provide information about an individual and his or her interests and accomplishments	May list publications or include the individual's résumé	URL will vary. May contain .com or .org or may contain a tilde (~)
Commercial	To promote goods or services	May provide news and information related to a company's products	.com

Evaluating the Content of a Web Site

When evaluating the content of a Web site, evaluate its appropriateness, its source, its level of technical detail, its presentation, its completeness, and its links.

Evaluate its appropriateness.   To be worthwhile, a Web site should contain the information you need. It should answer one or more of your search questions. If the site only touches upon answers to your questions but does not address them in detail, check the links on the site to see if they will lead you to more detailed information. If they do not, search for a more useful site.

Evaluate its source.   Another important step in evaluating a Web site is to determine its source. Ask yourself "Who is the sponsor?" and "Why was this site put up on the Web?" The sponsor of a Web site is the person or organization who paid for it to be created and placed on the Web. The sponsor will often suggest the purpose of a Web site. For example, a Web site sponsored by Nike is designed to promote its products, while a site sponsored by a university library is designed to help students learn to use its resources more effectively.

If you are not sure who sponsors a Web site, check its URL, its copyright, and the links it offers. The ending of the URL often suggests the type of sponsorship. The copyright indicates the owner of the site. Links may also reveal the sponsor. Some links may lead to commercial advertising, while others may lead to sites sponsored by nonprofit groups.

Evaluate its level of technical detail. A Web site should contain the level of technical detail that is suited to your purpose. Some sites may provide information that is too sketchy for your search purposes; others assume a level of background knowledge or technical sophistication that you lack. For example, if you are writing a short, introductory-level paper on threats to the survival of marine animals, information on the Web site of the Scripps Institution of Oceanography (http://www.sio.ucsd.edu) may be too technical and contain more information than you need. Unless you have some prevous knowledge in that field, you may want to search for a different Web site.

Evaluate its presentation. Information on a Web site should be presented clearly and should be well written. If you find a site that is not clear and well written, you should be suspicious of it. If the author did not take time to present ideas clearly and correctly, he or she may not have taken time to collect accurate information, either.

Evaluate its completeness. Determine whether the site provides complete information on its topic. Does it address all aspects of the topic that you feel it should? For example, if a Web site on important twentieth-century American poets does not mention Robert Frost, then the site is incomplete. If you discover that a site is incomplete, search for sites that provide a more thorough treatment of the topic.

Evaluate its links. Many reputable sites supply links to other related sites. Make sure that the links work and are current. Also check to see if the sites to which you are sent are reliable sources of information. If the links do not work or the sources appear unreliable, you should question the reliability of the site itself. Also determine whether the links provided are comprehensive or only present a representative sample. Either is acceptable, but the site should make clear the nature of the links it is providing.

| EXERCISE 13.13 | **Evaluating the Content of a Web Site** |

Directions *Evaluate the content of two of the following sites. Explain why you would either trust or distrust the site for reliable content.*

1. http://www.acaiinformation.biz/
2. http://www1.umn.edu/ohr/careerdev/resources/resume/index.html
3. http://fairus.org

Evaluating the Accuracy of a Web Site

When using information on a Web site for an academic paper, it is important to be sure that you have found accurate information. One way to determine the accuracy of a Web site is to compare it with print sources (periodicals and books) on the same topic. If you find a wide discrepancy between the Web site and the printed sources, do not trust the Web site. Another way to determine accuracy of the information on a site is to compare it with other Web sites that address the same topic. If discrepancies exist, further research is needed to determine which site is more accurate.

The site itself will also provide clues about the accuracy of its information. Ask yourself the following questions:

1. **Are the author's name and credentials provided?** A well-known writer with established credentials is likely to author only reliable, accurate information. If no author is given, you should question whether the information is accurate.

2. **Is contact information for the author included on the site?** Often, an e-mail address where the author may be contacted is provided.

3. **Is the information complete, or in summary form?** If it is a summary, use the site to find the original source. Original information has less chance of containing errors and is usually preferred in academic papers.

4. **If opinions are offered, are they clearly presented as opinions?** Authors who disguise their opinions as facts are not trustworthy.

5. **Does the site provide a list of works cited?** As with any form of research, sources used to put information up on a Web site must be documented. If sources are not credited, you should question the accuracy of the Web site.

It may be helpful to determine if the information is available in print form. If it is, try to obtain the print version. Errors may occur when the article or essay is put up on the Web. Web sites move, change, and delete information, so it may be difficult for a reader of an academic paper to locate the Web site that you used in writing it. Also, page numbers in print sources are easier to cite than those in electronic ones.

EXERCISE 13.14

Evaluating the Accuracy of a Web Site

Directions *Evaluate the accuracy of two of the following Web sites.*

1. http://gunscholar.com/
2. http://www.smokingsection.com/issues1.html#whatiss
3. http://147.129.226.1/library/research/AIDSFACTS.htm

Evaluating the Timeliness of a Web Site

Although the Web is well known for providing up-to-the-minute information, not all Web sites are current. Evaluate the timeliness by checking

◆ The date on which the Web site was posted (put on the Web)
◆ The date when the document you are using was added

◆ The date when the site was last revised

◆ The date when the links were last checked

This information is usually provided at the end of the site's home page or at the end of the document you are using.

Evaluating the Timeliness of Web Sites

Directions   *Evaluate the timeliness of two of the following Web sites, using the list above.*

1. http://www.rmc.sierraclub.org/ipg/curriss.htm/
2. http://www.mhric.org/mozart/index2.html/
3. http://www.genome.gov/10001676

SKILLS IN ACTION

Researching on the Web: Case Study

Analyze the following situation and answer the questions below.

A University of Washington film studies major is asked to choose five Web sites for the class home page of a course that deals with controversial filmmakers. She has found many interesting sites but is having difficulty deciding which would be the most appropriate.

1. What are the four most important factors the student should consider when choosing the Web sites?

2. How can she ensure that the sites offer insights into what makes each particular filmmaker controversial?

3. Some of the Web sites she has found are "fan"-based sites kept by people who are admirers of a particular filmmaker's work. Should any of these be included in her final list? Why or why not?

4. Some of the filmmakers include scenes in their films that could be considered inappropriately erotic or excessively violent. Some of the Web sites show stills of these scenes from the movies. What factors should the student take into account when deciding whether or not these Web sites are appropriate for the home page? What precautions might she take?

REVIEW — Five Key Points to Remember

1   **Use your textbooks' learning aids.** These will make your job easier by showing you what is important and helping you learn that material.

2   **Use the SQ3R study method.** SQ3R will improve your comprehension, improve your recall, and save you time in the long run.

3   **Pay attention to graphics.** Graphics consolidate, condense, emphasize, and summarize key information.

4   **Consider nontextbook assignments important.** Be sure to analyze each supplemental assignment and devise a strategy for reading and studying it.

5   **Evaluate Internet sources before using them.** Evaluate their purpose, content, accuracy, and timeliness.

The Work Connection

This table below shows excellent prospects for people entering various careers and occupations. Note that many of the high growth jobs listed require two or four years of technical training or college study to qualify for positions.

1. What trends does this table reveal?

2. List three factors in addition to growth opportunities, income, and steady employment that you have considered, or will consider, in choosing your career goals.

3. Does the information presented in this visual aid influence your thoughts and feelings about your chosen career path? Why or why not?

Table 2. Fastest growing occupations, 2006–16 [Numbers in thousands]						
2006 National Employment Matrix code and title	Employment		Change, 2006–16		Quartile rank by 2006 median annual wages	Most significant source of postsecondary education or training
	2006	2016	Number	Percent		
Network systems and data communications analysts..	262	402	140	53.4	VH	Bachelor's degree
Personal and home care aides................	767	1,156	389	50.6	VL	Short-term on-the-job training

(continues)

Table 2. Fastest growing occupations, 2006–16						
[Numbers in thousands]						
2006 National Employment Matrix code and title	Employment		Change, 2006–16		Quartile rank by 2006 median annual wages	Most significant source of postsecondary education or training
	2006	2016	Number	Percent		
Home health aides............................	787	1,171	384	48.7	VL	Short-term on-the-job training
Computer software engineers, applications	507	733	226	44.6	VH	Bachelor's degree
Veterinary technologists and technicians	71	100	29	41.0	L	Associate degree
Personal financial advisors....................	176	248	72	41.0	VH	Bachelor's degree
Makeup artists, theatrical and performance	2	3	1	39.8	H	Postsecondary vocational award
Medical assistants............................	417	565	148	35.4	L	Moderate-term on-the-job training
Veterinarians.................................	62	84	22	35.0	VH	First professional degree
Substance abuse and behavioral disorder counselors...................................	83	112	29	34.3	H	Bachelor's degree
Skin care specialists..........................	38	51	13	34.3	L	Postsecondary

H=High, L=Low, V =Very

The Web Connection

1. Academic Success: Reading Textbooks

   http://www.dartmouth.edu/~acskills/success/reading.html

   Dartmouth College offers several online handouts designed to help students read textbooks more effectively and efficiently. Two featured documents are "Six Reading Myths" and "Harvard Report on Reading." Read them over and discuss with your classmates how these documents apply to your current experiences. Offer each other suggestions for improving your reading skills.

2. Web Site Evaluation Worksheet

   http://www.pace.edu/library/pages/instruct/webevalworksheet.htm

   Print out this worksheet from Pace University Library and use it to evaluate a Web site that you use regularly. Notice that at the bottom of the site there are links to specialized criteria for specific types of Web pages. You might want to incorporate some of these into the worksheet you printed out.

3. Worst of the Web/Best of the Web

   http://www.worstoftheweb.com/

   http://www.webbyawards.com/webbys/current.php?season=13

   Explore some links from these sites and try to determine why they were given their respective "awards." Do you have sites that you return to over and over? What about them appeals to you? What types of sites do you avoid? Why?

14 Organizing and Synthesizing Course Content

Do You Know?

How can you reduce the amount of information you need to learn?

What techniques are useful for highlighting and annotating?

What strategies can you use to organize the information you have to learn?

When does it makes sense to take outline notes or to make maps to organize information?

How can you use your computer to synthesize course content?

Have you ever wondered how you will learn all the facts and ideas from your textbooks and your instructors' lectures? The key to handling this volume of information is a two-step process:

◆ You must reduce the amount to be learned by identifying what is important, less important, and unimportant to learn.
◆ You must organize and synthesize the information to make it more meaningful and easier to learn.

This chapter describes two strategies for reducing the information—textbook highlighting and marginal annotation—and three means of organizing information—note taking, mapping, and computer integration.

■ Textbook Highlighting and Annotation

Both textbook highlighting and marginal annotation are useful ways to condense textbook material and emphasize what is important.

Textbook Highlighting

Textbook highlighting is an extremely efficient way of making textbook review manageable. Especially when combined with annotation, it leads to a quick and easy way to review so that you do not have to reread everything when studying for an exam. If you highlight 20 percent of a chapter, you will be able to avoid rereading 80 percent of the material. If it normally takes two hours to read a chapter, you should be able to review a highlighted chapter in less than a half hour. Highlighting by itself, however, is not sufficient. The hour and a half you save, then, can be spent studying what you do not know, organizing and synthesizing the information, and preparing for your exam. To highlight textbook material most effectively, apply the guidelines below:

HOW TO HIGHLIGHT

Begin by analyzing the task.   Preview the assignment and define what type of learning is required. This will determine how much and what type of information you need to highlight.

Assess your familiarity with the subject.   Depending on your background knowledge, very little or thorough highlighting might be necessary. Do not waste time highlighting what you already know. In chemistry, for example, if you already have learned the definition of a mole, then do not highlight it.

Read first; then highlight.   Finish a paragraph or headed section before you highlight. Each idea may seem important as you first encounter it, but before you can judge its relative importance you must see how it fits with other ideas in the section.

Use the boldfaced headings.   Headings are labels that indicate the overall topic of a section. These headings serve as indicators of what is important to highlight. For example, under the heading "Objectives of Economic Growth," you should be certain to highlight each objective.

Highlight main ideas and only key supporting details.

Avoid highlighting complete sentences.   Highlight only enough so that your highlighting makes sense when you reread it. Notice that in Figure 14.1 on p. 307, an excerpt from a communication text, only key words and phrases are highlighted.

Maintain a reasonable pace.   If you have understood a paragraph or section, then your highlighting should be fast and efficient.

Develop a consistent system of highlighting.   Decide, for example, how you will mark main ideas, how you will distinguish main ideas from details, and how you will highlight new terminology. Some students use a system of brackets, asterisks, and circles to distinguish various types of information; others use different colors of ink, or combinations of pens and pencils. The specific coding system you create is unimportant; what is important is that you devise some consistent approach to highlighting. At first, you will need to experiment, testing out various systems. However, once you have settled on an effective system, use it regularly.

> **Adopt a 16–25 percent rule of thumb.**   Although the amount you highlight will vary from course to course, depending on your purposes, try to highlight no more than between 16 and 25 percent of any given page. If you exceed this figure, you may not be sorting ideas as efficiently as possible. Remember, the more you highlight, the smaller your time-saving dividends will be as you review. Figure 14.1 provides an example of effective highlighting.

FIGURE 14.1
Highlighting

Gossip

There can be no doubt that everyone spends a great deal of time gossiping. In fact, gossip seems universal among all cultures, and among some it's a commonly accepted ritual. Gossip refers to third party talk about another person; the word **gossip** "now embraces both the talker and the talk, the tattler and the tattle, the newsmonger and the newsmongering." Gossip is an inevitable part of daily interactions; to advise anyone not to gossip would be absurd. Not gossiping would eliminate one of the most frequent and enjoyable forms of communication.

In some instances, however, gossip is *unethical*. First, it's unethical to reveal information that you've promised to keep secret. Although this principle may seem too obvious to even mention, it seems violated in many cases. For example, in a study of 133 school executives, board presidents, and superintendents, the majority received communications that violated an employee's right to confidentiality. When it is impossible to keep something secret (Bok offers the example of the teenager who confides a suicide plan), the information should be revealed only to those who must know it, not to the world at large. Second, gossip is unethical when it invades the privacy that everyone has a right to, for example, when it concerns matters that are properly considered private and when the gossip can hurt the individuals involved. Third, gossip is unethical when it's known to be false, and is nevertheless passed on to others.

—DeVito, *The Interpersonal Communication Book,* p. 191

Overcoming Common Pitfalls

If highlighting is done incorrectly, it can waste valuable time and leave you inadequately prepared. Here are a few common mistakes to avoid.

◆ **Highlighting without a defined purpose.** Some students highlight because they feel it will help them learn, rather than identify specific information for subsequent review. Consequently, their review is unfocused and does not produce results. Be certain, then, to carefully assess the nature of the material and what you are expected to learn. For example, in a political

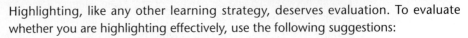

THINKING CRITICALLY
... About Highlighting

Highlighting, like any other learning strategy, deserves evaluation. To evaluate whether you are highlighting effectively, use the following suggestions:

1. Does your highlighting convey the key idea of the passage?

2. Can you follow the author's train of thought and progression of ideas by reading only the words highlighted?

3. Is the highlighting appropriate for your purposes?

4. How does your highlighting compare with that of a classmate? While each set of words you're highlighting will be different, each should reflect the same key ideas.

science course, are you focusing on trends, facts, and solutions to problems, or making comparisons and contrasts?

◆ **Highlighting too much.** This is the most common problem that students face. Operating on mistaken ideas about "better safe than sorry" or "too much is better than too little," they tend to highlight almost every idea on the page.

Highlighting nearly everything is about as effective as highlighting nothing, since no sorting occurs: key ideas are not distinguished from other, less important ones.

◆ **Highlighting too little.** Highlighting less than 10 percent per page may be a signal that you are having difficulty comprehending the material. Test your comprehension by trying to express the content of a given section in your own words. If you understand what you read but are highlighting very little, then you may need to refine or redefine your purpose for reading.

The Added Benefits of Highlighting

Highlighting is beneficial for several reasons:

◆ **Highlighting forces you to sift through what you have read to identify important information.** This sifting or sorting helps you weigh and evaluate what you read.

◆ **Highlighting keeps you physically active while you are reading and improves concentration.**

◆ **Highlighting can help you discover the organization of facts and ideas as well as their connections and relationships.**

◆ **Highlighting helps you determine whether you have understood a passage you have just read.** If you don't know what to highlight, you don't understand it.

A word of caution: Do not assume that what is highlighted is learned. You must process the information by organizing it, expressing it in your own words, and testing yourself periodically.

<table>
<tr><td>EXERCISE 14.1</td></tr>
</table>

Highlighting a Textbook Section

Directions *Choose a two- to three-page section from one of your textbooks and highlight it using the guidelines suggested above. Then evaluate the effectiveness of your highlighting as preparation for an objective exam on the material.*

Marginal Annotation

Highlighting alone often is not a sufficient means of identifying what to learn. It does not separate main ideas from examples or either of these from new terminology. Nor does it give you any opportunity to comment on or react to the material. Therefore, you need to make marginal annotations as well as highlight. Table 14.1 on p. 310 suggests various types of annotation used in marking a political science textbook chapter.

Figures 14.2 and 14.3 on p. 311 present two versions of the same paragraph. The first version has been highlighted, while the second has been both highlighted and annotated. Notice how the second version (Figure 14.3) more clearly conveys the meaning of the passage.

Summary Notes.   Writing summary words or phrases in the margin is another valuable form of annotation. It involves pulling together ideas and summarizing them in your own words. This process forces you to think, monitor your comprehension, and evaluate as you read, and it makes remembering easier.

Figure 14.4 on p. 312 illustrates effective use of summary notes to annotate a sample passage. First read the passage, and then study the marginal summary clues.

Summary clues are most effectively used in passages that contain long and complicated ideas. In these cases, it is simpler to write a summary phrase in the margin than to highlight a long or complicated statement of the main idea and supporting details. To write a summary clue, try to think of a word or phrase that accurately states in brief form a particular idea presented in the passage.

Recall Clues.   In Chapter 12 you learned to write recall clues in the margin of your lecture notes (see p. 261). A similar system will work for annotating and studying textbook chapters. Recall clues are words, phrases, or questions that you can use to test yourself on the material. Each recall clue summarizes a particular section of text. To study your text using recall clues, cover up the page,

TABLE 14.1 Marginal Annotations

Types of Annotation	Example
Circling unknown words	...redressing the apparent (asymmetry) of their relationship
Marking definitions	*def* [To say that the balance of power favors one party over another is to introduce a disequilibrium
Marking examples	*ex* [...concessions may include negative sanctions, trade agreements...
Numbering lists of ideas, causes, reasons, or events	components of power include ① self-image, ② population, ③ natural resources, and geography
Placing asterisks next to important passages	* [Power comes from three primary sources...
Putting question marks next to confusing passages	? → war prevention occurs through institutionalization of mediation...
Making notes to yourself	check def in soc text power is the ability of an actor on the international stage to...
Marking possible test items	] There are several key features in the relationship...
Drawing arrows to show relationships	↗ ...natural resources..., ...control of industrial manufacture capacity ↓
Writing comments, noting disagreements and similarities	can terrorism be prevented through similar balance? war prevention through balance of power is...
Marking summary statements	*sum* [the greater the degree of conflict, the more intricate will be...

exposing only the recall clues. Read the first recall clue and try to remember the information contained in the text. Continue working with the remaining recall clues on the page.

EXERCISE 14.2   Writing Annotations

Directions   *Review the textbook excerpt used in Figure 14.1 and add annotations.*

FIGURE 14.2
Highlighting

Influencing Public Opinion: Easy to Assume, Hard to Prove

Common sense suggests that long exposure to anything is likely to influence opinion. The average American spends twenty-eight hours and twenty-two minutes weekly glued to "the tube." (Contrary to popular opinion, teenagers are the least frequent TV viewers.) Thus Americans spend more time watching television than in any other single activity besides sleeping and working! On the average night, 100 million Americans—more than half the adult population—will be watching television.

Because of its pervasiveness, it is easy to *overestimate* the effects of the technotronic media on opinion change. For one thing, the vast majority of what people watch on television and read about in the papers is essentially nonpolitical. "Sitcoms," the NFL, etc. are not exactly high political drama. Even watching television news produces only about as much information as a single newspaper page.

In the early days of research on media impact, it was assumed that there would be direct, visible impacts of the media on public opinion, but efforts to prove such direct effects usually failed. Most media effects are subtle; the most obvious is on "agenda setting." People pay attention to what the media pays attention to; what the media says is important, we assume is important. Because the media sets our priorities, we tend to adopt its world view of political issues.[1]

FIGURE 14.3
Highlighting and Annotation

amount of TV watching

TV watching nonpolitical little effect on public opinion

major effects agenda setting

Influencing Public Opinion: Easy to Assume, Hard to Prove

Common sense suggests that long exposure to anything is likely to influence opinion. The average American spends twenty-eight hours and twenty-two minutes weekly glued to "the tube." (Contrary to popular opinion, teenagers are the least frequent TV viewers.) Thus Americans spend more time watching television than in any other single activity besides sleeping and working! On the average night, 100 million Americans—more than half the adult population—will be watching television.

Because of its pervasiveness, it is easy to *overestimate* the effects of the technotronic media on opinion change. For one thing, the vast majority of what people watch on television and read about in the papers is essentially nonpolitical. "Sitcoms," the NFL, etc. are not exactly high political drama. Even watching television news produces only about as much information as a single newspaper page.

In the early days of research on media impact, it was assumed that there would be direct, visible impacts of the media on public opinion, but efforts to prove such direct effects usually failed. Most media effects are subtle; the most obvious is on "agenda setting." People pay attention to what the media pays attention to; what the media says is important, we assume is important. Because the media sets our priorities, we tend to adopt its world view of political issues.

FIGURE 14.4
Passage Annotated with Summary Notes

chronemics: use
of time
3 types psych
time
  1. past
  2. present
  3. future
Examples of class
and experiences
  1. unskilled
  workers
  emphasze
  pleasure
  2. prof workers
  emphasze
  planning

Time Messages

The study of **temporal communication**, known technically as **chronemics,** concerns the use of time—how you organize it, react to it, and communicate messages through it. Consider, for example, **psychological time**: the emphasis you place on the past, present, or future. In a *past orientation,* you have special reverence for the past. You relive old times and regard the old methods as the best. You see events as circular and recurring, so the wisdom of yesterday is applicable also to today and tomorrow. In a *present orientation,* however, you live in the present: for now, not tomorrow. In a *future orientation,* you look toward and live for the future. You save today, work hard in college, and deny yourself luxuries because you're preparing for the future.

The time orientation you develop depends to a great extent on your socioeconomic class and your personal experiences. For example, parents with unskilled and semiskilled occupations are likely to teach their children a present-orientated fatalism and a belief that enjoying yourself is more important than planning for the future. Parents who are teachers, managers, or other professionals teach their children the importance of planning and preparing for the future, along with other strategies for success. In the United States, not surprisingly, future income is positively related to future orientation; the more future oriented you are, the greater your income is likely to be.

SKILLS IN ACTION

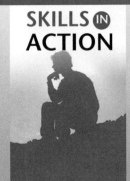

Highlighting and Annotating Your Textbook

Choose a three- to five-page section from one of your textbooks; then highlight and annotate it using the guidelines suggested in this section. Bring your textbook to the next class and trade with a classmate to compare highlighting and annotating skills. What did you and your classmate do well? What could you or your classmate have done better? To frame your discussion and thinking, ask yourself, "How well would this highlighting and annotating help me prepare for an exam?"

■ Note Taking to Organize and Condense Information

Although highlighting is usually a fast and efficient method of identifying and locating key information to be learned, it does little to help you organize information and relate or pull together ideas. Highlighting is of limited use in situations such as the following:

◆ Texts that deal with presentation and subsequent analysis of literary works or other documents

◆ Collections of readings (for example, "Readings in Psychology")

♦ Anthologies of literature
♦ Texts in technical fields such as electrical engineering
♦ Courses in which the text is used very selectively with only specific pages or sections assigned
♦ Very difficult, complicated material
♦ Reference material

Note taking has a number of benefits. It provides a truer test of your understanding of the material than does highlighting. While highlighting requires you to *recognize* what is important, note taking requires you to *express* it in words—a more difficult task that involves a higher level of thinking. Note taking enables you to organize the material for easier learning.

Note taking forces you to decide at once what is important. Since you cannot possibly record everything, you are forced to be selective. As you write, you have time to reflect on the ideas you are recording.

Developing Outline Notes

Use the outline form for note taking; it provides a visual representation of thought patterns and reflects the organization and development of ideas. Outline notes may be highly detailed or consist of a brief list of items; they may exhibit careful organization or be loosely structured. The type you write depends on how and why you are writing it.

Developing an outline involves two steps: (1) identifying how ideas relate and (2) grouping ideas together according to their connections. An effective outline, then, accomplishes two things:

♦ It shows the relative importance of ideas.
♦ It shows the relationships among these ideas.

An outline uses a listing order and a system of indentation. A standard format is shown below.

> **I. First Major Topic**
>   A. First major idea
>   1. First important detail
>   2. Second important detail
>   B. Second major idea
>   1. First important detail
>   a. Minor detail or example
>   b. Minor detail or example
>   2. Second important detail
> **II. Second Major Topic**
>   A. First major idea

A quick glance at the outline indicates what is most important, what is less important, and how ideas support or explain one another. When you write an outline for your own use, you do not necessarily have to follow the formal outline format of roman numerals, capital letters, and so forth (I., A., 1., a.). Instead you can use an informal system of indentation as shown in Figure 14.5. Here are a few suggestions for developing an effective outline.

- **Concentrate on the relative importance of ideas.** Do not worry about the numbering and lettering system. How you number or letter an idea, or whether you label it at all, is not as important as showing what other ideas it supports or explains.
- **Be brief.** Use words and phrases, never complete sentences.
- **Use your own words.** Don't lift most of the material from the text or lecture notes.
- **Make sure subentries are relevant.** All the information you place in sub-lists beneath a heading should support or explain the heading.
- **Align headings to reflect their relative importance.** Headings with the same indentation on the page should be of equal importance.

Outlining Using a Computer

Use the following tips for outlining using your computer:

- **Use the tab key to make indenting easy and systematic.**
- **Devise a system for using different typefaces to designate the relative importance of ideas.** Use caps for major topics and lowercase for details, for example.
- **Use symbols, such as asterisks or brackets, to mark important information and definitions.**
- **Use the cut-and-paste function to rearrange information and group together ideas on a specific topic.**

When to Use Outline Notes

Outline notes are particularly appropriate and effective in the following situations:

1. **Difficult material.** Outlining difficult or confusing material forces you to sort ideas, see connections, and express them in your own words, and it thus aids comprehension.

FIGURE 14.5
Informal Outline Notes

Time Management

– Analyze your college commitments

    ex. classes, labs, homework,

    online research

– Analyze your time commitments –

    hours per week

      ex. part-time job, transportation

   – Analyze Your Efficiency

     – notice wasted time, duplication

      of effort.

     – notice time traps

      ex-making small decisions

   – Principles of Time Management

    1) choose surroundings conducive to study

    2) Use peak periods of concentration

    3) do difficult tasks first

    4) Divide difficult tasks into manageable

      parts

    5) Build in short breaks

    6) Study for a course close to time when you

      attend class

    7) Avoid procrastination

2. **Interpreting and reacting.** When you are asked to write an evaluation of, reaction to, or critical interpretation of an article or essay, it is helpful to write a brief outline of the factual content. Your notes will reflect development and progression of thought and help you analyze the writer's ideas.

3. **Order and process.** In courses where order or process is important, outline notes are particularly useful. In data processing, for example, where sets of programming commands must be performed in a specified sequence, outline notes would organize the information.

4. **Classification.** In the natural sciences, where classifications are important, outlining is a helpful way to record and sort information. In botany, for example, you can use outline notes to list plant subgroups within each botanical category and keep track of similar characteristics.

EXERCISE 14.3

Writing Outline Notes

Directions   *Write a brief set of outline notes reflecting the organization and content of one or two pages of one of your textbooks.*

■ Mapping to Show Relationships

Mapping is a process of drawing a diagram to show how a topic and its related ideas are connected. It is a method of organizing and consolidating information, often to emphasize a particular thought pattern. The effectiveness of mapping depends on your individual learning style. Spatial learners will find it to be a particularly effective technique.

This section describes a general mapping procedure, called concept maps, and discusses five types of specialized maps: *time lines, process diagrams, part and function diagrams, organizational charts,* and *comparison* and *contrast charts.* Each utilizes one of the thought patterns discussed in Chapter 11.

Concept Maps

A concept map of Chapter 12, on lecture note taking, is shown in Figure 14.6. Take a moment now to refer to Chapter 12 before studying the map.

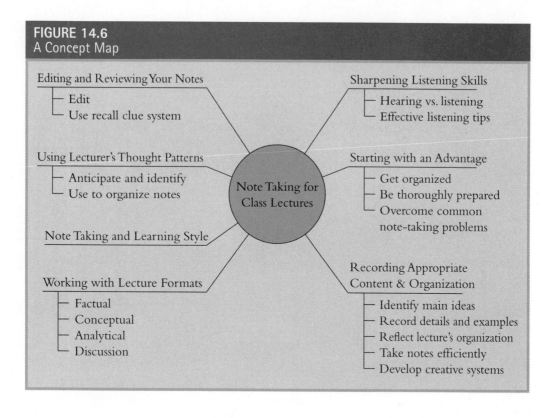

FIGURE 14.6
A Concept Map

Basically, a concept map is a form of outline that presents ideas spatially rather than in list form. Use the following steps in constructing a concept map:

1. **Identify the topic and write it in the center of the page.**

2. **Identify ideas, aspects, parts, and definitions that relate to the topic.** Draw each on a line radiating from the central topic.

3. **As you discover details that further explain an idea already recorded, draw a new line branching from the idea it explains.**

EXERCISE 14.4 **Drawing a Concept Map**

Directions *Choose a section of a chapter in this text that you have already read. Draw a concept map reflecting its overall content and organization.*

Concept maps can be drawn to organize any set of information. For example, you could draw a map to reflect chapter content. However, you can also draw maps to organize a section of a chapter, integrate several sets of lecture notes, or relate text and lecture notes on the same topic.

FIGURE 14.7
A Concept Map

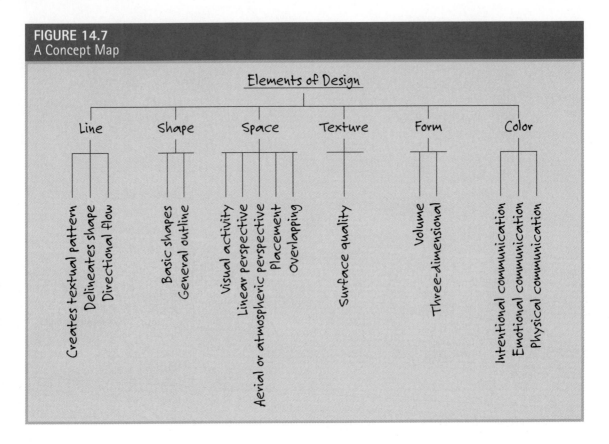

Concept maps can be simple or complex, brief or detailed, depending on the material you are mapping and on your purpose for mapping. Figure 14.7 shows a map an art student drew to integrate information on elements of design. Figure 14.8 shows a more detailed map of the cardiovascular system drawn for an anatomy and physiology course.

Specialized Maps

Each of the following maps relates to a specific thought pattern.

Time Lines

When studying a topic in which the sequence or order of events is a central focus, a time line is a useful way to organize the information. To map a sequence of events, draw a single horizontal line and mark it off in year intervals, just as a ruler is marked off in inches. Then write events next to the

FIGURE 14.8
A Concept Map

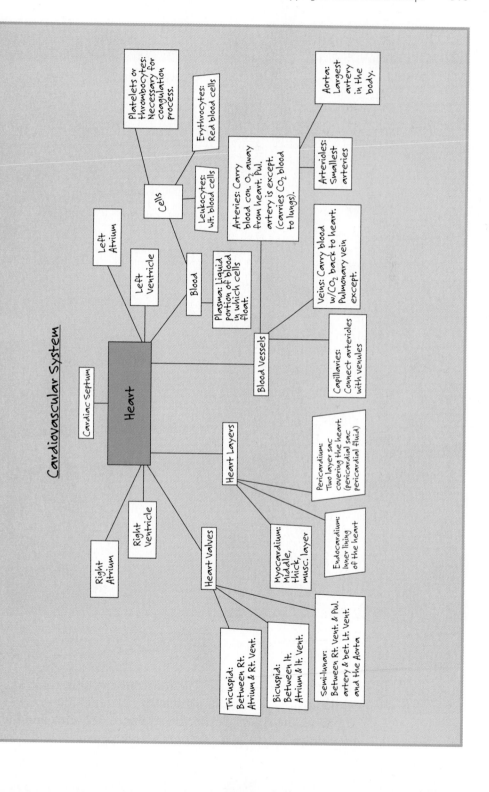

Cardiovascular System

Heart

Cardiac Septum

Left Atrium

Left Ventricle

Blood

Cells

Platelets or Thrombocytes: Necessary for coagulation process.

Erythrocytes: Red blood cells

Leukocytes: Wt. blood cells

Plasma: Liquid portion of blood in which cells float.

Blood Vessels

Arteries: Carry blood con. O$_2$ away from heart. Pul. artery is except. (carries CO$_2$ blood to lungs).

Aorta: Largest artery in the body.

Arterioles: Smallest arteries

Veins: Carry blood w/CO$_2$ back to heart. Pulmonary vein except.

Capillaries: Connect arterioles with venules

Right Atrium

Right Ventricle

Heart Valves

Heart Layers

Pericardium: Two layer sac covering the heart. (pericardial sac pericardial fluid)

Myocardium: Middle, thick, musc. layer

Endocardium: Inner lining of the heart

Tricuspid: Between Rt. Atrium & Rt. Vent.

Bicuspid: Between lt. Atrium & lt. Vent.

Semi-lunar: Between Rt. Vent. & Pul. artery & bet. Lt. Vent. and the Aorta

FIGURE 14.9
A Time Line

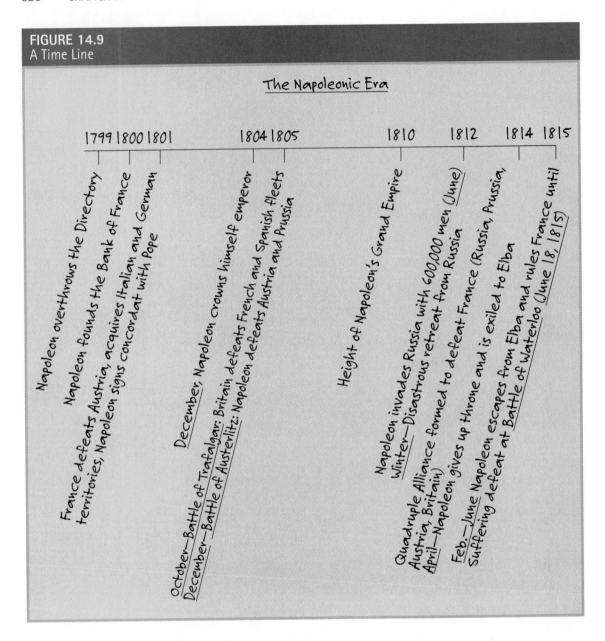

The Napoleonic Era

correct year. For example, the time line in Figure 14.9 was developed for a world history course in which the Napoleonic era was being studied. The time line shows clearly the sequence of events and helps you visualize their order.

EXERCISE 14.6

Drawing a Time Line

Directions   *The following passage reviews the ancient history of maps. Read the selection and then draw a time line that will help you visualize these historical events. (Remember that B.C. refers to time before Christ and that numbers increase as time moves back from history.) Compare your time line with that of a classmate.*

> In Babylonia, in approximately 2300 B.C., the oldest known map was drawn on a clay tablet. The map showed a man's property located in a valley surrounded by tall mountains. Later, around 1300 B.C., the Egyptians drew maps that detailed the location of Ethiopian gold mines and that showed a route from the Nile Valley. The ancient Greeks were early mapmakers as well, although none of their maps remain for us to examine. It is estimated that in 300 B.C. they drew maps showing the earth to be round. The Romans drew maps to tax land and to plan military tactics. The Romans drew the first road maps, a few of which have been preserved for study today. Claudius Ptolemy, an Egyptian scholar who lived around A.D. 160, drew one of the most famous ancient maps. He drew maps of the world as it was known at that time, including 26 regional maps of Europe, Africa, and Asia.

Process Diagrams

A **process diagram** is a chart that depicts the steps, variables, or parts of a process. For example, the diagram in Figure 14.10 might be used by a biology student. It describes the food chain and shows how energy is transferred through food consumption from lowest to highest organisms. Notice that this

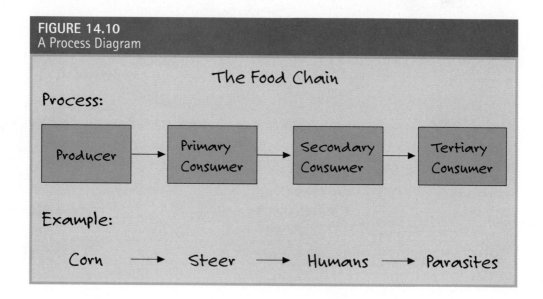

FIGURE 14.10
A Process Diagram

The Food Chain

Process:

Producer → Primary Consumer → Secondary Consumer → Tertiary Consumer

Example:

Corn → Steer → Humans → Parasites

student included an example as well as the steps in the process in order to make the diagram clearer. Figure 14.11 shows a more complicated process diagram. It describes the process for a person charged with a misdemeanor. Alternatives at each step are shown.

FIGURE 14.11
A Process Diagram

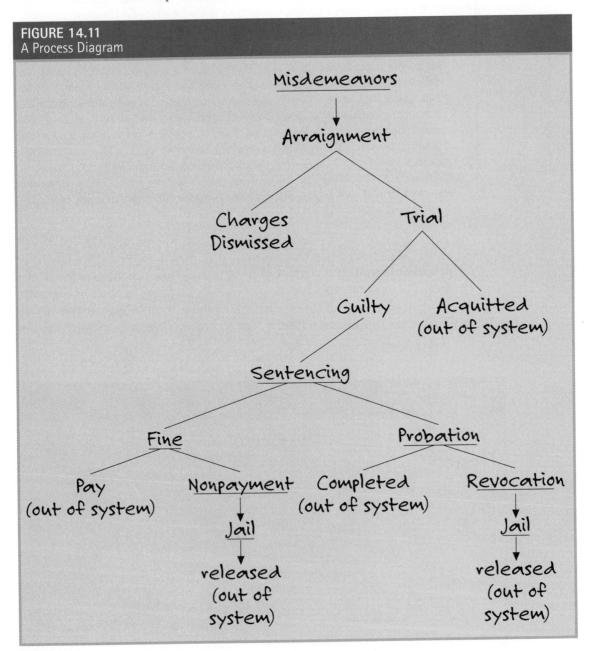

EXERCISE 14.7

Working Together

Drawing a Process Diagram

Directions *The following paragraph describes the process through which malaria is spread by mosquitoes. Read the paragraph and then draw a process diagram that shows how this process occurs. Compare your diagram with that of a classmate. Discuss any differences.*

Malaria, a serious tropical disease, is caused by parasites, or one-celled animals, called protozoa. These parasites live in the red blood cells of humans as well as in the female anopheles mosquitoes. These mosquitoes serve as hosts to the parasites and carry and spread malaria. When an anopheles mosquito stings a person who already has malaria, it ingests the red blood cells that contain the malaria parasites. In the host mosquito's body, these parasites multiply rapidly and move to its salivary glands and mouth. When the host mosquito bites another person, the malaria parasites are injected into the victim and enter his or her bloodstream. The parasites again multiply and burst the victim's blood cells, causing anemia.

Part and Function Diagrams: Classification

A **part and function diagram** is a drawing that labels the various parts and uses of a physical object. In a human anatomy and physiology course, for example, the easiest way to learn the parts and functions of the inner, middle, and outer ear is to draw the ear. To study, sketch the inner ear, and test your recall of each ear part and its function. A sample diagram is shown in Fig-ure 14.12 on p. 324.

EXERCISE 14.8

Working Together

Drawing a Part and Function Diagram

Directions *The following paragraph describes the earth's structure. Read the paragraph and then draw a diagram that will help you visualize how the interior of the earth is structured.*

At the center is a hot, highly compressed inner core, presumably solid and composed mainly of iron and nickel. Surrounding the inner core is an outer core, a molten shell primarily of liquid iron and nickel with lighter liquid material on the top. The outer envelope beyond the core is the mantle, of which the upper portion is mostly solid rock in the form of olivine, an iron-magnesium silicate, and the lower portion chiefly iron and magnesium oxides. A thin coat of metal silicates and oxides (granite) called the crust, forms the outermost skin.[2]

Organizational Charts

An **organizational chat** shows how a business or other group divides its personnel and/or responsibilities. Suppose in a business management course you are studying the organization of a small-market television station. If you drew and studied the organizational chart shown in Figure 14.13 (p. 325), the structure would become apparent and easy to remember.

FIGURE 14.12
A Part and Function Diagram

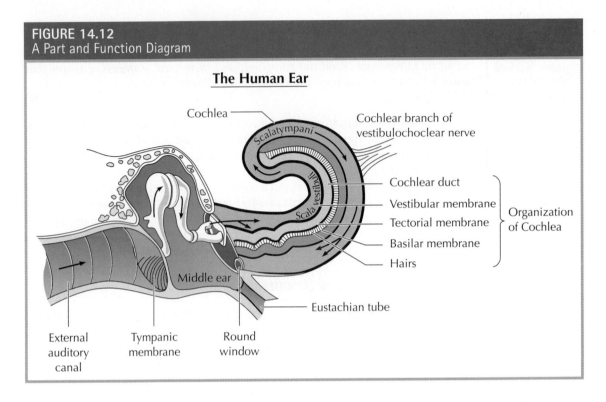

The Human Ear

Cochlea

Scalatympani

Cochlear branch of
vestibulochoclear nerve

Cochlear duct

Vestibular membrane

Tectorial membrane

Basilar membrane

Hairs

Organization
of Cochlea

Scala vestibuli

Scala

Middle ear

Eustachian tube

External
auditory
canal

Tympanic
membrane

Round
window

EXERCISE 14.9

Drawing an Organizational Chart

Directions   *The following paragraph describes one business organizational structure that is studied in business management courses. Read the paragraph and then
draw a diagram that will help you visualize this type of organization.*

It is common for some large businesses to be organized by place, with a
department for each major geographic area in which the firm is active. Businesses
that market products for which customer preference differs from one part of the
country to another often use this management structure. Departmentalization
allows each region to focus on its own special needs and problems. Often, the president of such a company appoints several regional vice-presidents, one for each
part of the country. Then each regional office is divided into sales districts, each
supervised by a district director.

Comparison and Contrast Charts

A **comparison and contrast chart** divides and groups information according
to similarities or common characteristics. Suppose in a business course
on marketing and advertising you are studying three types of market survey

FIGURE 14.13
An Organizational Chart

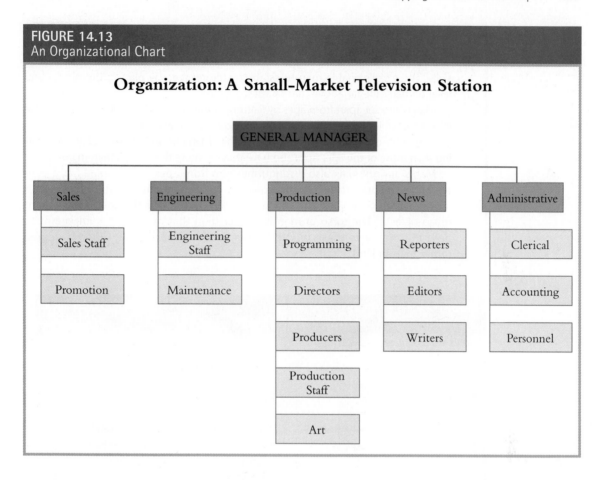

Organization: A Small-Market Television Station

techniques: mail, phone, and personal interview surveys. You are concerned with factors such as cost, level of response, and accuracy. To learn this information in an efficient manner, you could draw a chart such as the one shown in Figure 14.14 on p. 326.

Figure 14.14 on p. 326.

EXERCISE 14.10

Working
Together

Drawing a Comparison and Contrast Chart

Directions   *The following passage describes the major physical differences between humans and apes. Read the selection and then arrange the information into a chart that would make the information easy to learn. Compare your chart with that of a classmate.*

Numerous physical characteristics distinguish man from apes. While apes' bodies are covered with hair, man's body has relatively little hair. While apes often use both their hands and feet to walk, man walks erect. Apes' arms are longer than their legs, while just the reverse is true for man. Apes have large teeth, necessary for devouring coarse, uncooked food, and long canine teeth for self-defense and fighting. By comparison, man's teeth are small and short. The ape's brain is not as well developed as that of man. Man is capable of speech, thinking, and higher-level reasoning skills. These skills enable man to establish culture, thereby placing the quality and level of man's life far above that of apes.

Man is also set apart from apes by features of the head and face. Man's facial profile is vertical, while the ape's profile is *prognathous,* with jaw jutting outward. Man has a chin; apes have a strong lower jaw, but no chin. Man's nostrils are smaller and less flaring than those of the ape. Apes also have thinner, more flexible lips than man.

Man's upright walk also distinguishes him from apes. Man's spine has a double curve to support his weight, while an ape's spine has a single curve. Man's foot is arched both vertically and horizontally, but, unlike the ape's, is unable to grasp objects. The torso of man is shorter than that of apes. It is important to note that many of these physical traits, while quite distinct, differ in degree rather than in kind.

FIGURE 14.14
A Comparison and Contrast Chart

Market Survey Techniques

Type	Cost	Response	Accuracy
Mail	usually the cheapest	lower than phone or personal interview	problems with misunderstanding directions
Phone	depends on availability of 800 number	same as personal interview	problems with unlisted phones and homes w/out phones
Personal interview	most expensive	same as phone	problems with honesty when asking personal or embarrassing questions

SKILLS IN ACTION

Practicing Your Mapping Skills

Draw a map to illustrate the key points of the following passage. You will have to determine the best format for your map.

Tailoring the Marketing Mix for Global Markets

Marketers have several options as to the products they present in the global arena. They can sell the same product abroad that they sell at home, they can modify the product for foreign markets, or they can develop an entirely new product for foreign markets.

The simplest strategy is product extension, which involves offering the same product in all markets, domestic and foreign. This approach has worked successfully for companies including PepsiCo, Coca-Cola, Kentucky Fried Chicken, and Levis. Pepsi and Coke are currently battling for market share in both Russia and Vietnam, countries with small but growing soft-drink markets. Both firms are producing and selling the same cola to the Russian and Vietnamese markets that they sell to other markets around the world. Not all companies that have attempted it, however, have found success with product extension. When Duncan Hines introduced its rich, moist American cakes to England, the British found them too messy to hold while sipping tea. Japanese consumers disliked the coleslaw produced by Kentucky Fried Chicken; it was too sweet for their tastes. KFC responded by cutting the sugar in half.

The strategy of modifying a product to meet local preferences or conditions is product adaptation. Cosmetics companies produce different colors to meet the differing preferences of European consumers. French women like bold reds while British and German women prefer pearly pink shades of lipstick and nail color. Nestle's sells varieties of coffee to suit local tastes worldwide. Unilever produces frozen versions of local delicacies such as Bami Goreng and Madras Curry for markets in Indonesia and India.

Product invention consists of developing a new product to meet a market's needs and preferences. The opportunities that exist with this strategy are great since many unmet needs exist worldwide, particularly in developing and less-developed economies. Marketers have not been quick, however, to attempt product invention. For example, despite the fact that an estimated 600 million people worldwide still scrub cloths by hand, it was the early 1980s before a company (Colgate-Palmolive) developed an inexpensive, all plastic, manual washing machine with the tumbling action of an automatic washer for use in homes without electricity.

—Kinnear et al., *Principles of Marketing*, p. 132

■ Using a Computer to Synthesize Course Content

A computer's word processing capability makes it a useful study and learning aid. The following sections offer suggestions for using the computer to organize your study.

Organizing Notes from Textbook Reading

As you take notes on readings, your notes tend to follow the organization of the text. A computer's word processing program's cut-and-paste functions enable you to rearrange and reorganize your notes or outlines easily without retyping. It allows you to pull together information on a certain topic that is spread throughout one or more chapters.

Integrating Text and Lecture Notes

Students wrestle with how to integrate lecture and textbook notes or outlines. Some try leaving blank space in their lecture notes to add textbook notes; others try a two-column approach, taking lecture notes on half the page and leaving the remaining column blank for textual notes. Neither system works extremely well, though, since one never knows how much space to leave, and some space is always wasted, since lectures and text do not always parallel one another.

The computer offers an ideal solution to the integration of textual and lecture notes. The cut-and-paste option allows you to move sections of your notes to any desired place in the document. Thus, you can easily integrate text and lecture notes on each major topic. In Chapter 16, you will discover how to use these sets of notes to prepare for exams.

REAL STUDENTS SPEAK

Jamie Sturm

Kalamazoo College
Kalamazoo, MI

Background: Jamie is a senior at Kalamazoo, where he is studying for a bachelor's degree in international relations. He spent his junior year studying in China and the summer of 2009 in Ecuador.

Goals: To teach English abroad for 1–2 years, work for a large company like Honeywell or Coca Cola for an additional 1–2 years, obtain a master's degree, and possibly apply for a job in the U. S. Foreign Service.

Advice on Organizing Notes and Writing Outlines: In my opinion it's all about being able to say in your own words what you learned in class. I take extensive notes on the topic in class. I divide my notes into sections as I write using section headings and bullet points. When I read over the notes to study for tests, I read section by section and make sure that if I close my eyes I can explain to someone the information in that section. If I don't understand something and I'm studying with a classmate, I will ask questions and add in the answers. As I study, I highlight the information that is most important. If I have an essay exam, I sometimes write new notes, writing answers to possible questions in a bulleted form in the order I would write them in an essay.

Working Together

Working in groups of three, students should complete the following steps.

1. Each group should choose one academic discipline and read the corresponding section in Chapter 9 of this text.

2. Next, read a section of a textbook in that discipline. Assume this material will be included on an exam.

3. One group member should highlight and annotate the section; another should make outline notes; the third member should draw a map of its content.

4. Group members should review and critique one another's work and discuss the following questions:

   a. Which of the three methods used seemed most effective for this material?

   b. Might your answer to the above question depend on the type of exam you would have (objective or essay)?

   c. What advantages did each method seem to offer? What were its limitations?

5. Make a generalization about situations in which each can be used most effectively.

REVIEW   Five Key Points to Remember

1 **Highlight your textbooks to identify what is important to learn.** Use a textbook's headings to help you identify what is important.

2 **Use marking and annotation in addition to highlighting.** Develop a system that includes marginal annotations, as well as summary notes and recall clues.

3 **Write outline notes.** These will help you see relationships among ideas and discover their relative importance.

4 **Draw maps to show how ideas are connected.** Use concept maps for general information; use time lines, process diagrams, part and function diagrams, organizational charts, and comparison and contrast charts for material following a specific thought pattern.

5 **Use your computer to pull together course content.** Word processing is a great tool for reorganizing notes and integrating text and lecture material.

The Work Connection

How can you use the techniques you have learned in this chapter to market yourself to prospective employers? One way is to organize and synthesize information about yourself so you can respond effectively to help wanted ads. To gain an interview with a prospective employer, you first need to figure out what the job requires and then demonstrate in a résumé that you have the needed knowledge, skills, and accomplishments. Since most employers spend only about 20 to 30 seconds reading a résumé, you need to be able to organize and synthesize all your best points in a succinct format that directly responds to the points in a help wanted ad. Try the following steps.

1. Find a help wanted ad in a newspaper that lists at least three qualifications a successful job candidate should have. (An example of a qualification is "excellent written and verbal communication skills.") For each qualification, list experiences that demonstrate that you have the desired skills. List four to seven examples—from work, school, home, and extracurricular activities—that show you possess that qualification.

2. Which of your examples relate most directly to the qualification? Organize your examples from most important to least important. If some examples don't seem relevant, replace them with examples more closely related to the qualification. Stop when you have three solid examples for each qualification.

The Web Connection

1. Visual Organizers

   http://www.bucks.edu/~specpop/visual-org.htm

   Explanations and examples of various ways to graphically represent information are presented here at this site created by Bucks County Community College. Create several of your own visual organizers centered around your life. Try topics such as your schedule, your family history, future plans, or friends.

2. How to Read a Textbook

   http://www.uwmc.uwc.edu/freshman_seminar/read.htm#how

   Visit this site to find more tips on highlighting and writing margin notes from the University of Wisconsin, Marathon County. Practice on an old textbook from high school or from a used bookstore, garage sale, or library sale.

3. Concept Maps

   http://wik.ed.uiuc.edu/index.php/Concept_mapping#kinds_of_Concept_Maps

   Investigate the kinds of concepts maps listed in this Education Wiki from the University of Illinois at Urbana-Champaign. Using ideas, relationships, situations, and experiences from your own life, create a simple concept map of three different types.

15 Critical Reading and Thinking About Course Content

Do You Know?

How can you synthesize a number of different sources?

How can you distinguish between fact and opinion?

How do you evaluate differing viewpoints?

How can you evaluate generalizations?

How can you test hypotheses?

What critical questions can you ask to sort reliable information from unreliable information?

How can you evaluate the logic of an argument?

Critical reading and thinking skills are important when taking tests and exams. Many multiple-choice and essay exam questions measure your factual recall, but they also test your ability to think about and use what you have learned—to analyze, synthesize, evaluate, and apply course content.

Critical reading is also important when you take more advanced courses. You will find yourself working with many new kinds of material: research articles, essays, critiques, reports, and analyses. To these, you will be expected to respond critically by discussing, criticizing, interpreting, and evaluating the authors' ideas. You may need to assess the accuracy and completeness of information, identify persuasive techniques, or evaluate an argument. This chapter will help you pull together course content, evaluate what you are reading and learning, grasp implications, and make applications.

■ Synthesizing Information

Many writing assignments require you to synthesize, or pull together, information from a variety of sources. Synthesis is often required for in-class assignments, essay examinations, and term papers. Synthesizing is creating something new from a number of sources. Synthesizing information involves examining and inferring relationships among sources and then making those relationships explicit, usually in writing. Synthesis often results in a new idea, focus, or perspective.

Synthesis is required in a variety of academic situations:

♦ Integrating text and lecture notes on the same topic
♦ Summarizing information from several sources
♦ Reading several magazine articles on the same controversial issue and discussing pros and cons
♦ Answering an essay exam question based on notes, lectures, and class discussion of the same topic

Here are a few more specific examples of assignments that require synthesis. Notice that each implies a thought pattern.

Mass Communications

Discuss how the use of television may have affected public opinion toward the Vietnam War. Refer to at least three sources.

Literature

Select two twentieth-century American writers whose work you feel was influenced by the liberal attitudes of the 1960s. Discuss how this influence is evident in their writings.

Each of these assignments requires you to combine information or ideas. Each assignment, too, focuses on a type of relationship or thought pattern. The mass communications assignment asks you to infer a cause and effect relationship between television and public opinion. The literature assignment requires comparison and contrast between two writers.

The thought patterns you learned in Chapter 11 will be useful in synthesizing information. If, for example, you are synthesizing two or more articles that explain cultural differences in the status of women in the Middle East as compared to in the United States, you can expect each article to use a comparison and contrast and possibly a cause and effect pattern. The articles will contrast women's status in the two regions and possibly explain why the differences exist. To synthesize these articles you might make a comparison and contrast chart of differences and then rearrange it by grouping the differences according to categories such as public/social behavior, role in the family, dress, legal rights, and so forth. If the articles detail reasons for the differences, you might add a third column titled "Why?" or "Reasons."

The most useful patterns are cause and effect, comparison and contrast, and classification. Table 15.1 on p. 334 lists suggestions for using each of these three patterns to synthesize information.

TABLE 15.1   Synthesizing Information Using Patterns

Pattern	Suggestions
Cause and effect	1. Is the same cause and effect relationship described in all sources? 2. Can you construct a chain of events or happenings, each dependent on one another? 3. How do sources differ in attributing cause or describing effects?
Comparison and contrast	1. Identify ideas that are similar. Discover points of similarity. 2. Look for differences. Determine how and why the ideas or information differ. 3. Draw charts outlining similarities and differences.
Classification	1. Organize information into broad types or categories. 2. Look for similarities and differences among ideas. How are members of a group similar? How are they distinguishable from one another? 3. Look for overlap among categories. 4. List features of each category.

EXERCISE 15.1

Analyzing an Assignment

Directions   *Analyze the following assignment by identifying the thought pattern(s) and note-taking strategies to use in synthesizing the information:*

Using the periodical collection in the campus library, read three reports of a current national news event in *Time, U.S. News and World Report*, and one other periodical of your choice. Examine each, identifying factors such as completeness of coverage, political or social viewpoint, and amount of detail. Write a one-page paper evaluating the completeness and accuracy of each source.

SKILLS IN ACTION

Synthesizing Information Across Courses

College involves building on what you learn in one course to give you deeper perspectives in other courses. Consider the following statement, which you might read on the opinion page of your local newspaper:

"Though America has been fighting the 'War on Drugs' for decades, it seems clear that the drugs are winning. Every year thousands of people go to jail for selling or taking drugs. In the meantime, a very common drug—alcohol—is perfectly legal. And let's not even mention the abuse of prescription drugs, which is common and becoming even more common."

Suggest how this statement may be relevant to each of the courses you are taking, and how each course might treat this topic. For the sake of this exercise, assume you are taking the following courses:

Criminal Justice

Sociology

Psychology

Developmental Math/Pre-Algebra

Introduction to College Writing

■ Distinguishing Between Fact and Opinion

Facts are statements that can be verified—that is, proven to be true.

Opinions are statements that express feelings, attitudes, or beliefs and are neither true nor false. Here are a few examples of each.

Facts:

1. Martin Luther King, Jr., was assassinated in 1968.
2. Native Americans in the Great Plains were primarily meat eaters; herds of buffalo provided their main source of food.

Opinions:

1. If John F. Kennedy had lived, the United States would have made even greater advancements against the spread of communism in the 1960s.
2. By the year 2025, food shortages will be a major problem in most Asian countries.

Opinions are sometimes signaled by the use of such key words or phrases as *apparently, this suggests, some believe, it is likely that, seemingly, in my view* and *one explanation is.*

EXERCISE 15.2

Distinguishing Fact and Opinion

Directions   *Identify each of the following statements as either fact or opinion.*

1. Between 1945 and 1990, 203,432 persons were arrested for homicide in Mexico.
2. Job orientation should begin before an employee starts to work.
3. All the states have developed laws that require hospitals and health care workers to report each incidence of communicable or infectious disease.

4. A major step in developing assertive behavior is evaluating your own strengths and weaknesses.

5. The immune deficiency in AIDS (Acquired Immune Deficiency Syndrome) results from a decreased number of certain white blood cells called T-helper lymphocytes.

6. People caught in the throes of romantic love are drawn to thoughts of marriage as moths are drawn to light.

7. The state should curtail the liberty of the individual.

8. An infection is an illness produced by the action of microorganisms in the human body.

9. Virtue is its own reward.

10. A prominent theory among biologists is that humans are by nature instinctively aggressive.

Opinions can be divided into two categories: *informed opinions* and *uninformed opinions*. **Informed opinions** are made by people who are respected in their fields, whose learning and experience make them qualified to offer opinions that are *more likely* to be factual or to become factual. Noam Chomsky represents expert opinion in the field of linguistics, for example. **Uninformed opinions** are offered by those who have little or no background information and few qualifications. To determine whether an opinion is informed or not, ask yourself these questions:

◆ What job or title does this person hold? (For example, journalists will often give the professional title of the person they are quoting as a way of demonstrating that the opinion offered is an informed one.)

◆ What experience does this person have regarding the subject matter?

◆ What do other respected authorities think of this person?

◆ Is this the opinion of a respected organization of professionals, such as the AMA (American Medical Association) or U.S. BLS (Bureau of Labor Statistics)?

Textbook authors, too, often offer expert opinion, as in the following statement from an American government text.

Ample evidence indicates voters pay attention to economic conditions in making up their minds on election day: not only to their personal circumstances—whether they are employed or how secure their job is—but also to national economic circumstances.[1]

The author of this statement has reviewed the available evidence and is providing his expert opinion as to what the evidence indicates.

As you write papers, participate in class discussions, and answer exam questions, you will use facts to support your ideas. Opinions are one person's point of view that you are free to accept or reject. With the exception of expert ones, opinions have little use as supporting evidence.

A goal in many courses is to enable students to reexamine their existing beliefs, attitudes, and opinions. Opinions are useful in shaping and evaluating your own thinking. Exposure to both contradictory and supporting opinions provides background against which you can evaluate your own thinking. Expect your professors to ask challenging questions such as "Why do you think so?" and "What evidence do you have to support that opinion?"

| EXERCISE 15.3 | **Predicting Fact or Opinion** |

Working Together

Directions   *For each of the materials listed below, working in pairs, discuss and predict whether it will contain primarily fact or opinion.*

1. A book titled *Move Your Shadow: South Africa, Black and White,* written by Pulitzer prize–winning reporter Joseph Lelyveld, who lived in South Africa in the 1960s and again in the 1980s
2. An article titled "Advertising in the Year 2020"
3. A book titled *The Nazi Doctors: Medical Killing and the Psychology of Genocide* by Robert Lifton
4. An article in the *New England Journal of Medicine* titled "Control of Health Care Costs in the Next Decade"
5. A book titled *Secrets of Strong Families* by Nick Stinnett, which describes how to keep a family happy and together.

■ Evaluating Differing Viewpoints

College provides you with an opportunity to encounter new ideas and viewpoints. Some of these ideas may force you to reexamine your own values and beliefs and to reevaluate how you think about a particular issue. An instructor may examine a controversial or current topic or issue by asking you to examine or compare differing viewpoints. A sociology professor may, for example, assign several supplementary readings, each of which takes a different stance on capital punishment. Or, in a modern fiction class, you may consider various interpretations of Kurt Vonnegut's *Slaughterhouse Five.*

In examining differing viewpoints, try the following suggestions:

◆ Deliberately put aside or suspend temporarily what you already believe about a particular issue.

◆ Discover what similarities and differences exist among the various viewpoints.

◆ Identify the assumptions on which each view is based.

◆ Look for and evaluate evidence that suggests the viewpoint is well thought out.

◆ To overcome the natural tendency to pay more attention to points of view with which you agree and treat opposing viewpoints superficially,

REAL STUDENTS SPEAK

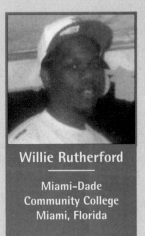

Willie Rutherford
—————
**Miami-Dade
Community College
Miami, Florida**

Background: Willie is a freshman at Miami-Dade Community College. He is taking a double major: an associate's degree in general education and an associate's degree in arts.

Goal: To become a registered nurse.

Advice on Problem Solving: I had a problem with my Reading 03 class. I was falling behind because I was not putting in enough time and effort. I was getting out of school early, doing other stuff, coming to class late, and not keeping up with the assignments. I stopped and thought to myself, What am I doing? I knew how to do the work, I just wasn't using my time wisely. So I organized a daily schedule. I wrote in all my classes, wrote in study time, and made sure I had some time for myself. I ended up passing my class and getting better scores on exams and quizzes. If you want to be successful, you have to use time wisely; you don't get it back.

deliberately spend more time reading, thinking about, and examining ideas that differ from your own.

◆ To analyze particularly complex, difficult, or very similar viewpoints, write a summary of each. Through the process of writing, you will be forced to discover the essence of each view.

Evaluating differing viewpoints is a way to pull together ideas and deal with differing, even contradictory, sources.

EXERCISE 15.4

**Working
Together**

Analyzing Viewpoints

Directions   *Determine how the three viewpoints on gun control expressed in statements 1 to 3 differ. Then break into small groups and discuss your responses.*

1.   Guns don't kill people, people kill people. Gun laws do not deter criminals. (A 1976 University of Wisconsin study of gun laws concluded that "gun control laws have no individual or collective effect in reducing the rate of violent crime.") A mandatory sentence for carrying an unlicensed gun, says Kates, would punish the "ordinary decent citizens in high-crime areas who carry guns illegally because police protection is inadequate and they don't have the special influence necessary to get a 'carry' permit." There are fifty million handguns out there in the United States already; unless you were to use a giant magnet, there is no way to retrieve them. The majority of people do not want guns banned. A ban on handguns would be like

Prohibition—widely disregarded, unenforceable, and corrosive to the nation's sense of moral order. Federal registration is the beginning of federal tyranny; we might someday need to use those guns against the government.[2]

2.   People kill people, but handguns make it easier. When other weapons (knives, for instance) are used, the consequences are not so often deadly. Strangling or stabbing someone takes a different degree of energy and intent than pulling a trigger. Registration will not interfere with hunting and other rifle sports but will simply exercise control over who can carry handguns. Ordinary people do not carry handguns. If a burglar has a gun in his hand, it is quite insane for you to shoot it out with him, as if you were in a quick draw contest in the Wild West. Half of all the guns used in crimes are stolen; 70% of the stolen guns are handguns. In other words, the supply of handguns used by criminals already comes to a great extent from the households these guns were supposed to protect.[3]

3.   [Statement by Edward Kennedy] We all know the toll that has been taken in this nation. We all know the leaders of our public life and of the human spirit who have been lost or wounded year after year. My brother, John Kennedy, and my brother, Robert Kennedy; Medgar Evers, who died so that others could live free; Martin Luther King, the apostle of nonviolence who became the victim of violence; George Wallace, who has been paralyzed for nearly nine years; and George Moscone, the mayor of San Francisco who was killed in his office. Last year alone, we lost Allard Lowenstein, and we almost lost Vernon Jordan. Four months ago, we lost John Lennon, the gentle soul who challenged us in song to "give peace a chance." We had two attacks on President Ford and now the attack on President Reagan.[4]

■ Evaluating Generalizations

A **generalization** is a statement made about a large group or class of items based on observation or experience with a portion of that group or class. Each of the following statements is a generalization:

- ◆ College freshmen are confused and disoriented during their first week on campus.
- ◆ Typewriter keyboards and computer terminal keyboards are similar.
- ◆ The courts, especially those in large cities, are faced with far more criminal cases than they can handle.

By visiting campuses and observing and talking with freshman students, you could make the generalization that freshmen are confused and disoriented. However, unless you observed and talked with *every* college student, you could not be absolutely certain your generalization is correct. Similarly, unless you contacted each large city court, you could not be certain of the accuracy of the third statement.

In many courses you will be expected to read and evaluate generalizations, as well as to make them yourself. Often, generalizations are followed by evidence that supports them, as in the following excerpt from a sociology text:

> An act considered deviant in one time period may be considered nondeviant in another. Cigarette smoking, for example, has a long history of changing normative definitions. Nuehring and Markle (1974) note that in the United States between 1895 and 1921, fourteen states completely banned cigarette smoking and all other states except Texas passed laws regulating the sale of cigarettes to minors. In the early years of this century, stop-smoking clinics were opened in several cities and antismoking campaigns were widespread. Following World War I, however, cigarette sales increased and public attitudes toward smoking changed. Through the mass media, the tobacco industry appealed to women, weight-watchers, and even to health seekers. States began to realize that tobacco could be a rich source of revenue, and by 1927 the fourteen states that banned cigarettes had repealed their laws. By the end of World War II, smoking had become acceptable, and in many contexts it was thought socially desirable. Today, once again, attitudes toward smoking have changed and it is considered less socially acceptable.[5]

The excerpt begins with two generalizations. The second generalization (sentence 2), which is supported throughout the remainder of the paragraph, is made in support of the first generalization, stated in the opening sentence.

Because writers do not always have the space to describe all available evidence on a topic, they often draw the evidence together themselves and make a general statement of what it shows. Generalizations that stand alone without any evidence to attest to their accuracy appear to be unsupported. The following paragraph makes numerous generalizations about the elderly.

> The lifestyles of the elderly vary greatly, depending on their social class and income. Women and blacks are the groups most likely to live in poverty. The most common source of income for the aged is Social Security. A minimal income is available to those not on Social Security through the Supplemental Security Income program. Income and class level greatly influence the health of the elderly.[6]

Without supporting evidence, you cannot evaluate the accuracy of the generalizations unless you research the topic yourself. You are left to rely on the credibility of the author to make accurate generalizations. In textbooks, where the author is an authority in his or her field, credibility is seldom a problem. However, when reading other information sources, do not assume automatically that all generalizations are supportable.

In many courses, you will be required to make generalizations by applying your knowledge to related, similar situations. Generalizing is an important skill—one that makes your learning usable and relevant in a variety of situations. Here are a few instances that require you to generalize:

◆ Solving math problems similar to sample problems solved in class
◆ Summarizing your experience with part-time jobs to make a generalization about the benefits of work experience
◆ Applying methods you learned in child psychology to control your niece's temper tantrums

Your generalization is usable and relevant when your experiences are sufficient in number to merit a generalization.

EXERCISE 15.5

Identifying and Analyzing Generalizations

Directions *Indicate which of statements 1 through 10 are generalizations. Then indicate what support or documentation would be necessary for you to evaluate their worth and accuracy.*

1. Fast food companies own large amounts of real estate.
2. Popular music artists have the highest incomes of all entertainers.
3. Big money can be made in every corner of the world, including the world of legitimate drug consumption.
4. Floor space in department stores is valued at $150 per square foot.
5. Creative products including paintings, engineering design plans, and musical scores are revised and revised again until they take final shape.
6. Intimacy is established through effective verbal communication.
7. Criminal lawyers work the longest hours of all types of lawyers.
8. The kidney produces an enzymelike substance known as renin that raises blood pressure.
9. *Quackery* refers to the use of unproved or disapproved methods or devices to diagnose or treat illnesses.
10. Heroin costs the addict more than $20 a day.

■ Testing Hypotheses

Suppose you arrive three minutes late to your biology class and find the classroom empty. You notice that the instructor's notes are on her desk and that most of the students have left their jackets or notebooks behind. So you form a hypothesis, a supposition to account for the observed circumstances and explain the absence of the class and instructor. You might hypothesize that the class went across the hall to the lab, for instance. A hypothesis, then, is a statement based on available evidence that explains an event or set of circumstances.

Here are a few examples of situations involving forming hypotheses:

◆ A nursing student is asked by her supervisor why she thinks patient X refuses to take his medication.
◆ A chemistry student must explain in her laboratory report why her experiment failed to produce expected results.
◆ A literature professor assigns a paper that requires you to develop and support a consistent theory explaining the symbolism used throughout a short story.

Hypotheses are simply *plausible* explanations. They are always open to confirmation, dispute, or refutation, usually by the addition of further information.

As you read textbook assignments, participate in class discussions, and conduct library research, you will frequently encounter hypotheses. In a political science course, for example, you might be asked to evaluate a theory or hypothesis that explains Stalin's popularity in Russia after Lenin's death. Or in a business and finance course, a class discussion may center on theories by Keynes and Friedman that explain why people choose to hold on to and not spend money. Evaluating a hypothesis is a two-part process. First, you must evaluate the evidence provided. Then you must search for information, reasons, or evidence that suggests the truth or falsity of the hypothesis. Ask questions such as these:

◆ Does my hypothesis account for all known information about the situation?
◆ Is it realistic—that is, within the realm of possibility and probability?

◆ Is it simple, or less complicated than, its alternatives? (Usually, unless a complex hypothesis can account for information not accounted for by a simple hypothesis, the simple one has greater likelihood of being correct.)

◆ What assumptions were made? Are they valid?

EXERCISE 15.6	**Developing Hypotheses**

Directions   *Develop hypotheses to explain each of situations 1 through 3.*

1. The book *What to Expect When You're Expecting* appeared on the *New York Times* best-seller list for at least 418 weeks.
2. McDonald's has expanded its operations to numerous foreign countries. It has become one of England's largest food service organizations.
3. There has been an increase in the number of children per couple in the United States.

THINKING CRITICALLY
. . . About Data and Evidence

You may have heard the term *spin doctor*. This is a phrase used to describe a public relations specialist whose job is to put a positive "spin" on bad news. Reading and thinking critically requires you to understand when information is being presented fairly, or when it is being "spun" for some purpose—to influence, to manipulate, to get votes, and so forth.

In general, information is the most reliable when it is based on solid *evidence*. Just as police look for evidence to discover who committed a crime, college students must look for evidence that supports any assertion being made by a writer. The following types of evidence are often considered relevant and valid:

1. **Personal experience or examples**. Personal experience can be very powerful. For example, no one understands cancer like a person who has suffered with the disease and survived. Keep in mind, however, that different people can experience the same event very differently, so be careful about overgeneralizing the experiences of one person.

2. **Statistical data**. Statistics and data are often collected by universities or professional research organizations, so these tend to be reliable. However, be wary of people using data in ways that try to hide the truth rather than clarify it. For example, a soda company may claim, "90 percent of the people in a taste test preferred our cola to our competitor's cola." This statement may be true, but what if the taste test were conducted at the company's headquarters?

(continues)

Wouldn't that create a different result than a taste test run in a more neutral location, such as a mall?

3. **Examples, descriptions of events, or illustrations.** Eyewitness reports are often considered reliable, but again remember that different people can interpret the same situation in different ways. Suppose you see a building burst into flames, then see a man run out of the building. You may think, "What a lucky man! He escaped from the burning building." Another person may think, "That man just started that fire to burn the building down and collect the insurance money." You need to do more investigating to discover whether either assumption is correct.

4. **Experimental evidence.** The results of scientific experiments are often considered valid because they are based on the *scientific method*, which very carefully prescribes the correct research method to achieve valid results. However, experiments are sometimes conducted improperly; and a wide variety of uncontrollable factors can influence the results of tests on human beings.

SKILLS IN ACTION

Analyzing Statements

Consider each of the following statements and the context in which it is made. How might you respond to each statement? What sort of information is missing that would help you weigh the evidence and evaluate the claim being made?

1. On the label of a bag of cookies:

   "CONTAINS 45% LESS FAT and 0 grams of TRANS FAT!"

2. In a printed political campaign flyer for mayoral candidate Mary Johnson:

   "Some people suspect my opponent, Joe Smith, of serious ethical breaches during his term as mayor. If you elect me as your mayor in the upcoming election, I promise to uphold the highest ethical standards."

3. In large print on the cover of a novel you see at the supermarket checkout:

   "This novel is a . . . wild and exciting . . . ride through the rough-and-tumble days of the Gold Rush . . . full of . . . adventure and excitement. . . . Memorable."—*The New York Times*

■ Asking Critical Questions

Suppose you received a phone call from someone saying you had just won a new car, and all you needed to do was pay a $200 claim fee to take ownership. Would you immediately write a check, or would you be suspicious and question the caller? Perhaps you would hang up, knowing it couldn't be true. As consumers we tend to be wise, alert, and critical—even suspicious. As readers, however, we tend to be much more tolerant and accepting. Many readers readily accept information and ideas presented in written form. This section of the chapter suggests questions that will help you become a more critical reader and thinker.

What Is the Source of the Material?

Determine from what book, magazine, reference book, newspaper, or online source the material you are reading was taken and then evaluate that source. Some sources are much more reliable and trustworthy than others.

Newspapers.   Most newspapers have an editorial page or section in which the newspaper's editors or contributors offer their opinions on important topics. Anything found on the opinion page is likely to offer only one viewpoint and to have some sort of agenda, so be aware of this. Also understand that some newspapers will tend to be more liberal in their views, while others will be more conservative politically. These tendencies show up not just on the editorial page but often in the way news stories are presented. The same is true for TV news broadcasts.

Magazines.   There are thousands of magazines in circulation. Some are quite serious and devoted to the interests of people with very specific hobbies, such as miniature dollhouses, scrapbooking, or toy trains. Such magazines can be excellent sources of information. At the other end of the spectrum are glossy magazines that focus on gossip and celebrities, such as *People* and *Us*. How do you think magazines in the latter category rate in terms of trustworthiness?

The Internet.   As we enter the second decade of the twenty-first century, the Internet is increasingly the first place people turn to for news and research. The key thing to remember about the Internet is that it is free and open to everyone. That means that anyone can create a Web page for any reason. So how can you tell which Web sites to trust and which are less reliable? In general, any Web site that ends in **.com** is a business-based Web site, which means it is trying to sell you something. In contrast, a Web site that ends in **.edu** is sponsored by a college or university, and the information appearing on that Web site is probably quite reliable. The same holds true for **.gov** Web addresses, which are run by organizations within the government. The government collects massive amounts of data and information each year, and it makes all this information available free to anyone who wants it. Nonprofit organizations, which are often philanthropic

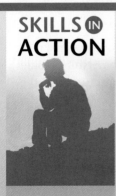

SKILLS IN ACTION

Evaluating Internet Sources

On your own or as part of a class discussion, evaluate the reliability of each of the following sources. Which exist solely for entertainment and should not be taken too seriously? Which would be acceptable as a reference in a research paper?

1. *The Washington Post* (newspaper)
2. The *National Enquirer* (newspaper/magazine)
3. *The Wall Street Journal* (newspaper)
4. *The Onion* (magazine)
5. *Soap Opera Digest* (magazine)
6. http://www.thesmokinggun.com
7. http://www.census.gov (Web site of the U.S. Census Bureau)
8. http://www.tmz.com
9. *The Journal of Economic Research*
10. Wikipedia (http://www.wikipedia.org)

organizations, use **.org** in their Web addresses and are often, but not always, reliable sources of information (anyone can buy a .org address, so be sure to evaluate sites carefully).

Blogs.   The word *blog* is short for *Web log*. A blog is basically an online diary for an individual, who uses the blog to comment on whatever topics he or she finds interesting. By its very definition, a blog is personal and opinionated. Blogs can be a good source of interesting reading. (For example, some famous economists, such as Paul Krugman and Gregory Mankiw, have very popular blogs. But Krugman is very liberal politically, while Mankiw is very conservative politically, so to get both sides of an issue you'd need to read *both* blogs.)

Scholarly journals.   Almost by definition, scholarly journals are excellent sources of information. So are the academic associations that produce them and serve as clearinghouses for important information in the discipline.

What Are the Author's Credentials?

Not everything that appears in print is accurate and competently reported. Consequently, you must assess whether the material you are reading is written by an expert in the field who can knowledgeably and accurately discuss the topic. In some materials, the author's credentials are footnoted or summarized at the end of the work. In journal articles, the author's college or university affiliation is often included. Authors also may establish their expertise or experience in the field within the material itself.

What Is the Author's Tone?

Have you ever noticed that people can sometimes say words that on paper would seem polite, but the tone of the words conveys a very different meaning? Consider a police officer who has pulled you over for speeding. He approaches the car and says to you, "Please step out of the car, sir (or ma'am)." Wouldn't a police officer saying these words *sound* very different from an employee at a car wash, who says the same words to you so that he can take your car through the car wash and then vacuum the interior?

Tone refers to how a writer sounds to readers and how the writer feels about his or her topic. (Note that we refer in this section to writers, but public speakers, such as journalists and politicians, also have very distinct tones when they speak.) Recognizing an author's tone will help you interpret and evaluate the message, as well as the message's intended effect on you.

Tone is revealed primarily through word choice and stylistic features such as sentence patterns and length. A writer can communicate surprise, disapproval, disgust, admiration, gratitude, or amusement, for example.

In your college experience, you will undoubtedly encounter many controversial issues and many speakers and writers who feel passionate about their beliefs. Be sure not to get carried away by the writer or speaker's tone or commitment. As a critical thinker, it is your job to analyze the words, the facts, and the tone to determine what their impact is on you, and whether or not you are being told the complete story.

Is the Author Biased?

Read each of the following statements and determine what they have in common:

◆ How can a sportsman, solely for his own pleasure, delight in the mutilation of a living animal?
◆ Laboratory experiments using live animals are forms of torture.
◆ The current vitamin fad is a distortion of sound medical advice.

Each statement reflects a **bias**—a partiality, preference, or prejudice for or against a person, object, or idea. Biased material is one-sided. Other facts, such as the advantages of using animals for laboratory research, or research that has confirmed the value of taking vitamins, are not mentioned. Notice, too, the use of emotional words such as *mutilation* and *torture*.

SKILLS IN ACTION

Thinking Critically About Tone

Develop your ability to think critically about tone by completing the following exercises.

1. Read each of the following statements; then describe its tone. Which words in the statement are clues to the tone?

   a. When you are backpacking, you can reduce the risk of back injury by adjusting your pack so that most of its weight is on your hip belt rather than your shoulder straps.

   b. Do you eat canned tuna? Then you are at least partially responsible for the deaths of thousands of innocent dolphins, who are mercilessly slaughtered by fisherman in their quest for huge schools of tuna.

   c. The penalty for creating and launching a computer virus should include a personal apology to every single person who was affected by the virus, and each apology should be typed—without errors!—on a manual typewriter.

   d. Our accumulating piles of solid waste threaten to ruin our environment, pointing to the urgent need for not only better disposal methods but also strategies to lower the rate of waste generation.

   e. All poets seek to convey emotion and the complete range of human feeling, but the only poet who fully accomplished this goal was William Shakespeare.

2. Consider the following situation: A highly populated city has decided to bulldoze an entire city block filled with burned-out tenement buildings and crumbling old factories. In their place, a developer is going to build a community of 300 upscale condominiums for people who work in the city and want to live close to their jobs.

   Write three different sentences that react to this news. Make the tone of your first sentence *outraged*. Make the tone of your second sentence *jubilant*. Make the tone of your third sentence *nostalgic*.

Much of what you read and hear expresses a bias. In many newspapers and magazine articles, nonfiction books, advertisements, and essays you will find the attitudes, opinions, and beliefs of the speaker or author revealed. As you listen to a history lecture, for example, you may discover the professor's attitude or bias toward particular historical figures, political decisions, or events.

Some writers reveal their attitudes directly by stating how they feel. Others do so less directly, expressing their attitudes through the manner in which they write. Through selection of facts, choice of words, and the quality and tone of description, they convey a particular feeling or attitude.

As you read or listen to biased materials, keep the following questions in mind:

◆ What facts were omitted? What additional facts are needed?
◆ What words create positive or negative impressions?
◆ What impression would I have if different words had been used?

| EXERCISE 15.7 | **Identifying Words that Indicate Bias** |

Directions   *In each of the following statements, underline the words and phrases that reveal the writer's bias. Indicate what additional information you would need to evaluate each.*

1. Now you can have room and comfort as well as a world-class road car for under $10,000.
2. The country has wasted a lot of money on purposeless space exploration.
3. The drunken behavior of sports fans at play-off games is a disgrace and insult to players and fans alike.
4. Shakespeare exhibited creative genius far beyond his contemporary playwrights by revealing insights into human behavior and its motivation.
5. Highgate University offers competitive athletic opportunities in football and basketball; its focus on academic excellence is unyielding; its emphasis on scholarship, outstanding; its commitment to equal opportunity, admirable.

Does the Author Make Assumptions?

An assumption is an idea or principle the writer accepts as true and makes no effort to prove or substantiate. Usually, it is a beginning or premise upon which he or she bases the remainder of the work. For example, an author may assume that television encourages violent behavior in children and proceed to argue for restrictions on watching TV. Or a writer may assume that abortion is morally wrong and suggest legal restrictions on how and when abortions are performed.

■ Examining an Argument

An argument is a logical arrangement and presentation of ideas. An **argument** addresses an issue and takes a position or makes a claim: the writer supports his or her position by offering reasons and supporting evidence. It is reasoned analysis, a tightly developed line of reasoning. Arguments are usually developed to persuade the reader to accept the claim or take a particular action. You will encounter arguments in various forms in various types of courses. Here are a few examples:

- ◆ An astronomy professor argues that extraterrestrial life is a statistical probability.
- ◆ An editorial in the college newspaper proposes that all grades be eliminated for first-year students in their first semester.
- ◆ A reading assignment for a political science course argues that terrorism is a necessary and unavoidable outgrowth of world politics.

Analyzing an Argument

Analyzing arguments is a complex and detailed process to which major portions of courses in logic are devoted. As a starting point, you might use the following guidelines as you encounter and analyze arguments:

- ◆ Analyze the argument by simplifying it. Reduce it to a list of statements or draw a map.
- ◆ What is the issue?
- ◆ What is the claim—the author's position on the issue?
- ◆ What reasons are offered in support of the claim?
- ◆ What types of evidence support each reason?
- ◆ Are the terms used clearly defined and consistently applied?
- ◆ Is the reasoning sound? (Does one point follow from another?)
- ◆ Are counterarguments recognized and refuted or addressed?
- ◆ What persuasive devices or emotional appeals does the author use (examples: appeal to sense of patriotism, appeal to authority)?

EXERCISE 15.8

Working **Together**

Analyzing Arguments

Directions *Analyze each of the following arguments by identifying the issue, the claim, and the reason(s) offered in support of the claim. Compare your answers with those of a classmate.*

1. Capital punishment deters crime. It also makes certain that the killer will never commit another crime. Therefore, capital punishment should be widely and consistently applied.
2. Voluntary euthanasia, permitting a person to elect to die, should never be legalized. First of all, our religious and cultural traditions and principles oppose it. Also, providing a terminally ill patient with the option to make a death decision adds to the person's pain and anguish. Finally, death decisions are irreversible, and we all have heard of cases in which unexpected, miraculous recoveries occur.
3. Sex education classes in public schools should be banned. They create interest in sex where it did not previously exist. Further, they encourage sexual deviance by making everything about sex seem natural. Also, these filthy classes detract from parental authority and autonomy.

Identifying Errors in Reasoning

To make their case, good arguments use good sources, verifiable facts, reliable statistics, and even more subjective things like personal experiences or research. But there are also many "tricks" that writers can use that are neither fair to the reader nor logical. They may sound reasonable upon a quick reading, but further thinking reveals their flawed reasoning. Here are some tricks you should be aware of.

***Ad hominem* ("against the man") arguments.**   An argument that attacks the holder of an opposing viewpoint, rather than the viewpoint itself, is an *ad hominem* argument. For example, the question "How can a woman who does not even hold a college degree criticize a judicial decision?" attacks the woman and her level of education, not her argument.

Bandwagon approach.   The appeal to do, believe, or buy what everyone else is doing, believing, or buying is known as the bandwagon effect. Commercials that claim that a car is the "#1 best-selling car in America" are using this type of argument. The problem is that the #1 best-selling car in America may not be the *best* car in America.

False authority and testimonials.   False authority involves using the opinion or action of a well-known or famous person to sell a product or state a message. We have all seen athletes and movie stars endorsing particular brands of clothing and shampoo. This type of appeal works on the notion that people admire celebrities and strive to be like them. But be careful here: Sometimes celebrities work for causes in which they believe strongly, such as animal rights or the campaign to free Tibet from China's rule. To think critically, you must consider the context of the message.

Circular reasoning.   Also known as "begging the question," circular reasoning involves using part of the conclusion as evidence to support it. For example, the statement "Cruel medical experimentation on defenseless animals is inhumane" engages in circular reasoning. So does the statement "Female police officers should not be sent to crime scenes because apprehending criminals is a man's job." Neither statement offers any true evidence for the case it is purporting to make.

Non sequiturs ("it does not follow").   A non sequitur is a conclusion that does not logically follow from the statements that precede it. Consider this sentence: "Because my doctor is young, I'm sure she'll be a good doctor." The second part of the sentence does not necessarily follow from the first—the fact that the doctor is young really has no bearing on whether or not she is a good doctor.

Either-or fallacy.   This fallacy, very common in the media, assumes that there are only two sides to a given issue, and that these sides can be very clearly described as "Yes" or "No." Consider the issue of violence on television. An either-or fallacy is to assume that violence on TV must be either allowed or completely banned. This fallacy does not recognize other alternatives, such as allowing violent programming only after (say) 10 p.m., restricting depictions of certain types of violence, and so forth.

Slippery slope.   The slippery slope involves objecting to something because it will inevitably lead to terrible consequences. The slippery slope starts out sounding logical but then devolves into grandiose generalizations. For example: "Smoking should be banned from movies, because teenagers will want to emulate movie stars and start smoking. Then, every teenager in America will end up smoking, and an entire generation will die from lung cancer." Watch for the slippery slope, particularly in political arguments, where they are very common.

Overgeneralizations.   Faulty arguments arise when people make hasty generalizations based on only a few observations. For example, an older person might see three teenagers playing basketball during school hours, then write a letter to the editor stating "There is clearly a problem with truancy among today's high school students." The fact that three students were playing hooky during school hours does not mean that truancy is necessarily an issue in the community.

EXERCISE 15.9

Evaluating Arguments

Directions   *Evaluate each of the following statements. Point out how the argument is misleading and which technique(s) are being used.*

1. There are a lot of Asian students in the honors chemistry class. Asians must be smarter than everyone else.
2. We should keep our town curfew at 10 p.m. If teenagers are allowed to roam the streets at night, vandalism will occur and old ladies will get mugged, and before you know it our nice quiet community will be filled with gangs and crack houses.
3. The Bill of Rights gives Americans the right to bear arms. It's as simple as that. Guns should be legal and should be available to whoever wants to own them.
4. Some people say that Bill Rodriguez would make a good governor, but he divorced his wife ten years ago. How can someone who's divorced represent the people of his state fairly?
5. Two million pet owners feed their pets VitaBrite tabs to keep their dogs healthy and increase longevity. Buy some today for your best friend.

SKILLS IN ACTION

Researching and Understanding Opposing Viewpoints

The best way to fully understand an issue is to have a fundamental comprehension of both sides of the issue. (And, often, there are more than two sides to any given story.) Only after you fully understand the issue can you make an informed opinion.

Following is a list of five controversial topics. Try to explain in your own words what the pros and cons of each topic are, but do not express your opinion. The goal of this exercise is to understand opposing arguments so that you can counter them with arguments that support your ultimate beliefs.

1. Gun control

2. Legalization of marijuana

3. The presence of undocumented immigrants in the United States

4. The bailout of large financial services companies by the U.S. government

5. The "outsourcing" of U.S. jobs to countries overseas

Working Together

Each student should write a one-page response to the following assignment.

Agree or disagree with the following statement:

Any person on welfare for more than a year lacks motivation and initiative.

Working in pairs, students should complete each of the following steps:

1. Exchange and read each other's papers.

2. Evaluate the paper using the following questions:

   a. Does the writer express opinions?

   b. Does the writer's viewpoint differ from your own? If so, how can you objectively evaluate the viewpoint?

   c. Does the writer make generalizations? If so, highlight them.

   d. What types of evidence does the writer provide to support his or her ideas?

   e. Is the writer biased?

   f. Evaluate the writer's argument. Is it logical and consistent?

REVIEW   Five Key Points to Remember

1 **Be sure to synthesize information within a course and between courses.** Make connections, discover relationships, and look for applications.

2 **Examine information.** Distinguish between fact and opinion, examine differing viewpoints, evaluate generalizations, and test hypotheses.

3 **Evaluate data and evidence.** Look at the following types of evidence: personal experience, statistics, examples, and experimental evidence.

4 **Ask critical questions.** Examine the source of information, the author's credentials, and bias, tone, and assumptions.

5 **Evaluate arguments.** Analyze an argument by examining its basic parts and looking for errors in reasoning.

The Work Connection

Your ability to organize, synthesize, and evaluate information will assist you in diverse ways throughout your entire life, whether you are choosing which field to major in, which car to buy, or which health insurance to select. Any complex decision requires knowing how pieces of information relate to one another. Choosing a career that you will enjoy involves making multiple decisions based on any number of variables. You can practice your skills of synthesizing and evaluating while doing career-related research on the World Wide Web. Try the following steps.

1. Go to the three Web sites listed below:

"Career Development eManual" by Marlene Bryan at the University of Waterloo:

http://www.cdm.uwaterloo.ca/index2.asp

"Conducting an Effective Job Search" at the Career Resource home page at Rensselaer Polytechnic Institute:

http://128.113.2.9/dept/cdc/handout/Jobsearch,%20Conducting%20an%20Effective.pdf

"Career Planning Process" by Pam Allen and Ellen Nagy at Bowling Green State University:

http://www.bgsu.edu/offices/sa/career/page18303.html

2. Read and compare the information about self-assessment (assessing your skills, values, and interests). Take notes or make maps about the self-assessment information at each site. Then synthesize the information in a paragraph or two so that you will remember the information that seems most important to you.

The Web Connection

1. "Fact or Opinion" Quizzes

   http://cuip.uchicago.edu/www4teach/97/jlyman/default/quiz/factopquiz.html
   http://dhp.com/~laflemm/RfT/Tut2.htm

   Pay attention to what you hear during the day and try to keep track of the facts and opinions. When do you hear one more than the other?

2. Charts and Graphs

   http://mcckc.edu/longview/ctac/GRAPHS.HTM

   The Critical Thinking Across the Curriculum Project from Longview Community College invites you to analyze the way statistical information is represented visually. Look through some newspapers and magazines with a friend to locate charts and graphs. Analyze their reliability based on the information presented in this site. What is your perception of the media's use of statistics?

3. Critically Analyzing Information Sources

   http://www.library.cornell.edu/olinuris/ref/research/skill26.htm

   This site from the Cornell University Library provides a well-organized, clear overview of evaluation techniques. Choose a magazine or newspaper article that interests you and apply these techniques to it.

16 Preparing for Exams

How do you organize your review so you will do your best on exams?

What is thematic study, and why is it effective?

What are helpful study strategies for particular types of exams?

What kinds of study strategies can you use in specific academic disciplines?

How can you control test anxiety?

Quizzes, midterm examinations, and finals are often the basis on which grades are awarded. However, they are also valuable thinking and learning experiences. Quizzes force you to keep up with reading and assignments and provide regular feedback on the quality of your learning. Longer examinations require you to consolidate and integrate concepts and information. Final exams force you to step back and retrace the direction of the course, noticing overall trends and patterns and integrating your learning.

Many students spend a great deal of time preparing for an exam, yet never seem to earn top grades. Some report that they spend more time studying than students who do earn the highest grades. Grades, however, have little to do with the *amount* of time spent studying. What is important is *how* study time is spent. This chapter will show you how to prepare for exams and earn the greatest dividends for the time you spend.

■ Organizing Your Review

The following suggestions will help you approach your study in an organized, systematic manner.

Organize Your Time

The amount of time you will need to spend is determined by your familiarity with the material and the amount of material the exam covers. In general, the longer the interval between exams, the longer you will need to spend in preparation. Organize your review sessions using the following suggestions:

Review at least one week in advance of the exam.   Set aside specific times for daily review. If the exam is in a difficult or troublesome subject, schedule extra study time.

Spend time organizing your review.   Make a list of all chapters, notes, and instructor's handouts that need to be reviewed. Divide the material by topic, planning what you will review during each session (see "Thematic Study," p. 359).

Review again the night before the exam.   Reserve time the night before the examination for a final, complete review. Do not study new material during this session. Instead, review the most difficult material, testing your recall of important facts or information for possible essay questions.

Attend the Class Before the Exam

Be sure to attend the class prior to the exam. During this class, the instructor may give a brief review of the material to be covered or offer last-minute review suggestions. Have you heard instructors make statements such as, "Be sure to look over . . ." or "Pay particular attention to . . ." prior to exams? Listen carefully to the instructor's answers to students' questions: these answers may provide clues about what the exam will emphasize.

Attend Review Classes

For final exams, particularly in mathematics or the sciences, professors occasionally offer optional review sessions. Be sure to attend these sessions: time spent there is likely to be more productive than time spent studying alone.

EXERCISE 16.1

Developing a Review Schedule

Directions   *Plan a review schedule for an upcoming exam. Include material you will study and when you will study it.*

Identify What to Study

Find out whether the examination will be objective, essay, or a combination of both. Also check your notes from the first several classes; some instructors describe their exams as part of their course introduction. If your instructor does not specify the type of exam, ask during or after class.

Find out as much as possible about what the examination will cover. Usually, your instructor will either announce the exam topics or specify the time span that the exam will cover. Some instructors expect you to recall text

TABLE 16.1 Review Strategies

Type of Material	Suggestions for Review
Textbook chapters	Reread highlighting and marking. Review chapter summary. Use your outlines, notes, summaries, or maps.
Lecture notes	Reread and mark important information. Use recall clues to self-test.
Supplementary assignments	Review purpose and relationship to course content. Review highlighting or summary notes.
Previous tests and quizzes	Mark all items you missed and look for a pattern of error. Identify types of questions you miss. Identify topics you need to study further. (See "Thinking Critically . . . About Returned Exams," p. 411.)
Instructor's handouts and class assignments	Note purpose of each item and to which lecture they correspond. Identify key points emphasized.

and lecture material; others expect you to summarize using their perspective on a particular subject; still others encourage you to think, discuss, recall, and disagree with the ideas and information they have presented. You can usually tell what to expect from quizzes and how classes have been conducted.

In preparing for an exam, use all sources of information, as shown in Table 16.1.

Assess Your Preparedness

Once you have collected and briefly looked over the materials listed in Table 16.1, you can estimate how well prepared you are and how much review and study time is necessary. If you are not caught up in your reading, highlighting, and homework assignments, make a list of what you have to do. Using this list, decide how to spend the first portion of your remaining study time. Try to get caught up as quickly as possible; double or triple your study time.

Also, identify your strengths and weaknesses. Identify topics for which you feel unprepared and lack confidence as well as those that you have mastered thoroughly. For example, a student taking Western civilization identified several topics in history that she felt were her weakest: the Protestant Reformation, exploration and colonization, and absolutism. Then she concentrated on these periods, organizing and consolidating events and trends for each.

THINKING CRITICALLY
. . . About Group Study

Some students find group study highly effective; others report that it is time-consuming and does not produce results. Use the following questions to decide whether group study would be effective for you:

1. Will group study force me to become more actively involved with the course content?

2. Will talking about, reacting to, and discussing the material help me learn?

3. Can I learn by explaining ideas to someone else? Does explaining an idea force me to think and test my own understanding?

4. What are the strengths of my learning style as discovered in Chapter 7? Am I strong in auditory or social learning, for example?

5. Can I prevent group study sessions from turning into social events where very little study occurs?

6. Can I avoid studying with the wrong people—those who spread negative attitudes (the "None of us understands this and we can't all fail" attitude, for example)?

7. Can I avoid studying with poorly prepared students—those who have not read the material carefully or attended class regularly?

EXERCISE 16.2   **Assessing Your Preparedness for an Exam**

Directions *For an upcoming exam, assess how well prepared you are by making a list of topics about which you feel confident and another list of those that will require further study.*

■ Thematic Study

Most students approach their study and review for exams in convenient but arbitrary units. During a study session, they may review a specific number of pages or a given number of lecture notes. While this approach is systematic, it is not the most conducive to learning. A more meaningful approach is to integrate text and lecture material using a method called *thematic study.*

In thematic study, you focus on topics, or themes. You pull together all available material on a given topic and learn it as an organized body of information.

In essence, thematic study means studying by topic. For instance, for a macro-economics test, a student's topics included aggregate demand and aggregate supply, real and nominal GNP, and indexes to measure price changes.

Why Thematic Study Is Effective

Thematic study forces you to think in the following ways:

- ◆ **It forces you to decide what topics are important**, to sift and sort and make decisions about course content.
- ◆ **It forces you to integrate information, recognize similarities, and reconcile differences** in approach and focus between text and lecture.
- ◆ **It forces you to organize the information** from a variety of sources into a meaningful set.
- ◆ **It forces you to practice the skills** that you are required to use when you take exams. Exams require you to draw upon information from all sources. Thematic study forces you to do this in advance; consequently, you are better prepared when you take an exam.

Selecting Themes

The key to selecting worthwhile, important themes is your ability to grasp an overview of the course and understand how and where specific pieces of information fit into the big picture. To get an overview of the course, try the following suggestions:

Think about how and why the material was covered in the order it was presented. How does one class lecture relate to the next? To what larger theme are the lectures connected? For class lectures, check the course outline or syllabus that was distributed at the beginning of the course. Since it lists major topics and suggests the order in which they will be covered, your syllabus will be useful in discovering patterns.

Focus on the progression of ideas in the textbook. Study the table of contents to see the connections among chapters you have read. Often, chapters are grouped into sections based on similar content.

Study relationships. Ask yourself: "Where is the information presented in this chapter leading?" and "How does this chapter relate to the next?" Suppose in psychology you had studied a chapter on personality traits; next, you were assigned a chapter on abnormal and deviant behavior. In this situation, the chapter on personality establishes the standard or norm by which abnormal and deviant behavior are determined.

Do not let facts and details camouflage important questions, issues, and problems. Remember to ask yourself, "What does this mean? How is this information useful? How can this be applied to various situations?" Once you have identified the literal content, stop, react, and evaluate its use, value, and application.

Identify predominant thought patterns.   Evident in both text and lecture material are patterns that point directly to key topics.

EXERCISE 16.3

Working Together

Identifying Topics for Thematic Study

Directions   *Assume you are to have an examination based on the first four chapters of this book. List the major topics you would review during thematic study. Compare and discuss your list with that of a classmate.*

EXERCISE 16.4

Identifying Topics for Thematic Study

Directions   *For an upcoming exam in one of your courses, identify several topics for thematic study.*

How to Prepare Study Sheets

The study sheet system is a way of organizing and summarizing complex information by preparing mini-outlines on each topic. It is most useful for reviewing material that is interrelated and needs to be learned as a whole rather than as separate facts. Several types of information should be reviewed on study sheets:

◆ Theories and principles
◆ Complex events with multiple causes and effects
◆ Controversial issues—pros and cons
◆ Summaries of philosophical issues
◆ Trends in ideas or data
◆ Groups of related facts

The sample study sheet in Figure 16.1 (p. 362) was made by a student preparing for an exam in a communications media course. You will notice that the study sheet organizes the advantages and disadvantages of the various types of media advertising and presents them in a form that invites easy comparison of the various media types.

To prepare a study sheet, first select the information to be learned. Then outline the information, using as few words as possible. Group together important points, from both your text and lecture notes, that relate to each topic. Try to use one or more thought patterns as a means of organization.

The computer is an excellent aid to thematic study. If, as suggested in Chapter 14, you are able to type both your textbook and lecture notes into a computer file, then the preparation of study sheets is easily done. Using the computer's copy and paste function, you can collect information from various sets of text and lecture notes on a given topic.

FIGURE 16.1
A Sample Study Sheet

Forms of Media Advertising

Media form	Advantages	Disadvantages
1. Newspapers	- widely read - regional flexibility - offer use of inserts	- little buyer selectivity
2. Magazines	- better appearance than newspapers - longer life - people do reread	- advance commitment required - may have to buy entire national circulation
3. TV	- reaches 95% of households - can produce favorable product images - can choose stations	- commercial clutter (must compete with other ads)
4. Radio	- inexpensive - can afford high level of repetition - geographic selectivity - can change ads frequently	- short lived (can't reread) - people don't listen to the ads
5. Outdoor Advertising	- large amount of repetition - low cost per exposure	- copy must be short
6. Online Advertising	- can be visually appealing - inexpensive to create - can target the audience	- copy must be short - some consumers unfamiliar with it

EXERCISE 16.5 **Preparing a Study Sheet**

Directions *Prepare a study sheet for one of the themes you identified in Exercise 16.3.*

Review Strategies

Many students review by rereading their notes and text highlighting. Rereading is a passive, inactive approach that seldom prepares you well for any exam. Instead, review for an exam should be a dress rehearsal for the exam itself. Think of a theater company preparing to perform a play. In rehearsal they practice the conditions of their actual performance. Likewise, in preparing for an exam you should practice the actual exam situation. You must, in effect, test yourself by asking questions and answering them. Since the exam is written, it is helpful to *write,* not just to mentally construct, answers.

Asking the Right Questions

As you review, be sure to ask questions at each level of thinking, especially those at the applying, analyzing, evaluating, and creating levels. Refer to

REAL STUDENTS SPEAK

Christina Olivo

Western New England
College (WNEC)
Springfield,
Massachusetts

Background: Christina is a sophomore at WNEC pursuing a double major in elementary education and psychology.

Goals: To obtain a master's degree in elementary education and teach reading to elementary students 3rd grade and under for five years, returning to school later to pursue a doctorate in education or psychology with the goal of becoming a reading specialist.

Advice on Taking Exams: I usually start preparing for exams about five days in advance. I read and highlight information and then write it out. I usually make outlines and then make them into paragraphs. For one history class, I had to write an essay. The professor gave us five questions and gave two on the exam. I practiced writing essay answers to all of them in advance. I also make index cards and quiz myself on them.

TABLE 16.2   Sample Questions Based on the Study Sheet in Figure 16.1

Level of Thinking	Sample Questions
Remembering and Understanding	What percentage of households does TV reach?
	Which media offer regional flexibility?
Applying	What types of products could be most effectively advertised in each media form?
Analyzing	Why don't people listen to the ads on the radio?
Evaluating	How did the author decide what is low cost?
Creating	What are the similarities between radio and newspaper advertising?

Chapter 2 for a review of each of these levels. Refer to Table 16.2 for sample questions you could ask at each level if you were preparing for an exam on the media advertising material covered in Figure 16.1.

Remembering and Understanding questions.   These levels require recall of facts; remembering dates, names, definitions, and formulas falls into these categories. The five "W" questions—*Who? What? Where? When?* and *Why?*—are useful to ask.

Applying questions.   This level of thinking requires you to use or apply information. The two following questions best test this level:

◆ In what practical situations would this information be useful?

◆ What does this have to do with what I already know about the subject?

Analyzing questions.   Analyzing involves seeing relationships. Ask questions that test your ability to take ideas apart, discover cause and effect relationships, and discover how things work.

Evaluating questions.   This level involves making judgments and assessing value or worth. Ask questions that challenge sources, accuracy, long-term value, importance, and so forth.

Creating questions.   This level involves pulling ideas together or creating something new. Ask questions that force you to look at similarities and differences.

How to Test Yourself

To test yourself, follow these steps.

◆ **Review each study sheet several times, asking questions at the various levels of thinking.**

◆ **As you find information that is difficult, unclear, or unfamiliar, mark it for later reference and further study.**

◆ **Jot appropriate questions in the margin or on the back of the study sheet.** You may wish to refer to these as you predict questions for essay exams (see p. 367).

◆ **Write answers to each of your questions.** This process will clarify your thinking and help you learn the information.

◆ **Critique your answers.** First verify the correctness and completeness of factual information. Then analyze and think about your response. Did you really answer the questions? What related information might you have included? What are the implications of what you have said?

◆ **Review both questions and answers periodically.**

Some students find it useful to write their questions using a computer. Each question is entered in a test preparation file, and answers are typed on a separate line below. Some information can be copied from lecture and/or textbook note files to save time. Review of questions and answers is simple using the scroll function. You can position each question at the bottom of the screen, without the answer showing. Then test your recall by writing the answer (on paper) or through mental review. Finally, to check your recall, scroll down to review the answer.

EXERCISE 16.6	**Writing Questions**

Directions   *Choose a textbook chapter on which you are currently working. Write questions at each level for several main topics covered.*

■ Strategies for Particular Types of Exams

While basic study and review strategies are the same for all types of examinations, there are specific techniques to use as you prepare for objective exams, essay exams, open-book exams, take-home exams, problem-solution exams, and final exams.

Preparing for Objective Exams

Objective exams are those that require a brief right or wrong answer. These include multiple choice, true/false, matching, and fill in the blank.

Objective tests often require mastery of a great deal of factual data—information at the knowledge and comprehension levels. Often, too, test items require you to apply, analyze, and evaluate these facts. An effective way to prepare for an exam in which a large amount of factual learning is required is to use an index card system.

Using Index Cards

Step 1.   Using 3 × 5-inch index cards (or small sheets of paper), write names of terms, laws, principles, or concepts on the front of the card and facts and details about them on the back. To review the significance of important events in a history course, for example, write the event on the front of one card and its importance on the back. To learn definitions, record the word on the front and its meaning on the back. The sample index cards shown in Figure 16.2 were prepared for an economics examination.

FIGURE 16.2
Sample Index Cards

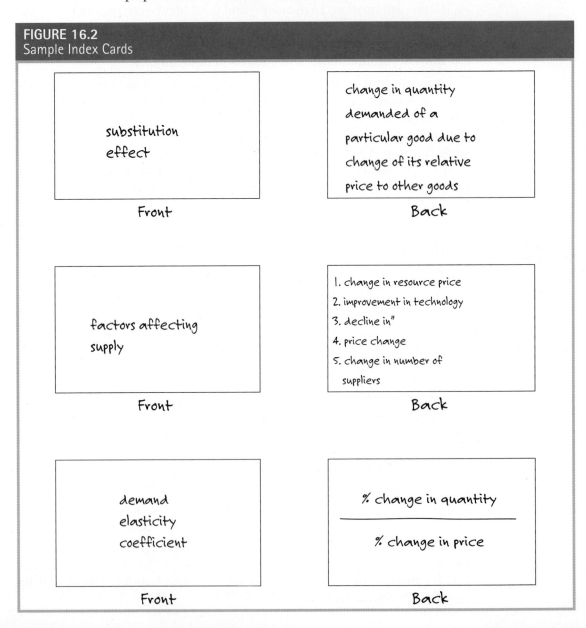

substitution
effect

Front

change in quantity
demanded of a
particular good due to
change of its relative
price to other goods

Back

factors affecting
supply

Front

1. change in resource price
2. improvement in technology
3. decline in"
4. price change
5. change in number of
   suppliers

Back

demand
elasticity
coefficient

Front

% change in quantity
——————————————
% change in price

Back

Step 2. To study each of these cards, look at the front and try to recall what is written on the back. Then, turn the card over to see if you were correct. As you work, sort them into two stacks—those you know and those you cannot remember.

Step 3. Go back through the stack that you did not know, study each, and retest yourself, again sorting the cards into two stacks. Continue with this procedure until you are satisfied that you have learned all the information. Review the index cards several times a day on each of the three or four days before the exam. On the day of the exam, do a final, once-through review so that the information is fresh in your mind.

This index card system has several advantages:

◆ **Writing helps you learn,** so preparing the cards is also a learning process.
◆ **You spend time learning what you do not know** and avoid wasting time reviewing already learned material.
◆ **Cards are more effective than lists of material.** If you study a list of items, you run the risk of learning them in a fixed order. When a single item appears out of order on the exam, you may not remember it. Sorting and occasionally shuffling your index cards eliminates this problem. You can carry cards in a pocket or purse and study them in spare moments.

EXERCISE 16.7 | **Preparing Index Cards**

Directions   *Choose a course in which you expect to take an objective examination. Prepare a set of index cards for one chapter you have studied.*

Preparing for Essay Examinations

Essay examinations demand complete recall; you begin with a blank sheet of paper on which you must answer the question. Reviewing for an essay exam is a process of concentrated thematic study.

Predict possible questions.   Predicting essay questions is a process of analyzing the relationships that exist within the material (see Chapter 11) and writing questions that concern these relationships. Use the themes you identified as a guide. As you predict questions, be sure to include all course material; avoid trying to second-guess the instructor as to the content of the exam. The following suggestions will assist you in predicting possible essay questions:

◆ **Reread your course syllabus or objectives.** The major headings or objectives refer to the important issues. For example, a sociology course objective might be "Students will understand the concept of socialization and the roles of the family, peer, and reference groups." This objective identifies the key topic and suggests what you need to know about it.

◆ **Study your textbook's table of contents and the organization of individual chapters.** Notice important topics that run through several chapters. In a marketing textbook, you might discover that chapters on the impact of technology, federal regulations, and consumer-protection legislation all relate to the market environment.

◆ **Study your notes.** Identify lecture topics and group them into larger subjects or themes. In a psychology course, for example, individual lectures on developmental disabilities, creativity, and IQ could be grouped together under mental abilities.

◆ **Evaluate previous exams to see what key ideas were emphasized.** For example, in a history course you may find on each exam questions on the historical significance of events.

◆ **Listen carefully when your instructor announces, discusses, or reviews for the exam.** He or she is likely to reveal important information. Make detailed notes and study them later. Your biology instructor might say, "Be sure to review the structure of plants, as well as their reproduction, development, and growth cycles." This remark indicates that these topics will be on the exam.

Write rough draft answers.   Once you have identified possible exam questions, the next step is to practice answering them. Do not take the time to write out full, complete sentences. Instead collect and organize the information you would include in your answer and record it in brief note or outline form, listing the ideas you would include. Form these ideas from information in your textbook and class notes that relates to the question. Figure 16.3 shows a sample essay question and a rough draft answer.

Use key word outlines.   As a convenient way to remember what your draft answer includes, make a key word outline of your answer. For each idea in your draft, identify a key word that will trigger your memory of that idea. Then list and learn these key words. Together, these words form a mini-outline of topics and ideas to include in an essay on this topic. A key word outline is shown in Figure 16.4 on p. 370.

Predicting and answering possible examination questions is an effective technique for several reasons.

◆ **Predicting forces you to analyze the material, not just review it.**

◆ **Drafting answers forces you to express ideas in written form.** Through writing you will realize relationships, organize your thoughts, and discover the best way to present them.

◆ **You will save time while taking the exam.** If you have already collected and organized your thoughts, then you can use the time those processes would have taken to prepare a more complete, carefully written answer.

FIGURE 16.3
A Sample Essay Question and Rough Draft Answer

Question: Discuss the organized social life of monkeys and apes.

Rough draft response:

Social Structure developed for following advantages:
- group can spot predators & rally a defense
- foraging for food is more efficient if done in groups
- access to opposite sex is assured for reproduction
- groups permit socialization and learning from elders

Social structure organized according to following principles
- infants and young are dependent on mother
  • longer than most animals
  • allows for learned behavior to occur
  • "   " juvenile play – imp't for
  • social bonds as adults
- adults hold social rank in group
  • males dominate
  • hierarchy often more significant among
       males than females

Sexual bonding occurs among mating adults
- breeding occurs only during specific seasons
- males are aware of estrous cycle of female

Grooming – acceptable form of social contact
- functions 1. remove parasites
            2. establish and maintain social relationships

The computer is a useful tool for predicting and answering essay exam questions. The word-processing function enables you to rearrange information, thereby experimenting with various means of organizing and consolidating it. The various typographic features (boldfaced print, italics, underlining) enable you to add visually striking (and easy to remember) points of emphasis. For example, you might highlight key points or place key words in boldfaced print.

FIGURE 16.4
A Sample Key Word Outline

Advantages
Defense
Food
Reproduction
Learning
Principles
Dependency
Social Rank
Sexual Bonding
Grooming

Predicting and Answering an Exam Question

Directions   *Select a course in which you expect to have an essay examination or an essay question on your next exam. Predict and record possible essay questions. Then choose one question and prepare a rough draft answer and key word outline.*

Preparing for Open-Book Exams

Open-book exams are those that allow you to refer to your textbook or lecture notes during the exam. At first, this type of exam may seem easy, almost a give-away. Some students make the mistake of doing little or no preparation. Actually, an open-book exam is often an essay exam in which the instructor will assess your ability to interpret, evaluate, react to, or apply a given body of information. The focus is on your ability to think about and use available information.

Organization of information is the key to preparing for open-book exams. Time is usually limited and often a key factor in taking an open-book exam. If you have to waste time on an exam searching for a piece of information, it can affect the quality of your answer. Study sheets (see p. 361) are effective because they draw together and organize information by topic. One useful addition to your study sheets is page references, from both your texts and lecture notes, allowing you to check your source for information on a particular topic, if needed.

Preparing for Take-Home Exams

Take-home exams are a variation of the open-book exam. The instructor allows you to leave the classroom and work on it for a specified period of time, usually several days. Usually, more extensive, complete answers are expected. Some instructors may expect research as well. A more carefully written, concise, and clear response is expected than for in-class writing. Be sure at the time the exam is distributed to clarify, as best you can, what is expected in terms of length, sources to be used, and format. If the exam consists of only one question, the take-home exam closely resembles the assignment of a paper in terms of what is expected.

Preparing for Problem-Solution Exams

Exams in mathematics and in some of the sciences, such as chemistry and physics, consist primarily or exclusively of problems to solve. Here are a few suggestions on how to prepare for such exams:

◆ **Organize problems by types, and outline strategies for solving each type.** Anticipate possible variations on each type.
◆ **Prepare study sheets that include formulas and principles.** Also include conversions and constants.
◆ **Review by practicing solving problems—not by reading through sample problems and their solutions.**
◆ **Identify types of problems with which you have had trouble either on homework assignments or on quizzes, and spend extra time with these.** Try to identify at what stage or step in the solution process your difficulty occurs.
◆ **Give yourself a practice exam, selecting items from homework or previous quizzes.** Complete the exam within the same time limit you will have for the actual exam.

Preparing for Final Exams

Final exams differ from other types of exams in two respects: They are longer and more comprehensive, covering a larger body of material. What is more important, however, is that they often emphasize the integration of course content. To prepare for final exams, use the following suggestions:

1. **Begin your study well in advance.** Finals usually are given roughly within a one-week time period, usually immediately following the last class of the term.

2. **Condense all course materials.** Prepare a master study sheet from your individual study sheets, drawing together and relating various topics.

3. **Focus on large ideas.** Concentrate on concepts, trends, historical perspectives, principles, methods, patterns, and long-range effects—instead of individual facts. Try to identify themes that run through much or most of the course content. The theme of self-identity, for example, may pervade a Native American history course; a theme of revolution and change may be the focus of a course on eighteenth-century American literature.

4. **Review outlines of course content.** Refer once again to your course syllabus or outline and your textbook's table of contents to reestablish an overview of the course. In preparing for a final exam, recall the "big picture" in order to avoid the mistake of becoming lost or overwhelmed by detail.

5. **Anticipate essay questions.** If your final will include essays, try to predict and answer these questions. Essays on finals often are targeted to areas of major emphasis. As a starting point, ask yourself these questions:

   ◆ What key ideas, themes, or processes has the professor been discussing all semester?
   ◆ Where does everything seem to be leading?
   ◆ What long-lasting, beneficial ideas, processes, or principles have we learned?
   ◆ To what topics has the professor devoted considerable time in class lectures or discussions?

Review previous exams and quizzes.   Identify topics and your areas of weakness for more intensive review. Look for patterns, trends, types of questions, and areas of emphasis.

| EXERCISE 16.9 | ### Predicting Final Exam Questions |

Directions   *Using all the material you have covered up to this point in one of your courses, predict several essay questions that might appear on a final examination in that course.*

SKILLS IN ACTION

Expanding Your Exam Comfort Zone

This section has discussed six different types of exams: *objective exams, essay exams, open-book exams, take-home exams, problem-solution exams,* and *final exams.*

On which types of exams do you tend to score the best? The worst? Examine the reasons behind your relative success (or failure) at each type of exam. For those types of exams on which you tend to do less well, create a specific list of the problems you encounter, and then propose a solution for each. For example, if you tend to run out of time on essay exams, your proposed solution might be "Put my watch on the desk and allot X minutes to each question. Even if I'm not done with the question at that time, I need to move on."

■ Strategies for Specific Academic Disciplines

A key to becoming a top student is to study for each exam differently. Since each course, each instructor, and each lecture is different, each exam will also be different and require slightly different types of preparation. Be sure to check your course syllabus for clues about what is important in the course. An examination in a literature course is quite unlike an examination in business management; an exam in mathematics is very different from one in political science. Table 16.3 (p. 374) offers suggestions for preparing for examinations in various academic disciplines. As you read this table, keep in mind that these strategies are general guidelines, not rules to follow. They may not always work, depending on the specific course, how the professor conducts it, and the types of exams given.

EXERCISE 16.10   ### Adapting Study Strategies

Directions   *List the courses in which you are currently enrolled. For each course, predict the next type of exam you will have and the major topics it will cover. Then describe how you will approach each, emphasizing how you will modify your approach to suit the subject matter.*

■ Controlling Test Anxiety

Do you get nervous and anxious just before an exam begins? If so, your response is perfectly normal; most students feel some anxiety before an exam. In fact, research indicates that some anxiety is beneficial and improves your performance by sharpening your attention and keeping you alert.

TABLE 16.3 Tips on Studying for Exams in Various Academic Disciplines

Academic Discipline	Emphasis/Focus of Study
Social sciences	Exams often contain both objective and essay questions. Objective exams test basic knowledge of theories, principles, concepts; essay questions may be on applications or a case study. Learn specialized vocabulary. Focus on relationships: comparisons and contrasts, causes and effects, sequences.
Sciences	Make lists of themes and principles covered; consider various situations in which these may be applied. Identify types of problems you expect to be covered and practice solving them. In the life sciences, be certain to learn and understand classifications.
Mathematics	Practice solving problems. Identify troublesome problem types and concentrate on them. Try to anticipate variations on general problem types. Memorize formulas.
Literature and the arts	Focus on trends and patterns demonstrated through series of works. Be certain to learn full names of works and the correct spelling of authors' or artists' names. Compare and contrast various works and authors or artists. Expect most exams to require essay answers. Note characteristics and features of particular works as well as themes and significant issues.
Career fields	Focus on applications: how is the information to be used? Anticipate questions that apply information to hypothetical situations or case studies. Learn procedures and processes and distinguish when each is appropriate.

Research also shows that very high levels of anxiety can interfere with performance on a test. Some students become highly nervous and emotional and lose their concentration. Their minds seem to go blank, and they are unable to recall material they have learned. They also report physical symptoms: their hearts pound, they find it difficult to swallow, they break out in a cold sweat.

Test anxiety is a very complicated psychological response to a threatening situation. It may be deeply rooted and related to other problems and past experiences. The following suggestions are intended to help ease your test anxiety. If these suggestions do not help, the next step is to discuss the problem with a counselor.

Be Sure Test Anxiety Is Not an Excuse

Many students say they have test anxiety when the truth is that they have not studied and reviewed carefully or thoroughly. The first question, then, that you must answer honestly is this: Are you really *unprepared* for the exam and therefore justifiably anxious?

Get Used to Test Situations

Here are a few ways you can simulate test situations to reduce your own test anxiety:

- ◆ **Become familiar with the building and room in which the test is given.** Visit the room when it is empty and take a seat. Visualize yourself taking a test there.
- ◆ **Develop practice or review tests.** Treat them as real tests and do them in situations as similar as possible to real test conditions.
- ◆ **Practice working with time limits.** Set an alarm clock while taking practice or review tests and work only until it rings.
- ◆ **Take as many tests as possible, even though you dislike them.** Always take advantage of practice tests and in-chapter exercises. Buy a review book for the course you are taking, or a workbook that accompanies your text. Treat each section as an exam and have someone else correct your work.

Control Negative Thinking

Major factors that contribute to test anxiety are worry, self-doubt, and negative thinking. Just before and during an exam, anxious students often think such things as, "I won't do well," "I'm going to fail," or "What will my friends think of me when I get a failing grade?" This type of thinking is a predisposition for failure; you are telling yourself that you expect to fail. By doing this, you are blocking your chances for success. One solution to this problem is to send yourself

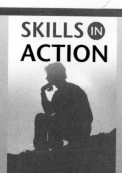

SKILLS IN ACTION

Controlling Anxiety Through Breathing Exercises

People experiencing anxiety or stress frequently end up taking short, shallow breaths, which only serves to heighten their anxiety. You will be amazed at how taking long, deep breaths can slow down your heart rate and make you feel more relaxed very quickly. Try the "square breathing" method: (1) Take a deep breath; (2) hold it for the count of four; (3) exhale; (4) hold it for the count of four. Breathe deeply through your nostrils and mouth. All that oxygen is good for your brain and good for your relaxation!

positive rather than negative messages. Say to yourself, "I have studied hard and I deserve to pass" or "I know that I know the material" or "I know I can do it!"

Compose Yourself Before the Test Begins

Before you begin the test, take 30 minutes or so to calm yourself, to slow down, and to focus your attention. Take several deep breaths, close your eyes, and visualize yourself calmly working through the test.

Working Together

Suppose that your study skills instructor has just announced that in three weeks there will be a major exam on all the material you have learned so far in his course. Form groups of four students to answer the following questions:

1. Based on the chapters of this book (and any other books) you have studied and your instructor's lectures, identify at least three to five topics for thematic study.
2. What type of exam seems appropriate for the material?
3. List topics, definitions, and types of problems that would make good exam questions.
4. Predict possible essay questions, if appropriate.
5. Discuss how you should schedule your study over the next three weeks.

REVIEW   Five Key Points to Remember

1 **Organize your review.** Attend review classes, plan your time, and identify what to study.

2 **Use thematic study.** Focus on large topics and how they relate to one another. Create study sheets and use them to test yourself.

3 **Prepare for objective exams.** Your task is to recognize correct information.

4 **Prepare for essay exams.** Your task is to organize information and present it clearly.

5 **Adapt your study strategies for particular disciplines.** Consider how each course is organized and what is emphasized by your instructor (see course syllabus) and your textbook.

The Work Connection

How does practicing effective study techniques for exams prepare you to win the job you want? Just as an exam in a college course shows your instructor that you have studied and thought about the course material, a job interview showcases your careful preparation and interest in the job for which you are applying. Career specialists recommend the following steps to prepare for a successful interview:

◆ Learn about the organization.

◆ Have a specific job or jobs in mind.

◆ Review your qualifications for the job.

◆ Prepare answers to broad questions about yourself such as "Tell me a little about yourself" and "What do you consider your strong and weak points?"

◆ Review your résumé.

◆ Practice an interview with a friend, relative, or career counselor.

  1. Review this chapter. List five specific ideas that will help you organize your interview preparation.

  2. Respond in writing (five to seven sentences) to the two broad questions given as examples in the list above. Think about how you can use your responses to demonstrate your competence and self-confidence to an interviewer.

The Web Connection

1. Preparing for Exams

   http://www.adm.uwaterloo.ca/infocs/study/preparing.html

   The University of Waterloo presents suggestions for successful studying. Figure out what you can do now to start preparing for your next exam.

2. Ten Traps of Studying

   http://campushealth.unc.edu/index.php?option=com_content&task=view&id=470&Itemid=65

   Avoid these studying traps with help from the University of North Carolina at Chapel Hill. Print out the list and highlight the traps that apply to you. Make a list of the strategies you can use to improve your study habits. Post the list where you can see it often.

3. Overcoming Test Anxiety

   http://www.studygs.net/tstprp8.htm

   Read over and print out these simple ways to avoid and deal with test anxiety. Put a check mark next to the suggestions you already use. Highlight the ones you would like to try. Evaluate their effectiveness. Add new ones and share them with your classmates.

17 Reasoning Skills for Objective Exams

Taking exams demands keen thinking and reasoning skills. These skills often distinguish top students from hardworking, above-average ones, or the A students from the B students. This chapter will show you how to approach all types of exams with an advantage and how to apply thinking and reasoning skills to objective exams. Rate your present level of skill in taking exams by completing the questionnaire shown in Figure 17.1.

■ Starting with an Advantage

Be sure to approach an exam in a confident, organized, and systematic manner. Unless you feel as if you have the situation under your control, you will probably not do well on the exam, regardless of how much you have prepared or how well you think and reason. Here are several useful tips to give you an important advantage.

Bring the Necessary Materials

Take along any materials you might be asked or allowed to use. Be sure you have a watch and an extra pen, and take several number two pencils in case you must make a drawing or diagram or fill in an electronically scored answer sheet. Take paper—you may need it for computing figures or writing essay answers. Take along anything you have been allowed to use throughout the semester, such as a calculator, conversion chart, or dictionary. If you are not sure whether you may use them, ask the instructor.

FIGURE 17.1
Rate Your Test-Taking Strategies

Respond to each of the following statements by checking "Always," "Usually," or "Never."

	Always	Usually	Never
1. Do you preview your entire exam paper before beginning?	❑	❑	❑
2. Do you allocate and keep track of time while taking the exam?	❑	❑	❑
3. Do you review the exam once you've finished?	❑	❑	❑
4. Do you avoid changing answers frequently unless you are certain that your first answer is wrong?	❑	❑	❑
5. Do you always read all of the choices on a multiple-choice exam before choosing the answer?	❑	❑	❑
6. Do you use the point value of short-answer questions as a guide to how much information to provide?	❑	❑	❑
7. Do you read the directions before beginning the exam?	❑	❑	❑
8. Do you avoid reading too much into a test question?	❑	❑	❑
9. Do you look for key words that qualify the meaning of true/false items?	❑	❑	❑
10. Do you look for clues in the question that suggest how to answer it?	❑	❑	❑

If you answered "Usually" or "Never" to more than one or two of the items, this chapter will help you improve your objective test-taking skills.

Time Your Arrival Carefully

Arrive at the examination room a few minutes early, in time to get a seat and get organized before the instructor arrives. If you are late, you may miss instructions and feel rushed as you begin the exam. If you arrive too early (15 minutes ahead), you risk building anxiety. You may see panic-stricken students questioning each other, trading last-minute memory tricks, and worrying about how difficult the exam will be.

Sit in the Front of the Room

The most practical place to sit for an exam is in the front. There, you often receive the test first and get a head start. Also, it is easier to concentrate and avoid distractions, such as a student dropping papers, someone whispering, or the person in front who is already two pages ahead of you.

Listen Carefully to Your Instructor's Directions

Your instructor may give specific instructions that are not included in the exam's written directions. If these are detailed instructions, and the instructor does not write them on the chalkboard, jot them down on your exam paper or on scrap paper. Note any changes in the questions you were given or in the point value of questions or sections. Listen critically to any instructions or comments your instructor adds; you might detect valuable hints about what your instructor considers to be an important focus or about specific information to include in your answers.

Preview the Exam

Before you answer any of the questions, quickly page through the exam, noticing the directions, the length, the type of questions, the general topics covered, the number of points the questions are worth, and where to put your answers.

Plan Your Time

After previewing, you will know the number and types of questions included. The next step is to estimate how much time you should spend on each part of the exam, using the point distribution as your guide. If, for example, an exam has 30 multiple-choice questions worth one point each and two essay questions worth a total of 70 points, you should spend twice as much time on the essay questions as on the multiple-choice items. If the point distribution is not indicated on the test booklet, ask the instructor. As you plan your time, allow four to five minutes at the end of the exam to read through what you have done, answering questions you skipped, and making any necessary corrections or changes. To keep track of time, always wear a watch.

If you are taking an exam with the question and point distribution shown below, how would you divide your time? Assume the total exam time is 50 minutes.

Type of Question	Number of Questions	Total Points
Multiple-choice	25	25
True/false	20	20
Essay	1	55

You probably should divide your time as indicated.

Previewing	1–2 minutes
Multiple-choice	10 minutes
True/false	10 minutes
Essay	25 minutes
Review	3–4 minutes

Avoid Reading Too Much into the Question

Most instructors word their questions so that what is asked for is clear. A common mistake students make is to read more into the question than is asked for. To avoid this error, read the question several times, paying attention to how it is worded. If you are uncertain of what is asked for, try to relate the question to the course content, specifically the material you have studied. Do not look for hidden meanings or trick questions.

SKILLS IN ACTION

Allotting Your Time on Exams

For each of the exams described below, estimate how you would divide your time:

1. Time limit: 75 minutes

Type of Question	Number of Questions	Total Points	Minutes
Multiple-choice	20	40	___
Matching	10	10	___
Essay	2	50	___

2. Time limit: 40 minutes

Type of Question	Number of Questions	Total Points	Minutes
True/false	15	30	___
Fill-in-the-blank	10	30	___
Short-answer	10	40	___

■ Skills for Objective Exams

The most common types of objective exam questions are multiple-choice and true/false, although some instructors include matching and fill-in-the-blank items as well.

General Suggestions

Here are a few general suggestions to follow in approaching all types of objective exams:

Read the directions.   Often, an instructor will want the correct answer marked in a particular way (for example, underlined rather than circled). The directions may contain crucial information that you must be aware of in order to answer the questions correctly. In the items below, if you did not read the directions and assumed the test questions were of the usual type, you could lose a considerable number of points.

> *True/False Directions:* Read each statement. If the statement is true, write a T in the blank to the left of the item. If the statement is false, add and/or subtract words that will make the statement correct.

> *Multiple-Choice Directions:* Circle all the choices that correctly complete the statement.

Leave nothing blank.   Before turning in your exam, check through it to be sure you have answered every question. If you have no idea about the correct answer to a question and there is no additional penalty for wrong answers, guess. You might be right! On a true/false test, your chances of being correct are 50 percent; on a four-choice multiple-choice question, the odds are 25 percent. The odds improve if you can eliminate one or two of the choices.

Students frequently turn in tests with some items unanswered because they leave difficult questions blank, planning to return to them later. Then, in the rush to finish, they forget them. To avoid this problem, when you are uncertain, choose what looks like the best answer, and mark the question number with an X or check mark so you can return to it; then, if you have time at the end of the exam, give it further thought. If you run out of time, you will have an answer marked.

Look for clues.   If you encounter a difficult question, choose what seems to be the best answer, mark the question with an X or check mark so that you can return to it, and keep the item in mind as you go through the rest of the exam. Sometimes you will see some piece of information later in the exam that reminds you of a fact or idea. For example, a psychology student could not recall a definition of behaviorism for a short-answer question. Later in the examination, a multiple-choice item mentioned the psychologist Skinner. The student remembered that Skinner was a behaviorist and knew enough about him to reason out an answer to the short-answer item. At other times, you may notice a piece of information that, if true, contradicts an answer you had already chosen.

Write your answers clearly.   If your instructor cannot be sure of the answer you wrote, he or she will mark it wrong. Answer with capital letters on multiple-choice and matching tests to avoid confusion. Write or print responses legibly in fill-in-the-blank tests. Be sure that your answers to short-answer questions are not only written neatly, but are also to the point and express complete thoughts.

Check over your answers before you turn in the exam.   As mentioned earlier, reserve some time at the end of the exam for reviewing your answers. Check to be sure you didn't use the same matching-test answer twice. Be sure your multiple-choice answers are written in the correct blanks or marked in the correct place on the answer grid. One answer marked out of sequence could lead to a series of answers being in error. If there is a separate answer sheet, verify that your fill-in-the-blank and short answers correspond with the correct question numbers.

Don't change answers without a good reason.   When reviewing your answers during an exam, don't make a change unless you have a reason for doing so. Very often your first impressions are correct. If clues from a later test item prompt your recall of information for a previous item, change your answer.

True/False Tests: Making Judgments

True/false tests require you to make judgments, based on your knowledge and information about the subject, about the correctness of each item. The following suggestions will help you make more accurate judgments and reason the answer with a higher degree of accuracy:

Watch for qualifying words and phrases.   Watch for words that qualify or change the meaning of a statement; often, just one word makes it true or false. Consider for a moment a simplified example:

- ◆ All students are engineering majors.
- ◆ Some students are engineering majors.

Of course, the first statement is false, whereas the second is true. While the words and statements are much more complicated on most true/false exams, you will find that one word often determines whether a statement is true or false.

- ◆ *All* paragraphs must have a stated main idea.
- ◆ Spelling, punctuation, and handwriting *always* affect the grade given to an essay answer.
- ◆ When taking notes on a lecture, try to write down *everything* the speaker says.

In each of the examples above, the word in italics modifies—or limits—the truth of each statement. When reading a true/false question, look carefully for limiting words such as *all, absolutely, some, none, never, completely, only, always, usually, frequently,* and *most of the time.* Close attention to these words may earn you several points on an exam.

Read two-part statements carefully.   Occasionally, you may find a statement with two or more parts. In answering these items, remember that both or all parts of the statement must be true in order for it to be correctly marked "True." If part of the statement is true and another part is false, as in the following example, then mark the statement "False."

The World Health Organization (WHO) has been successful in its campaign to eliminate smallpox and malaria.

While it is true that WHO has been successful in eliminating smallpox, malaria is still a world health problem and has not been eliminated. Since only part of this statement is true, it should be marked "False."

EXERCISE 17.1   ## Analyzing True/False Items

Directions   *Read each of the following statements and underline the portion that is not true:*

1. Although thinking is a single-dimensional skill, most students can improve their thinking skills.

2. Patterns are difficult to recognize in most college lectures, but it is important to record as many key points as possible.
3. Problem solving and decision making are similar processes; each depends on the other for success.
4. Because textbooks are highly structured, it is usually possible to learn efficiently by rereading.

Look for negative and double-negative statements. Test items that use negative words or word parts can be confusing. Words such as *no, none, never, not,* and *cannot* and prefixes such as *in-, dis-, un-, il-,* or *ir-* are easy to miss and always alter the meaning of the statement. Make it a habit to underline or circle negative words as you are reading examination questions.

Statements like the following that contain two negatives are even more confusing:

> It is not unreasonable to expect that some welfare applicants feel that their privacy has been violated.

In reading such statements, remember that two negatives balance or cancel each other out. So "not unreasonable" can be interpreted to mean "reasonable."

Make your best guess. When all else fails and you are unable to reason out the answer to an item, use these three last-resort rules of thumb:

◆ **Absolute statements tend to be false.** Since very few things are always true, with no exceptions, your best guess is to mark statements that contain words such as *always, all, never,* or *none* as false.

◆ **Mark any item that contains unfamiliar terminology or facts as false.** If you have studied the material thoroughly, trust that you would recognize as true anything that was a part of the course content.

◆ **When all else fails, it is usually better to guess true than false.** It is more difficult for an instructor to write plausible false statements than true statements. As a result, many exams have more true items than false.

EXERCISE 17.2	Analyzing True/False Items

Working Together

Directions *The following true/false items are based on content presented in this text. Working in pairs, read each item; then locate and underline the word(s) or phrase(s) that, if changed or deleted, could change the truth or falsity of the statement. Indicate whether the statement is true or false by marking T for true and F for false.*

_____ 1. Decision making is primarily a process of discovering alternatives.
_____ 2. A table never displays more than two sets of data.
_____ 3. Critical thinking is often defined as the careful, deliberate evaluation of ideas and information for the singular purpose of establishing their importance.

_____ 4. Most students avoid taking responsibility for their grades by shifting the blame to others.

_____ 5. Previewing rarely enables you to focus your attention on a reading assignment.

_____ 6. Process and procedure are usually important in mathematics courses.

_____ 7. A study sheet is most useful for reviewing material that is interrelated.

_____ 8. Falling behind on reading assignments is often a sign of academic difficulty.

_____ 9. Active learning is primarily a discrimination task.

_____ 10. Retrieval of information from memory depends exclusively upon its relevance and meaningfulness.

Matching Tests: Discovering Relationships

Matching tests require you to select items in one column that can be paired with items in a second column. The key to working with matching tests is to discover the overall pattern or relationship between the two columns. Begin by glancing through both columns before answering anything to get an overview of the subject and the topics the test covers. Are you asked to match dates with events, terms with meanings, people with accomplishments, causes with effects? In the following excerpt from a literature test, determine the relationship that exists:

Column 1	Column 2
1. Imagery	a. "One short sleep past, we wake eternally and Death shall be no more; Death, thou shalt die."—Donne
2. Simile	b. "We force their [children's] growth as if they were chicks in a poultry factory." —Toynbee
3. Personification	c. "And many a rose-carnation feeds with summer spice the humming air." —Tennyson

Use the following suggestions to answer matching items:

◆ **Answer the items you are sure of first, lightly crossing off items as they are used.** This process of elimination will make it easier to match the remaining items. Try each item that remains with each of the remaining answers in the other column. Each time you eliminate another item, repeat this procedure.

◆ **Don't choose the first answer that seems correct; items later in the list may be better choices.** Often, there are several possible matches for each item. You must choose the *best* match. In order to do this, you need to look at all possible matches, not just the first good match.

◆ **Make the list with the longer choices your starting point.** If the first column consists of short words or phrases and the second is lengthy definitions or descriptions, save time by reverse matching; that is, look for the word or phrase in column 1 that fits each item in column 2.

◆ **Use clues to narrow down the possible matches.** Match terms with definitions or synonyms that are the same part of speech. Look for a synonym for a term among the possible definitions. Key in on the meanings of familiar word parts in unknown terms to help you make a match. Try to "think outside the box" by applying your powers of logic and your everyday knowledge.

Short-Answer Tests: Listing Information

Short-answer tests require you to write a brief answer, usually in list or brief sentence form, such as asked by the following example:

List three events that increased U.S. involvement in the Vietnam War.

In answering short-answer questions, keep the following in mind:

◆ **Use the point distribution as a clue to how many pieces of information to list.** For a nine-point item asking you to describe the characteristics of a totalitarian government, give at least three ideas.
◆ **Plan what you will say before starting to write.**
◆ **Use the amount of space provided,** especially if it varies for different items, as a clue to how much should be written. If you are asked to list three causes or to describe four events, number your answers so each point is clear and easy to identify.
◆ **Write your answer in sentence and paragraph form.** Unless you are specifically directed to "list," express your answer in complete sentences. If the answer requires more than one sentence, structure it as a paragraph with a topic sentence and supporting details.

Fill-in-the-Blank Tests: Factual Recall

Test questions that ask you to fill in a missing word or phrase within a sentence require recall of information rather than recognition of the correct answer. Therefore, it is important to look for clues that will trigger your recall. Here are a few suggestions:

◆ **Look for key words in the sentence.** Use them to determine what subject matter and topic are covered in the item. Here is a sample item: "Kohlberg devised a _____ to chart the course of 'moral development.'" In this item you should focus on "Kohlberg," "chart," and "moral development."
◆ **Decide what type of information is required.** Is it a date, name, place, new term?
◆ **Use the grammatical structure of the sentence to determine the type of word called for.** Is it a noun, verb, or qualifier? In the above item you must supply a noun. The correct answer is "stage theory," a noun phrase. If the blank is preceded by "an," the answer should be a noun beginning with a vowel.

REAL STUDENTS SPEAK

Adesola Sonaike

Armstrong Atlantic
State University
Savannah, Georgia

Background: Adesola graduated from high school in Nigeria at age 16 and came to the United States with her brother to attend college. She took reading and writing classes in her first year at Armstrong and went on to earn first a bachelor's and then a master's degree in chemistry. She currently works as a lab technician in a water-testing laboratory.

Goal: To get a degree in pharmacy and help people here and in her native Nigeria.

Advice on Taking Multiple-Choice Exams: In some classes, math for example, tests were easy because I just had to memorize formulas and things. For other subjects, I learned how to eliminate wrong answers on multiple-choice tests. I would read the question and then read the answers and recognize that some of the answers were wrong; they didn't correlate with the question they were asking. I would eliminate the wrong ones and then choose an answer. If I didn't know the answer I would guess. I also did the easiest questions first so I had more time to go back and do the difficult ones.

Multiple-Choice Tests: Recognizing Correct Answers

Multiple-choice is the most frequently used type of exam and often the most difficult to answer. The following suggestions should improve your success in taking this type of exam:

Begin by reading each question as if it is a fill-in-the-blank or short-answer question.   Cover up the choices and try to answer the question from your knowledge of the subject. In this way, you will avoid confusion that might arise from complicated choices. After you have formed your answer, compare it with each of the choices, and select the one that comes closest to your answer.

Read all choices before choosing one.   Do not stop with second or third choices, even if you are certain that you have found the correct answer. Remember, on most multiple-choice tests your job is to pick the *best* answer, and the last choice may be a better answer than any of the first three.

Read combination choices.   Some multiple-choice tests include choices that are combinations of previously listed choices, as in the following item:

The mesodermal tissue layer contains cells that will become

a. skin, sensory organs, and nervous systems.
b. skin, sensory organs, and blood vessels.

    c. bones and muscle.

    d. stomach, liver, and pancreas.

    e. a and c

    f. b, c, and d

    g. a, c, and d

The addition of choices that are combinations of the previous choices tends to make answers even more confusing. Treat each choice, when combined with the stem, as a true or false statement. As you consider each choice, mark it true or false. If you find more than one true statement, then select the choice that contains the letters of all the true statements you identified.

Use logic and common sense.   Even if you are unfamiliar with the subject matter, you can sometimes reason out the correct answer. The following test item is taken from a history exam on Japanese-American relations after World War II:

Prejudice and discrimination are

    a. harmful to our society because they waste our economic, political, and social resources.

    b. helpful because they ensure us against attack from within.

    c. harmful because they create negative images of the United States in foreign countries.

    d. helpful because they keep the majority pure and united against minorities.

Through logic and common sense, it is possible to eliminate choices *b* and *d.* Prejudice and discrimination are seldom, if ever, regarded as positive, desirable, or helpful since they are inconsistent with democratic ideals. Having narrowed your answer to two choices, *a* or *c,* you can see that choice *a* offers a stronger, more substantial reason why prejudice and discrimination are harmful. The attitude of other countries toward the United States is not as serious as a waste of economic, political, and social resources.

Examine closely items that are very similar.   Often, when two similar choices are presented, one is likely to be correct. Carefully compare the two choices. First, try to express each in your own words, and then analyze how they differ. Often, this process will enable you to recognize the right answer.

Pay special attention to the level of qualifying words.   As noted for true/false tests, qualifying words are important. Since many statements, ideas, principles, and rules have exceptions, be careful in selecting items that contain such extreme qualifying words as *best, always, all, no, never, none, entirely,* and *completely,* all of which suggest that a condition exists without exception. Items containing words that provide for some level of exception, or qualification, are more likely to be correct. Here are a few examples of such words: *often, usually, less, seldom, few, more,* and *most.* Likewise, numerical answers that are about in the middle of a range of choices are probably correct.

In the following example, notice the use of the italicized qualifying words:

In most societies

a. values are *highly* consistent.
b. people *often* believe and act on values that are contradictory.
c. *all* legitimate organizations support values of the majority.
d. values of equality *never* exist alongside prejudice and discrimination.

In this question, items *c* and *d* contain the words *all* and *never,* suggesting that those statements are true without exception. Thus, if you did not know the answer to this question based on content, you could eliminate items *c* and *d* on the basis of the level of qualifiers.

Some multiple-choice questions require application of knowledge or information.   You may be asked to analyze a hypothetical situation or to use what you have learned to solve a problem. In answering questions of this type, start by crossing out unnecessary information that can distract you. In the following example, distracting information has been eliminated.

~~Carrie is comfortable in her new home in New Orleans.~~ When she gets ~~dressed up~~ and leaves her home and goes to the supermarket ~~to buy the week's groceries~~, she gets nervous and angry and feels that something is going to happen to her. She feels the same way when walking ~~her four-year-old~~ son ~~Jason~~ in the park ~~or playground~~.

Carrie is suffering from

a. shyness.
b. a phobia.
c. a personality disorder.
d. hypertension.

Jot down the essence.   If a question concerns steps in a process or order of events or any other information that is easily confused, ignore the choices and use the margin or scrap paper to jot down the information as you can recall it. Then select the choice that matches what you wrote.

Avoid the unfamiliar.   Avoid choosing answers that are unfamiliar or that you do not understand. A choice that looks complicated or uses difficult words is not necessarily correct. If you have studied carefully, a choice that is unfamiliar to you or contains unfamiliar terminology is probably incorrect.

Eliminate choices that are obviously false.   Treat each choice in a troublesome question like you would a statement on a true/false test. Follow the procedures on p. 384 to pare down the number of probable answers.

Choose the longest or most inclusive answers.   As a last resort, when you do not know the answer and are unable to eliminate any of the choices as wrong, guess by picking the one that seems most complete and contains the most information. This is a good choice because instructors are usually careful to make the correct answer complete. Thus, the answer often becomes long or detailed.

Be careful of "all of the above" and "none of the above" questions. This type of question can be particularly difficult, since it usually involves five choices and can lead to confusion. To make it easier, first try to eliminate "all of the above." If even *one* choice is incorrect, "all of the above" will be incorrect. If you think that at least *one* of the choices is correct, you can eliminate "none of the above." If you think two choices are correct but you are unsure of the third one, you should choose "all of the above." When questions such as these occur only a few times in a test, "all" or "none" is probably the correct choice.

Make educated guesses.   In most instances, you can eliminate one or more of the choices as obviously wrong. Even if you can eliminate only one choice, you have increased your odds on a four-choice answer from one in four to one in three. If you can eliminate two choices, you have increased your odds to one in two, or 50 percent. Don't hesitate to play the odds and make a guess—you may gain points.

Choose a midrange number.   When an item asks you to select a number, such as a percentage or other statistic, choose a midrange number. Test writers often include both choices that are higher and lower than the correct answer.

| EXERCISE 17.3 | ## Answering Multiple-Choice Items |

Directions   *The following multiple-choice items appeared on an exam in psychology. Study each item and use your reasoning skills to eliminate items that seem incorrect and then, making an educated guess, select the best answer.*

_____ 1. Modern psychological researchers maintain that the mind as well as behavior can be scientifically examined primarily by
   a. observing behavior and making inferences about mental functioning.
   b. observing mental activity and making inferences about behavior.
   c. making inferences about behavior.
   d. direct observation of behavior.

_____ 2. Jane Goodall has studied the behavior of chimpanzees in their own habitat. She exemplifies a school of psychology that is concerned with
   a. theories.
   b. mental processes.
   c. the individual's potential for growth.
   d. naturalistic behavior.

———— 3. If a psychologist were personally to witness the effects of a tornado upon the residents of a small town, what technique would he or she be using?
 a. experimentation
 b. correlational research
 c. observation
 d. none of the above

———— 4. A case study is a(n)
 a. observation of an event.
 b. comparison of similar events.
 c. study of changes and their effects.
 d. intense investigation of a particular occurrence.

———— 5. Events that we are aware of at a given time make up the
 a. unconscious.
 b. subconscious.
 c. consciousness.
 d. triconscious.

———— 6. Unlocking a combination padlock
 a. always involves language skills.
 b. always involves motor skills.
 c. never involves imaginable skills.
 d. seldom involves memory skills.

THINKING CRITICALLY
. . . About Practicum Exams

Often, exams in technical fields such as computer science, accounting, nursing, engineering, and medical technology take the form of practicums. In this type of exam, you are required to perform a task or solve a problem that simulates one you might encounter on the job. For example, a computer science student might be required to "debug" a faulty computer program. A nursing student might be required to install a number of intravenous devices. In preparing for practicum exams ask yourself the following questions:

1. **What tasks will I probably be asked to perform?** Consider any classroom demonstration your instructor presented. Review any lab assignments or class projects you carried out.

2. **What procedures are involved with these tasks?** Determine the process or steps you were taught for each task. Review your class notes on them. Prepare a summary sheet listing the steps in order. Write out an index card for each step, shuffle the cards, and then practice arranging them in the right order.

Rehearse the steps mentally or write them out from memory to test yourself. Draw diagrams or sketches depicting the process. Picture yourself carrying out these procedures.

3. **How can I improve my performance of the task?** Repeatedly carry out the task while you review the steps or procedures you learned. Work with another student so that you can observe and evaluate each other's techniques.

SKILLS IN ACTION

Using All Your Exam-Taking Skills

Each question below contains a hint that helps you eliminate incorrect choices and determine the correct answer. Explain what this hint is and give the correct answer to the question.

True/False Questions

1. A psychology test always measures behavior. T/F

   Explanation of hint: _____

   Answer: _____

2. Thomas Jefferson was the primary author of the Declaration of Independence and the first president of the United States. T/F

   Explanation of hint: _____

   Answer: _____

Fill-in-the-Blank Questions

3. The type of memory that contains information for only a short period is called _____ memory.

   Explanation of hint: _____

   Answer: _____

4. Information that is condensed and organized with headings indented to reflect their relative importance is known as an _____.

   Explanation of hint: _____

   Answer: _____

Multiple-Choice Questions

5. You can best improve your memory by

   a. reading about memory.
   b. taking a lot of courses at one time.

(continues)

    c. practicing saying, seeing, and hearing the information you want to remember.

    d. listening more attentively to lectures.

Explanation of hint: _____

Answer: _____

6. Information can be transferred from your short-term to your long-term memory by

    a. repeating it.

    b. elaborative rehearsal.

    c. taking notes on it.

    d. all of the above

    e. none of the above

Explanation of hint: _____

Answer: _____

7. Which is the best estimate of the percentage of Americans suffering from a psychological disorder?

    a. 5 percent

    b. 10 percent

    c. 20 percent

    d. 40 percent

Explanation of hint: _____

Answer: _____

■ Achieving Success with Standardized Tests

At various times in college, you may be required to take standardized tests. These are commercially prepared; they are usually lengthy, timed tests that are used nationally or statewide to measure specific skills and abilities. Your score on these tests is used to compare your performance with that of large numbers of other students throughout the country or state. The SAT and ACT are examples of standardized tests you may have already taken. Many graduate schools require one or more standardized tests as part of their admission process. The most common is the Graduate Record Examination (GRE). Others are the Medical College Admission Test (MCAT), the Law School Admission Test (LSAT), and the Graduate Management Admission Test (GMAT). Licensing and certification exams are also a form of standardized test. Tests you take to obtain credentials as a CPA, nurse, or public school teacher are examples. Standardized tests are also given as admission tests for specialized training or employment: police, firefighters, and postal employees often take qualifying written exams.

Preparing for the Test

◆ **Find out as much as possible about the test.** Meet with your advisor or check the career center to obtain brochures and application forms. Find out about its general contents, length, and timing. Determine its format and the scoring procedures used. Know when and where the test is given.

◆ **Take a review course.** Find out if your college offers a preparatory course of review sessions to help you prepare for the test.

◆ **Obtain a review book or CD.** Review books or CDs are available to help you prepare for many standardized tests. Purchase these at your college bookstore, a large off-campus bookstore, or through the Internet.

◆ **Begin your review early.** Start to study well ahead of the exam, so that you can fit the necessary review time into your already hectic schedule.

◆ **Start with a quick overview of the test.** Most review books contain a section that explains the type of questions on the test and offers test-taking strategies. If a brief review of the subject matter is offered, read through it.

◆ **Take practice tests.** To become most comfortable with the test, take numerous timed practice tests and score them. Make your practice tests as much like the actual test as possible. Work at a well-lighted desk or table in a quiet setting and time yourself carefully.

◆ **Review your answers.** Thoroughly review the questions you answered incorrectly. Read through the explanations given in your review book and try to see why the indicated answer is best.

◆ **Keep track of your scores.** Keep a record of both your total score and subtest scores on practice tests. This will help you judge your progress and can give you insights into areas of weakness that require extra review.

Taking the Test

◆ **Arrive prepared at the exam room.** Get to the testing site early so you can choose a good seat and become comfortable with the surroundings. Wear a watch, bring two sharpened pencils with erasers (in case one breaks), and two pens (in case one runs out of ink).

◆ **Get organized before the timing begins.** Line up your answer sheet and test booklet so you can move between them rapidly without losing your place. Carefully fill out your answer sheet.

◆ **Skim the instructions.** This can save you valuable time. If you have prepared yourself properly, you should be very familiar with the format of the test and the instructions. A quick reading of the directions will be all that is necessary to assure yourself that they have not changed.

◆ **Work quickly and steadily.** Most standardized tests are timed, so the pace you work at is a critical factor. You need to work at a fairly rapid rate, but not so fast as to make careless errors.

◆ **Don't expect to get everything right.** Unlike classroom tests or exams, you are not expected to get all of the answers correct.

◆ **Find out if there is a penalty for guessing.** If there is none, then use the last 20 or 30 seconds to randomly fill in an answer for each item that you have not had time to do. The odds are that you will get one out of every five correct. If there is a guessing penalty, guess only if you can narrow the answer down to two choices. Otherwise, leave it blank.

◆ **Check your answer sheet periodically.** If you have skipped a question, make sure that later answers match their questions. If the test has several parts, check to see that you are marking answers in the correct answer grid.

◆ **Don't just stop if you finish early.** If you have time left over, use it. Complete marked questions you skipped. Review as many answers as you can. Check over your answer sheet for stray marks, and darken your answer marks.

REVIEW   Five Key Points to Remember

1 **The first few minutes you spend on an exam are important.** Be sure to preview the exam and plan your time before beginning the first item.

2 **True/false items involve making judgments based on your knowledge and experience.** Watch for qualifying words and phrases, read two-part statements carefully, and pay attention to negative or double-negative statements.

3 **Matching tests require you to discover relationships.** Discover the relationship between the columns before beginning.

4 **Short answer and fill-in-the-blank items focus on factual information.** Look for clues in the statement to help you know what information to supply.

5 **Multiple-choice exams focus on recognition of the right answer.** Use your reasoning skills to eliminate wrong answers.

Working
Together

Each class member should write five multiple-choice items based on Chapter 8 of this book. Working in groups, students should review the items, comparing their reasoning for each item, and identify the level of thinking each item required.

The Work Connection

Becoming familiar with the format of objective exams may prove useful when you apply for a job. Some employers give a variety of tests as part of their pre-employment process. *Aptitude tests* measure your ability to perform job functions; *integrity tests* predict your attitudes, work ethic, and personality; and *psychological tests* provide in-depth information about you. Hunter and Hunter (1984) found that how applicants do on ability tests predicts future job success better than job interviews, previous employment history, education, or reference checks.[1] Familiarity with objective exams will be an advantage if your prospective employer uses objective tests to measure, for example, such basic skills as the ability to solve problems, use words precisely, or do basic math.

1. If you were to take a test now on your mastery of basic language and math skills, how well do you predict you would do? Why?

2. Aside from the study skills course in which you are currently enrolled, what other courses or campus services can help you learn how to do well on objective tests? List two or three ways you can improve your test-taking skills.

The Web Connection

1. Practice Test Made by Students

   http://www.mtsu.edu/~studskl/practest.html

   Students from Middle Tennessee State University created this practice test that reviews how to take true/false and multiple-choice exams. Test yourself!

2. Test-Taking Strategies

   http://campushealth.unc.edu/index.php?option=com_content&task=view&id=469&Itemid=65

   The University of North Carolina, Chapel Hill, offers some useful tips for taking exams that involve solving math or science problems. List some other specialized tests (for example, a driver's license test) and specific preparation techniques. Try to think of tests that are given outside of the academic realm.

3. Test-Taking Strategies

http://www.life.arizona.edu/academicsuccess/tips/testtakingtips.pdf

The University Learning Center at the University of Arizona offers tips to apply before, during, and after a test. Review all the tips and then complete the exercises under the section, "Apply What You Have Learned."

18 Taking Essay Exams

Do You Know?

How should you organize your approach to essay exams?

How do you analyze essay exam questions?

How do you outline your essay answers?

How do you write an effective essay answer?

How can you succeed at writing competency tests and exit exams?

While objective exams such as multiple-choice and true/false tests require primarily that you *recognize* correct answers, essay exams require you to demonstrate higher-level thinking skills through writing. Essay exams provide a greater opportunity to demonstrate your learning and to distinguish yourself as an excellent student. Your essays reveal a great deal about your level of mastery of the course content as well as your ability to organize, synthesize, and apply it. Essay exams measure your ability to think about the subject and communicate those thoughts in written form.

The manner in which you approach an essay exam, and how carefully you read the questions and organize and write your answers, can influence your grade by as much as 10 or 15 points. The primary purpose of this chapter is to discuss each of these aspects of taking essay exams. Suggestions for achieving success on writing competency tests and exit exams are also presented.

■ Writing Effective Essay Exams

Essay answers are usually rated on two factors: content and form. It is not enough, then, simply to include the correct information. The information must be presented in a logical, organized way that demonstrates your understanding of the subject. There can be as much as one whole letter grade difference between a well-written and a poorly written essay even though both contain the same basic information. This section offers suggestions for earning as many points as possible on essay exams.

REAL STUDENTS SPEAK

Nakasha Kirkland
———
Armstrong Atlantic
State University
Savannah, Georgia

Background: Nakasha has a bachelor's degree in music, and recently graduated with a master's degree in education with a concentration in math and science from Armstrong Atlantic State.

Goal: She is now pursuing her goal of teaching 6th grade mathematics at Hubert Middle School.

Advice on Doing Well on Essay Exams: I make sure I cover all the points before I'm out of time. To get started, I try to quickly jot down everything I want to cover—all the main points. Then I break it down and take each idea and expand on it, writing a paragraph for each important idea.

Organizing Your Approach

Here are a few suggestions to help you approach essay exams in an organized, systematic manner:

Read the directions. Before reading any of the essay questions, be certain to read the general directions first. They may tell you how many questions to answer, how to structure your answers, what the point distribution is, or what the minimum or maximum length of your answer should be.

Plan your time. If you have to answer two essay questions in a 50-minute class session, allot yourself 20 to 25 minutes for each one. There is a strong tendency to spend the most time on the first question, but you should guard against it. Keep track of time so that you are able to finish both questions. Allow a few minutes at the end of an in-class exam to check and proofread your answers. Allow more time for a final exam.

Know the point value of each question. If that information is not included on the exam, ask the instructor. Use this information to budget your time and to decide how much to write for each question. Suppose you are taking an exam that has three questions with the following values:

Question 1: 20 points

Question 2: 30 points

Question 3: 50 points

Because question 3 is worth half the total points, you should spend approximately half of your time on it. Divide the remaining time nearly equally on questions 1 and 2. Point distribution can suggest how many ideas to include in your answer. For a 20-point question, your instructor probably expects four or five main points ($4 \times 5 = 20$), since most instructors don't work with fractions of points. If you can think of additional ideas to include and time permits, include them because point distribution is only an indicator, not a rule for length.

If you have a choice, select carefully.   When the directions specify a choice of questions to answer, select those on which you will be able to score the most points. Some essay questions are more difficult than others; some require specific, exact information, while others call for a reasoned, logical interpretation or evaluation. Take time to make a careful choice. A few moments spent at the beginning may well save you the time it takes to switch from one question to another should you realize midway that you are not able to prepare an adequate response.

Answer the easiest question first.   Assuming the questions are of equal point value, answer the easiest question first. Knowing you are doing well will build your self-confidence and help you approach the remainder of the exam with a positive attitude. You will be able to complete the easiest question fairly quickly, leaving the remainder of time to be divided among the more difficult questions.

Make notes as you read.   As you read a question the first time, you may begin to formulate an answer automatically. Jot down a few key words that will bring these thoughts back when you are ready to organize your answer.

Analyze the question.   Well-written essay questions define the topic and suggest what kinds of information to include, as shown in the following item.

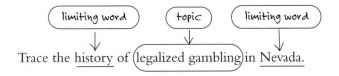

Here the topic, legalized gambling, is clearly defined, and it is limited or restricted in two ways: (1) you are concerned only with its history—not its status today, or its effects; and (2) you are concerned only with the state of Nevada. Also notice the word "trace." It suggests the method of development to use in writing this essay. Since *trace* means to track something through time, you should use chronological order to develop your answer.

Here are a few more examples: The topics have been circled and the restricting or limiting words have been underlined.

Develop the habit of looking for and marking or circling key words as you analyze essay questions.

List several categories of speeches and describe their primary functions and uses.

Describe the basic differences between the reproductive cycles of angiosperms and gymnosperms.

Compare the purpose and function of analytical reports and research reports.

Watch for questions with several parts.   Students often fail to answer all parts of an essay question. Most likely, they become involved with answering the first part and forget to complete the remaining parts. Questions with several parts come in two forms. The most obvious form is shown in the following example:

For the U.S. invasion of Panama, discuss the (a) causes, (b) immediate effects, and (c) long-range political implications.

A sample of a less obvious form that does not stand out as a several-part question is shown below:

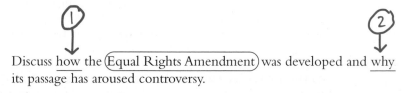

Discuss how the Equal Rights Amendment was developed and why its passage has aroused controversy.

When you find a question of this type, circle the topic and underline the limiting words (as in the example) to serve as reminders of what to focus on.

Use thought patterns as clues to content and organization.   Essay questions contain one or more clue words that indicate the predominant thought pattern(s) to use in organizing, constructing, and writing your answer. These words specify what approach you are to take in answering the question. They indicate whether you are to make comparisons, summarize, explain, or answer in some other way. Here is a sample essay question:

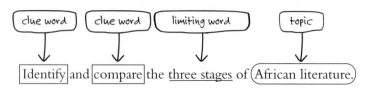

Identify and compare the three stages of African literature.

The topic of this essay question, African literature, is limited to a consideration of its three stages. The clue words "identify" and "compare" specify what type of response is called for. They tell you *what* to say about the stages of African literature. First you are to identify—that is, name and briefly describe—each stage. Then you are to compare the three stages, describing their similarities. The most commonly used clue words, and the thought patterns they often suggest, are summarized in Table 18.1.

TABLE 18.1 Essay Exam Questions

Thought Pattern	Clue Word	Example	Information to Include
Chronological	Trace	Trace the history of the foreign exchange market.	Describe the development or progress of a particular trend, event, or process in chronological order.
Process	Describe	Describe how an advertisement is produced and prepared.	Tell how something happened, including how, who, where, and why.
Comparison	Compare	Compare the causes of air pollution with those of water pollution.	Show how items are similar as well as different; include details or examples.
Contrast	Contrast (differentiate)	Contrast the health care system in the United States with that in England.	Show how the items are different; include details or examples.
Cause and effect	Prove	Prove that ice is a better cooling agent than air when both are at the same temperature.	Give reasons or evidence, or establish that a concept or theory is correct, logical, or valid.
Cause and effect	Justify	Justify the decision to place economic sanctions on Iraq.	Give reasons that support an action, event, or policy.
Listing	Discuss	Discuss the effectiveness of drug rehabilitation programs.	Consider important characteristics and main points.
Listing	Enumerate	Enumerate the reasons for U.S. involvement in the Persian Gulf War.	List or discuss one by one.
Definition	State (illustrate)	State Boyle's Law and illustrate its use.	Explain, using examples that demonstrate or clarify a point or idea.
Definition	Define	Define thermal pollution and include several examples.	Give an accurate meaning of the term with enough detail to show that you really understand it.
Classification	Diagram	Diagram the stamen and pistil of a lily.	Make a drawing and label its parts.

(continues)

TABLE 18.1

Thought Pattern	Clue Word	Example	Information to Include
Various patterns	Criticize	Criticize the current environmental controls to combat air pollution.	Make judgments about quality or worth; include both positive and negative aspects, explaining or giving reasons for your judgments.
Various patterns	Evaluate	Evaluate the strategies our society has used to treat mental illness.	React to the topic in a logical way. Discuss the merits, strengths, weaknesses, advantages, or limitations of the topic, explaining your reasons.
Various Patterns	Summarize	Summarize the arguments for and against offering sex education courses in public schools.	Cover the major points in brief form; use a sentence and paragraph form.

EXERCISE 18.1   **Analyzing Essay Questions**

Directions   *Read each of the following essay questions. In each question, underline the topic, circle the limiting word(s), and identify the thought pattern(s) the question suggests.*

1. Discuss the long-term effects of the trend toward a smaller, more self-contained family structure.
2. Trace the development of monopolies in the late nineteenth and early twentieth centuries in America.
3. Explain one effect of the Industrial Revolution upon each of three of the following:
   a. transportation
   b. capitalism
   c. socialism
   d. population growth
   e. scientific research
4. Discuss the reason why, although tropical plants have very large leaves and most desert plants have very small leaves, cacti grow equally well in both habitats.
5. Describe the events leading up to the War of 1812.
6. Compare and contrast the purposes and procedures in textbook marking and lecture note taking.
7. Briefly describe a complete approach to reading and studying a textbook chapter that will enable you to handle a test on that material successfully.
8. List four factors that influence memory or recall ability, and explain how each can be used to make study more efficient.

9. Summarize the techniques a speaker or lecturer may use to emphasize the important concepts and ideas in his lecture.

10. Explain the value and purpose of the previewing technique, and list the steps involved in prereading a textbook chapter.

Constructing Your Answer

As soon as they have finished analyzing the question, many students immediately begin to write the answer. A far better technique is to take a few moments to think about, plan, and organize your ideas. Since you are working within a time limit, you might not be able to revise your answer. Consequently, it is even more important than usual to plan your essay carefully before you begin.

Outline.   Make a brief word or phrase outline of the ideas you want to include in your answer. After you have read and marked each question, jot down ideas you'll include in your essay on the back of the exam, or on a separate sheet of paper that you won't turn in. If the question is one that you predicted, jot down the outline of your draft essay, making adjustments and additions to fit the actual question. Arrange your ideas to follow the method of development suggested in the question. Number them to indicate the order in which you'll present them in your essay. Keep in mind, too, the point value of the essay, and be sure to include sufficient ideas and explanations.

One student made these notes in response to the following question:

Identify the stages of sleep and describe four sleep disorders.

Stages	Disorders
1 wakefulness	4 hypersomnia
2 quiet sleep	1 insomnia
3 REM sleep (active)	2 sleepwalking
	3 night terrors

As you write your essay, other ideas may occur to you. Add them to your list so they won't slip from your mind.

Rearrange the outline.   Study your word outline and rearrange its order. You may want to put major topics and important ideas first and less important points toward the end. Or you may decide to organize your answer chronologically, discussing events early in time near the beginning of the essay and mentioning more recent events near the end.

If the point value of the essay is given, use that information as a clue to how many separate points or ideas may be expected. For example, for an essay worth 25 points, five major points may be expected.

If you are having difficulty recalling needed information or if you should suddenly "go blank," try a technique called brainstorming. Basically, it involves writing a list of anything and everything you can think of related to the topic. Then review your list; you are likely to find some ideas you can use in your answer.

EXERCISE 18.2   **Predicting Essay Questions**

Directions *For a course you are currently taking, predict an essay question you think your instructor is likely to include on a midterm or final exam. Underline the limiting word(s), circle the topic, and box in the clue word(s); then construct and revise an outline of your answer to this question.*

SKILLS IN ACTION

Outlining Your Essay Exam

Many students underestimate the importance of outlining their answers before they begin writing an essay exam. The following are three topics of general interest. Choose one and create an outline for an answer that you think would get you an A.

1. Describe three ways that the cell phone has changed communication styles and how these changes are affecting society as a whole.

2. Compare and contrast two different styles of music, such as classical and hip-hop, describing the typical audience for each type of music and what draws people to each type of music.

3. American zoos are often divided into different sections. Identify at least three sections of a typical zoo and explain the types of wildlife that are usually on display in those sections. Also explain the general environment of each section—for example, is it light or dark, wet or dry? Why?

Writing Your Answer

The appearance, organization, and correctness of your essay influence your grade. Numerous experiments have been done; most indicate that well-organized, correctly written papers receive nearly one letter grade higher than papers that express the same content but do so in a poorly organized, error-filled manner. An effective essay answer should follow correct paragraph form, use complete sentences, and clearly present ideas in a logical format. You should begin your answer with a thesis statement and then explain and support it in several paragraphs.

Write a clear thesis statement.   The thesis statement you write for essay tests should be simple and straightforward. It should clearly state the main point your essay is intended to explain. Often, simply rephrasing the question is sufficient. Here are two examples:

Essay Question	Thesis Statement
Explain how advertising differs from publicity.	Advertising differs from publicity in three primary ways.
Discuss the practical applications of Newton's three laws of motion.	Newton's laws of motion have many practical applications.

Other times, it might be appropriate to include additional information. In the following example, the question provided structure to which the writer added more information.

Essay Question	Thesis Statement
Explain the differences between primary and secondary groups.	Primary groups differ from secondary groups in their purpose, membership, level of interaction, and level of intimacy.

Always make your thesis statement as direct, concise, and specific as possible. Your goals should be to announce to your instructor that you know the answer to the question and to indicate how it will be organized.

EXERCISE 18.3

Working **Together**

Writing Thesis Statements

Directions   *Working with a classmate, write a thesis statement for each of the following essay questions.*

1. Discuss how books differ from other print media in communicating to the public.
2. Describe the types of long-term memory.
3. Criticize the current state of mental health services in the United States.
4. Explain how communication is affected by the Internet.
5. Compare Thurstone's model of intelligence with Guilford's.

Make your main points stand out.   You can do this most easily by writing a separate paragraph for each major supporting detail. Begin each paragraph with a topic sentence that introduces its main point. For example, your thesis statement might be:

There are four social factors that may affect the consumer buying process.

Your topic sentences could then read as follows:

Paragraph 1: First, social role and family influence are factors that affect consumer decisions.

Paragraph 2: Reference groups are a second social factor.

Paragraph 3: Social class also affects the consumer's purchase decisions.

Paragraph 4: Finally, cultures and subcultures affect buying decisions.

Due to the large volume of essays that many instructors must read in a short period of time, they tend to skim for the key ideas rather than to read everything. Therefore, it is best to make your main points easy to find, at the beginning of each paragraph. For lengthy answers or multipart questions, you can use headings, the numbering from the question, or space between the different parts of your answer, to make your key points obvious.

Develop your main points.   Instructors often criticize essay answers because they fail to explain or to support ideas fully. If you include only one major idea per paragraph, you will avoid this danger and force yourself to explain the major points. Also, if you answer an essay question with the intent of convincing your instructor that you have learned the material, then you are likely to include enough explanation.

You should take care to provide relevant and sufficient explanation of the topic sentence of each paragraph. In other words, each detail you include should directly support your topic sentence and there should be enough details to make your topic sentence understandable and convincing. Providing too much information is better than including too little. For the sample above on consumer buying, you should explain or define each social factor and then discuss how it affects buying behavior.

Refer to the sample essay answer shown in Figure 18.1 to see how the thesis statement, main points, and supporting details come together in an essay answer.

Write a brief conclusion.   A concluding sentence is an effective way to reemphasize your main points in a lengthy essay.

Proofread your answer.   Be sure to leave enough time to proofread your answer. Check for errors in spelling, punctuation, and grammar. If time permits, make minor revisions. Pay attention to sentences that do not make sense, and write your changes as neatly as possible. If you think of an important fact to add, do so.

Table 18.2 (p. 410) summarizes these and further suggestions for presenting a correctly written essay answer.

If You Run Out of Time

Despite careful planning, you may run out of time before you can finish writing one of the essays. If this happens, try to jot down the major ideas that you would discuss fully if you had time. Often, your instructor will give you partial credit for this type of response, especially if you mention that you ran out of time.

FIGURE 18.1
A Sample Essay Question and Answer

ESSAY QUESTION

Crime is a human act that violates criminal law. Identify the various categories of crime. Describe and provide an example of each.

ANSWER

<u>There are five categories of crime. Each violates one or more aspects of criminal law.</u> <u>The first of these categories is index crime.</u> Index crimes are those identified by the Federal Bureau of Investigation as serious crimes. They include criminal homicide, rape, robbery, burglary, aggravated assault, larceny, auto theft, and arson. — Thesis Statement

— Main Point #1

Supporting Details

<u>The second type of crime is white-collar crime.</u> These crimes may be committed by corporations or individuals, usually within the course of daily business. The criminals are often affluent and respectable citizens. Some examples are embezzlement and income tax evasion. — Main Point #2

Supporting Details

<u>A third type of crime is professional crime.</u> Professional crimes are committed by criminals who pursue crime as a day-to-day occupation. They often use skilled techniques and are respected by other criminals. Shoplifters, safecrackers, or cargo highjackers are examples of professional criminals. — Main Point #3

Supporting Details

<u>Organized crime is a fourth type of crime.</u> Organized crime involves the sale of illegal goods and services and is conducted by criminals who organize into networks. Organized crime is often transmitted through generations and does not depend on particular individuals for its continuation. Organized crime often involves political corruption. Examples of organized crime are gambling, narcotics sales, and loan sharking. — Main Point #4

Supporting Details

<u>A fifth type of crime is victimless crime.</u> These crimes involve willing participants; there is no victim other than the offender. Examples include drug use, prostitution, and public drunkenness. — Main Point #5

Supporting Details

If You Don't Know the Answer

Despite careful preparation, you may be unable to answer a particular question. If this should happen, do not leave a blank page; write something. Attempt to answer the question—you may even hit upon some partially correct information. However, the main reason for writing something is to give the instructor the

TABLE 18.2 Tips and Techniques for Presenting Essay Answers

Tips	Techniques
Use correct paragraph form.	Explain one idea per paragraph.
Begin your answer with a thesis statement.	Write a sentence that states what the entire essay will discuss.
Make your main points easy to find.	State each main point in a separate paragraph; use headings; number ideas; use blank space to divide ideas.
Include sufficient explanation.	Provide several supporting details for each main point.
Avoid opinions and judgments.	Include only factual information unless otherwise requested.
Make your answer readable.	Use ink; use 8½ × 11-inch paper; number your pages; write on one side; leave margins and spaces between lines.
Proofread your answer.	Read through your answer to check grammar, spelling, and punctuation. Make minor revisions if time permits.

opportunity to give you at least a few points for trying. If you leave a completely blank page, your instructor has no choice but to give you zero points. Usually losing full credit on one essay automatically eliminates one's chances of getting a high passing grade.

EXERCISE 18.4

Writing an Essay Answer

Directions   *Use the outline you constructed in Exercise 18.2 to write an answer to the essay question you predicted.*

EXERCISE 18.5

Working Together

Evaluating Essay Answers

Directions   *Exchange essays with another student and evaluate the essays by discussing how well each meet the following criteria:*

1. Use of complete sentences and paragraph form
2. Clarity of thesis statement
3. Ease of locating main points
4. Quality of supporting details
5. Organization of the essay

THINKING CRITICALLY
. . . About Returned Exams

Most students do not pay enough attention to returned exams. If you usually file away returned exams for future reference once you have noted your grade, STOP. You can learn a lot by analyzing a returned exam. Use the following questions to guide your analysis:

1. **Where did you lose your points?** Make a list of topics on which you lost points. Do you see a pattern? Can you identify one or more topics or chapters that were particularly troublesome? If so, review that material now, and make a note to review it again before your final exam.

2. **What type of questions did you miss?** If the exam had several parts, where did you lose the most points (essay or multiple-choice, for example)? Adjust your study and review strategies accordingly, using the suggestions in Chapter 16.

3. **What level of thinking (see Chapter 2, p. 42) was required in the questions you missed?** Did you miss knowledge and comprehension questions? If so, you will need to spend more time on factual recall. If you missed questions that require analysis, then you should adjust your study plan to include more thought and reflection. If you missed questions that require synthesis, then you should devise study strategies that force you to pull information together. If you missed application questions, spend more time looking at practical uses and applications of course content. If you missed evaluation questions, ask more critical questions about course content.

■ Achieving Success with Competency Tests and Exit Exams

Your college may require that you pass competency tests in such skill areas as reading, writing, and mathematics. You should think of tests such as these as readiness tests, since they assess the skills required in more advanced college courses. Competency tests and exit exams are intended to ensure that you will not be placed in courses for which you are inadequately prepared or that are too difficult for you. You should, of course, try your best with these types of tests, but you shouldn't be upset if you don't score at the required level. It is best to be sure you possess the necessary skills before you attempt more difficult courses.

The suggestions given in this section focus on competency tests and exit exams in writing, but also apply to other tests.

Find Out About the Test

Find out as much as possible about the test ahead of time, so you will feel confident and prepared for the test. You'll want to know

◆ what skills the test measures
◆ what kinds of questions are included (for example, will you write an essay or correct errors in paragraphs?)
◆ the number of questions there are
◆ if there is a time limit and, if so, what it is
◆ how the test is scored (do some skills count more than others?)
◆ if you are to write an essay, whether you are expected to revise or recopy it

Your instructor should be able to answer many of these questions. In addition, talk with other students who have taken the test. They may be able to offer useful tips and advice.

Make Your Final Preparations for the Test

Since competency tests and exit exams in writing are usually taken right after you have finished a writing course, you should be well prepared for them already. Only a few last-minute matters remain.

Essay tests.   If your test requires you to write an essay, the following suggestions will help:

1. Review all papers your instructor has graded in order to identify and make a list of your most common errors. When you revise and proofread your competency-test answers, check for each of these errors.

2. Before you go into the exam, construct a mental checklist that you can use for revising your essay. If time permits, jot your list down on scrap paper during the exam and use it to revise your essay.

3. Plan how to divide your time if your test is timed. Estimate how much time you will need for each step in the writing process. Gauge your time on a practice test. Wear a watch to the exam, and check periodically to see that you're on schedule.

4. Take a practice test. Ask a classmate to make up a topic or question for you to write about that is the same type as the questions that will be on the test. Observe the time limit that will be used on the test. Finally, ask your classmate to evaluate your essay.

Error-correction tests.   If your test requires you to edit or correct another writer's sentences or paragraphs, do the following:

1. Review your graded papers from the course. The errors you made when you wrote them are likely to be those you'll have difficulty spotting on the test.

2. If time permits, read each sentence or paragraph several times, looking for different types of errors each time. For example, read it once looking for spelling errors, another time to evaluate sentence structure, and so forth.

3. Practice with a classmate. Write sample test items for each other. Pay attention to the kinds of errors you fail to spot; you're likely to miss them on the test as well.

4. If you are taking a state exam, practice manuals or review books may be available. Check with your college bookstore. Take the sample tests and work through the practice exercises. Note your pattern of errors and, if necessary, get additional help from your instructor or your college's academic skills center.

REVIEW Five Key Points to Remember

1 **Analyze essay exams before you begin.** Study the directions, note the point values, and plan your time.

2 **Analyze each question.** Look for clue words and limiting words. Use thought patterns as a guide.

3 **Write a brief outline of your answer before answering the question.** Use it to guide your writing.

4 **Make sure your answer is detailed and well organized.** Include a clear thesis statement, use correct paragraphing, and be sure to explain each of your main points.

5 **If time permits, reread your answer.** Check for completeness and correctness. Be sure you have answered the question fully.

Working Together

Each class member should write a response to the following essay question. Then, form groups of four or five students and follow each step listed below:

Problem solving is a vital and important skill. Describe the problem-solving process and illustrate its use in a particular academic situation.

(continues)

1. Group members should read and evaluate each other's essays. Specifically, they should rate each answer and award it a grade of A, B, C, or D based on each of the following criteria:

    a. Correct and complete information (refer to Chapter 16)

    b. Sufficient detail and explanation

    c. Clear organization of ideas

    d. Effectiveness of thesis statement

    e. Grammatical correctness and readability

2. Group members should defend, compare, contrast, and discuss each other's ratings.

The Work Connection

What personal characteristics and skills have been identified as vital to a person's employability? From 34 studies of the qualities employers desire most in employees, the following are the top five characteristics for getting and keeping a job:

1. Dependability/responsibility

2. Positive attitude toward work

3. Conscientiousness, punctuality, efficiency

4. Interpersonal skills, cooperation, working as a team member

5. Self-confidence, positive self-image

In a review of the studies, Kathleen Cotton noted that "virtually *all* of the employers in these studies cited 'dependability,' 'responsibility,' and 'positive attitude toward work' as vital."[1]

Analyze one of the following essay questions and make notes about how you would answer it:

1. Choose one of the traits listed above and illustrate its importance to employers.

2. As an employer, how would you know if your employee had a positive attitude toward work? Explain.

The Web Connection

1. Answering Essay Questions

   http://www.coun.uvic.ca/learning/exams/essay-questions.html

   This site from the University of Victoria presents more tips for approaching essay questions on exams. Print out this list and choose the ideas that you think would be most useful to you. Then mark the ones that you find the least useful. Would the usefulness of the tips depend on the subject matter being tested?

2. Reasons to Review Tests

   http://www.mtsu.edu/~studskl/rtrned.html

   Middle Tennessee State University offers a dozen practical reasons to look over your returned tests. When else might it be useful to examine your mistakes? Create a chart that describes some mistakes you have made in school, at home, and on the job. What did you do? Why was it wrong? How did you fix it? What did you learn?

3. Planning the Final Exam Period

   http://www.conestogac.on.ca/learningcommons/learningskills/handouts/exam_preparation.pdf

   This site from Conestoga College provides advice on how to deal with finals week. Read over the material and then answer the questions.

References

Sylvan Barnet, *A Short Guide to Writing About Art.* Boston: Little, Brown, 1989.

Bettina Lankard Brown, "Career Resilience." *ERIC Clearinghouse on Adult, Career, and Vocational Education,* Digest 178, 1996.

Careers and Employment Online, "The Use of Psychological Tests in Candidate Selection: An Overview." At www.careers.unsw.edu.au/careered/Vocational%20Assessment/psych_testing.html.

Sabra Chartrand, "Employees Devise New Strategies to Test Job Applicants," *New York Times,* December 14, 1997.

Sabra Chartrand, "A World Where Language and 'Soft Skills' Are Key," *New York Times,* April 6, 1997.

Carolyn Corbin and James D. Henry, "Conquering Career Codependence." At http://www.cweb.com/21stcentury/welcome.html.

Carolyn Corbin, "Employment in the 21st Century." Speech to the National Association of Colleges and Employers, May 29, 1998. At http://www.jobweb.org/nace/nm98/may29.shtml.

DeVry Institute of Technology, a division of DeVry University, "Survival of the Fittest." *Directions* newsletter, 1997.

Rebecca J. Donatelle, *Access to Health, 7th ed.* San Francisco, CA: Benjamin Cummings (Pearson), 2002.

Robert B. Ekelund and Robert D. Tollison, *Economics.* Boston: Little, Brown and Co., 1986.

J. Ross Eshleman and Barbara G. Cashion, *Sociology: An Introduction.* Boston: Little, Brown and Co., 1985.

Walter S. Jones, *The Logic of International Relations, 5th ed.* Boston: Little, Brown and Co., 1985.

Brenda Kemp and Adele Pilitteri, *Fundamentals of Nursing.* Boston: Little, Brown and Co., 1984.

Edward M. Kennedy, "The Need for Handgun Control." *Los Angeles Times,* April 5, 1981.

Robert L. Lineberry, *Government in America, 3rd ed.* Boston: Little, Brown and Co., 1986.

Elaine P. Maimon, *Writing in the Arts and Sciences.* Cambridge, MA: Winthrop Publishers, 1981.

George Miller, "The Magic Number. Seven Plus or Minus Two: Some Limits on Our Capacity for Processing Information," *Psychological Review* 63 (1956).

Robert C. Nickerson, *Fundamentals of Structured COBOL.* Boston: Little, Brown and Co., 1984.

Edward M. Reingold and Wilfred J. Hansen, *Dale Structures.* Boston: Little, Brown and Co., 1983.

Rosemary A. Rosser and Glen L. Nickolson, *Educational Psychology.* Boston: Little, Brown and Co., 1984.

Frederick A. Russ and Charles A. Kirkpatrick, *Marketing.* Boston: Little, Brown and Co., 1982.

Adam Smith, "Fifty Million Handguns." *Esquire,* April 1981.

Star Tribune, "Part III: The coming trauma" of "On the Edge of the Digital Age." *Star Tribune,* 1996. At http://startribune.com/stonline/html/digage/main3.html.

Endnotes

Chapter 2
1. Corbin and Henry; 2. Corbin.

Chapter 4
1. Donatelle, p. 285, adapted; 2. Chartrand. *New York Times,* December 14, 1997.

Chapter 5
1. Chartrand. *New York Times,* April 6, 1997.

Chapter 6
1. DeVry.

Chapter 7
1. Ekelund and Tollison, p. xxv.

Chapter 8
1. Miller, pp. 81–97; 2. Spitzer, pp. 641–656; 3. Brown.

Chapter 9
1. Maimon, pp. 4–5; 2. Barnet, pp. 21–22.

Chapter 10
1. Reingold and Hansen, p. 334; 2. Russ and Kirkpatrick, p. 5; 3. *Star Tribune*; 4. *Star Tribune*; 5. *Star Tribune*.

Chapter 11
1. Lineberry, p. 316; 2. Kemp and Pilitteri, p. 194; 3. Nickerson, p. 121; 4. Lineberry, p. 276; 5. Jones, p. 183; 6. Jones, p. 185; 7. Jones, p. 364; 8. Jones, p. 278; 9. Jones, p. 5; 10. Rosser and Nickolson, p. 81; 11. Jones, 376; 12. Jones, p. 370.

Chapter 13
1. Weaver, pp. 215–218.

Chapter 14
1. Lineberry; 2. Berman and Evans, p. 145.

Chapter 15
1. Lineberry, p. 547; 2. Smith; 3. Smith; 4. Kennedy; 5. Eschelmen and Cashion, p. 165; 6. Eschelmen and Cashion, p. 313.

Chapter 17
1. http://www.careers.unsw.edu.au/careered/ Vocational%20Assessment/psych_testing.html.

Chapter 18
1. Cotton.

Credits

Text Credits

Chapter 2

p. 44: Richard L. Weaver, *Understanding Interpersonal Communication*, Sixth Edition, pp. 283–284. Copyright © 1993 HarperCollins College Publishers. Reprinted by permission.

p. 45: Kenneth Neubeck, *Social Problems: A Critical Approach*, p. 247. Glenview, IL: Scott, Foresman, 1979.

p. 47: Tim Curry, Robert Jiobu, and Kent Schwirian, *Sociology for the Twenty-First Century*, Second Edition, p. 207. Upper Saddle River, NJ: Prentice-Hall, 1999.

p. 49: "Indipreneur"™ is trademarked by Carolyn Corbin. Used by permission.

p. 49: Carolyn Corbin and James D. Henry, "Conquering Career Codependence." http://www.cweb.com/21stcentury/welcome.html.

p. 49: Carolyn Corbin, from speech "Employment in the 21st Century" to the National Association of Colleges and Employers, May 29, 1998.

Chapter 4

p. 81: MyPyramid: Steps to a Healthier You. U.S. Department of Agriculture, Center for Nutrition Policy and Promotion, April 2005. http://www.mypyramid.gov/downloads/MiniPoster.pdf.

p. 87: Rebecca Donatelle, *Access to Health*, Seventh Edition, p. 285. San Francisco: Benjamin/Cummings, 2002.

p. 102: Sabra Chartrand, "Employers Devise New Strategies to Test Job Applicants," *The New York Times*, December 14, 1997.

Chapter 5

p. 115: Sabra Chartrand, "A World Where Language and 'Soft Skills' Are Key," *The New York Times*, April 6, 1997.

Chapter 6

p. 131: DeVry Institute of Technology, from "Survival of the Fittest" from *Directions* newsletter, 1997. Used by permission of DeVry Institute of Technology, a division of DeVry University.

Chapter 7

p. 149: Robert Ekelund and Robert Tollison, *Economics*, p. xxv Boston: Little, Brown and Company, 1986.

Chapter 8

p. 155: George Miller, "The Magic Number. Seven Plus or Minus Two: Some Limits on Our Capacity for Processing Information," *Psychological Review* 63 (1956): 81–97.

p. 159: H. F. Spitzer, "Studies in Retention," *Journal of Educational Psychology* 30 (1939): 641–656.

p. 168: Bettina Lankard Brown, "Career Resilience," *ERIC Clearinghouse on Adult, Career, and Vocational Education*, Digest 178, 1996. http://www.uncg.edu/edu/ericcass/career/digests/dig178.htm.

Chapter 9

p. 170: Elaine p. Maimon, *Writing in the Arts and Sciences*, pp. 4–5. Cambridge, MA: Winthrop Publishers, 1981.

p. 174: Josh R. Gerow, *Psychology: An Introduction*, Fifth Edition, pp. 305–306. New York: Longman, 1997.

p. 188: Sylvan Barnet, *A Short Guide to Writing About Art*, pp. 21–22. Boston: Little, Brown and Company, 1989.

Chapter 10

p. 197: Edward M. Reingold and Wilfred J. Hansen, *Data Structures*, p. 334. Copyright © 1983 by Edward M. Reingold and Wilfred J. Hansen. Reprinted by permission of Little, Brown and Company.

p. 202: Frederick A. Russ and Charles A. Kirkpatrick, *Marketing*, p. 5. Copyright © 1982 by Frederick A. Russ and Charles A. Kirkpatrick. Reprinted by permission of Little, Brown and Company.

p. 208: *Star Tribune*, "Part III: The Coming Trauma" of "On the Edge of the Digital Age" from the *Star Tribune*. Copyright © 1996 Star Tribune. http://www.startribune.com/stonline/html/digage/main3.htm.

Chapter 11

p. 228: Robert L. Lineberry, *Government in America*, Third Edition, p. 316. Copyright © 1986 by Robert Lineberry. Reprinted by permission of Little, Brown and Company.

p. 228: Brenda Kemp and Adele Pilitteri, *Fundamentals of Nursing*, p. 194. Boston: Little, Brown and Company, 1984.

p. 228: Robert C. Nickerson, *Fundamentals of Structured COBOL*, p. 121. Boston: Little, Brown and Company, 1984.

p. 228: Lineberry, p. 276.

p. 232: Walter S. Jones, *The Logic of International Relations*, Fifth Edition, p. 183. Boston: Little, Brown and Company, 1985.

p. 232: Jones, p. 185.

p. 236: Jones, p. 364.

p. 236: Jones, p. 278.

p. 236: Jones, p. 5.

p. 236: Rosemary Rosser and Glen Nickolson, *Educational Psychology*, p. 81. Boston: Little, Brown and Company, 1984.

p. 236: Jones, p. 376.

p. 237: Jones, p. 370.

Chapter 12

p. 257: John Keats, "Ode on a Grecian Urn."

Chapter 13

p. 274: Josh R. Gerow, *Psychology: An Introduction*, Fifth Edition. New York: Longman, 1997.

p. 275: Thomas C. Kinnear, Kenneth L. Bernhardt, and Kathleen A. Krentler, *Principles of Marketing*, Fourth Edition. New York: Longman, 1995.

p. 279: Raymond A. Dumont and John M. Lannon, *Business Communications*. Copyright © 1985 by Raymond A. Dupont and John M. Lannon. Reprinted with permission of Little, Brown and Company.

p. 284: Richard L. Weaver, *Understanding Interpersonal Communication*, Sixth Edition, pp. 215–218. Copyright © 1993 HarperCollins College Publishers. Reprinted by permission.

p. 288: Figure "U.S. Advertising Spending by selected media, 2006-2010" from Jason Pontin, "But Who's Counting?" *Technology Review*, March/April 2009, p. 67. Copyright 2009 by MIT Technology Review. Reproduced with permission of MIT Technology Review in the format Textbook via Copyright Clearance Center.

p. 289: Barbara Walton Spradley, *Community Health Nursing*, Second Edition. Copyright © 1985 by Barbara Walton Spradley. Reprinted by permission of Little, Brown and Company.

p. 290: James M. Henslin, *Social Problems*, Sixth Edition, p. 366. Copyright © 2003. Reprinted by permission of Pearson Education, Inc., Upper Saddle River, NJ.

p. 290: Henslin, p. 454.

p. 291: Henslin, p. 153.

p. 292: Robert J. Ferl, Robert A. Wallace, and Gerald p. Sanders, *Biology: The Realm of Life*, Third Edition.

Copyright © 1996 Addison Wesley Educational Publishers, Inc. Reprinted by permission of Addison Wesley Educational Publishers, Inc.

p. 293: Robert L. Lineberry, *Government in America*, Third Edition. Copyright © 1986 by Robert Lineberry. Reprinted by permission of Little, Brown and Company.

p. 297: Consumer Reports Site Map, Copyright 2009 by Consumers Union of U.S., Inc. Yonkers, NY 10703-1057, a nonprofit organization. Reprinted with permission from ConsumerReports.org® for educational purposes only. No commercial use or reproduction permitted. www.ConsumerReports.org.

p. 303: *Monthly Labor Review*, vol. 130, no. 11 (November 2007), p. 95.

Chapter 14

p. 307: Joseph A. DeVito, *The Interpersonal Communication Book*, Ninth Edition, p. 191. New York: Longman, 2001.

p. 311: Robert L. Lineberry, *Government in America*, Third Edition. Copyright © 1986 by Robert Lineberry. Reprinted by permission of Little, Brown and Company.

p. 311: Robert L. Lineberry, *Government in America*, Third Edition. Copyright © 1986 by Robert Lineberry. Reprinted by permission of Little, Brown and Company.

p. 312: Joseph A. DeVito, *Interpersonal Messages: Communication and Relationship Skills*, pp. 169, 171. Boston: Pearson Allyn and Bacon, 2008.

p. 323: Louis Berman and J.C. Evans, *Exploring the Cosmos*, Second Edition, p. 145. Boston: Little, Brown and Company, 1977.

p. 324: Carl E. Rischer and Thomas A. Easton, *Focus on Human Biology*, Second Edition. Copyright © 1995 by HarperCollins College Publishers, Inc. Reprinted by permission.

p. 327: Thomas C. Kinnear, Kenneth L. Bernhardt, and Kathleen A. Krentler, *Principles of Marketing*, fourth edition, p. 132. New York: Longman, 1995.

Chapter 15

p. 336: Robert L. Lineberry, *Government in America*, Third Edition, p. 547. Copyright © 1986 by Robert L. Lineberry. Reprinted by permission of Little, Brown and Company.

p. 338: Adam Smith, from "Fifty Million Handguns," *Esquire*, 1981. Copyright © 1981 by Adam Smith. Reprinted with permission of *Esquire*.

p. 339: Adam Smith, from "Fifty Million Handguns," *Esquire*, 1981. Copyright © 1981 by Adam Smith. Reprinted with permission of *Esquire*.

p. 339: Senator Edward Kennedy, "The Need for Handgun Control," *Los Angeles Times,* April 5, 1981. Reprinted by permission of Senator Edward Kennedy.

p. 340: J. Ross Eshleman and Barbara G. Cashion, *Sociology: An Introduction*, p. 165. Boston: Little, Brown and Company, 1985.

p. 340: Eshleman and Cashion, p. 313.

Chapter 18

p. 414: Kathleen Cotton, from "Developing Employability Skills" from *School Improvement Research Series*. Reprinted by permission of the Northwest Regional Educational Laboratory School Improvement Research Series, Portland, Oregon.

Photo Credits

p. 1 (top right): age footstock/Art Life Images; **(right):** Pictor International/Alamy; **(bottom):** Burgess Bievins/ Getty Images; **p. 5 (left):** Norbert Rosing/Animals/ Animals; **(right):** Daniel J. Cox/Corbis; **p. 7:** Kathrin Ziegler/Getty Images; **p. 40:** Flame/Corbis; **p. 55:** Dennis MacDonald; **p. 99:** Asia Images/Getty Images; **p. 146:** age footstock/Art Life Images.

Index